TRACING THE ROLES OF SOFT LAW IN HUMAN RIGHTS

Tracing the Roles of Soft Law in Human Rights

Edited by

STÉPHANIE LAGOUTTE
THOMAS GAMMELTOFT-HANSEN
and
JOHN CERONE

OXFORD
UNIVERSITY PRESS

OXFORD
UNIVERSITY PRESS

Great Clarendon Street, Oxford, OX2 6DP,
United Kingdom

Oxford University Press is a department of the University of Oxford.
It furthers the University's objective of excellence in research, scholarship,
and education by publishing worldwide. Oxford is a registered trade mark of
Oxford University Press in the UK and in certain other countries

First Edition published in 2016

Published in the United States of America by Oxford University Press
198 Madison Avenue, New York, NY 10016, United States of America

British Library Cataloguing in Publication Data
Data available

Library of Congress Control Number: 2016957536

ISBN 978–0–19–879140–9

Preface

As the cover picture to this volume is intended to convey, soft law and clay seem to share certain properties. It naturally lends itself to being shaped and moulded by those working with it. Over time it may eventually vitrify into 'hard law'. Yet, as most scholars attempting to grapple with it have come to realize, the concept of soft law often remains amorphous, difficult to pin down.

The idea for this volume emerged at the 2013 Association of Human Rights Institutes conference in London, where Stéphanie Lagoutte and Thomas Gammeltoft-Hansen started comparing notes and discussing the impact of soft law across different human rights issues, in turn raising larger questions and showing the need for a more systematic treatment of this contested concept within international human rights law. Subsequently, John Cerone, at the time serving as Distinguished Raoul Wallenberg Chair in Human Rights and Humanitarian Law across the waters at Lund University, joined the editorial group, further refining the conceptual framework.

The editors would like to thank each of the contributors for their constructive engagement in this project and their critical comments during the animated authors' workshop held at the Danish Institute for Human Rights in October 2014. Some of the contributions were presented at the 2014 Association of Human Rights Institutes Research Conference in Copenhagen, and we are indebted to Martin Scheinin, serving as discussant, for his insightful comments on each of the papers.

Financial support for the authors' workshop and publication process has kindly been provided by the Danish Institute for Human Rights. We would also like to acknowledge Kareem Padraig A. McDonald for his tireless work preparing the final manuscript, and Nikolas Feith Tan for his help convening the authors workshop. Last, but not least, we are very grateful to Nicole Leyland and Emma Endean-Mills and others at Oxford University Press for their continuing assistance and support in the editorial process.

Stéphanie Lagoutte, Thomas Gammeltoft-Hansen, and John Cerone
Copenhagen, 27 June 2016

Table of Contents

List of Contributors

Editors

Stéphanie Lagoutte is Senior Researcher at the Danish Institute for Human Rights. She holds a Doctoral degree in law from the University of Paris 1, Panthéon-Sorbonne and a Ph.D. in Law from the University of Aarhus. She has taught and published within the field of European Human Rights Law, including on the reform of the European Court of Human Rights, human rights, and family law as well as religious freedom. Most of her work focuses on the duties and role of the state in human rights protection. She has coordinated research projects with partners from developing countries, especially in West Africa. In 2012–14 she worked in close cooperation with the UN Working Group on Human Rights and Business focusing on state duties under the UN Guiding Principles on Human Rights and Business.

Thomas Gammeltoft-Hansen is Research Director at the Danish Institute for Human Rights and Executive Chairman of the Association of Human Rights Institutes (AHRI). He holds a Doctoral degree in law from Aarhus University, an M.Sc. in forced migration from the University of Oxford and an MPhil in political science from the University of Copenhagen. In addition to his academic work, Thomas Gammeltoft-Hansen serves as member of the Danish Refugee Appeals Board and has served as adviser and consultant to a number of international organizations, governmental institutions, and European NGOs. Book publications include *The Power of Legality: Practices of International Law and their Politics* (Cambridge University Press, forthcoming); *Access to Asylum: International Refugee Law and the Globalisation of Migration Control* (Cambridge University Press, 2011/13), *The Migration Industry: The Commercialisation of International Migration* (Routledge, 2013), and *Sovereignty Games: Instrumentalizing State Sovereignty in Europe and Beyond* (Palgrave, 2008).

John Cerone is Paul Martin Senior Professor in International Affairs & Law at the University of Windsor Faculty of Law and Visiting Professor of International Law at the Fletcher School of Law and Diplomacy. He has been Distinguished Chair in Human Rights & Humanitarian Law at the Raoul Wallenberg Institute, a fellow at the Max Planck Institute for Comparative Public Law and International Law and a visiting scholar at the International Criminal Court. He has also been a Fulbright scholar at both the Danish Institute for Human Rights and the Tokyo University of Foreign Studies. He has worked for a number of different international organizations, including the United Nations, OSCE, Amnesty International, and the International Crisis Group, and has served as a legal adviser to international criminal courts. In 2009 he was appointed special adviser to the first US delegation to the UN Human Rights Council.

Other Authors

Mátyás Bódig is Senior Lecturer at the Law School of the University of Aberdeen, UK. Previously, he worked as Associate Professor at the University of Miskolc (Hungary) and Senior Research Fellow at the Institute for Legal Studies of the Hungarian Academy of Sciences in

Budapest. In Aberdeen, he is founding member of the Centre for Citizenship, Civil Society and Rule of Law, and Programme Coordinator for L.L.M. in Human Rights. Dr Bódig has established himself as a legal theorist, and his publications span from jurisprudential methodology, through conceptual legal theory and political philosophy to international human rights law. His current research revolves around the methodological profile of doctrinal legal scholarship, the patterns of doctrinal development in international human rights law, and the integration of political ideals (e.g. the rule of law) into international norms.

Megan Bradley is Assistant Professor of Political Science and International Development Studies at McGill University. She is the author of *Refugee Repatriation: Justice, Responsibility and Redress* (Cambridge University Press, 2013), and the editor of *Forced Migration, Reconciliation and Justice* (McGill-Queen's University Press, 2015).

Christoph Good is Senior Research Fellow at the Centre for Human Rights Studies of the University of Zurich and Lecturer for International Law at the Andrássy University Budapest. Christoph studied law at University St Gallen where he obtained his Ph.D. with a study on the idea of human rights and humanitarian law in the works of Emer de Vattel (1714–67). He is, among other things, co-author of the *Baseline Study about Business and Human Rights in Switzerland* (2014) as well as the study *Corporate Social Responsibility—Rahmenbedingungen für die Förderung und Integration von menschenrechtlichen Inhalten in ein modernes CSR-Verständnis* (2015) by the Swiss Centre of Expertise in Human Rights. He is currently working on the role of corporations in international law and the appearance of corporate human rights standards in the global governance discourse.

Felipe Gómez Isa is Professor of Public International Law and Researcher at the Institute of Human Rights of the University of Deusto (Bilbao). He is National Director of the European Master in Human Rights and Democratization, EMA, organized by forty-one European Universities in the framework of the European Inter-University Centre for Human Rights and Democratization (EIUC, Venice, Italy). He is also the Spanish representative to the UN Working Group for the elaboration of an Optional Protocol to the Convention on the Elimination of All Forms of Discrimination against Women (New York, 1998 and 1999). Felipe is Visiting Professor at Washington College of Law of American University (Washington, DC), at Universidad Externado de Colombia (Bogotá), at Peoples' Friendship University of Russia (Moscow), and at the René Cassin Institute of Human Rights (Strasbourg). His publications include *The Right to Development in International Law* (Deusto, 1999), *Privatisation and Human Rights in the Age of Globalisation* (Intersentia, 2005), and *Freedom from Want from a Local Perspective: Evolution and Challenges Ahead* (Cambridge, 2011).

Sally Holt is Senior Research Fellow and Deputy Director of the Centre on Human Rights in Conflict at the University of East London.

Anette Faye Jacobsen is Senior Researcher at the Danish Institute for Human Rights. She holds a Ph.D. in legal and political history from the University of Copenhagen. Her specialization in the human rights field is on children's rights internationally and domestically. Her interests also include democracy, governance, and human rights implementation at the local level. Anette's academic publications cover a variety of fields including child protection, history of legal and political theory, customary law, political rights, history of education, history of child rights, and the Conventions of the Rights of the Child.

Peter Vedel Kessing is Senior Researcher at the Danish Institute for Human Rights and lecturer at the Faculty of Law of the University of Copenhagen. He specializes in and has published extensively on security law, armed conflict, counter-terrorism, and human rights. He has worked with international human rights projects for several years. In addition, he has served as: a judge in a Danish District Court; Head of the International Law Department at the Danish Red Cross; and a member of the Danish Refugee Board. He has also worked with international refugee law and cooperation in the Danish Ministry of Interior and for the UNHCR.

Ekaterina Yahyaoui Krivenko is a Lecturer at the Irish Centre for Human Rights at the School of Law of the National University of Ireland. Currently she leads the project 'International Protection of Human Rights as a Constitutional Issue: Promises, Problems and Prospects'. Her research interests include: general public international law; global governance; international constitutionalism/rule of law; human rights with emphasis on gender; Islam and human rights; international refugee and migration law; comparative law and legal cultures; feminist analyses of law; and law and humanities.

Debra Long is a Senior Research Associate at the Human Rights Implementation Centre of the University of Bristol Law School. She is a UK qualified lawyer and her specialist areas are the rights of persons deprived of their liberty and the prevention of torture and other ill-treatment. Her work has a particular focus on the African human rights system. At the regional level, Debra was one of the principal drafters of the Robben Island Guidelines on the prevention of torture in Africa. Debra is also part of the Africa research team on The Human Rights Implementation Project (HRLIP), a collaborative project between four leading academic human rights Centres (Bristol, Essex, Middlesex, and Pretoria) and the Open Society Justice Initiative. The project aims to examine the factors which impact on implementation of decisions from individual complaints to the UN and regional human rights bodies.

Kasey L. McCall-Smith is a Lecturer in Public International Law at the School of Law at the University of Edinburgh. She is a US qualified lawyer and holds a Ph.D. and L.L.M. in Public International Law. Her research focuses on treaty law and how treaties impact law and policy at the domestic level. Kasey also actively researches international human rights law, including the influence of the UN human rights treaty bodies on domestic law, and is interested in the increasingly blurred distinction between public and private international law in terms of business and human rights protection. Kasey has published multiple articles that cut across these issues, including her most recent article 'Severing Reservations' in the *International Comparative Law Quarterly*. At the School of Law, she codirects the Human Rights L.L.M. programme and serves on the Global Justice Academy steering committee.

Rachel Murray is Professor of International Human Rights Law, founder and Director of the Human Rights Implementation Centre at the University of Bristol Law School. Her specialist areas are human rights in Africa (particularly the African Charter and its Commission; the African Court on Human and Peoples' Rights; and the African Union), national human rights institutions, the Optional Protocol to the UN Convention against Torture (OPCAT), and human rights implementation. Rachel is a Fellow of the Human Rights Centre at the University of Essex and a member of the AHRC's Peer Review College. Rachel is the Principal Investigator on The Human Rights Implementation Project (HRLIP), a collaborative project between four leading academic human rights Centres (Bristol, Essex, Middlesex, and Pretoria) and the Open Society Justice Initiative. The project aims to examine the factors which impact on implementation of decisions from individual complaints to the UN and regional human rights bodies.

Bruce 'Ossie' Oswald is an Associate Professor in the Melbourne Law School at the University of Melbourne. He is also the Director of the Asia Pacific Centre for Military Law (APCML). His interests in law and practice are in the areas of international humanitarian law, peace operations, state building, accountability and responsibility, and the application of human rights law to military operations. He also served as legal adviser to the Danish government during the Copenhagen Process and helped draft the ensuing Principles and Guidelines on the Handling of Detainees in International Military Operations.

John Packer is Associate Professor of Law and Director of the Human Rights Research and Education Centre at the University of Ottawa.

Zdenka Machnyikova is an independent consultant. The authors served together in the Office of the OSCE High Commissioner on National Minorities from the mid-1990s to mid-2000s in the positions, respectively, of Senior Legal Adviser then Director, Legal Officer, and Senior Legal Adviser. They contributed substantially to the evolving approach and work of the High Commissioner both overall and in his specific engagements (i.e. vis-à-vis individual states, with relevant intergovernmental and other organizations, and in terms of the High Commissioner's series of general Recommendations). They subsequently contributed to and remain engaged with the Initiative on Quiet Diplomacy aimed at sharing the High Commissioner's experience with, and building capacities amongst, the relevant institutions of other IGOs. They continue to advise various parties in matters of interethnic relations, diversity management, and conflict prevention, management, and resolution.

Angela Sherwood is a Ph.D. Candidate in Law at King's College London. She has worked and published on issues of forced migration, as well as co-led research on durable solutions to internal displacement. Her research interests cover themes related to international law and internal displacement; post-colonialism and land rights movements; and addressing social and economic rights violations in displacement contexts.

Léticia Villeneuve is a DPhil Candidate in International Relations at the University of Oxford, where she studies as a Rhodes Scholar and Doctoral Fellow of the Social Sciences and Humanities Research Council of Canada. Her current research looks at the creation and use of non-binding instruments by state and non-state actors, especially in the field of human rights.

Introduction

Tracing the Roles of Soft Law in Human Rights

Thomas Gammeltoft-Hansen, Stéphanie Lagoutte, and John Cerone

1. Introduction

It has become commonplace to argue that we live in an era of unprecedented proliferation in the development of international law. Importantly, however, an increasing part of the normative standards generated through world politics and other international practice has taken the form of non-binding agreements and other instruments short of positive international law. This new realm of 'soft law' can be seen to shape and impact upon the content of international law in multiple ways: from being a first step in a norm-making process, to providing detailed rules and more technical standards required for the interpretation and the implementation of existing rules of positive law. This is especially the case in the area of human rights. While relatively few human rights treaties have been adopted at the UN level in the last two decades, the number of declarations, resolutions, conclusions, and principles has grown almost exponentially. In some areas, soft law has come to fill a void in the absence of treaty law, exerting a degree of normative force notwithstanding its non-binding character. In others areas, soft law seems to have become the battleground for interpretative struggles to both expand and delimit human rights protection in the context of existing regimes.

Despite these developments, little attention has been given to soft law within legal scholarship on human rights. A better understanding of how soft law shapes and affects different branches of international human rights law may not only provide a more dynamic picture of the current state of international human rights law, it may also help to unsettle and critically question certain political and doctrinal beliefs. The importance of these questions is not just theoretical but also practical. Hence, the book aims to serve also as a guide to human rights practitioners and inform strategic decision-making by surveying the ways in which soft law has actually been used in concrete cases and by discussing factors that influence the weight accorded to soft law in various contexts.

This book springs from a sense that the roles performed by soft law are both more ambiguous and multifaceted than what is ordinarily assumed. First, can it still be presumed that soft law necessarily leads to an expansive interpretation of international human rights law? In a number of recent cases, states have increasingly relied on soft law to either hedge against or directly backtrack on what they see as activist courts or politically undesirable interpretative developments, suggesting that soft law may equally confine the application of well-established hard law standards or hinder the development of hard law. Secondly, is soft law starting to move beyond its traditional role as an auxiliary tool for the interpretation of international law? In some areas today, soft law constitutes a primary reference point, and yet there seem to be no immediate prospects for codification or crystallization of soft law into hard law. States may prefer the sometimes contradictory language of soft law instruments in order to retain political manoeuvring room. Resistance to codification of certain categories of norms, for example those purporting to regulate the conduct of corporations, may also stem from the inability of scholars and practitioners to reconcile these soft law standards with the fundamental building blocks of general international law. To the extent that this remains the case, should we rather think of certain soft law regimes as *sui generis*—not just complementing but in some cases also challenging positive international law?

The central purpose of this volume is to openly explore the roles of soft law in both established and emerging human rights regimes. Section 2 proceeds with some reflections on the (im)possibility and politics related to clearly defining soft law in the field of human rights. Section 3 sets out a more practice-oriented, bottom-up approach to examining soft law across different fields, and introduces the questions that are raised in this volume. On this basis a tentative framework for analysing the roles of soft law in emerging and established human rights regimes is set out. Section 4 outlines the structure of the volume and the individual contributions.

2. Defining Soft Law in International Law

Despite its common usage, the notion of soft law continues to cause confusion and contestation among international lawyers. Some scholars resist the term, arguing that it has come to signify a too wide and disparate set of phenomena, making any single definition or taxonomy impossible.[1] Others argue that the conjunction of the two words 'soft' and 'law' inevitably invites attempts to ascribe legality to political documents, threatening to undermine the status of positive international law proper and blur the boundary between law and politics.[2] Both the definition and standing of soft law have, thus, been the subject of substantial doctrinal debate.

[1] See John Cerone's chapter in this volume for more information. See also: J. Ellis, 'Shades of Grey: Soft Law and the Validity of Public International Law', *Leiden Journal of International Law* vol. 25 (2012): 313–34; Salem H. Nasser, *Sources and Norms of International Law* (Berlin: Galda and Wilch Verlag, 2008).

[2] P. Weil, 'Towards Relative Normativity in International Law?', *American Journal of International Law* vol. 77 (1983): 413–42; J. Klabbers, 'The Undesirability of Soft Law', *Nordic Journal of International Law* vol. 67 (1998): 381–91.

The term itself would seem to indicate a residual category—not quite positive international law, but somehow aspiring thereto or at least thought to influence legal interpretation.[3] A common approach is thus to define soft law in the negative, as lacking one or several properties normally ascribed to international law; for example precise normative content, enforceability, and formal legal status.[4]

While such a multi-dimensional model can be useful in terms of more clearly distinguishing between different types of soft law for purposes of legal interpretation, it also significantly expands the ambit of what may be characterized as soft law. It may, for instance, imply the elevation of rules and instruments traditionally considered outside the boundary of international law,[5] notably texts authored by and/or addressed to non-state actors, such as the Montreux Document on military and security companies,[6] or the Maastricht Principles on extraterritorial obligations of states.[7] This is an issue of particular importance in the field of human rights, where NGOs and scholars have a strong presence and long history in terms of advancing human rights issues.

Such a definition may secondly imply a downgrading of formally hard law commitments lacking a sufficient degree of normative precision or enforceability so as to be de facto non-binding. Despite important institutional developments in international human rights law in terms of review, petition, and adjudication, effective enforcement is still lacking in many areas. Similarly, important parts of international human rights law—notably in the area of economic, cultural, and social rights—have always built on aspirational commitments and principles of collective responsibility that, despite on-going developments, are not easily implemented or adjudicated.

The issue of definition thus also raises obvious political questions: do we risk overreaching and thus conflating law and politics in a way that fundamentally undermines the privileged position of human rights law as a subset of positive international law?[8] Or, vice versa, are we selling short those parts of international human rights law that do not resemble traditional treaty language?[9]

[3] Andrew T. Guzman and Timothy L. Meyer, 'International Soft Law', *Journal of Legal Analysis* vol. 171 (2010): 171–225, at 172.

[4] C. Chinkin, 'Normative Development in the International Legal System', in *Commitment and Compliance: The Role of Non-binding Norms in the International Legal System*, ed. D. Shelton (Oxford: Oxford University Press, 2000); K. C. Wellens and G. M. Borchardt, 'Soft Law in European Community Law', *European Law Review* vol. 14 (1989): 267–321, at 285; M. Adelstam, 'Soft Law in the State Aid Policy Area', in *Soft Law in Governance and Regulation*, ed. U. Mörth (Cheltenham: Elgar Publishing, 2004): 11–36 at 17; Ellis (2012).

[5] Nasser (2008) and Ellis (2012).

[6] *The Montreux Document on Pertinent International Legal Obligations and Good Practices for States Related to Operations of Private Military and Security Companies during Armed Conflict* (17 Sept. 2008).

[7] *Maastricht Principles on Extraterritorial Obligations of States in the area of Economic, Social and Cultural Rights* (28 Sept. 2011).

[8] Klabbers (1998); G. Noll, *Negotiating Asylum: The EU Acquis, Extraterritorial Protection and the Common Market of Deflection* (The Hague: Martinus Nijhoff, 2000).

[9] As pointed out by Weil: 'A rule of treaty or customary law may be vague, "soft"; but ... it does not thereby cease to be a legal norm.' Weil (1983): 414.

From a more conceptual perspective, any attempt to define soft law simply as 'not-hard law' could be argued to run all the same risks of other negative definitions in international law.[10] The criteria applied vary considerably among scholars,[11] and the definitional problem is thus pushed back into a larger discussion of the concept of international law, its functions and its transformation.[12]

The contributions to this volume show that the roles of soft law often challenge the boundaries of international human rights law, both in term of its nature and its fields of application. While some lawyers have greeted these developments and corresponding 'new sources of international law' with optimism,[13] others see the fragmentation of international law as a 'legal jungle' of incoherent interpretation that may end up creating obligations *ex nihilo*, and consequently advocate in favour of legal non-proliferation.[14]

The doctrinal debate over the increased use of soft law seems to reflect a more fundamental rift between those keen to uphold international law as a system that produces foreseeable and determinable outcomes, based on a limited yet objectively identifiable and binding set of international obligations,[15] and those who accept that the expansion of international norms, with varying normative density, implies a more subjective and dynamic interpretation.[16]

[10] See e.g.: P. Alston, 'The "Not-a-Cat" Syndrome: Can the International Human Rights Regime Accommodate Non-state Actors?', in *Non-state Actors and Human Rights*, ed. P. Alston (Oxford: Oxford University Press, 2005): 3–6; P. Alston, 'The "Not-a-Cat" Syndrome: Re-thinking Human Rights Law to Meet the Needs of the Twenty-first Century', in *Progressive Governance for the XXI Century* (Florence: European University Institute and New York University School of Law, 2000) (proceedings of the conference involving Presidents Clinton and Cardozo, Prime Ministers Blair, D'Alema, and Jospin, and Chancellor Schroeder): 128–44.

[11] Scholars vary considerably in terms of the criteria to be applied however. Chinkin proposes (1) legal form, (2) precision, (3) authorship, (4) addressees, (5) theory of responsibility, and (6) enforcement. See: Chinkin in Shelton (2000); Wellens and Borchardt, and later, Aldestam apply four criteria: (1) binding requirement of certain conduct or omission formulated by subjects with authority and following pre-established procedures; (2) knowledge, ability, and will of the addressees to comply; (3) precision of the norm; and (4) means to enforce the norm. See: Karel C. Wellens, and G. M. Borchardt, 'Soft Law in European Community Law', *European Law Review* vol. 14 (1989): 267–321 at 285; Adelstam (2004): 11–36 at 17. More recently, Ellis talks about: (1) Normativity and Justiciability, (2) Enforceability, (3) Precision, and (4) Formal legal status. See: Ellis (2012): 313–34.

[12] Ellis (2012); Nasser (2008): 12.

[13] E. Riedel, 'Standards and Sources: Farewell to the Exclusivity of the Sources Triad in International Law', *European Journal of International Law* vol. 2 (1991): 58–84 at 62; G. Von Glahn, *Law among Nations: An Introduction to Public International Law* (New York: Macmillan, 1981).

[14] A number of scholars have written on and enumerated different viewpoints in this ongoing debate. See in particular: K. Nicolaidis and J. L. Tong, 'Diversity or Cacophony? The Continuing Debate of New Sources of International Law', *Michigan Journal of International Law* vol. 25 (2004): 1349–75 at 1361; J. H. H. Weiler and Andreas L. Paulus, 'The Structure of Change in International Law or is There a Hierarchy of Norms in International Law?', *European Journal of International Law* vol. 8 (1997): 545–65; C. Leben, 'Symposium: The Changing Structure of International Law Revisited: By Way of Introduction', *European Journal of International Law* vol. 8 (1997): 399–408; and J. A. C. Salcedo, 'Reflections on the Existence of a Hierarchy of Norms in International Law', *European Journal of International Law* vol. 8 (1997): 583–95.

[15] Weil (1983): 77; J. Klabbers, 'The Redundancy of Soft Law', *Nordic Journal of International Law* vol. 65 (1996): 167–82; Klabbers (1998).

[16] U. Fastenrath, 'Relative Normativity in International Law', *EJIL* vol. 4 (1993): 305–40, at 324.

2.1 Stipulating a definition

Notwithstanding these difficulties, the term 'soft law' remains widely accepted and used by the international legal community, and thus warrants a basic definition.[17] For the purpose of the present volume, the term soft law is understood to refer to rules (prescribing conduct or otherwise establishing standards) that are in the process of becoming, though may not ultimately become, binding rules of international law, in the form of any of the established sources of international law—customary law, general principles of law, or as an authentic (binding) interpretation of a rule of treaty law.

Of course, any normative statement, irrespective of its source, has *some* possibility of becoming a rule of international law. However, a normative statement will become a rule of soft law only once it acquires a degree of traction. For the purpose of this study, the term soft law refers to rules that are already in the process of incubation, that are emerging rules of international law, and that are viable candidates for crystallizing into hard law. While non-state actors, such as NGOs and academics, may have an important role to play in identifying and clarifying soft law, this traction must ultimately come in the form of acceptance by the authors of international law—states.

The only criteria used to delimit the concept of soft law for the purposes of the present study are that the content be formulated as a rule and that the rule be in the process of incubation.[18] The term 'soft law instruments' then may be understood as referring to any instrument with normative content that by its form and provenance provides support sufficient to establish the minimum threshold of traction for at least some of the norms contained therein to be regarded as soft law.

Last, but not least, this volume deals with the roles of soft law in international human rights law. By this we mean the corpus of international and regional principles and standards, binding and non-binding, that govern the protection of human rights, including UN and regional treaties, declarations, and principles adopted by states, relevant case law from international and regional courts, as well as recommendations, observations, and other decisions adopted by human rights organs and monitoring bodies. Related fields such as international criminal law and international humanitarian law are only dealt with in this volume insofar as the issues under examination are linked to international human rights protection.

3. The Roles of Soft Law in International Relations

The central purpose of this volume is not doctrinal, however, but essentially concerned with understanding human rights law as a constantly developing legal

[17] A. Boyle, 'Soft Law in International Law-Making', in *International Law*, ed. M. D. Evans (Oxford: Oxford University Press, 2010): 122–40 at 122–5; Guzman and Meyer (2010): 171; Shelton (2000).

[18] A more extensive taxonomy is elaborated in John Cerone's chapter in this volume.

system. The core questions that we ask are: what specific roles soft law plays across different areas of human rights law, and what impact it has had, and is likely to have, on the development of international human rights law. Further, does the role of soft law in human rights differ from that in public international law more generally? Although international human rights law is generally considered a subset of public international law,[19] the specificities of human rights law may, nonetheless, impact both legal developments and interpretation.[20] On the one hand, the strong *telos* of human rights law may be understood to provide a progressive role for soft law in the development of new and existing human rights regimes. On the other hand, soft law may also serve to reduce the specificities of international human rights law by aligning interpretation more closely with general international law.

The historical lack of strong enforcement institutions in the human rights field may, similarly, have granted soft law a privileged position in resolving interpretative uncertainties. However, as stronger human rights institutions and a more complex web of arbitration at both the national and international level have developed, is the importance of soft law similarly waning? Such institutions may naturally continue to be informed by and emphasize the importance of soft law developments, yet in this process soft law may also become a tool for states to resist or hedge against judicial or quasi-judicial supervision. Soft law may furthermore be a preferred means by both states and non-state actors in order to respond more quickly, with less paucity and more flexibility. Yet, it can also be used to block or delay the subsequent development of hard law instruments and, hence, reduce the legal quality of the protection they otherwise could afford individuals in international human rights law.

This is why this volume aims to trace the roles of soft law both more generally and through specific case studies across human rights issues. This phenomenon must be documented and its effects must be analysed thoroughly—beyond the perfunctory discourse.

From what precedes, we can assume that soft law fulfils at least two main functions in international human rights: it can be norm-filling and norm-creating.

First, soft law is *norm-filling* in areas where there are already legally binding standards. If human rights treaties cast a relatively wide net, where the particularities of certain cases or political practices often fall somewhere in the cracks, soft law serves as a tool to fill interpretative gaps and uncertainties. Soft law is not a substitute for hard law in any of these instances, yet it plays a crucial role in

[19] While in the past, much human rights scholarship retained a rather distant relationship to general international law, the 'integrationist' position is today more commonly accepted. See notably: International Law Association, Committee on International Human Rights Law and Practice, 'Final Report on the Relationship between General International Law and International Human Rights Law' (72nd Conference of the International Law Association, Rio de Janeiro, 2008); M. T. Kamminga and M. Scheinin, *The Impact of Human Rights Law on General International Law* (Oxford: Oxford University Press, 2009).

[20] See e.g.: M. K. Addo, 'The Legal Nature of International Human Rights', in *International Studies in Human Rights*, vol. 104 (Leiden/Boston: Martinus Nijhoff Publishers, 2010); B. Simma, 'International Human Rights and General International Law: A Comparative Analysis', in *Collected Courses of the Academy of European Law*, vol. 4, Book 2 (The Hague: Kluwer Law International, 1995): 153–236; A. Pellet, '"Human Rightism" and International Law', *Italian Yearbook of International Law* (2000): 3–16.

creating a common understanding of the existing rules, and their interpretation. Hence, 'soft law formulates and reformulates the hard law of human rights treaties in the application of this law to specific states and cases'.[21] The assumption in such cases is often that soft law will have a positive effect in terms of expanding human rights protection. In the traditional, liberal view international human rights law is seen as a continuously developing project paving the way for increased protection, international governance, and a gradual willingness of states to submit to international judiciaries and other independent third party supervision. While human rights treaties may have their shortcomings, the task of human rights institutions, NGOs, and advocates is to assist states to gradually fill these gaps through soft law, judicial outcomes, best practices, and general interpretation. Consequently, soft law initiatives are often couched in larger institutional settings, allowing human rights institutions to frame the agenda and stressing civil society as an important voice in this process.

In recent years, however, states themselves seem to be taking on an active role in promoting soft law, not with the intention of furthering human rights standards, but rather as a reaction to what is seen as political or unrealistic interpretative developments by international human rights institutions and judiciaries. For instance, in 2012, the Committee of Ministers of the Council of Europe unanimously adopted the Brighton Declaration emphasizing that the European Court of Human Rights is to have due regard to the state's 'margin of appreciation' when reviewing decisions taken by national authorities.[22]

Second, soft law is *norm-creating* in areas where there are currently no binding international standards. Soft law has helped pave the way for hard law as shown by the many declarations recognizing the existence of rights which, for many years, have been the inevitable prelude to legally binding instruments. As far as the international human rights law-making process is concerned, soft law is 'a necessary mechanism related to the traditional consensual nature of international law formation'.[23] Both among practitioners and human rights scholars there is often an implicit assumption that soft law in this category will eventually solidify or lead to 'norm cascade'.[24] This builds on the idea that the existence of non-binding norms and the consensus that emerges as states begin to comply with them appears to stimulate the development of legally binding norms.[25]

[21] D. Shelton, 'Commentary and Conclusions' (on human rights and soft law), in Shelton (2000): 449–63 at 461.

[22] The declaration made at the end of the High Level Conference meeting at Brighton on 19 and 20 Apr. 2012 at the initiative of the United Kingdom Chairmanship of the Committee of Ministers of the Council of Europe.

[23] D. Shelton, 'Commentary and Conclusions' (on human rights and soft law), in Shelton (2000): 449–63 at 461.

[24] J. Ruggie, UN Doc. A/HRC/4/35, 19 Feb. 2007, 'Report of the Special Representative of the Secretary-General on the Issue of Human Rights and Transnational Corporations and Other Business Enterprises'; M. Finnemore and K. Sikkink, 'International Norm Dynamics and Political Change', *International Organization* vol. 52 (1998): 887–917.

[25] D. Shelton, 'Commentary and Conclusions' (on human rights and soft law), in Shelton (2000): 449–63 at 461.

Yet, on a number of current issues, practice has yet to prove that treaty codification, or even hardening of the rules into customary international law, is necessarily the end point. States and, for example, corporations, may prefer the political flexibility provided by a soft law framework. Substantial criticism has also been raised by legal scholars arguing that the hardening of, for example, the UN Guiding Principles on Business and Human Rights not only poses problems in terms of the transposition of primary obligations, it even threatens to erode the very foundations of international law.[26]

Furthermore, there is an inherent difficulty in identifying the growing role of these kinds of soft law within the traditional international public law paradigm. Even though it is acknowledged that soft law plays an important role in attempting to define the human rights commitments of a variety of actors, the actual *legal* consistency of such commitments are often inconsistent and do not bring about clear legal consequences for breach. In that sense, rather than simply paving the way for codification into hard law, we may well see certain soft law regimes end up as the ultimate and authoritative determinations of open-ended legal questions.

Finally, many international instruments emanating from non-state actors have emerged in the past decades and are often considered as soft law standards for these actors (e.g. international agreements on corporate social responsibility, framework agreements or codes of conduct signed by international trade union organizations, employers' organizations, companies, etc.). When dealing with business, trade, economics, or transnational sectors such as the Internet, many scholars are now talking about new actor-oriented models and multi-level, multi-layer, and multi-player governance structures and mechanisms. In such a global setting, multi-stakeholder models and new actors are playing an increasing role in international norm-creation processes.[27]

What this will mean for the future development of international law at large is still unclear. Some hope that soft law may pave the way for new subjects of international law, while others argue that state-centrism is likely to remain the epistemic starting point in the current legal and political order, and remains an appropriate and sufficient normative framework to guide the majority of situations, where the exercise of public power is carried out by states' own authorities and within their respective national boundaries. Even if the latter perspective prevails, this does not mean that we will not see gradual and potentially far-reaching developments. When confronted with human rights abuses committed by non-state actors in states unable to provide victims with remedy and redress, the statist framework may be easier

[26] C. Parker and J. Howe, 'Ruggie's Diplomatic Project and its Missing Regulatory Infrastructure', in *The UN Guiding Principles on Business and Human Rights: Foundations and Implementation*, ed. R. Mares (The Hague: Brill, 2012): 273–301; S. Deva, 'Treating Human Rights Lightly: A Critique of the Consensus Rhetoric and the Language Employed by the Guiding Principles', in *Human Rights Obligations of Business: Beyond the Corporate Responsibility to Respect?*, ed. S. Deva and D. Bilchitz (Cambridge: Cambridge University Press, 2013): 96–7. See also: Stéphanie Lagoutte's chapter in this volume.

[27] M. C. Kettemann, *The Future of Individuals in International Law: Lessons from International Internet Law* (The Hague: Eleven Publishing International, 2013): 12.

to sidestep by retaining a *sui generis* soft law regime than overcome by a process of treaty codification or crystallization that would make non-state actors fully-fledged subjects of international human rights law.

4. Structure of the Volume

The opening chapter, by *John Cerone*, examines the concept of 'soft law' and its relationship to binding international human rights law. While there is no universally accepted definition of the term, the phrase is nonetheless commonly used by international and human rights lawyers. Acknowledging the very different understandings of the roles and usages of soft law traced by the authors to this volume, a working definition is nonetheless important to delimit the scope of the study and establish the framework of the subject matter to be analysed. To this end, this chapter attempts a definition of both the terms 'soft law' and 'soft law instrument' in order to establish a common vocabulary for the ensuing chapters.

The remainder of the volume charts its course in two parts. Part I includes case studies that explore the diversity of roles soft law has played within 'developed' human rights regimes (i.e. regimes where there are established hard law standards), its progressive and regressive effects, and the role that different actors play in the incubation process. In her contribution *Kasey McCall-Smith* examines the introduction of general comments into domestic legal systems. As a universally applicable form of soft law produced by the treaty bodies, general comments have unparalleled potential to shape universal human rights. Soft law produced by the treaty bodies contains rules that are in the process of incubation and therefore norm-filling as they aid in interpreting the hard law standards set forth in the core human rights treaties. Though states often ignore treaty body jurisprudence, there is strong evidence that it is nonetheless influential in the domestic sphere by virtue of the increasing references to general comments in domestic court opinions and policy debates. Yet, the persisting question is whether the use of treaty body jurisprudence at the domestic level refines or distorts the development of universal human rights standards.

Ekaterina Yahyaoui Krivenko analyses the role of soft law in the process of emergence and gradual recognition of violence against women as a human rights concern at the universal level. Her analysis shows that in the context of the CEDAW Committee soft law is used not only to bolster the interpretation of existing human rights standards, but also to support normative developments related to new forms of violence against women not recognized at the time of drafting of the Convention. Her chapter highlights the dialectical relationship between law and non-law. Instead of approaching these as binary opposites, the CEDAW Committee applies the soft law prohibition of violence against women as an intermediary concept to link newer forms of violence against women to the Convention.

Some of the most important current developments in our understanding of human rights are currently happening in the area of economic and social rights.

In his chapter, *Mátyás Bódig* examines the role of the CESCR Committee and its general comments in facilitating this process. Most authors agree that the Covenant on Economic, Social and Cultural Rights suffers from a flawed doctrinal design and important drafting deficiencies. Yet, the soft law of the CESCR general comments has served to better articulate relevant human rights obligations and as such serves as an important tool for addressing these issues. The Committee may, however, equally be accused of human rights activism in its effort to push current interpretation and develop new rights, most notably the right to water. While many states are unsympathetic to the Committee's work, general comments are nonetheless reflected in the periodic reports and there are signs that CESCR soft law is becoming a more widely accepted model for articulating the content of economic and social rights.

The proliferation and multifaceted nature of soft law within the human rights field identified in the volume is perhaps nowhere more evident than in the work of the African Commission on Human and Peoples' Rights covered in the chapter by *Debra Long and Rachel Murray*. The African Commission as a quasi-judicial, monitoring body generates a range of soft law instruments. These instruments reflect the variety of reasons identified in the volume for which soft law may be developed, and the diverse types of instruments that may be categorized as 'soft law instruments', but which may have very different persuasive force or purpose in practice. In that sense, they may be considered useful additions to the human rights 'armoury', which the African Commission, and others working in the field of human rights, can draw upon to encourage states to comply with their human rights obligations. Moreover, notably, these instruments are designed to influence not only state behaviour but also the strategy and policy of the African Commission itself in respect of a particular issue. As the authors point out, however, there is a problem with the degree of traction that these soft law instruments have gained at the national and regional levels.

While the Guiding Principles on IDPs and most other soft law instruments in the human rights field have been developed in close collaboration with, for example, NGOs and relevant international organizations, the Principles and Guidelines on the Handling of Detainees in International Military Operations is a unique example of a state-centric approach to developing soft law, with no institutional anchoring and very limited involvement by civil society. In his chapter *Bruce 'Ossie' Oswald* revisits the Copenhagen Process and reflects on the nature of the Principles and the extent to which the state-led process influenced the content of the Principles and Guidelines. He argues that the Principles and Guidelines may be seen as an example of a new mode of soft law development in areas where states have serious concerns and do not trust the existing human rights machinery to develop interpretation. That said, the Principles and Guidelines also highlight how difficult it is to establish the appropriate relationship between human rights and international humanitarian law, and it remains to be seen how they will be used to fill perceived or actual gaps in the law concerning taking and handling of detainees in military operations.

Taking a more critical perspective, *Peter Vedel Kessing* argues that in the area of armed conflict soft law tends to play the role of a 'norm-excluder' rather than a norm-filler or norm-creator as is ordinarily the case in the field of international human rights law. It is remarkable that many new soft law instruments, including the Copenhagen Principles and Guidelines, deliberately delimit or exclude human rights, even though there is a strong consensus among judicial bodies and international organizations that international human rights law is a relevant legal source in times of armed conflict. The fact that these instruments are often developed by a small group of selected experts/organizations and a few selected states in a closed and non-transparent process entails a higher risk that these instruments will lead to fragmentation and polarization.

In the last chapter in this part of the volume *Megan Bradley and Angela Sherwood* show how the development of the Guiding Principles on Internal Displacement in 1998 created a soft law standard that was essential to establishing the IDP issue on national and international agendas, and to making progress in understanding and better protecting the rights of IDPs. The global number of internally displaced persons is currently the highest since this group of people was first systematically recorded. A number of national laws and policies, as well as a regional convention, have further been developed using the Guiding Principles as a normative reference on how to protect and assist IDPs. Yet, as the authors show, the extent of domestic implementation varies considerably. While the Guiding Principles are often hailed as a success story in international fora, they tend to be contested or overlooked as a matter of domestic practice and struggle to exert influence in complex post-conflict and post-disaster contexts where even domestic laws are often not systematically and equitably applied.

Part II traces the role of soft law in emerging areas of international human rights law, where there is no substantial treaty codification of norms. The chapters in this part all examine the relationship between soft and hard law, the role of different actors in formulating new soft law and the potential for eventual codification. The UN Declaration on the Rights of Indigenous Peoples is one such case. In his chapter, *Felipe Gómez Isa* analyses how indigenous peoples have used soft contemporary international law in their efforts to put an end to historically rooted patterns of subjugation, dispossession, and cultural assimilation. The UNDRIP, adopted in 2007 by the UN General Assembly, has to be seen as the culmination of a long and difficult journey in which indigenous peoples themselves and their representatives have been the driving force and key participants. Many of the provisions enshrined in the Declaration simply reaffirm existing customary rules of international law, while others point to future developments. Irrespective of the uncertain legal nature of the UNDRIP, it has thus become an unavoidable point of reference when implementing indigenous peoples' rights.

Nuancing this view, *Léticia Villeneuve* points out that although the UNDRIP is an important milestone, its adoption was also opposed by four important countries: Australia, Canada, New Zealand, and the United States. Looking through these countries' positions and motives for opposing the UNDRIP, she argues that commitment to a soft law instrument may involve a more complex decision-making process than conventional human rights theory suggests, at least for the states involved. Her chapter shows that the four opposing states' declarations directly map onto the potential developments foreseen for a soft law instrument, as each state voiced clear objections to all potential avenues through which the UNDRIP could follow the lead of the previous 'hardening' of provisions in soft law instruments. Such 'hardening' may undermine the perceived benefits of soft law instruments in terms of their flexibility and adaptability. The more soft law advocates attempt to stretch the limits of state consent after the adoption of a soft law instrument and attempt to push for the recognition of binding obligations arising from it, the likelier the chances that it will cause a backlash from states and nourish a reluctance to commit to further instruments. Soft law could thus fall prey to its own success.

The UN Guiding Principles on Business and Human Rights is another example where soft law arguably takes on a primary role in the human rights field. Introducing non-state actors as quasi duty-bearers in a set of human rights standards endorsed by the Human Rights Council, they have been met with both enthusiasm and resistance from states and legal scholars. In her chapter *Stéphanie Lagoutte* argues that the Guiding Principles are a challenging, and sometimes confusing, instrument for public international law and international human rights law in terms of form and content. It is therefore important to clarify the nature and the contents of the Guiding Principles and analyse the effects of the emergence of such soft law instruments. She acknowledges that the Guiding Principles have played a catalyst role in restating and bringing together relevant human rights obligations in a set of soft law standards addressing both states and business enterprises. Yet, by associating corporate social responsibility discourse and actual legal obligation in the same instrument, it also becomes more difficult to distinguish the mandatory elements from the voluntary ones within the field of human rights and business.

Following on from this, *Christoph Good* argues that the Guiding Principles may be analysed in terms of different objectives in relation to the wider international human rights framework. In addition to the classical preparatory function of soft law (that is expressed in the concrete case in the expectation to harden the corporate obligation to respect human rights), the Guiding Principles may also be seen as an example of soft law filling a more pragmatic role to ensure an output-oriented, multi-layer governance approach. This process is characterized by institutionalized stakeholder involvement and a general openness towards alternative regulative approaches. It may be too early to tell whether the Guiding Principles will induce a sustainable behavioural change of states and corporations, yet the use of soft law ended the deadlocked international discussions on how to frame the corporate responsibilities in the business and human rights nexus. Furthermore, this functional turn is not limited to the Guiding Principles, but may be disseminated as an underlying benchmark into wider human rights processes at the international, regional, and national level.

Anette Faye Jacobsen examines the role soft law plays in relation to development agencies' and non-state actors' policies and programmes. As in other areas, soft law is seen as a means to elaborate and expand on existing hard law, and, gradually, to bring about new norms. Soft law is thus extensively referenced by development organizations, NGOs, and activists to strengthen civil society's influence on governmental policies and decision-making. In that sense soft law may indeed be argued to expand the human rights field at the political and discursive levels. Yet, to what extent it actually leads to improved and expanded application of human rights protections depends on the context, and the expansive trend carries with it a risk that state actors may try to stifle the influence of international and regional human rights institutions in order to counter normative developments.

Chapter 14, by *Sally Holt, Zdenka Machnyikova, and John Packer*, examines the issue of minority rights and their implementation. This is an area that has relied heavily on soft law instruments to expand the scope, reach, and implementation of human rights protection. Vague provisions of hard law instruments have been given substantial specificity in content, and whole areas—such as language rights and rights of effective participation—have emerged with their own sub-elements with important implications for minority protection and good governance. Their case study indicates that less dogmatic approaches and constructive engagement, with interpretative intermediaries, may result in greater and more sustained gains in the effective enjoyment and realization of human rights. More broadly, this is an example of the dynamic interplay between international norms and domestic behaviour, where the two orders of law positively intersect generating voluntary compliance and sustained performance. Despite its status, soft law may thus have 'hard effects', and the process by which this area has evolved may provide lessons for the effective implementation and realization of human rights in other areas.

1

A Taxonomy of Soft Law

Stipulating a Definition

John Cerone

1. Introduction

There is no universally accepted definition of the term 'soft law'. Indeed, as noted in the Introduction, the very notion of soft law is disputed. Nonetheless, the phrase is commonly used by international lawyers and is generally understood to refer to certain categories of norms, and at least some of these norms are having an undeniable impact on the interpretation, application, and development of international human rights law.

Existing definitions for the term soft law are varied, inconsistent, and at times incoherent from the perspective of international law. Some definitions encompass any behaviour-affecting, or potentially behaviour-affecting, norms that are not themselves existing rules of international law (i.e. that do not have the status of binding legal rules according to the established sources of international law). Other definitions are limited to particular formulations set forth in certain types of instruments, irrespective of whether their content reflects existing law. Still others would include even vague or non-justiciable obligations in unquestionably hard law sources, such as treaties.[1] There are countless other usages of the term, including, but not limited to, various permutations of the foregoing.[2]

In order to delimit the scope of the volume, and consequently to establish the framework of the subject matter to be analysed, the present chapter stipulates a formulation for a core meaning of the term 'soft law', as well as a definition for the phrase 'soft law instrument'. In addition to serving the purpose of framing the subject matter, the formulation of a definition also serves the broader purpose of facilitating communication by clarifying our understanding of what we mean when

[1] Note, however, that a provision in a treaty may reflect soft law vis-à-vis states that are not bound by that rule (e.g. because they are not parties to that treaty).

[2] J. Ellis, 'Shades of Grey: Soft Law and the Validity of Public International Law', *Leiden Journal of International Law* vol. 25 (2012): 313–34, at 315; J. Klabbers, 'The Redundancy of Soft Law', *Nordic Journal of International Law* vol. 65 (1996): 167–82 at 168; D. Shelton, 'Normative Hierarchy in International Law', *American Journal of International Law* vol. 100 (2006): 291–323 at 319.

we use this phrase. We may have different understandings of the roles and usages of soft law, and indeed even of what properly constitutes soft law, but it is essential to have a common vocabulary in order to understand these differences.

2. 'Soft' and 'Law'

The words composing the phrase provide a starting point for understanding some of the existing conceptions and usages of this term. Some definitions focus on the word 'soft' as giving the phrase distinctive meaning. According to such definitions, 'soft' law is a type of law—that is, a law that is in some sense 'soft'.

This camp is then subdivided between those who adopt a binary approach between law and non-law, and those who view law as more of a continuum. Some adopt a binary approach, where something is either law or not law. For those adhering to this more positivist approach, 'soft law' refers to rules of positive law that are recognized as such, but nonetheless may be considered soft in their commands.[3] This softness might be attributable to, for example, vague language, non-justiciable formulations, or an exclusive reliance on auto-interpretation by the subject of obligation. For those who adopt this approach, there is no such thing as a soft law instrument, for it is not the character of the instrument that makes it soft. In order for something to be called soft law, it must be existing international law according to the established sources.

Others within this camp reject the binary approach and rather see a broader spectrum of law than what is formulated in Article 38 of the ICJ Statute.[4] For this second group, soft law need not be law established in accordance with the traditional doctrine of sources. Soft law may thus not be legally binding in the technical sense, but the adherents of this view tend to accord the binding/non-binding dichotomy less significance, instead viewing a spectrum of normativity and behaviour-influencing capacity. They view all of it as a type of 'law' because the norms are typically formulated as rules and are intended to, and often do, guide behaviour. The 'softness' of a norm, formulation, or instrument could be in terms of, inter alia, specificity, onerousness, enforceability, justiciability, normativity, or 'bindingness'.[5]

Rather than seeing soft law as a type of law, a third approach, which is also the approach of the present author, is to not regard 'soft law' as law at all.[6] This conception also adopts a positivistic, binary perspective, but is the inverse of the

[3] P. Weil, 'Towards Relative Normativity in International Law', *American Journal of International Law* vol. 77 (1983): 413–42 at 414.

[4] See e.g.: D. Shelton (ed.), *Commitment and Compliance: The Role of Non-binding Norms in the International Legal System* (Oxford: Oxford University Press, 2000).

[5] See e.g.: G. Shaffer and M. Pollack, 'Hard Versus Soft Law in International Security', *Boston College Law Review* vol. 52 (2011): 1147–241 at 1160; C. Christine, 'The Challenge of Soft Law: Development and Change in International Law', *International and Comparative Law Quarterly* vol. 38 (1989): 850–66 at 851.

[6] See e.g.: Klabbers (1996): 167–82.

positivistic perspective described above, in that it entirely excludes positive law from the ambit of soft law and includes only rules that do not have the status of existing international law according to the established sources. According to this view, the term 'law' in the phrase soft law does not describe the status of the rule itself, but instead refers to the form or provenance of the rule and may also reflect its relationship to and potential relevance in the international legal system. In this sense, the rule is described as 'soft' precisely because it is not itself law, but is still referred to as 'law' because it may exert an influence on law or may achieve some of the effects that law seeks to achieve.

All three of the above approaches are reflected in usage of the term 'soft law' by both academics and practitioners, though most common usages seem to correspond to the second and third conceptions.

Another variation in usage should be noted. Most of the views formulated above conceive of soft law as a category of norms; however, the term is also used to describe a category of instruments[7]—generally, instruments that are adopted in an intergovernmental setting and that set forth rules of behaviour or other normative standards, but that are not legally binding. This usage would not correspond to the notion of soft law set forth in the first conception above, as that conception is limited to norms that formally have the status of positive law, but it would overlap with the second and third conceptions. However, as one use of the term refers to the norms themselves and the other refers to the type of instrument, the usages are not coextensive. As such, the terms 'soft law' and 'soft law instrument' will each be defined separately in sections 3 and 4.

3. Soft Law Defined

The central challenge in defining the term 'soft law', at least for present purposes, is to develop a definition that is sufficiently precise to have some legally relevant meaning, to ensure a common understanding, and to facilitate clear communication, while at the same time remaining fluid enough to be informed by the very work undertaken by the authors of this volume.

As this book examines the uses of soft law in law and legal process, it is essential to formulate a core definition that, while still corresponding to prevailing usages of the term by international lawyers, remains coherent in a legal context. As such, the term soft law strictly understood will be limited to rules that have some recognizable status within the international legal system and, more precisely, within the framework of the established sources of international law as reflected in Article 38 of the Statute of the International Court of Justice.

The most suitable definition for the present enquiry is one that adopts the binary view between law and non-law while admitting the vast diversity of relationships

[7] J. d'Aspremont, 'The Politics of Deformalization in International Law', *Göttingen Journal of International Law* vol. 3 (2011): 503–50 at 526–7; Klabbers (1996): 168.

and effects that non-law norms can have to and upon existing law. At the same time, to say that this definition adopts a binary view as to whether a given norm is law or not, does not exclude a spectrum of relative softness/hardness. The soft law spectrum in this sense is the spectrum beginning from the point at which a rule begins to find authoritative acceptance and through its progressive hardening/crystallization as it gains increasing acceptance. Here, within this spectrum of norms that are in the process of incubation, is the realm of soft law in the strict sense. Once a rule fully crystallizes into, or pursuant to, one of the Article 38 sources of international law, it thereafter ceases to be soft law.

The adoption of this binary approach is particularly important in the field of international human rights law. Considerations of enforceability, precision, measurability, justiciability, onerousness, availability of redress or recourse to other fora, likelihood of sanction or penalty, and the like, are irrelevant to the issue of whether the given obligation exists as a matter of applicable law. A treaty obligation to make a voluntary pledge is still a binding legal obligation. A treaty obligation to endeavour to make a voluntary pledge is still a binding legal obligation. If the binary approach were instead rejected in favour of an assessment of 'softness' according to the foregoing considerations, the concept of soft law could potentially encompass much of human rights treaty law, rendering the central enquiry of the present study incoherent.

For purposes of this volume, then, the term soft law is understood to refer to rules (prescribing conduct or otherwise establishing standards) that are in the process of becoming, though may not ultimately become, binding rules of international law in the form of any of the established sources of international law—customary law, general principles of law, or as a binding interpretation of a rule of treaty law. This definition refers to the rules themselves, and not the instruments in which they may be found. (The term 'soft law instrument' will be defined in section 6.)

Softness therefore does not refer to degree of precision, onerousness, enforceability, justiciability, availability of redress or recourse to other fora, or likelihood of sanction or penalty. Softness instead will be understood in relation to the degree of hardening of a norm into an existing rule of international law. Soft law, in this sense, may be grounded in the broader concept of *lex ferenda*. While recognizing that the latter is a distinct concept, it helps to situate our notion of soft law in the context of the international legal system, enabling the concept to be useful in lawyering while retaining much of the scope encompassed by usage.

4. Situating Soft Law within the Broader Context of *Lex Ferenda*

The International Court of Justice has at times expressly drawn a distinction between *lex ferenda* and *lex lata*. While these terms might have a sharper meaning in a domestic legal context, with its typically more precise and clearly defined modes of law-making, their application in the context of international law-making warrants closer examination.

Ferenda is the gerundive form of the verb *ferre*, meaning 'to carry' or 'to bear'. *Ferre legem* is thus to carry or to bear a law; that is, to bring forth or to propose a law for adoption. The gerundive signifies futurity or necessity. *Lex ferenda* thus refers to a law which is to be brought forth or should be brought forth. Similarly, the phrase *de lege ferenda* means 'concerning a law which is to be brought forth'. *Lata*, on the other hand, is the (irregular) past participle of *ferre*. Thus, the phrase *lex lata* refers to a law that has already been brought, that is, existing law.

While *lex lata* is synonymous with existing law, the term *lex ferenda* is not identical to the proposed definition of soft law. In the national legal context, within which the line where non-law passes into law is arguably much sharper than in the international legal system, the concept of *lex ferenda* is generally reserved for proposals for legislative change and indicates nothing about the status or likelihood of their progression toward law. In contrast, in the international legal system, with its more diffuse systems of law-making, there is a greater coincidence between the categories of *lex ferenda* and soft law as defined in section 3.

This coincidence can be seen in the ICJ's Advisory Opinion on the Legality of the Threat or Use of Nuclear Weapons.[8] After acknowledging the consistent practice of non-use of nuclear weapons, the Court turned to the issue of *opinio juris*. The Court surveyed a number of General Assembly resolutions declaring the illegality of the use of nuclear weapons, but noted that several of the resolutions were adopted with substantial numbers of negative votes and abstentions. It concluded, 'thus, although those resolutions are a clear sign of deep concern regarding the problem of nuclear weapons, they still fall short of establishing the existence of an *opinio juris* on the illegality of the use of such weapons'.[9] The Court then went on to point out that these resolutions 'reveal[] the desire of a very large section of the international community to take, by a specific and express prohibition of the use of nuclear weapons, a significant step forward along the road to complete nuclear disarmament',[10] essentially constituting a *lex ferenda*. The Court concluded, 'The emergence, as *lex lata*, of a customary rule specifically prohibiting the use of nuclear weapons as such is hampered by the continuing tensions between the nascent *opinio juris* on the one hand, and the still strong adherence to the practice of deterrence on the other.'[11] The Court's use of the term *lex lata* is in contrast with both the general concept of *lex ferenda* and the more specific category of soft law—in this case an emerging prohibition supported by a nascent *opinio juris* reflected in, inter alia, General Assembly resolutions.

Thus, in the context of the more diffuse and evolutionary international legal system, the term *lex ferenda* may bear a richer meaning. It connotes not just a law

[8] Legality of the Threat or Use of Nuclear Weapons Advisory Opinion, 1996 ICJ 226 (8 July).

[9] Legality of the Threat or Use of Nuclear Weapons Advisory Opinion, 1996 ICJ 226 (8 July), para. 71.

[10] Legality of the Threat or Use of Nuclear Weapons Advisory Opinion, 1996 ICJ 226 (8 July), para. 73.

[11] Legality of the Threat or Use of Nuclear Weapons Advisory Opinion, 1996 ICJ 226 (8 July), para. 73.

for the future, but a law that is being carried forward into the future—a rule that is in the process of becoming law. Here we can borrow a metaphor from Professor Georges Abi-Saab, who has described customary international law as a parasitic plant, latching onto whatever champion comes along to carry it forward. Soft law then consists of law *in statu nascendi*, those rules of the *lex ferenda* that have at least begun the process of hardening.

A contemporary and oft-cited example of soft law in the realm of human rights is the emerging prohibition of the death penalty as an aspect of the right to life. In addition to an increasing state practice of abolishing the death penalty accompanied by expressions of the requisite *opinio juris*, this soft law norm is reflected in numerous treaties and resolutions of intergovernmental organizations. The latter are commonly categorized as 'soft law instruments', though some would save this denomination for sets of norms adopted in more particular forms, such as guidelines, declarations, principles, recommendations, or other code-like instruments. In any event, as the norm is still 'soft', it is not yet legally binding as such; that is, on those states that have not accepted it in some established form (e.g. by being a party to one of the Protocols abolishing it). It also remains open for states at this stage to contend for eventual persistent objector status; hence the insistence of the United States on explicitly reserving its position when the issue of capital punishment arises in intergovernmental fora.

A critical issue in this 'spectrum view' of norms as they progress toward law is that of momentum and the related shifting burden of inertia. In the early stages of this progression toward law, states need not object to a norm with which they disagree, and indeed, as noted, the norm may never progress beyond this embryonic stage. However, if and as the number of states supporting the norm approaches a critical mass, states will need to speak up if they wish to prevent it from hardening. The momentum generated by the increasing support for the norm shifts the burden of inertia. Silence will now be deemed acquiescence. As the norm hardens, the burden on the objector increases. If it becomes clear that the battle to prevent hardening will be lost and the norm is on track to become law, a state seeking an exemption from its application may contend for persistent objector status.

This spectrum view of the hardening of international norms is broadly accepted. Nonetheless, reasonable minds, and even different sittings of the same international court, will differ as to when a critical mass of state acceptance has been reached, both as a general proposition and with reference to particular instances.

5. The Soft Law Threshold

Of course, any normative statement, irrespective of source, has *some* possibility of becoming a rule of international law. An idea proposed by a student in a university lecture hall, a proposition from a political party manifesto, a tenet of religious faith, a dictum in a national court decision, a normative assertion set forth in a human rights NGO's advocacy document, or a rule formulated by a transnational working group of law professors. Any of these could be the genesis for an eventual rule of soft law.

However, a normative statement will be considered a rule of soft law only once it acquires a degree of traction. For purposes of this study, the term soft law refers to rules that are already in the process of incubation, that are emerging rules of international law, that are viable candidates for crystallizing into hard law. This traction must come in the form of acceptance by the authors of international law—states.

Any attempt to define this point of traction raises a number of further questions. How much acceptance is sufficient to meet this threshold, in terms of degree, directness, and proximity? Can the necessary support be expressed through intergovernmental bodies, and, if so, what are the criteria for determining the necessary institutional pedigree and what is the necessary degree of proximity between the intergovernmental body and the will of states? Will the requisite degree of acceptance vary based on the character and function of the norm at issue, for example whether it is a new rule emerging in a sparsely populated field, or whether it is a refining rule in a densely regulated area of international law? Must there be affirmative support, or express acceptance, or would mere acquiescence suffice? Does the burden of inertia shift, and if so, at what point, in what contexts, and based on what factors?

No precise lines can be drawn, and any analysis would be highly context dependent. Just as it is impossible to come up with a precise formula for determining when a rule of soft law has crystallized into hard law,[12] so it is impossible to define with precision the moment at which a proposed rule has achieved sufficient traction to fall within the category of soft law.[13]

The principal and essential factor, of course, is acceptance by states. At least some degree of state acceptance is necessary for a norm to be considered soft law as defined here. Other, related factors might include: the intent of the authors, the proximity of the authors to states, the number and representativeness of states involved, institutional pedigree and imprimatur, the normative character of the rule as formulated, whether the rule is formulated in terms of rights or obligations, the nature and form of the instrument in which the rule appears, whether the new

[12] The law is in a constant state of flux. This is particularly true of international law. Attempting to ascertain and interpret the applicable rules of international law in a given factual context at a particular moment in time is like trying to paint a picture of the precise location of an object that is constantly in motion.

[13] A recent example of this ambiguity would be the so-called Copenhagen Process Principles and Guidelines. The Principles and Guidelines were created in an intergovernmental setting, but with limited participation. The Principles were drafted in consultation with, and ultimately acknowledged by, a select group of states invited by Denmark to participate in a conference for this purpose. The Principles expressly declare that they do not alter the applicable rules of international law. It would seem that such a caveat would preclude these principles from qualifying as soft law by their simple formulation and acknowledgement by states. However, at least one domestic court has subsequently invoked the Principles in support of interpreting and applying rules of international humanitarian law. Could this manifestation of state acceptance be sufficient to bring the cited Principles into the realm of soft law? The Copenhagen Principles are discussed in the chapters by Bruce Oswald and Peter Vedel Kessing in this volume.

rule is framed as an interpretation of an existing rule, and the character and status of those to whom the rule is addressed. These additional factors may themselves indicate state acceptance, or may influence the degree of state acceptance regarded as sufficient to establish the rules as soft law.

As soft law in the strict sense comprises the norms as such, the above factors are not tied to any particular form. Any evidence of state acceptance of the rule would qualify as evidence of soft law. Similarly, any evidence of customary law would also be evidence of soft law, including, for example, the subsidiary means for determining rules of international law described in Article 38(1)(d) of the ICJ Statute.

While there may be vast differences of opinion regarding the point at which a rule satisfies the definition in section 3, the purpose of this chapter is simply to clarify our general conception of soft law. Thus, the only criteria used to delimit the concept of soft law for the purposes of the present study are that the content be formulated as a rule and that the rule has acquired traction, and, as such, is in the process of incubation.

6. 'Soft Law Instruments'

This definition of soft law is, and is intended to be, broad. It is not limited to norms derived from any particular source, formulated by any particular actor, or set forth in any particular type of instrument.

According to this understanding of soft law then, there are no instruments that are soft law as such. The rules reflected in a UN General Assembly Declaration, for example, may be soft law, and the form and provenance of such instruments may provide the necessary degree of support to establish the soft law character of the norms contained therein, but the instrument itself would not be soft law.

Nonetheless, the term 'soft law' is commonly used as a descriptor for certain types of instruments, including, but not limited to, normative statements in formally non-binding texts adopted by states in a multilateral setting. In addition, as this study focuses on the way in which soft law is being used, much of the practice surveyed involves recourse to codifications and other instruments as evidence to support or promote the existence of the relevant norms.

The term 'soft law instruments' then may be understood as referring to any instrument with normative content that by its form and provenance provides support sufficient to establish the minimum threshold of traction for at least some of the norms contained therein to be regarded as soft law.

There is an extensive catalogue of instruments that may be deemed to have at least some evidentiary weight as soft law. Of particular significance in the field of human rights, there are resolutions and other pronouncements of representative organs of IGOs (including declarations, principles, rules, and guidelines),[14] opinions of experts (or anyone else for that matter) that have been endorsed by

[14] See Felipe Gómez Isa's chapter in this volume.

states directly or through IGO organs,[15] ad hoc intergovernmental processes for the elaboration of standards,[16] and treaty body jurisprudence (including general comments/recommendations, views, enquiries).[17] One might also include in this category decisions of regional and international courts and quasi-judicial bodies, in relation to those that are not parties to the particular dispute. Each of these types of instruments reflects at least some of the factors identified here.

7. Implications of Opting for a Legal, Positivist Conception of Soft Law

In opting for a definition that is tied into the established framework of international law, certain factors that are sometimes cited as soft law parameters must be viewed in light of the requirements for the development of international law. For example, that a set of norms influences behaviour does not alone indicate the soft law character of those norms, as there are plenty of other types of norms that influence behaviour that are in no sense legal. Consideration also has to be given to author, addressee, formulation, and acceptance by states in terms of practice and sense of legal obligation. Thus, a set of human rights guidelines developed by NGOs and subsequently implemented by corporations, without more (e.g. state acceptance, involvement, regulation), would not qualify as soft law, irrespective of the intended or actual impact they had on changing the behaviour of the target audience.

This brings us to the issue of non-state actors. It is well-established that international law may impose legal obligations and confer legal rights on non-state actors. However, states remain the exclusive authors[18] of international law. Thus, rules formulated by NGOs, academics, and other non-state actors cannot be soft law if they are not already in the process of incubation.[19] The texts that they produce would not be soft law instruments as the authors are not endowed with any law-making power. Nonetheless, such rules and texts may have a relationship with soft law. They may reflect existing soft law norms or contribute to the development of new soft law norms by influencing state practice and *opinio juris*. The texts produced by these non-state actors could also be subsequently adopted in an intergovernmental setting, potentially converting them into soft law instruments. Indeed, in practice,

[15] See the chapters by Stéphanie Lagoutte, Christoph Good, Debra Long and Rachel Murray, and Megan Bradley and Angela Sherwood in this volume.

[16] See the chapters by Peter Vedel Kessing and Bruce Oswald in this volume.

[17] See the chapters by Kasey McCall-Smith and Mátyás Bódig in this volume.

[18] This would include of course those entities empowered by states to create new rules of international law. While intergovernmental organizations increasingly engage in law-making, their authority to do so can and must be traced back to states.

[19] This proposal of rules, or interpretations thereof, by academics and other non-state actors must be distinguished from the use of academic writings 'as subsidiary means for the determination of rules of law', within the meaning of Art. 38(1)(d) of the ICJ Statute. The latter are not sources of international law, but merely provide evidence of what the rules are, with the rules themselves having their legal foundation in Art. 38(1)(a)–(c).

there is substantial input by non-state actors in the development of soft law instruments, and some such instruments find their origins in meetings convened by non-state actors.

Thus, while such rules and texts would not qualify as soft law or soft law instruments as defined in this chapter, they are potentially highly relevant to the generation and use of soft law. As such, and to this extent, they constitute part of the subject matter examined in this volume.

Finally, and as noted in this chapter, law is excluded from this definition of soft law. However, just as there will be different views as to whether a norm has gained sufficient traction to enter the realm of soft law, so will there be different views at the other end of the spectrum—as to whether, and at what point, a norm has passed from the realm of soft law into law.[20] Indeed, much of the work undertaken by the authors focuses on precisely this point.

And, again, to say that soft law is not law, is not to say that it is irrelevant to legal analysis. As will be amply demonstrated in the chapters of this volume, soft law can and does have legal effects.[21]

[20] A contemporary example of such difference of views is reflected in the US letter to the ICRC following the publication of the latter's Study on Customary International Humanitarian Law. See: 'Joint letter from John Bellinger and William Haynes to Jakob Kellenberger on Customary International Law Study', *International Legal Materials* vol. 46 (2007): 9. ('The Study's summary states: "It appears that the United States is a 'persistent objector' to the first part of this rule. In addition, France, the United Kingdom and the United States are persistent objectors with regard to the application of the first part of this rule to the use of nuclear weapons." However, the weight of the evidence—including the fact that ICRC statements prior to and upon conclusion of the Diplomatic Conference acknowledged this as a limiting condition for promulgation of new rules at the Conference; that specially affected States lodged these objections from the time the rule first was articulated; and that these States have made them consistently since then—clearly indicates that these three States are not simply persistent objectors, but rather that the rule has not formed into a customary rule at all.')

[21] See the Introduction to this volume and: J. d'Aspremont, *Formalism and the Sources of International Law* (Oxford: Oxford University Press, 2011): 149.

PART I

ESTABLISHED HUMAN RIGHTS REGIMES

2

Interpreting International Human Rights Standards

Treaty Body General Comments as a Chisel or a Hammer

*Kasey L. McCall-Smith**

1. Introduction

Human rights treaties are standard-setting yet these standards are open-textured and evolutionary; therefore interpretative tools must be engaged in order to flesh out the true extent of states' obligations, particularly as these obligations evolve to reflect rights in the modern world. The human rights treaty bodies embedded in each of the UN human rights treaties comprise experts in the field specific to each treaty and represent a unique feature of the core treaties in that they are the primary interpreters of the treaties at the international level. Human rights treaty bodies have contributed a great deal to the development of measurable international human rights obligations. Through the functions confirmed by their respective treaties, treaty bodies have a range of options by way of which they can inform states parties about the evolving nature of human rights protection. From issuing general comments, to appraising states' periodic reports, or reaching final views on individual communications—what will be referred to collectively throughout this chapter as 'jurisprudence'—there is no lack of soft law to be found. Though many states often ignore treaty body jurisprudence, there is unmistakable evidence that it is creeping into the domestic realm by virtue of increasing reference to this jurisprudence in domestic court opinions and policy debates. The persisting question is whether the use of treaty body jurisprudence at the domestic level refines or distorts the development of universal human rights standards.

Human rights treaty bodies are invested by their respective treaties with the competence to assess the implementation of treaty obligations. As will be examined below, the various methods by which treaty bodies may engage in this assessment are outlined in each treaty and the competences of each supervisory mechanism

* The author is indebted to Professor Alan Boyle and Dr James Harrison for comments on previous versions and Sean Molloy for research assistance.

varies, albeit only slightly. The jurisprudence produced through the exercise of these competences is a form of soft law that can respond to the legal and social environment more flexibly and guide interpretation and state practice in the international sphere. In other words, the soft law produced by the treaty bodies is norm-filling.[1] However, it is when these soft instruments are introduced into domestic legal systems that they are truly tested, especially when the instruments are used in a peculiar manner.[2] The impact of these references sustains the concept of soft law put forward by this volume—that treaty body instruments contain rules which are in the process of incubation.[3] The judicial practices surveyed herein suggest that these incubating rules—or more accurately, interpretations of the minimalist binding rules found in the treaties themselves—are gaining traction. It also supports the oft-repeated maxims that human rights treaties do not exist in a vacuum[4] and are 'living instruments'[5] which makes evolutionary interpretation necessary.

This chapter explores the introduction of treaty body jurisprudence into domestic legal systems. Specifically, it considers the use of general comments.[6] The contribution begins with a brief introduction of the treaty bodies as it is the nature of these bodies that warrants consideration of their jurisprudence as a legitimate interpretative tool. It will then deliver an overview of references to treaty body general comments in the case law across a selection of jurisdictions, including the UK and South Africa, as well as Europe as a supranational jurisdiction. Finally, it will analyse the impact that these domestic engagements with treaty body jurisprudence have on the interpretation of international human rights standards. It will consider

[1] See the Introduction to this volume.

[2] The same observation can be said of domestic court application of treaty interpretation rules generally. See e.g.: H. P. Aust, A. Rodiles, and P. Staubach, 'Unity or Uniformity? Domestic Courts and Treaty Interpretation', *Leiden Journal of International Law* vol. 27 (2014): 75–112 at 84.

[3] See the chapter by John Cerone in this volume.

[4] See e.g.: *Hassan v. United Kingdom*, 29750/09 [2014] ECHR 1162 (16 Sept. 2014), para. 77; *Cyprus v. Turkey*, 25781/94 [2014] ECHR 478 (12 May 2014), para. 23; *Marguš v. Croatia*, 4455/10 [2014] ECHR 523 (27 May 2014), para. 129; *Neulinger and Shuruk v. Switzerland* [2010] ECHR 1053 (6 July 2010), para. 131; F. Hampson, Working paper submitted pursuant to Sub-Commission decision 1998/113, UN Doc. E/CN.4/Sub.2/1999/28 (1999), para. 13.

[5] *Jaloud v. The Netherlands*, 47708/08 [2014] ECHR 1292 (20 Nov. 2014), para. 121; *O'Keeffe v. Ireland*, 35810/09 [2014] ECHR 96 (28 Jan. 2014), concurring opinion of Judge Ziemele, para. 11; *X and others v. Austria*, 19010/07 [2013] ECHR 148 (19 Feb. 2013), para. 139; *Loizidou v. Turkey (Preliminary Objections)* [1995] 20 EHRR 99, para. 71; A. Boyle and C. Chinkin, *The Making of International Law* (Oxford: Oxford University Press, 2007): 155; D. Kinley and R. Chambers, 'The UN Human Rights Norms for Corporations: The Private Implications of Public International Law', *Human Rights Law Review* vol. 6 (2006): 447.

[6] Throughout this chapter the term 'general comments' will be used collectively in reference to both general comments and general recommendations as in practice both terms refer to the same form of treaty body jurisprudential product. See e.g.: International Covenant on Civil and Political Rights (ICCPR), 999 UNTS 171, 16 Dec. 1966, Art. 40(4): 'The Committee shall study the reports submitted by the States Parties to the present Covenant. It shall transmit its reports, and such *general comments* as it may consider appropriate, to States Parties' (emphasis added). The Convention on the Elimination of All forms of Discrimination against Women (CEDAW) 1249 UNTS 13, 18 Dec. 1979, Art. 21(1): 'The Committee shall ... report annually to the General Assembly of the United Nations on its activities and may make suggestions and *general recommendations* based on the examination of reports and information received from the States Parties' (emphasis added). Similar statements can be found in each of the core UN human rights treaties discussed in this chapter.

whether the outcome of a court case that has relied upon general comments contributes to or detracts from the strength of the treaty body outputs. It is posited that in instances where rights are progressively recognized for protection, general comments serve as a chisel to aid in refining rights. In instances where the judiciary disregards or distorts treaty body guidance, it is suggested that the general comments act more as a hammer that weakens a particular right. Thus it is extremely important that treaty bodies take special care when drafting their opinions, comments, and reports; therefore some attention will be given to the issue of treaty body drafting.

As an interpretative tool, treaty body general comments enrich the understanding of human rights obligations, and it is clear that state organs are increasingly willing to entertain these views in order to better define human rights at the domestic level. As an increasingly authoritative form of soft law, general comments are shaping the way in which domestic courts interpret international human rights standards. What is not clear is whether the unwieldy nature of domestic interpretations bolsters or undermines these standards.

2. Human Rights Treaty Bodies

Human rights treaty bodies are the embedded international institutions of the UN human rights treaties and the primary monitoring and enforcement mechanisms of the texts' obligations. All of the treaty bodies review periodic reports and are authorized to issue general comments as they may consider appropriate. Essential to the perceived legal value of the treaty bodies' jurisprudence is the independent, expert, non-political status of the bodies.

Each of the treaty bodies' membership election processes is crafted to guarantee that an unbiased authority exercises oversight over the universal human rights treaties. The treaty body election guidelines seek to achieve equitable geographical distribution in addition to representation of different types of civilizations and legal systems among the states parties, which helps ensure that no one region or culture dominates. Essential to the execution of their duties is the requirement that members act in their personal capacities, not as representatives of their governments, despite being nominated by them.

It has been suggested that experts working together in the international context 'can facilitate the resolution of global policy issues by narrowing the range within which political bargains could be struck'.[7] For example, typical members of the CEDAW Committee have been active in the areas of gender equality and women's issues and this is reflected by their curriculum vitae. Picciotto observed that 'delegating specific issues to specialists who would deal with them in a depoliticized fashion … is a means of implementing policies that have been formulated through

[7] S. Picciotto, 'Constitutionalizing Multilevel Governance?', *International Journal of Constitutional Review* vol. 6 (2008): 457–79 at 459.

political processes ... [and] understood as a response to the problems of governing ever more complex societies'.[8] The treaty bodies exist to ensure specific rights are implemented into a variety of social, cultural, and political jurisdictions. The combination of a highly varied membership and specialists in the field, both mandated by committee election guidelines, provides an essential element of legitimacy to the work of the treaty bodies. Without the treaty bodies supervising implementation, human rights treaties would be in danger of becoming merely aspirational.

3. Treaty Body Jurisprudence

States parties have a duty of good faith to cooperate with the treaty body as recognized by general principles of treaty law.[9] It is essential that treaty bodies interpret the obligations in light of the domestic situation on the ground, including introduction of new law or reconciliation with existing law. The interaction between a treaty body and a state party is very much an exclusive, interactive process and is best understood as an ongoing dialogue. Thus, treaty bodies function primarily on a bilateral plane.[10] The exception to this rule is the practice of issuing general comments or recommendations, which are intended specifically to provide useful information to all states parties regarding how convention obligations should be implemented.

General comments often are viewed as the 'attendant product' to guide states on the scope of treaty obligations.[11] In light of the concerns of many states about interference with state sovereignty, the treaty bodies' obligations to make general comments is possibly the strongest language available to indicate that they are singularly responsible for guiding states' compliance with a treaty despite the fact that this practice has been repeatedly harpooned by states as an over-extension of their powers.[12] General comments address the entirety of states parties, rather than individual states as with the communications or periodic reporting procedures, and they range from mundane matters of internal treaty body functioning to elucidating the appropriate means of protecting particular rights.[13]

[8] Picciotto (2008): 457–79 at 459.

[9] Vienna Convention on the Law of Treaties (Vienna Convention), 1155 UNTS 331, 23 May 1969, Art. 26. This is also typically noted within each of the treaty texts.

[10] N. Rodley, 'United Nations Human Rights Treaty Bodies and Special Procedures of the Commission on Human Rights: Complementary or Competition?', *Human Rights Quarterly* vol. 25 (2003): 882–908 at 887.

[11] Rodley (2003): 906.

[12] See e.g.: Observations by the United States of America and the United Kingdom on General Comment No. 24(52), UN Doc. A/50/40 (1995); reprinted in *Human Rights Law Journal* vol. 16 (1995): 423.

[13] Rodley (2003): 888; H. J. Steiner, 'Individual Claims in a World of Massive Violations: What Role for the Human Rights Committee?', in *The Future of UN Human Rights Treaty Monitoring*, ed. P. Alston and J. Crawford (Cambridge: Cambridge University Press, 2000): 15–53 at 22.

3.1 General comments—evolving practice

The practice of issuing general comments began in 1981 with the Human Rights Committee pursuant to ICCPR Article 40.[14] Eight of the nine core UN human rights treaty bodies have issued a combined 153 general comments on various aspects of their respective treaties.[15] These include the CERD Committee[16] (thirty-five comments), the Human Rights Committee (HRC)[17] (thirty-five comments), the ESCR Committee[18] (twenty-three comments), the CEDAW Committee[19] (thirty-four comments), the CAT Committee[20] (three comments), the CRC Committee[21] (nineteen comments, including one draft comment published June 2015), the Committee on Migrant Workers[22] (two comments), and the newest treaty body to commence operation, the Committee on the Rights of Persons with Disabilities (two comments). Most recently, the ESRC Committee adopted General Comment 23 on the right to justice and favourable conditions of work in March 2016.[23]

The debate amongst observers of the UN human rights regime assigns disparate levels of importance to these comments as a form of soft law. Some view them as authoritative interpretations of the treaties while others view them as unsystematic and unfounded statements deserving no recognition in the law.[24] Though there is far from consensus on the determination of exactly what legal weight general comments carry, it is evident that they have influenced the protection of human rights and enriched the human rights dialogue.

[14] For a more complete overview of the history of general comments see: H. Keller and L. Grover, 'General Comments of the Human Rights Committee and their Legitimacy', in *UN Human Rights Treaty Bodies: Law and Legitimacy*, ed. H. Keller and G. Ulfstein (Cambridge: Cambridge University Press, 2012): 116–98 at 121–7; P. Alston, 'The Historical Origins of the Concept of "General Comments" in Human Rights Law', in *The International Legal System in Quest of Equity and Universality: Liber Amicorum Georges Abi-saab*, ed. L. Boisson de Chazournes and V. Gowlland-Debbas (2001): 763, reprinted in H. J. Steiner, P. Alston, and R. Goodman, *International Human Rights in Context: Law, Politics, Morals* (3rd edn) (Oxford: Oxford University Press, 2008): 873.

[15] As of 3 Jan. 2016.

[16] The treaty body established by Art. 8 of the Convention on the Elimination of all forms of Racial Discrimination (CERD), 669 UNTS 195, 21 Dec. 1965.

[17] The treaty body established by Art. 28, ICCPR.

[18] The treaty body overseeing the International Covenant on Economic, Social and Cultural Rights (ICESCR), 993 UNTS 3, 26 Dec. 1966, was established by ECOSOC Resolution 1985/17, 28 May 1985. Prior to the resolution, reports were submitted directly to the UN Economic and Social Council pursuant to Art. 16 of the Covenant.

[19] The treaty body established by Art. 18 of CEDAW.

[20] The treaty body established by Art. 17 of the Convention on the Prevention of Torture and Other Cruel, Inhuman or Degrading Treatment or Punishment (CAT), 465 UNTS 85, 10 Dec. 1984.

[21] The treaty body established by Art. 43 of the Convention on the Rights of the Child (CRC), 1577 UNTS 3, 20 Nov. 1989.

[22] The treaty body established by Art. 72 of the Convention for the Protection of the Rights of Migrant Workers and Their Families (CRMW), 2220 UNTS 3, 18 Dec. 1990.

[23] ESRC Committee, General Comment No. 23 on the Right to Just and Favourable Conditions of Work (Art. 7), UN Doc. E/C.12/GC/23 (2016). General Comment information updated 28 June 2016.

[24] Keller and Grover (2012): 118–19.

3.1.1 Guiding principles on general comments

The guiding principles on formulating comments, an amalgamation of the procedure and practice that has developed since 1981, indicate that they should be directed to states parties, promote cooperation between states parties, summarize the experience the treaty body has gained reviewing the states parties' periodic reports, and focus the attention of the states parties on matters that would improve implementation of the treaty obligations.[25] They are intended to provide 'significant normative guidance' on aspects of implementation of the treaty.[26] Furthermore, the subjects should be limited to those involving implementation of obligations related to periodic reports, guarantee of the treaty rights, article specific questions, or suggestions relating to cooperation between states parties.[27] General comments are most often expository in style and the language typically reflects the expertise of the treaty body in dealing with the treaty obligations under its supervision.[28] In maintaining a formula, albeit a vague one, it is intended that states will more readily accept comments adhering to the guidelines.

The lack of a clear definition of 'general comment/recommendation' in the treaties coupled with the vague guidelines has resulted in diverse subject matters ranging from implementation of CERD Article 6[29] (access to effective remedy) to the practice of reservations to the ICCPR[30] and CEDAW.[31] What is important to reiterate is that the treaty bodies are carrying out their duties under the treaty texts. The issue of transmitting comments, as with many aspects in the human rights regime, was left undefined intentionally so that practices could develop as the human rights movement spread. However, it is now clear that the practice is firmly established and accepted by the majority of states parties.[32]

3.2 General comments—points of contention

The issuing of general comments has traditionally been the point at which states articulate opposition to treaty bodies as they often view the practice as going beyond the treaty into the realm of developing new law.[33] General comments air the problems that surface during the review of periodic reports and, though they are not state-specific, the fact that reports and comments are publicly available enables

[25] Alston (2001): 876. [26] Keller and Grover (2012): 124.

[27] Alston (2001): 876.

[28] See e.g.: Rodley (2003): 888–9, discussing the HRC's general comment on ICCPR Art. 7.

[29] CERD Committee, General Recommendation No. 26: Article 6 of the Convention, UN Doc. A/55/18, annex V (2000).

[30] HRC, General Comment No. 24: Issues Relating to Reservations Made upon Ratification or Accession to the Covenant or the Optional Protocols Thereto, or in Relation to Declarations under Article 41 of the Covenant, UN Doc. CCPR/C/21/Rev.1/Add.6, 4 Nov. 1994.

[31] CEDAW Committee, General Recommendation No 4: Reservations, UN Doc. HRI/GEN/1/Rev.9, vol. 2 (2008).

[32] G. Ulfstein, 'Law-Making by Human Rights Treaty Bodies', in *International Law-Making: Essays in Honour of Jan Klabbers*, ed. R. Liivoja and J. Petman (London: Routledge, 2014): 249–58 at 252.

[33] Keller and Grover (2012): 118.

the easy association of themes and, therefore, may be embarrassing to states with less than commendable rights records. This, in turn, causes offended states parties to argue the lack of legal basis for the comment.[34] Alston appropriately identified general comments as a 'double-edged sword' for states parties who launch attacks criticizing their legitimacy as it not only draws attention to their disagreement with the opinion and authority of the commenting committee, but also highlights the committee's interpretation of the controversial right, thus establishing a benchmark for other states parties.[35]

Much of the opinion surrounding general comments has turned on the drafting and the process by which the comment is adopted;[36] comments specifically derived from treaty documents have met far less criticism than those that are more creative with the execution of a treaty body's remit. Examples of both can be found in the 2008 General Comment 33[37] of the HRC, which deals with states parties' obligations pursuant to the Optional Protocol[38] to the ICCPR (OP-ICCPR). The HRC notes that under Article 2 of the OP-ICCPR that a state party is obliged to provide the author of a complaint with an effective remedy when the Committee determines that there has been a violation of the ICCPR. By grounding their statement in the treaty text, states parties are reminded of the obligations to which they have agreed in becoming a party to the Covenant. Paragraph 19, by contrast, refers to the HRC's rules of procedure as a basis for implementing interim measures where it is thought that irreparable harm is likely to occur before the Committee is able to develop its final views on the complaint. Though linked back to its purpose under the OP-ICCPR and obviously an important tool, using the rules of procedure as a basis for obliging a state to comply with a Committee decision is far weaker than using the actual obligation to which the state has subscribed.

3.3 Summary

A mounting hazard for states, which is equally a windfall for human rights protection, is that treaty body jurisprudence often is viewed as a form of developing law and increasingly is being cited by domestic courts and regional human rights organs, thus incorporating this jurisprudence into the corpus of case law and

[34] See e.g.: Observations by the Governments of the United States and the United Kingdom on Human Rights Committee General Comment No. 24 (52) Relating to Reservations, UN Doc. A/50/40 (1995); reprinted in *Human Rights Law Journal* vol. 16 (1995).

[35] Alston (2001): 763 and 874 of reprinted version.

[36] Keller and Grover (2012): 119.

[37] HRC, General Comment No 33: The Obligations of States Parties under the Optional Protocol to the International Covenant on Civil and Political Rights, UN Doc. CCPR/C/GC/33 (2008).

[38] Optional Protocol to the International Covenant on Civil and Political Rights, 999 UNTS 171, 16 Dec. 1966. HRC General Comment 34 notes at para. 3: 'The preamble to the Optional Protocol states that its purpose is "further to achieve the purposes" of the Covenant by enabling the Human Rights Committee, established in part IV of the Covenant, "to receive and consider, as provided in the present Protocol, communications from individuals claiming to be victims of violations of any of the rights set forth in the Covenant." The Optional Protocol sets out a procedure, and imposes obligations on States parties to the Optional Protocol arising out of that procedure, in addition to their obligations under the Covenant.'

moving it to a less 'soft' form of law, particularly in common law jurisdictions. This use of treaty body jurisprudence may be more appropriately referred to as 'liquid' law in the domestic context as it aids in filling the gaps in and among the hard law that governs rights assessment. In these situations, the legal opinion of a treaty body can be validated by the court and can lend legitimacy to existing and future treaty body opinions. It is to this phenomenon that this chapter will now turn.

4. General Comments in Domestic Courts

There is a strong argument to rely heavily on the opinions of the treaty bodies as interpretative tools in light of the special nature of both the treaty bodies and the nature of the rights their constitutive treaties are designed to protect. It must be acknowledged, however, that as far as the codified rules of treaty interpretation are concerned, the 1969 Vienna Convention on the Law of Treaties does not mention the treaty-specific monitoring mechanisms. Treaty bodies had not begun to operate at the time the Vienna Convention was adopted, thus it would have had no cause to address such mechanisms.[39] This underscores the point that international law and human rights law, particularly, are dynamic and evolving and thus updates must be considered in order to maintain a coherent system.

This section examines the increasing recognition of general comments as interpretative tools by a selection of domestic courts. The caveat, which must be set forth from the outset, is that the following is an extremely preliminary overview of the case law derived from three distinct jurisdictions. It is by no means comparative between them, nor exhaustive in any way. Particularly, the following gives a perfunctory overview of general comments as introduced into the UK, South African, and European systems.

4.1 United Kingdom

The UK is party to CERD,[40] ICESCR,[41] ICCPR,[42] CEDAW,[43] CAT,[44] the CRC,[45] and the CRPD.[46] Thus, opinions stemming from the associated treaty

[39] Though the treaty bodies were functioning prior to the entry into force of the Vienna Convention in 1980. In its Guide to Practice on Reservations to Treaties the International Law Commission specifically recognizes the role of treaty bodies in monitoring and determining issues related to human rights treaty interpretation, see Report of the International Law Commission on its 63rd session, Guide to Practice on Reservations with commentary, UN Doc. A/66/10/Add.1 (2011), 3.2 and 3.2.1. For an examination of this competence: K. L. McCall-Smith, 'Reservations and the Determinative Function of the Human Rights Treaty Bodies', *German Yearbook of International Law* vol. 54 (2011): 521–64.

[40] The UK signed on 11 Oct. 1966 and ratified on 7 Mar. 1969.

[41] The UK signed on 16 Sept. 1968 and ratified on 20 May 1976.

[42] The UK signed on 16 Sept. 1968 and ratified on 20 May 1976.

[43] The UK signed on 22 July 1981 and ratified on 7 Apr. 1986.

[44] The UK signed on 15 Mar. 1985 and ratified on 8 Dec. 1988.

[45] The UK signed on 19 Apr. 1990 and ratified on 16 Dec. 1991.

[46] The UK signed on 26 Feb. 2009 and ratified on 7 Aug. 2009.

bodies should be acknowledged and observed 'in good faith' in accordance with the Vienna Convention on the Law of Treaties, though none of these treaties has been officially incorporated into UK law. The trend of referencing treaty body documentation in the UK began shortly after the adoption of the Human Rights Act[47] in 1998. It, however, has taken some time for the products of the treaty bodies to evolve into and become accepted as more mainstream interpretative tools in the UK domestic legal system. Since the inception of the UK Supreme Court, intermittent reference to the treaty bodies has increased and this has trickled down to lower courts in their efforts to maintain coherence with the rulings of the highest court.

Article 2 of the Human Rights Act 1998 largely shapes the assessment of human rights and the expansion of rights in the UK. Article 2 provides:

2 Interpretation of Convention rights.

(1) A court or tribunal determining a question which has arisen in connection with a Convention right must take into account any—
- (a) judgment, decision, declaration or advisory opinion of the European Court of Human Rights,
- (b) opinion of the Commission given in a report adopted under Article 31 of the Convention,
- (c) decision of the Commission in connection with Article 26 or 27(2) of the Convention, or
- (d) decision of the Committee of Ministers taken under Article 46 of the Convention,

whenever made or given, so far as, in the opinion of the court or tribunal, it is relevant to the proceedings in which that question has arisen.

Thus whilst it outlines specifically that UK courts must take into account the jurisprudence of the European Court of Human Rights and opinions of other European Convention on Human Rights organs, there is no direct reference to jurisprudence emanating from the UN treaty bodies. However, this omission has not prevented British courts from utilizing treaty body jurisprudence in the course of interpreting human rights issues that come before them.

In the early months of 2014 the UK Supreme Court reflected on general comments in a handful of cases. For example, *Kennedy v. The Charity Commission*[48] recounted the evolution of the freedom of expression under Article 10 of the ECHR and how it has been expanded to include access to information in order to facilitate expression, particularly in the context of a public watchdog.[49] The Court noted that the European Court of Human Rights relied on General Comment No. 34 in which the Human Rights Committee[50] (HRC) underscored that 'the right of access to information includes a right whereby the media has access to information on

[47] UK, *Human Rights Act 1998: Elizabeth ll. Chapter 42* (London: The Stationery Office, 1998), 'An Act to give further effect to rights and freedoms guaranteed under the European Convention on Human Rights'.

[48] *Kennedy v. The Charity Commission* [2014] 2UKSC 20, [2014] WLR 808.

[49] *Kennedy v. The Charity Commission* [2014] 2UKSC 20, [2014] WLR 808, para. 186.

[50] The Human Rights Committee is the monitoring mechanism attached to the ICCPR.

public affairs'.[51] Thus the Supreme Court 'confidently conclude[d] that a right to require an unwilling public authority to disclose information can arise under article 10'[52] because the right of access goes hand in hand with freedom of expression, as outlined in the HRC's interpretation of Article 19 of the ICCPR. This does not mean that limitations cannot be put in place through legislation, such as those limitations established by the Freedom of Information Act. It, however, demonstrates that in the UK the domestic evaluation of the freedom of expression tracks the interpretation provided by the HRC in its general comment. This linkage strengthens and refines the shared universal dimensions of the right to free expression.

Examination of free movement protected by ICCPR Article 12 is a recurrent theme on which a multitude of UK courts have looked to the treaty bodies for guidance. For example, an administrative judge invoked the HRC's General Comment No. 27 on Freedom of Movement in the 2010 *Agyeman* case.[53] The judge pointed out that despite the fact that the ICCPR was not incorporated into domestic law, the HRC's interpretation of the Article 12 freedom of movement in paragraphs 19 and 21 of the general comment were rights flowing to British subjects by virtue of their citizenship.[54] Specifically, the focus was the deprivation of the right of a person to enter his own country. The dicta of the case recognized that this right is set forth in domestic, European, and international law, though it is not an unfettered right. As outlined in the comment, the interference with an individual's right to return to his country of residence may only be interfered with to the extent that is 'reasonable in particular circumstances'.[55] In this case, the Court determined that the claimant in the case had to accept the difficulties with which he dealt in relation to obtaining a new British passport. It reasoned that the difficulties were justified in light of the security concerns of the age in which we live, even for a British citizen returning home. Thus the general comment, once again, was used to refine the outer limits of a right by highlighting the restrictions that the state might legitimately employ in the protection of free movement.

Immigration and asylum actions are possibly the most frequent cases to invoke the opinions of the treaty bodies in the UK, but this is largely due to the frequency of such cases both at the administrative and higher court levels. In 2012, the UK Supreme Court examined *RT & KM (among others) v. Secretary of State*,[56] a series of cases revolving around asylum-seeking refugees from Zimbabwe who did not only claim not to support the current Zimbabwean regime but simply had no political views whatsoever. The applicants argued that if returned to Zimbabwe it would

[51] HRC, General Comment No. 34: Article 19: Freedoms of Opinion and Expression, UN Doc. CCPR/C/GC/34 (2011), para. 18.

[52] *Kennedy v. The Charity Commission* [2014] 2UKSC 20, [2014] WLR 808, para. 190.

[53] *Derrick Agyeman v. Secretary of State for Foreign and Commonwealth Affairs, Secretary of State for the Home Department*, CO/8185/2006, [2010] EWHC 2180 (Admin) (11 Aug. 2010), at para. 13.

[54] *Derrick Agyeman v. Secretary of State for Foreign and Commonwealth Affairs, Secretary of State for the Home Department*, CO/8185/2006, [2010] EWHC 2180 (Admin) (11 Aug. 2010), paras 12–13.

[55] HRC, General Comment No. 27: Freedom of Movement, UN Doc. CCPR/C/21/Rev.1/Add.9 (1999), para. 21.

[56] *RT & KM (among others) v. Secretary of State* [2012] UKSC 38, [2012] 4 All ER 843.

be necessary for them to lie and profess support for the regime in order to avoid persecution in light of the Zimbabwean authority's view that 'you are either with us or against us'.[57] The Court underscored that there was 'no support in any of the human rights jurisprudence for a distinction between the conscientious non-believer and the indifferent non-believer'.[58] Thus, the Court determined that the claimants should not be denied asylum simply because they had no political views nor should the alternative to asylum be that the claimants live a lie in their home state simply to avoid persecution. In considering the exercise of the right to freedoms of thought, conscience, and religion as well as the freedom of expression, the Court tracked the HRC's approach to these rights in General Comment No. 22 on Article 18 (30 July 1993) and in General Comment No. 34 on Article 19 (12 September 2011).[59] By referencing the HRC jurisprudence spanning several decades, the UK Supreme Court demonstrates an appreciation for the evolving nature of the right and the multifaceted dimensions in which the right may be implicated.[60] It is clear that the Court worked to maintain a consistent interpretation of the rights involved by paying great deference to the rights as outlined in the HRC's comments. By utilizing the HRC interpretation of the right to freedom of thought, conscience, and religion the Court aids in building a broad consensus on the expansive nature of the right.

Continuing a long line of asylum and immigration cases specifically involving children, in early March of 2011 a Civil Court of Appeal judge found that five paragraphs of the CRC Committee's General Comment No. 6 on Treatment of Unaccompanied and Separated Children Outside their Country of Origin[61] were particularly relevant in *DS (Afghanistan)*.[62] The specificity with which the judge referred to the general comment left no room for questioning the importance of the comment as a tool for interpreting the validity of government actions. The previous month, the Supreme Court had noted in *ZH (Tanzania)* that the most relevant legislation to the question of the effects of deportation on a child was Article 3(1) of the CRC. Article 3(1) establishes the 'best interests of the child' as the primary consideration for all actions involving children.[63] Though a different child-related immigration/asylum issue was asked from that in *DS (Afghanistan)*, both courts relied on the best interests of the child derived directly from the CRC and elaborated upon by the CRC Committee's general comments.[64] Notably, the

[57] *RT & KM (among others) v. Secretary of State* [2012] UKSC 38, [2012] 4 All ER 843, para. 44.

[58] *RT & KM (among others) v. Secretary of State* [2012] UKSC 38, [2012] 4 All ER 843, para. 45, relying on *HJ (Iran) v. Secretary of State for the Home Department* [2011] 1 AC 596.

[59] *RT & KM (among others) v. Secretary of State* [2012] UKSC 38, [2012] 4 All ER 843, para. 33.

[60] HRC, General Comment No. 22 on Article 18 (30 July 1993); HRC, General Comment No. 34 on Article 19 (12 Sept. 2011).

[61] CRC Committee, General Comment No 6: Treatment of Unaccompanied and Separated Children Outside their Country of Origin, UN Doc. CRC/GC/2005/6 (2005).

[62] *DS (Afghanistan) v. Secretary of State for the Home Department* [2011] EWCA Civ 305, para. 65.

[63] *ZH (Tanzania) (FC) v. Secretary of State for the Home Department* [2011] UKSC 4, para. 23.

[64] *DS (Afghanistan) v. Secretary of State for the Home Department* [2011] EWCA Civ 305, para. 22; *ZH (Tanzania) (FC) v. Secretary of State for the Home Department* [2011] UKSC 4, para. 23.

ZH (Tanzania) opinion also cited the CRC Committee's General Comment No. 6 and articulated that:

> Exceptionally, a return to the home country may be arranged, after careful balancing of the child's best interests and other considerations, if the latter are rights-based and override best interests of the child. Such may be the case in situations in which the child constitutes a serious risk to the security of the State or to the society. Non-rights based arguments such as those relating to general migration control, cannot override best interests considerations.[65]

With the Supreme Court recognizing the CRC Committee's opinion, it is no wonder that the decision created a great ripple effect. Following on from *ZH (Tanzania)*, the *Mansoor* case, in a very similar fact pattern and relying heavily on that case, repeated the acceptance of CRC General Comment No. 6.[66] The *Mansoor* decision noted that the UK Supreme Court has adopted:

> the approach recommended by international bodies, including the general comments of the rights of the child and the UNHCR guidelines, to the extent that a rights-based approach must be brought into being in order to justify accumulation of factors which could be said to outweigh the best interests of the child as a primary consideration in these cases.[67]

Thus, the progeny of *ZH (Tanzania)* continues to reinforce the strength of treaty body general comments as an integral consideration for interpreting UK law, whether as some form of evolving law or as an interpretative tool.

The use of general comments by the UK judiciary presented here demonstrates that these treaty body products aid in developing a more complete picture of international human rights obligations. British courts do not always utilize the chisel approach. The *Agyeman* case could be viewed as diminution of rights in the restrictions it places on access to passports. However, human rights are not guaranteed unfettered exercise when a legitimate restriction is deemed necessary. The selection of cases here highlights the potential for a common interpretation of international human rights driven by treaty body general comments.

4.2 South Africa

In 1995, a South African court opined in the *Makwanyane* case that both non-binding, as well as binding, international law 'may be used as tools of interpretation'[68] in keeping with section 39 of the state's (now former) Constitution—which

[65] *ZH (Tanzania) (FC) v. Secretary of State for the Home Department* [2011] UKSC 4, para. 27.

[66] *The Queen on the application of Mansoor v. Secretary of State for the Home Department* [2011] EWHC 832 (Admin), para. 27, citing UN CRC, General Comment No. 6 on the Treatment of Unaccompanied and Separated Children Outside their Country of Origin, UN Doc. CRC/GC/2005/6 (2005), para. 86.

[67] *The Queen on the application of Mansoor v. Secretary of State for the Home Department* [2011] EWHC 832 (Admin), para. 27, citing UN CRC, General Comment No. 6 on the Treatment of Unaccompanied and Separated Children Outside their Country of Origin, UN Doc. CRC/GC/2005/6 (2005), para. 32.

[68] *S v. Makwanyane and another*, 1995 (3) SA 391 (CC) (1995 (2) SACR 1; 1995 (6) BCLR 665), para. 35.

is reflected in the current Constitution, also in Article 39.[69] The 1995 decision provided a list of potential sources of international law including instruments produced by the HRC,[70] despite the fact that the state had not yet ratified the ICCPR. At present, South Africa is party to CERD,[71] ICCPR,[72] CEDAW,[73] CAT,[74] CRC,[75] CRPD,[76] and the ICESCR.[77] Since the passage of the 1996 South African Constitution[78] the Constitutional Court has been particularly willing to utilize general comments in an effort to interpret rights stemming from the Constitution's Bill of Rights (Articles 7–39). Interestingly, the South African courts for many years have tended to invoke general comments of the Committee on Economic, Social and Cultural Rights (ESCR Committee) most often despite only having ratified the ICESCR on 12 January 2015.

In 2000, the Constitutional Court employed relevant international law, including a general comment issued by the ESCR Committee, as a tool of interpretation when considering the socio-economic right of access to housing in *South Africa v. Grootboom*.[79] The Court incorporated paragraph 10 of General Comment No. 3 on The Nature of States Parties' Obligations into the opinion verbatim to establish that the 'minimum core obligation' is necessary to determine whether a state is in violation of its obligations under the ICESCR, as outlined by the ESCR Committee. The minimum core obligation was eventually determined to be outside the scope of the case.[80] The dicta, however, proved useful in subsequent examinations of alleged violations of economic and social rights. Many human rights observers took issue with the Court for its failure to employ a 'minimum essential level' of an economic, social, and cultural right,[81] as outlined by the ESCR Committee in General Comment No. 3.[82] Effectively the opinion severed an essential component

[69] Art. 39, para. 1, of the current Constitution of the Republic of South Africa reads as follows: 'When interpreting the Bill of Rights, a court, tribunal or forum— ... (b) must consider international law; and (c) may consider foreign law.'

[70] Art. 39, para. 35, of the current Constitution of the Republic of South Africa.

[71] South Africa signed on 3 Oct. 1994 and ratified on 10 Dec. 1998.

[72] South Africa signed on 3 Oct. 1994 and ratified on 10 Dec. 1998.

[73] South Africa signed on 29 Jan. 1993 and ratified on 15 Dec. 1995.

[74] South Africa signed on 29 Jan. 1993 and ratified on 10 Dec. 1998.

[75] South Africa signed on 29 Jan. 1993 and ratified on 16 Jun. 1995.

[76] South Africa signed on 30 Mar. 2007 and ratified on 30 Nov. 2007.

[77] South Africa signed on 3 Oct. 1994 and ratified on 12 Jan. 2015.

[78] Adopted on 18 Dec. 1996 and became effective on 4 Feb. 1997.

[79] *South Africa v. Grootboom*, 2001 (1) SA 46 (CC) (4 Oct. 2000).

[80] 'There may be cases where it may be possible and appropriate to have regard to the content of a minimum core obligation to determine whether the measures taken by the State are reasonable. However, even if it were appropriate to do so, it could not be done unless sufficient information is placed before a Court to enable it to determine the minimum core in any given context. In this case, we do not have sufficient information to determine what would comprise the minimum core obligation in the context of our Constitution. It is not in any event necessary to decide whether it is appropriate for a Court to determine in the first instance the minimum core content of a right.' *South Africa v. Grootboom*, 2001 (1) SA 46 (CC) (4 Oct. 2000), at 66.

[81] E.g.: D. Davis, 'Socio-economic rights in South Africa: The Record of the Constitutional Court after Ten Years', *ESR Review* vol. 5 (2004): 3–7; Institute for Democracy in Africa (IDASA), 'The Women's Budget', Budget Brief No. 111, (October 2002), <http://oppenheimer.mcgill.ca/IMG/pdf/10-09_Fondements_Pleniere_Grootboom.pdf> (last accessed 3 Jan. 2015).

[82] ESCR Committee, General Comment No. 3: The Nature of States Parties' Obligations, UN Doc. E/1991/23, Annex III at 86 (1991), para. 10.

of the realization of economic and social rights identified by the ESCR Committee, thereby inhibiting the development of a universal interpretation of the right to adequate housing.[83] The Court opted for a test of reasonable legislative (and other) measures within its available resources to progressively realize the right to housing. Whilst in many ways *Grootboom* was a major victory in the fight to have economic, social, and cultural rights recognized and substantiated in a court of law, it is a sad note that eight years after Irene Grootboom's 'victory' she died in a shack in Cape Town without any indicia of her right to housing having been fulfilled. The realization of the right was not achieved in part due to the state's failure to employ the ESCR Committee's outlined 'minimum essential level'.

The ESCR Committee has issued two general comments on the right to adequate housing. The Constitutional Court has employed both general comments in subsequent efforts to flesh out the duties imposed on the state by Article 26 of its Constitution, particularly in relation to displaced individuals. Article 26(1) of the Constitution provides that '[e]veryone has the right to have access to adequate housing'. The South African Constitutional right to 'access' adequate housing is somewhat different from the right as introduced by ICESCR Article 11(1). General Comment No. 7, The Right to Adequate Housing,[84] was utilized by the Constitutional Court in the 2009 *Joe Slovo Community*[85] forced evictions case. It drew upon the treaty body's interpretation of appropriate measures to establish the obligation of the state to provide housing for those persons subject to a legitimate forced eviction.

> [E]victions should not result in people being rendered homeless. And where the people affected by the eviction are unable to provide for themselves, the [government] must take all appropriate measures, to the maximum of its available resources, to ensure that adequate alternative housing, resettlement or access to productive land, as the case may be, is available.[86]

Comment No. 7 was also used to define the duty of the government, including procedural protections, when relocating people under South Africa's PIE[87] policy.[88] Previously, in *Mpange v. Sithole*,[89] the Court had relied upon the ESCR Committee's 1991 General Comment No. 4 on the Right to Adequate Housing[90]

[83] It must be acknowledged, also, that the South African right is phrased 'right to *have access* to adequate housing' (emphasis added) whilst the international obligation is the 'right to adequate housing' which some argue are two different concepts.

[84] ESCR Committee, General Comment No. 7: The Right to Adequate Housing (Art. 11(1) of the Covenant): Forced Evictions, UN Doc. HRI/GEN/1/Rev.9 (vol. 1), paras 7, 16.

[85] *Residents of Joe Slovo Community, Western Cape v. Thubelisha Homes and others* (CCT 22/08) (2009).

[86] *Residents of Joe Slovo Community, Western Cape v. Thubelisha Homes and others* (CCT 22/08) (2009), para. 32.

[87] Prevention of Illegal Eviction from and Unlawful Occupation of Land Act (PIE), Act 19 of 1998.

[88] *Residents of Joe Slovo Community, Western Cape v. Thubelisha Homes and others* (CCT 22/08) (2009), paras 36–37.

[89] *Mpange and others v. Sithole* (07/1063) [2007] ZAGPHC 201 (22 June 2007).

[90] ESCR Committee, General Comment No. 4: The Right to Adequate Housing (Art. 11(1) of the Covenant), UN Doc. E/1992/23 (1991), para. 8.

to examine the duties imposed on the state by Article 26 of its Constitution with respect to the right to adequate housing.[91] Particularly the *Mpange* Court noted the interrelatedness of adequate housing and other fundamental rights, such as human dignity, as the ESCR Committee outlined in General Comment No. 4.[92] Underscoring the relationship to human dignity is particularly important in light of the Constitutional Court's recognition of human dignity as the 'central value of the objective normative value system established by the Constitution'.[93] It also emphasized the ESCR Committee's stress on the need for effective domestic legal remedies in order to comply with ICESCR obligations.[94] These references to general comments are a step forward; however, the South African experience highlights that domestic use of these soft law instruments does not always equate to the successful implementation of a universal minimum standard of human rights.

More recently, in April 2011, the Constitutional Court used HRC General Comment No. 3[95] and ESCR Committee General Comment No. 13[96] to frame the importance of and basic right to education. The comment further aided the Court's interpretation of a private party's obligation to not infringe the right of education under the Bill of Rights. In *Juma Musjid Primary School*[97] the Court established that the Member of the Executive Council for Education for KwaZulu-Natal, a representative of the government, failed to comply with the positive obligation to 'respect, protect, promote and fulfil'[98] the right to a basic education despite its recognized status as an empowerment right and 'the primary vehicle by which economically and socially marginalized adults and children can lift themselves out of poverty and obtain the means to participate fully in their communities'.[99] In this instance, the treaty bodies' interpretations helped consolidate the international minimum standards required to fulfil the right to education.

It is not only the South African Constitutional Court that has relied upon general comments in pursuit of abiding by Article 39 of the state's Constitution. In 2008, the High Court of South Africa relied upon ESCR Committee General Comment No. 15 on The Right to Water[100]—derived from Articles 11 and 12—to determine

[91] *Mpange and others v. Sithole* (07/1063) [2007] ZAGPHC 201 (22 June 2007), para. 51.

[92] *Mpange and others v. Sithole* (07/1063) [2007] ZAGPHC 201 (22 June 2007), para. 51.

[93] *Mpange and others v. Sithole* (07/1063) [2007] ZAGPHC 201 (22 June 2007), para. 53. On this point: A. Chaskalson, 'Human Dignity as a Foundational Value of our Constitutional Order', *South African Journal of Human Rights* vol. 16 (2000): 193–206.

[94] *Mpange and others v. Sithole* (07/1063) [2007] ZAGPHC 201 (22 June 2007), para. 52.

[95] HRC, General Comment No. 3, Art. 2 Implementation at the National Level, Doc. HRI/GEN/1/Rev.1 at 4 (1994).

[96] ESCR Committee, General Comment No. 13, The Right to Education, UN Doc. E/C.12/1999/10 (1999).

[97] *Juma Musjid Primary School & others v. Essay N.O. and others* (CCT 29/10) [2011] ZACC 13 (11 Apr. 2011).

[98] *Juma Musjid Primary School & others v. Essay N.O. and others* (CCT 29/10) [2011] ZACC 13 (11 Apr. 2011), para. 45.

[99] *Juma Musjid Primary School & others v. Essay N.O. and others* (CCT 29/10) [2011] ZACC 13 (11 Apr. 2011), para. 41, quoting the ESCR Committee, General Comment No. 13, UN Doc. HRI/GEN/1/Rev.9 (vol. 1).

[100] UN Doc. HRI/GEN/1/Rev.9 (vol. 1).

that 'the State is obliged to provide free basic water to the poor'[101] despite there being no express right to water under international or South African law.[102] This case exemplified the Court's readiness to recognize the interrelatedness and indivisibility of human rights and the fact that gaps related to the realization of rights must often be filled using all available tools of interpretation.

The courts of South Africa have firmly established the role of treaty body jurisprudence as an interpretative tool and indispensable source of law. Though the use of general comments has not consistently represented a step forward in the universal standard of certain rights addressed by the South African courts, progress definitely can be charted. As the courts tease out the true meaning of the protections provided in the South African Bill of Rights, the interpretative guidance provided by general comments, and other treaty body jurisprudence, will continue to be an unparalleled tool.

4.3 Europe as a supranational jurisdiction

The European Court of Human Rights (ECtHR) was the quickest to consider treaty body jurisprudence as a supporting source in the course of evaluating complaints of human rights abuse. This swift uptake can be attributed to the prominence of the European Convention on Human Rights[103] (ECHR), to which all forty-seven Council of Europe member states subscribe. The ECHR has guided domestic European jurisdictions since its adoption in 1950. Both the Council of Europe and the European Union, which have an overlapping membership of twenty-eight states, maintain human rights as a primary policy objective. Therefore, it is unsurprising that the ECtHR has often utilized the soft law promulgated by the treaty bodies in its efforts to normalize the interpretation of rights and aid in the development of universal human rights standards.

As the primary court of review of human rights violations in Europe, the ECtHR has referred to the opinions of various treaty bodies on many occasions. The cases discussed here represent a sampling of those where a general comment was invoked as an interpretative tool. In 2014 the ECtHR applied HRC General Comment No. 20,[104] in concert with other international law, in *Marguš v. Croatia*[105] to assess

[101] *S v. Mazibuko* (A1246/2006) [2008] ZAGPHC 106 (18 Apr. 2008), paras 36–7, see specifically para. 40.

[102] *S v. Mazibuko* (A1246/2006) [2008] ZAGPHC 106 (18 Apr. 2008), para. 45. The right to water, as indicated in General Comment No. 15, is derived from Art. 11 of the ICESCR, which enunciates a non-exhaustive list of rights that must be insured in order to uphold the right to an adequate standard of living. See ESCR Committee, General Comment No. 15: The Right to Water (Arts 11 and 12 of the International Covenant on Economic, Social and Cultural Rights), UN Doc. HRI/GEN/1/Rev.9 (vol. 1), paras 2–6.

[103] European Convention for the Protection of Human Rights and Fundamental Freedoms (ECHR), 4 Nov. 1950, ETS No. 005, 213 UNTS 221, as amended by Protocol Nos 11 (ETS No. 155) and 14 (CETS No. 194), entry into force 1 June 2010.

[104] HRC, General Comment No. 20: Prohibition of Torture, or Other Cruel, Inhuman or Degrading Treatment or Punishment, Art. 7, 30 Sept. 1992 at <http://tbinternet.ohchr.org/_layouts/treatybody-external/TBSearch.aspx?Lang=en&TreatyID=8&DocTypeID=11> (last accessed 3 Jan. 2016).

[105] *Marguš v. Croatia*, ECtHR (GC) [2014] ECHR 523.

the issue of the right not to be tried for the same charges and the right to a fair trial in light of an amnesty granted to the claimant. Following General Comment No. 20, the ECtHR recognized that though some states have granted amnesties for acts of torture, such amnesties violate the duty of states under the ICCPR to investigate and prevent acts prohibited by ICCPR Article 7. Thus in this instance, the ECtHR utilized the general comment to reinforce the need to limit the use of amnesties in order to ensure justice for the victims of torture or other prohibited treatment. *Marguš* represents one of a growing line of cases focused on refining the prohibition against torture and the multifarious ways in which the breach of the right might be manifested.[106]

The ECtHR examined the extent to which threats constitute torture in 2010 in *Gäfgen v. Germany*.[107] As part of its evaluation the Court referenced a 2001 report by the UN Special Rapporteur for the Commission on Human Rights. The report reminded governments that the prohibition of torture related also to acts that cause mental suffering, including intimidation and threats, as pointed out in HRC General Comment No. 20. It also referenced HRC General Comment No. 7[108] (which was replaced by No. 20) to confirm the importance of the principle of effective protection and remedy for victims of torture or ill-treatment, including the inadmissibility of statements or confessions obtained by torture or other prohibited treatment.[109] The impact of General Comment Nos. 7 and 20 continue to resonate in cases throughout both the Council of Europe and European Union systems.

In *Baka v. Hungary*,[110] the ECtHR sat in a unique position as it heard an application by one of its former members relating to the independence of the judiciary. The Court relied heavily on HRC General Comment No. 32 on the right to equality before courts and tribunals and to a fair trial to outline the international guidance on what ICCPR Article 14 required in the context of independence of the judiciary and protecting judges from political influence.[111] The ECtHR ultimately found that Baka's ECHR Article 10 rights had been violated. In doing so, the ECtHR confirmed an international standard for the independence of the judiciary.

The 2005 *Hirst*[112] judgment referred to HRC General Comment No. 25(57)[113] which detailed the requirement that states provide detailed information on any

[106] E.g.: *Othman (Abu Qatada) v. United Kingdom* [2012] ECHR 56, which examined the extent of the prohibition against torture. In the case the Court explicitly referred to concluding observations, another form of soft law, by both the Committee Against Torture and the HRC, in addition to a General Comment, paras 107–108, 147–151, 156, and 158.

[107] *Gäfgen v. Germany*, 22978/05 [2010] ECHR 759 (1 June 2010).

[108] HRC, General Comment No. 7: Torture or Cruel, Inhuman or Degrading Treatment or Punishment, 30 May 1982 at <http://tbinternet.ohchr.org/_layouts/treatybodyexternal/TBSearch.aspx?Lang=en&TreatyID=8&DocTypeID=11> (last accessed 3 Jan. 2016).

[109] *Gäfgen v. Germany*, 22978/05 [2010] ECHR 759 (1 June 2010), paras 67, 70–71.

[110] *Baka v. Hungary* (Chamber) [2014] ECHR 528.

[111] HRC, General Comment No. 32: Article 14: Right to Equality before Courts and Tribunals and to a Fair Trial, UN Doc. CCPR/C/GC/32 (2007), paras 19–21.

[112] *Hirst v. United Kingdom*, ECtHR (GC), No. 74025/01, judgment 6 Oct. 2005, para. 27.

[113] Participation in Public Affairs and the Right to Vote, UN Doc. CCPR/C/21/Rev.1/Add.7

legislation that was the basis of suspending the right to vote.[114] The case involved prisoners' voting rights in the UK and the Court ultimately held that the UK was in violation of ECHR Protocol No. 1, Article 3 due to the broad blanket ban depriving prisoners of the right to vote. In another 2005 case, *Öcalan v. Turkey*, the ECtHR recognized the findings of the HRC in *Reid v. Jamaica*, which were based on its General Comment No. 6: Article 6 (Right to Life),[115] as 'international developments concerning the death penalty'.[116] Thus the Court noted the changing views of the international community at large as set forth by the HRC general comment.

A distinguishing feature of the ECtHR is its ability to stay on top of the large amount of information coming out of the treaty bodies and to employ it without delay. One reason for this may be the number of judges—currently four—sitting on the ECtHR that formerly served as members of a treaty body.[117] It could also be the increasing cross-fertilization of information across international human rights mechanisms. Whatever the reason, the ECtHR has demonstrated a deft capacity to engage the jurisprudence of the treaty bodies in its navigation of international human rights standards.

For instance, the Court used the 2007 General Comment No. 10 of the CRC Committee and the 2008 General Comment No. 2 of the CAT Committee in the November 2008 *Salduz v. Turkey*[118] judgment to elaborate the relevant law concerning legal assistance to minors in police custody. It expressly incorporated two paragraphs of the CRC Committee comment[119] and one from the CAT comment[120] to interpret the extent of Turkey's obligation to provide assistance, legal or otherwise, in cases involving juveniles and the general right of access to a lawyer while in police custody. Regarding general comments as interpretative tools, *Salduz* is particularly interesting in that it featured two comments that were issued after the commencement of the case, which highlights the evolving nature of the tools that are essential to rights protection.

The use of general comments quite often reflects the interrelatedness and indivisibility of human rights as recognized in a broad range of treaties. HRC General Comment No. 29: States of Emergency (Article 4)[121] was used in 2009 to assist in

[114] *Hirst v. United Kingdom*, ECtHR (GC), No. 74025/01, judgment 6 Oct. 2005; *Baka v. Hungary* (Chamber) [2014] ECHR 528, para. 27.

[115] HRC, General Comment No. 6: Article 6 (Right to Life), 30 Apr. 1982, <http://tbinternet.ohchr.org/_layouts/treatybodyexternal/TBSearch.aspx?Lang=en&TreatyID=8&DocTypeID=11> (last accessed 3 Jan. 2016).

[116] *Öcalan v. Turkey*, ECtHR (GC), No. 46221/99, judgment 12 May 2005, para. 60.

[117] Judge Boštjan Župančič was a member of the CAT Committee (1995–8); Judge Linos-Alexandre Sicilianos was a member of the CERD Committee (2002–9); Judge Helen Keller was a member of the HRC (2008–11); Judge Iulia Antoanella Motoc was a member of the HRC (2006–13).

[118] (ECtHR) App. 36391/02, 27 Nov. 2008.

[119] CRC Committee, General Comment No. 10: Children's Rights in Juvenile Justice, UN Doc. CRC/C/GC/10 (2007), paras 49, 52.

[120] CAT Committee, General Comment No. 2: Implementation of Article 2 by States Parties, UN Doc. CAT/C/GC/2 (2008), para. 13.

[121] HRC, General Comment No 29: State of Emergency (Article 4), UN CCPR/C/21/Rev.1/Add.11 (2001).

determining the legal standard used to measure when a state could claim a legitimate derogation to the ECHR. The applicants in the case alleged unlawful detention, which was countered by the UK with an argument that it was derogating from certain ECHR obligations (as outlined in the Anti-terrorism, Crime and Security Act 2001). Primary questions in the cases leading to the ECtHR hearing were the actual existence of a valid 'public emergency' and the duration of the derogation to Article 5 of the ECHR. As noted in the Comment No. 29, '[m]easures derogating from the provisions of the Covenant must be of an exceptional and temporary nature'.[122] The Court ultimately held that despite there being a public emergency worthy of derogation and that the derogation was not of an unreasonable duration in keeping with accepted law, including General Comment No. 29, the 'derogation measures were disproportionate in that they discriminated unjustifiably between nationals and non-nationals'.[123] Thus, it was necessary to mix and match the various international obligations and standards to get to the heart of the breach of the obligation.

The approach of the ECtHR in referencing a wide range of treaty body jurisprudence, as demonstrated in *Neulinger*, reinforces the common mantra that a human rights convention 'cannot be interpreted in a vacuum but must be interpreted in harmony with the general principles of international law'.[124] The *Neulinger* decision relied upon HRC General Comments Nos 17 and 19, among several other international documents, to tease out the meaning of the 'best interests of the child'[125] and the decision has resonated across many European states. The position of the ECtHR, as well as other supranational human rights courts, is unique in the potential for its decisions, and the reasoning articulated therein, to influence the states within its regulatory system. Giving pride of place to treaty body instruments as means of determining human rights standards at the European level strengthens the 'soft' nature of this jurisprudence and underscores its value as an interpretative tool.

5. Conclusion

It is clear that domestic and supranational judicial opinions are referencing the general comments of the human rights treaty bodies. Whether introduced by zealous human rights defenders, NGO amicus briefs, or the judges themselves, it cannot be denied that the interpretations of human rights conventions by the treaty bodies are gaining traction in domestic courts. What legal value attaches to the comments in light of this phenomenon is less clear. This is particularly true when

[122] *Case of A and others v. United Kingdom*, App. 3455/05, 19 Feb. 2009, citing HRC General Comment 29, para. 2.

[123] *Case of A and others v. United Kingdom*, App. 3455/05, 19 Feb. 2009, citing HRC General Comment 29, paras 181, 190.

[124] *Neulinger v. Switzerland* (2010) 28 BHRC 706, para. 131.

[125] *Neulinger v. Switzerland* (2010) 28 BHRC 706, paras 49–56.

the comments are employed to achieve different aims from those the treaty body originally intended or where a court opts not to adopt the treaty body's approach.

In some instances the use of general comments is norm-filling and aids in refining the universal interpretation of human rights. In others, a court's failure to follow the reasoning of the treaty body suggests that the right is subject to alternative or selective interpretations. The reluctance of domestic judiciaries to follow the international interpretation may shatter the promise of a unified global human rights interpretation. However, as discussed in this chapter, the UK cases[126] concerning the approach to immigration and asylum involving children demonstrate that in those instances where the highest court in a jurisdiction has opted to use general comments to refine the extent of a right it is certain that lower courts will follow suit. Does this indicate broadening of the available interpretative tools or should these examples be treated as mere throwaway observations? The evolution of the international human rights system has occurred in many ways not conceived at its inception in 1948. The impact of general comments must be included in this observation and only time will reveal the true interpretative power of this form of treaty body jurisprudence.

[126] See the discussion of: *ZH (Tanzania) (FC) v. Secretary of State for the Home Department* [2011] UKSC 4; *DS (Afghanistan) v. Secretary of State for the Home Department* [2011] EWCA Civ 305; *The Queen on the application of Mansoor v. Secretary of State for the Home Department* [2011] EWHC 832.

3

The Role and Impact of Soft Law on the Emergence of the Prohibition of Violence against Women within the Context of the CEDAW

Ekaterina Yahyaoui Krivenko

1. Introduction

Despite the absence of an explicit legal provision, the Convention on the Elimination of All Forms of Discrimination against Women (CEDAW)[1] is commonly understood and interpreted as integrating a prohibition of violence against women.[2] Therefore, there is a contradiction inherent in the absence of any recognition of the issue of violence against women as a human right in a binding instrument and the broad belief in the acceptance of it as a part of established human rights law. In the absence of a binding instrument, the question of the status of prohibition of violence against women in human rights law becomes central. Arguably, the prohibition of violence against women as a human rights issue has undergone a significant change since the time of the adoption of the CEDAW. The role of the CEDAW Committee in this process cannot be denied. In this context, it is important to enquire about the role of soft law as well as tactics and mechanisms used by the CEDAW Committee that allowed for such a smooth and almost invisible sliding of the prohibition of violence against women into the realm of recognized human rights obligations. The continuing impact of the soft law on human rights development in this area is equally important. Relatedly, investigating these issues will also shed new light on the nature of soft law itself.

[1] Convention on the Elimination of All Forms of Discrimination against Women (New York, 18 Dec. 1979, 1249 UNTS 13).

[2] Defining violence against women is a difficult task. Preliminarily, violence against women can be defined as 'violence that is directed against a woman because she is a woman or that affects women disproportionately', General Recommendation 19: Violence against Women, 11th Session, 1992, Contained in Compilation of General Comments and General Recommendations Adopted by Human Rights Treaty Bodies, HRI/GEN/1/Rev.9, vol. 2 (27 May 2008): 331, para. 6. For a more detailed discussion of the definition, see section 2.1 of this chapter.

The CEDAW does not contain any provision addressing violence against women despite lobbying by some NGOs and governments during the drafting process. Initially, the issue of violence against women was addressed in the CEDAW General Recommendation 12 adopted in 1989,[3] General Recommendation 19 of 1992,[4] and subsequently in the famous General Assembly (GA) Declaration on the Elimination of Violence against Women (DEVAW) of 20 December 1993.[5] In the jurisprudence of the CEDAW Committee and its concluding observations, the Committee addressed the issue of violence against women from the very beginning of its activities despite the apparent lack of an express legal provision allowing it to do so.

Focusing on the issue of violence against women and on the particular approach chosen by the CEDAW Committee to address this issue, this contribution will explore the development of the prohibition of violence against women from non-law (recognition of violence against women as a societal problem)[6] to soft law (understood here as a normative statement with some degree of traction),[7] on the one hand, and from soft law to hard law, on the other.

2. Definitions and Historical Background

2.1 Definition

The concept of violence against women is very broad and can potentially cover a variety of phenomena. Even at the level of a general definition, there are some divergences between the existing definitions. At the universal level, two definitions are the most important: the definition formulated by the CEDAW Committee in General Recommendation 19[8] and the definition contained in the DEVAW.[9]

[3] General Recommendation 12: Violence against Women, 8th Session, 1989, Contained in International Human Rights Instruments. Compilation of General Comments: 324.

[4] General Recommendation 19: Violence against Women, 11th Session, 1992, Contained in Compilation of General Comments and General Recommendations Adopted by Human Rights Treaty Bodies, HRI/GEN/1/Rev.9, vol. 2 (27 May 2008).

[5] Adopted by UN GA Resolution 48/104 of 20 Dec. 1993, A/RES/48/104.

[6] I would like to emphasize that the term 'non-law' is used here in its commonsense meaning: recognizing a societal problem and addressing it without using any legal tools. Of course, it would be interesting to see how this exclusion of violence against women from legal regulation plays out against the theories of non-legality. However, the author believes, this is better done within the framework of a separate article. For conceptualization of non-legality in international law in general, see e.g.: F. Johns, *Non-Legality in International Law* (Cambridge: Cambridge University Press, 2013).

[7] The definition of soft law that this chapter adopts is in line with the view presented by the editors in the introduction to this volume. In addition, this chapter also refers to the nature of the instrument in some instances where the legal status of the instrument influences the soft or hard law nature of a particular normative statement and the degree of traction that it attracts.

[8] General Recommendation 19: Violence against Women, 11th Session, 1992, Contained in Compilation of General Comments and General Recommendations Adopted by Human Rights Treaty Bodies, HRI/GEN/1/Rev.9, vol. 2 (27 May 2008): 331, para. 6.

[9] '[A]ny act of gender-based violence that results in, or is likely to result in, physical, sexual or psychological harm or suffering to women, including threats of such acts, coercion or arbitrary deprivation

Significantly, two regional treaties addressing violence against women are currently in force: the Council of Europe Convention on Preventing and Combating Violence against Women and Domestic Violence (Istanbul Convention)[10] and the Inter-American Convention on the Prevention, Punishment, and Eradication of Violence against Women (Belem Do Para Convention).[11] These two conventions contain their own definitions of violence against women that are very similar to each other and to the two above-mentioned definitions.[12] The common elements of all these definitions are: the fact that violence is based on gender; the consequences of violence that encompass not only physical harm, but also psychological harm or suffering; and the emphasis that both public and private violence falls under the ambit of international law. These core elements can be regarded as uniting factors. The crucial element is that of 'based on gender'. The definition of 'gender' itself is a very difficult task if taken seriously.[13] Therefore, the understanding and recognition of violence against women, as well as its various forms and manifestations, will depend on the evolving and changing understandings of gender. The link to gender in defining violence against women has been the subject of criticism.[14] As the definition contained in General Recommendation 19 demonstrates, it is possible to define violence against women without relying on the concept of gender. The definition of the Protocol to the African Charter on Human and Peoples' Rights on the Rights of Women in Africa also makes no reference to gender. This document, in line with the CEDAW Committee's definition, defines violence against women as 'all acts perpetrated against women which cause the physical, sexual, psychological, and economic harm'.[15]

The available definitions of violence against women are quite broad and can potentially cover many rights violations that are already recognized under other

of liberty, whether occurring in public or in private life.' Adopted by UN GA Resolution 48/104 of 20 Dec. 1993, A/RES/48/104, Art. 1.

[10] Council of Europe Convention on Preventing and Combating Violence against Women and Domestic Violence, CETS No 210, adopted 11 May 2011, in force 1 Aug. 2014.

[11] Inter-American Convention on the Prevention, Punishment, and Eradication of Violence against Women, A-61, adopted 9 June 1994, in force 5 Mar. 1995.

[12] Art. 1 of the Belem do Para Convention reads as follows: 'For the purposes of this Convention, violence against women shall be understood as any act or conduct, based on gender, which causes death or physical, sexual or psychological harm or suffering to women, whether in the public or the private sphere.' The Istanbul Convention provides several definitions in Art. 3 and separately deals with violence against women (Art. 3(a)), domestic violence (Art. 3(b)), and gender-based violence (Art. 3(d)).

[13] The term 'gender' usually refers to the social construction of roles and responsibilities of men and women. See e.g.: UNESCO, Division of Gender Equality, Office of the Director-General, *Priority Gender Equality Guidelines* (2011): 5. However, it can have a more restricted and a broader, complex meaning. For a more restrictive approach to gender, see e.g.: Rome Statute of the International Criminal Court (Rome, 17 July 1998, 2187 UNTS 3) Art. 7(3). To appreciate the complexities of the notion of gender, see e.g.: J. Butler, *Gender Trouble: Feminism and the Subversion of Identity* (New York: Harper Perennial, 1993).

[14] See e.g.: A. Edwards, *Violence against Women under International Human Rights Law* (Cambridge: Cambridge University Press, 2013): 21–5.

[15] Protocol to the African Charter on Human and Peoples' Rights on the Rights of Women in Africa, 11 July 2003, CAB/LEG/66.6 (13 Sept. 2000); 1 Afr. Hum. Rts LJ 40 (2001) Art. 1(j).

general or specific treaties such as the CEDAW. However, thanks to the definitions' focus on gender and women, they can help identify and recognize new forms of harm that otherwise remain invisible due to the male standard still prevalent in human rights law.[16] The attitude of the CEDAW Committee is indicative of the deliberate use of this function in relation to the prohibition of violence against women. When the Committee can approach a particular situation from a perspective of another, more specific right embodied in the CEDAW, it will not resort to the language of violence against women. However, when it is faced with issues that are more difficult to subsume under other articles of the Convention, domestic violence being the prominent example, prohibition of violence against women becomes the dominant narrative.

The focus of this contribution is not on the definition as such. However, it will become clear that the broad vision of violence against women as it emerged in human rights discourse plays an important role in this author's interpretation of the role and impact of soft law in this regard.

2.2 Historical background

Violence against women is as old as the history of humanity. However, an examination of international law instruments, documents, and discussions reveals that official international law history of violence against women starts with the adoption of the CEDAW in 1979. Nevertheless, this does not mean that the issue of violence against women was unknown or non-existent before the CEDAW Committee started its work. This section examines the discourse on violence against women prior to the adoption of the CEDAW as well as the attitude towards the issue of violence against women during the drafting process. This examination will shed more light on the circumstances of the emergence of the issue of violence against women as a human rights issue and serve as a background for the discussion on further developments. At this stage the issue of violence against women is not yet 'in the process of becoming'[17] a binding rule in international law, but a societal problem to discuss and understand.

2.2.1 Violence against women prior to the adoption of the CEDAW

At the official interstate level, the issue of violence against women was addressed for the first time in 1975, at the First UN Women's Conference in Mexico City. This conference is linked to the declaration by the UN of the year 1975 as International Women's Year[18] and the subsequent decade (1976–85) as Decade for Women: Equality, Development, and Peace.[19] One hundred and thirty-three

[16] For a clear overview and analysis, see e.g.: D. Otto, 'Lost in Translation: Re-scripting the Sexed Subjects of International Human Rights Law', in *International Law and its Others*, ed. A. Orford (Cambridge: Cambridge University Press, 2006): 318–56.

[17] See the Introduction to this volume, section 2.1.

[18] United Nations General Assembly, Resolution, 18 Dec. 1972, A/RES/27/3010.

[19] United Nations General Assembly, Resolution, 16 Dec. 1976, A/RES/31/136.

states participated in the conference in Mexico City organized by the UN. UN specialized agencies and some NGOs were also invited to attend.[20] The outcomes of the conference are contained in its report. There are three types of substantive outcomes: Plans of Action,[21] Resolutions and Decisions,[22] and a Declaration.[23] The report of the conference contains four references to violence against women in total. However, the World Plan of Action, the main outcome document of the conference, contains no such reference. Two of the references appear in resolutions adopted by the conference: one in relation to health[24] and another related to communication media.[25] Violence is also mentioned as the root cause of inequality in the opening address of the conference.[26] Importantly, all these statements are not framed as normative statements, but as observations about the reality of women's lives. The statement with regard to violence against women that has some normative connotations appears only in the summary of the discussions by the delegates: 'It was also suggested that there should be more effective legislation to protect women against all forms of physical violence.'[27] However, even this statement is a mere suggestion by one delegate that, as the Plan of Action indicates, was not followed up in 1975. Therefore, we can observe that in 1975 the awareness of violence against women as a matter of concern at the international level existed. However, the nature of the instruments in which it was mentioned, as well as the language used, make it difficult to affirm the existence of any level of normative commitment. States certainly expressed some level of normative commitment to combat some most obvious forms of violence against women, such as exploitation of prostitution,[28] but violence against women as a phenomenon was not yet defined in official documents.

[20] For a full list of participants and attendees see the Report of the World Conference of the International Women's Year, Mexico City, 19 June–2 July 1975, E/CONF.66/34, 120–123.

[21] Report of the World Conference of the International Women's Year, Mexico City, 19 June–2 July 1975, E/CONF.66/34, 8–72.

[22] Report of the World Conference of the International Women's Year, Mexico City, 19 June–2 July 1975, E/CONF.66/34, 73–113.

[23] Declaration of Mexico on the Equality of Women and their Contribution to the Development and Peace; Report of the World Conference of the International Women's Year, Mexico City, 19 June–2 July 1975, E/CONF.66/34, 2–7.

[24] 'Considering that Governments should be aware of the particular forms of violence and cruelty, both physical and mental, that are perpetuated against women.' Report of the World Conference of the International Women's Year, Mexico City, 19 June–2 July 1975, E/CONF.66/34, 78.

[25] 'Likewise requests those in charge of the mass communication media to cease projecting and gradually eliminate commercialized, tasteless and stereotyped images of women, particularly in pornographic publications, the use of such images in depicting sexual crimes and crimes of violence, and the dissemination of any material tending to create prejudices and negative attitudes with regard to the changes necessary for the revaluation of the role of women and to transmit an image of men's and women's roles that is as varied as possible.' Report of the World Conference of the International Women's Year, Mexico City, 19 June–2 July 1975, E/CONF.66/34, 93, para. 4.4.

[26] Report of the World Conference of the International Women's Year, Mexico City, 19 June–2 July 1975, E/CONF.66/34, 124.

[27] Report of the World Conference of the International Women's Year, Mexico City, 19 June–2 July 1975, E/CONF.66/34, 133, para. 70.

[28] Sexual exploitation and trafficking of women is the earliest recognized form of violence against women. See the Convention for the Suppression of the Traffic in Persons and of the Exploitation of the Prostitution of Others, 21 Mar. 1950, 96 UNTS 271.

Leading up to the adoption of the CEDAW, there were actors outside the UN that were working on the issue of violence against women, including academics and NGOs.[29] One of the most notable examples is an initiative called International Tribunal on Crimes against Women. This initiative, in which more than 2,000 women from over forty countries participated, took place from 4 to 8 March 1976 in Belgium. The report contains testimonies of women about a variety of violations of women's rights, including a chapter on violence against women (chapter 12).[30] This chapter includes accounts of domestic violence, rape, assault, femicide, torture, to mention just a few. Several accounts in other chapters can also be regarded as relevant to the issue of violence against women, especially forced sterilizations and forced motherhood. The organizers intentionally scheduled this event just after the end of the UN proclaimed International Women's Year in order to demonstrate their dissatisfaction with the way the official UN discourse addressed women's issues, especially the issue of violence against women. They were also very critical of the Mexico City conference, arguing that it had not sufficiently addressed important issues.

Thus, violence against women, its different forms and levels of severity, were well documented and widely known by the time the CEDAW's drafting process started. There was a strong movement and a powerful campaign emphasizing the international nature of the problem.[31] However, at the level of the official discourse, the degree of normativity of statements contained in the Report of the First UN Women's conference was quite low. The CEDAW was adopted four years after the conference in Mexico City. Why does the Convention contain no reference at all to the issue of violence against women? Does this indicate lack of consensus and normative commitment? In order to answer this question, the drafting process and the broader context of the adoption of the Convention need to be examined.

2.2.2 Prohibition of violence against women in the drafting process

Similarly to many UN drafting processes, the CEDAW's emergence is generally well documented. Nevertheless, it is not possible to trace the details and reasons for some decisions in the drafting process because not every single word was recorded and not all concerns or objections were expressed clearly, officially, and in writing.[32]

[29] For a general overview of activism around the issue of violence against women prior to the adoption of the CEDAW as well as during the drafting process, see e.g.: J. Joachim, 'Shaping the Human Rights Agenda: The Case of Violence against Women', in *Gender Politics in Global Governance*, ed. M. K. Meyer and E. Prügl (London: Rowman & Littlefield, 1999): 142–60; L. Kelly, 'Inside Outsiders', *International Feminist Journal of Politics* vol. 7 (2005): 477–80 at 471. The book by Niamh Reilly also contains some useful insights, but it focuses mostly on NGO campaigns in the early 1990s and afterwards: N. Reilly, *Women's Human Rights: Seeking Justice in a Globalising Age* (Cambridge: Polity Press, 2009), ch. 4 deals with the issue of violence against women.

[30] D. E. H. Russel and N. Van Den Ven, *Crimes against Women: Proceedings of the International Tribunal* (Berkley: Russel Publications; 1st published 1976, edn consulted: 3rd, 1990).

[31] For an example see the letter of Simone de Beauvoir to the International Tribunal on Crimes against Women reproduced in the proceedings in Russel and Van Den Ven (1990): 5.

[32] See similar observations in: L. A. Rehof, *Guide to the Travaux Préparatoires of the United Nations Convention on the Elimination of All Forms of Discrimination against Women* (Dordrecht/Boston/London: Martinus Nijhoff Publishers, 1993): 3.

Not a single draft version of the CEDAW contains a reference to violence against women or the physical harm of women. It is surprising to see how many discussions revolved around harmful working conditions and harm to maternal health, while the discussion on other, more serious types of harm women suffer, including physical violence, is absent. The only provision that can be classified as a certain type of violence against women, and that prompted one proposal that came closer to the broader issue of violence against women, is the provision dealing with trafficking of women and exploitation of prostitution that later became Article 6 of the CEDAW. Within the context of the discussion of this provision, Belgium proposed the inclusion of 'attacks on the physical integrity of women' into the text of the Convention[33] so that the relevant provision would read as follows: 'Each State Party agrees to take all appropriate measures, including legislation, to combat all forms of traffic in women, exploitation of prostitution of women and attacks on the physical integrity of women.'[34] This proposal was not retained due to insufficient support.[35] It is difficult to identify the precise reasons for lack of support for this provision because available documents contain no indication of the expressly stated reasons for lack of support. The only exception is the following statement by the representative of Pakistan: 'The Belgian amendment addressed itself to a further aspect of the problem, but it was not the only one. Accordingly, it was preferable to keep to the basic text.'[36] This explanation is not very clear either. It indicates however, that even this proposal was thought as related to the issue of trafficking and exploitation of women for prostitution, not the broader issue of violence against women. Taking into account the above described general context two conclusions can be drawn. First, since the gravity and severity of different forms of violence against women were widely known also at the official UN level, the lack of support for inclusion of an express provision addressing violence against women cannot be attributed to a careless, inattentive drafting or lack of understanding or knowledge. Secondly, an overview of the official statements on the issue of violence against women indicates that the level of normativity of these statements was very low and clearly beyond the degree of traction required for qualifying these statements as soft law. Therefore, it can be concluded that at the time of the adoption of the CEDAW there was no consensus on the existence of an international obligation to combat violence against women as a human rights issue. The issue of violence against women was present on the official international agenda as a problem to study and understand. At most, it

[33] International Instruments Relating to the Status of Women. Draft Convention on the Elimination of Discrimination against Women. Working Paper Prepared by the Secretary General, Corrigendum, 14 Sept. 1976, E/CN.6/591/Add.1/Corr.1: 2.

[34] International Instruments Relating to the Status of Women. Draft Convention on the Elimination of Discrimination against Women. Working Paper Prepared by the Secretary General, Addendum, 25 Aug. 1976, E/CN.6/591/Add.1: 4.

[35] The discussion and objections are captured in Commission on the Status of Women, 26th session, Summary Records of the 638th meeting, 20 Sept. 1976, E/CN.6/SR.638, paras 40–49. The reasons for opposition are not stated, except the statement by the representative of Pakistan.

[36] Commission on the Status of Women, 26th session, Summary Records of the 638th meeting, 20 Sept. 1976, E/CN.6/SR.638, para. 41.

can be suggested that the Convention's drafters were advising states to devise national strategies to more effectively address the needs of victims of violence against women (and particularly domestic violence) within existing national judicial frameworks.

An additional argument in favour of this interpretation results from the general context of the drafting process. It is well documented that various drafts of the CEDAW contained many controversial provisions. However, these provisions were not excluded in the final Convention, but rather drafted in very vague language. Thus, the issues that were raised but then excluded are those on which no consensus or agreement could be reached even at a very basic level.[37] One could even say that due to the lack of any serious discussion of the proposals for the inclusion of violence against women into the text of the CEDAW, the consensus existed that this is not a human rights issue that governments are willing to address in a hard law international instrument.

The issue of violence against women was addressed during the Second UN Women's Conference in Copenhagen, held just a year after the adoption of the CEDAW. The Report of the Copenhagen Conference adopted in 1980, and its Programme of Action, is the only official document with some normative value dating back prior to the beginning of the work of the CEDAW Committee in 1982 that mentions violence against women as an issue of international relevance.[38]

The Copenhagen Conference was the second in a series of four UN organized conferences on the status of women.[39] One hundred and forty-five states participated in the conference. The main outcome of the conference is its Programme of Action.[40] As during the first conference, a number of decisions and resolutions on some specific areas considered of importance were adopted.[41] The language of the decisions and resolutions is also 'soft'. For example, Resolution No. 5 on Battered Women and Violence in the Family addressed two of its four recommendations to the Secretary General with a view of studying violence against women.[42] The remaining two recommendations were addressed to states, urging them to adopt measures aimed at protecting victims of domestic violence within existing national judicial systems.[43]

[37] Examples of such issues alongside violence against women include the proposed reference to children born out of wedlock in Art. 16 and to inheritance in the same provision. For details see e.g.: Rehof (1993): 181–6.

[38] Report of the World Conference of the United Nations Decade for Women: Equality, Development and Peace, Copenhagen, 14–30 July 1980, A/CONF.94/35. The Programme of Action is the first document in the report, at 2–59.

[39] The first conference was held in 1975 in Mexico City. The third and fourth conferences were held in 1985 in Nairobi and in 1995 in Beijing respectively.

[40] Report of the World Conference of the United Nations Decade for Women: Equality, Development and Peace, Copenhagen, 14–30 July 1980, A/CONF.94/35, 2–59.

[41] Report of the World Conference of the United Nations Decade for Women: Equality, Development and Peace, Copenhagen, 14–30 July 1980, A/CONF.94/35, 60–112.

[42] Report of the World Conference of the United Nations Decade for Women: Equality, Development and Peace, Copenhagen, 14–30 July 1980, A/CONF.94/35, 67–8, recommendations 1 and 2.

[43] Report of the World Conference of the United Nations Decade for Women: Equality, Development and Peace, Copenhagen, 14–30 July 1980, A/CONF.94/35, 68, recommendations 3 and 4.

Under the rubric of priority areas for action, the Programme of Action called on states to promote research on causes of violence against women.[44] This indicates that while violence against women had become of concern to the UN and states, it had not yet reached even the lowest normative threshold. Otherwise the Programme of Action mentions violence against women as an issue of concern under educational and health-related issues. The strongest language is employed under the rubric 'legislative measures':

> Legislation should also be enacted and implemented in order to prevent domestic and sexual violence against women. All appropriate measures, including legislative ones, should be taken to allow victims to be fairly treated in all criminal procedures.[45]

However, this provision is not included in the priority areas identified by the conference in its Programme of Action. Moreover, it is directed at two types of violence against women only: domestic violence and sexual violence. Thus, prior to the beginning of the work of the CEDAW Committee, the issue of violence against women was not absent from the international agenda. However, its normative content was very light, perhaps even below the soft law threshold. Therefore, this can be viewed as additional evidence in favour of the argument that the lack of inclusion of any reference to violence against women in the CEDAW is due to the lack of normative consensus on the issue and even perhaps indicates that the consensus of the time was to regard the issue of violence against women as irrelevant to legal human rights commitments.

Section 3 examines the strategy adopted by the CEDAW Committee that allowed for the inclusion of violence against women as part and parcel of international human rights law.

3. Bringing Violence against Women into the CEDAW

The CEDAW Committee was at first very reluctant to assume an active role. Despite a clear provision allowing it to 'make suggestions and general recommendations',[46] it was slow to issue general recommendations that went beyond simple comments on states' reports or reporting obligations, despite the existence of this practice in the work of the Human Rights Committee.[47] The Human Rights Committee

[44] Notably, the document calls upon states to 'Promote research into the extent and the causes of domestic violence with a view to eliminating it; take measures to eliminate glorification of violence against and sexual exploitation of women in the mass media, literature and advertising; provide effective help for women and children who are victims of violence, for example, by the establishment of centres for treatment, shelter and counselling victims of violence and sexual assault.' Report of the World Conference of the United Nations Decade for Women: Equality, Development and Peace, Copenhagen, 14–30 July 1980, A/CONF.94/35, para. 163.

[45] Report of the World Conference of the United Nations Decade for Women: Equality, Development and Peace, Copenhagen, 14–30 July 1980, A/CONF.94/35, para. 65.

[46] Convention on the Elimination of All Forms of Discrimination against Women (New York, 18 Dec. 1979, 1249 UNTS 13), Art. 21(1).

[47] For a detailed discussion of this reluctance and related issues, see e.g.: E. Evatt, 'Finding a Voice for Women's Rights: The Early Days of CEDAW', *The George Washington International Law Review* vol. 34 (2002–3): 515–53 at 537–42 in particular.

adopted five general comments in 1981 and four general comments in 1982, the year when the CEDAW Committee started its work.

The CEDAW Committee addressed the issue of violence against women in two general recommendations: General Recommendation 12 adopted in 1989 and General Recommendation 19 adopted in 1992.[48]

3.1 General Recommendation 12

Remarkably, General Recommendation 12 is the first substantive recommendation adopted by the Committee. All previous recommendations dealt with technical issues related to the states' reporting obligations such as provision of statistical data and other relevant information, and the structure and content of reports. In the second introductory paragraph, General Recommendation 12 makes reference to a resolution of the Economic and Social Council of the UN (ECOSOC) from which it apparently derives its legitimacy. The ECOSOC resolution entitled 'Efforts to eradicate violence against women within the family and society' was adopted in 1988.[49] It addresses the issue of violence against women as a crime prevention issue and calls for more research and better understanding of the phenomenon. The resolution is remarkable in one particular regard: the language of the introductory paragraphs expressly links its subject matter to existing states' human rights obligations. In doing so, it mentions the Covenant on Economic Social and Cultural Rights, Nairobi Forward-looking Strategies for the Advancement of Women, General Assembly resolution on domestic violence, a report of the Secretary-General on efforts to eradicate violence against women, and some other events and documents, but is silent on the existence and relevance of the CEDAW, despite the fact that the CEDAW is already in force and its Committee active. Thus, the CEDAW Committee in adopting its first general recommendation on violence against women performs an important creative move: it reminds the international community and international institutions about its own existence and relevance while simultaneously deriving legitimacy and 'a right to speak' from these international institutions. The language and terms of the ECOSOC resolution can be regarded as a further indication of the almost non-existent level of recognition by states of violence against women within the CEDAW prior to the beginning of the CEDAW Committee's work on the issue.

In the General Recommendation, the Committee addressed four recommendations to states linked to their reporting obligations. The recommendations were aimed at providing the Committee with more information on particular aspects of states' efforts to combat violence against women. This included: legislation that was in force; other measures adopted to eradicate violence; existence of support services

[48] General Recommendation 19: Violence against Women, 11th Session, 1992, Contained in Compilation of General Comments and General Recommendations Adopted by Human Rights Treaty Bodies, HRI/GEN/1/Rev.9, vol. 2 (27 May 2008).

[49] ECOSOC, Efforts to Eradicate Violence against Women within the Family and Society, 1 July 1988, E/RES/1988/27.

for victims of violence; and relevant statistical data. This was the main content of the General Recommendation in line with the Committee's previous practice of addressing mainly states' reporting obligations in its general comments. However, the first sentence of the recommendation that appears as a simple introductory statement is crucial and marks a turn in the CEDAW Committee's attitude. It reads as follows: 'Considering that articles 2, 5, 11, 12, and 16 of the Convention *require* the States parties to act to protect women against violence of any kind occurring within the family, at the work place or in any other area of social life.'[50] Structurally, this sentence is just an introduction to the recommendations that the Committee addresses to states. However, with this sentence, the Committee makes an unambiguous determination that inscribes the requirement of combating all forms of violence against women into other provisions of the CEDAW in an attempt to make it part and parcel of hard law. This is quite a big move forward, if we consider the background of the adoption of the CEDAW, and especially the fact that even a reference to attacks on the physical integrity of women[51] did not get enough support. Thus, from the very beginning of its activities, the CEDAW Committee simply assumed, or pretended, that violence against women was a matter within its competence and that it was also covered by various provisions of the CEDAW, creating obligations for states parties. The attitude of the CEDAW Committee is that it is performing a norm-filling function by articulating soft law standards on violence against women. However, against the background of the historical development sketched above, the Committee's actions can be regarded as norm-creating. From now on states have to address certain issues that they were unwilling to include in the text of the CEDAW during the drafting process.

3.2 General Recommendation 19

Between the adoption of the first general recommendation on violence against women in 1989 and the second general recommendation on this issue in 1992 the Committee adopted six recommendations, none of which mentioned the issue of violence against women. Interestingly, in 1990, the Committee adopted General Recommendation 14 on female circumcision,[52] which does not mention violence against women. This is particularly significant in light of the fact that female circumcision is mentioned as one of the forms of violence against women in General Recommendation 19 adopted just two years later.[53] However, in General Recommendation 14, female circumcision is framed exclusively as a health and educational issue. The Committee required states to report on measures to combat

[50] General Recommendation 12.

[51] The proposal did not specify the type of attacks or the area of their application (e.g.: domestic sphere). The proposal aimed at including something similar to the right to liberty and security of the person in the CEDAW.

[52] General Recommendation 14: Female Circumcision, 9th Session, 1990, Contained in Compilation of General Comments: 326.

[53] General Recommendation 19, para. 11.

female circumcision under Article 10 of the CEDAW devoted to education and Article 12 dealing with health issues.[54]

The general recommendation of the CEDAW on violence against women adopted in 1992 is more detailed and to the point. It is the first in a series of general recommendations addressing specific issues related to the CEDAW's implementation that are precise, detailed, and quite long compared to all previous general recommendations. In this general recommendation the Committee clarifies its reasoning with regard to the relationship between violence against women and various provisions of the CEDAW. Rather clearly, the Committee affirms that 'the full implementation of the Convention required States to take positive measures to eliminate all forms of violence against women'.[55] The Committee also affirmed for the first time that the definition of discrimination against women in Article 1 of the CEDAW includes gender-based violence, that is, 'violence that is directed against a woman because she is a woman or that affects women disproportionately'.[56] Other articles of the CEDAW discussed in this general recommendation are: Articles 2, 3, 5, 6, 10(c), 11, 12, 14, and 16. Thus, the extent and amount of links established between various provisions of the CEDAW and the obligation to eradicate violence against women grew from one general recommendation to another. An additional important step needs to be highlighted. In this general recommendation, the CEDAW Committee established a link between violence against women and the principle of non-discrimination for the first time. This became one of the main strategies for addressing violence against women as an international human rights hard law obligation not only within the context of the CEDAW, but also beyond.[57]

3.3 Analysis of the CEDAW Committee's strategy

The strategy adopted by the CEDAW Committee to affirm the existence of the prohibition of violence against women in human rights law is based on links between different provisions of the CEDAW, most importantly the prohibition of discrimination, and consequences of violence against women. This strategy suggests that the prohibition of violence against women is part and parcel of the already existing hard law. This produced some positive results, as the remainder of the chapter will demonstrate. However, the preceding discussion around the position of states towards the issue of violence against women puts it in a new light. Seemingly, the Committee sidestepped the soft law stage in the development of the prohibition of violence against women propelling it immediately into the realm of hard law. As mentioned previously, the outcome of the Copenhagen Conference in 1980 indicated that the prohibition of violence against women did not even attract the degree of traction required for a soft law standard, not to speak of hard law. When

[54] General Recommendation 14, section d. [55] General Recommendation 19, para. 4.

[56] General Recommendation 19, para. 6. General Recommendation 12 did not mention Art. 1 (definition of discrimination) among articles that require states to combat violence against women. See also: General Recommendation 12.

[57] For a detailed discussion of this strategy, see e.g.: Edwards (2013): 140–97.

adopting General Recommendation 19 in 1992 the Committee also noted that 'not all the reports of States parties adequately reflected the close connection between discrimination against women, gender-based violence, and violations of human rights and fundamental freedoms',[58] something that states were required to do at least since the adoption of General Recommendation 12 in 1989. Two observations are important in this regard. First, the reluctance of states to comply with the Committee's 1989 recommendations can be due to their inexperience with reporting, but can also indicate an unwillingness to follow the Committee's view on the place of prohibition of violence against women in the CEDAW. This would mean that, at that stage, the prohibition of violence against women still did not attract enough traction to be considered a soft law rule, or, alternatively, was very close to being accepted as a soft law standard but not yet as a part of hard law. In any case, these developments indicate a very rapid growth in the level of traction attracted by the prohibition of violence against women that can, at least partially, be explained by the dressing up of norm-creation as simply a norm-filling exercise performed by the CEDAW Committee.

Secondly, the intimate connection established by the Committee between the prohibition of violence against women and the existing articles of the Convention, especially the principle of non-discrimination, leads to the problem of only certain types of violence against women being included in the existing norms, leaving other forms of violence against women in the realm of non-law. As stated previously, violence against women is defined very broadly and can take a variety of forms that are not immediately apparent. Some new forms can either arise or become apparent over time. It is not possible to assume that all forms of violence against women will necessarily fit into the framework of the existing human rights obligations. Therefore, in the remaining parts of this chapter, particular care should be applied in order not to be led away from the broad understanding of violence against women by the rhetoric of inclusion of the prohibition of violence against women into existing human rights standards. It is important to keep in mind the fate of those forms of violence against women that do not easily fit into the existing human rights standards.

4. Attempts at Framing Violence against Women as Hard Law

The straightforward language adopted by the CEDAW Committee in its general recommendations but especially in General Recommendation 19 leads to a proposition that the prohibition of violence against women has perhaps achieved the transition from soft to hard law or has even become hard law without ever passing through the soft law stage. This section examines this proposition in light of subsequent developments in the practice of the Committee and states' reactions to it. However, before examining the practice of the Committee, some remarks

[58] General Recommendation 19, para. 4.

about the attitude towards violence against women in general human rights law are required.[59] The understanding of the overall reaction of general human rights law to the approach of the Committee is necessary for an adequate interpretation of the subsequent developments within the CEDAW. It is equally important to highlight that developments related to the issue of violence against women in general human rights law are a consequence of the efforts of the CEDAW Committee described above and broader efforts leading to the adoption of the CEDAW itself.

4.1 General international law and violence against women

After the CEDAW Committee issuing General Recommendation 19 in 1992, the next significant step in framing the discussion on violence against women occurred with the adoption of the DEVAW in 1993.[60] Technically speaking, from a positivist point of view, this marked the appearance of a recognized soft law instrument. The adoption of the declaration was a result of the movement led by the Commission on the Status of Women and the ECOSOC that advocated the adoption of an international instrument on violence against women. A notable expression of this advocacy was ECOSOC Resolution 1991/18 Violence against Women in All its Forms.[61] In this resolution, ECOSOC recommended the adoption of an international instrument 'expressly' addressing violence against women. The objective behind this recommendation went beyond the creation of a simple resolution or a soft law instrument. Contrary to the previously mentioned ECOSOC resolution of 1988, this time ECOSOC acknowledged the existence of the CEDAW and the work of its Committee on the issue of violence against women. However, it also noted that the CEDAW 'does not expressly address violence against women'.[62] Thus, it became clear that the objective was to come up with a binding instrument, rather than soft law. Therefore, the absence of any follow up after the adoption of the DEVAW can again be interpreted as absence of the required consensus at the international level for the transition of the prohibition of violence against women from soft to hard law. However, thanks to the adoption of the DEVAW, at least the soft law nature of the prohibition of violence against women can now be safely affirmed.

Other developments in relation to the prohibition of violence against women at the international law level can be identified in some specific areas of human rights law. For instance, some forms of violence against women are framed as issues related to the prohibition of torture or as a right to life.[63] Refugee law adjudication also contributed significantly to bringing attention to various forms of violence against

[59] It is not the objective of this chapter to trace the reception of the prohibition of violence against women in general human rights law. This would require at least another article. A very valuable and most up-to-date source of information on the developments surrounding the issue of violence against women in general human rights law remains the already mentioned book by A. Edwards (2013).

[60] Adopted by UN GA Resolution 48/104 of 20 Dec. 1993, A/RES/48/104.

[61] ECOSOC, Resolution 1991/18, 30 May 1991.

[62] ECOSOC, Resolution 1991/18, 30 May 1991, last introductory paragraph.

[63] For a discussion of these developments: Edwards (2013): 198–303.

women and framing them as human rights issues.[64] Other human rights bodies followed the strategy of framing violence against women as violations of other already well-established human rights standards. However, this development does not mean that violence against women in all its forms and manifestations became part of established human rights law. This simply indicates that some forms of violence against women can be addressed, to some extent, under the existing hard law standards. There is still uncertainty in regard to whether the prohibition of violence against women in its entirety, and not simply some of its forms, has accomplished the transition from soft to hard law.

4.2 The CEDAW Committee and uncertainty in relation to violence against women

The recurring difficulty to clearly ensure the transition of the prohibition of violence against women from soft to hard law did not stop the CEDAW Committee from systematically raising the issue with states parties when considering complaints submitted by individuals and reports by states. How did the Committee approach this task? What strategies and language allow it to address the issue despite apparent lack of international consensus for the adoption of a specific hard law instrument on the issue? The overall strategy of the Committee remained the same as the one adopted at the very beginning of its work on the topic: to subsume the prohibition of violence against women under other substantive provisions of the CEDAW, with the prohibition of discrimination being the most general and the most far-reaching. However, it is important to take a closer look at the way the Committee employed this strategy and to consider the responses of states. In the following pages such an analysis is provided with a discussion of the jurisprudence under the CEDAW and the Committee's consideration of states' reports.

4.2.1 CEDAW jurisprudence and the prohibition of violence against women

Table 3.1 summarizes all the cases that can be regarded as raising issues related to violence against women based on the definition formulated in General Recommendation 19. In total, up to now, the Committee has issued decisions in thirty-six cases. Out of these thirty-six cases, twenty-four are selected as relevant to the issue of violence against women. It should be noted that cases 7 and 9 are less obvious examples of violence against women. Case 7 is more easily couched in terms of women's access to health services. However, since the applicant invoked the issue of violence against women, it is included in the table. In case 9, the applicant framed the issue mainly in terms of the right to housing. However, domestic

[64] See e.g.: M. Randall, 'Refugee Law and State Accountability for Violence against Women: A Comparative Analysis of Legal Approaches to Recognizing Asylum Claims Based on Gender Persecution', *Harvard Women's Law Journal* vol. 25 (2002): 281–318; L. S. Alfredson, *Creating Human Rights: How Non-Citizens Made Sex Persecution Matter to the World* (Philadelphia: University of Pennsylvania Press, 2009).

Table 3.1 CEDAW jurisprudence showing invocation of violence against women

	Case No.	Type of issue	Violence against women invoked/ mentioned by		
			Applicant	State	Committee
1	CEDAW/C/36/D/2/2003	Domestic violence	X	X	X
2	CEDAW/C/36/D/4/2004	Coerced sterilization	X		X
3	CEDAW/39/D/5/2004	Honour killing	X	X	X
4	CEDAW/39/D/6/2004	Honour killing	X	X	X
5	CEDAW/38/D/10/2005	Domestic violence in home country			X
6	CEDAW/42/D/15/2007	Forced prostitution, trafficking			
7	CEDAW/49/D/17/2008	Pregnancy related health	X		
8	CEDAW/46/D/18/2008	Rape	X		X
9	CEDAW/51/D/19/2008	Housing linked to domestic violence		X	
10	CEDAW/49/D/20/2008	Domestic violence	X		X
11	CEDAW/50/D/22/2009	Denial of abortion			
12	CEDAW/49/D/23/2009	Mistreatment in detention			X
13	CEDAW/50/D/26/2010	Domestic violence in home country			
14	CEDAW/51/D/25/2010	Abuse by a former spouse in home country			
15	CEDAW/52/D/32/2010	Domestic violence	X		X
16	CEDAW/53/D/31/2011	Rape and domestic violence	X	X	X
17	CEDAW/55/D/33/2011	Circumcision in home country	X		X
18	CEDAW/55/D/35/2011	Rape in home country	X	X	X
19	CEDAW/55/D/40/2012	Sexual harassment in home country	X	X	X
20	CEDAW/56/D/44/2012	Domestic violence	X		
21	CEDAW/57/D/34/2011	Rape			
22	CEDAW/57/D/39/2012	Rape in home country		X	
23	CEDAW/58/D/47/2012	Domestic violence			X
24	CEDAW/58/D/30/2011	Sexual assault			

Note: Shaded lines refer to cases that were declared inadmissible.

violence was an important element of the circumstances that led to the ultimate denial of the access to housing that the Committee had to assess. Moreover, the state felt compelled to mention its policies with regard to combating violence against women. Therefore, the case is included in the table. Finally, case 11 is a good example of violence against women that can be controversial in some settings. In this case, a 13-year-old victim of sexual abuse suspecting pregnancy attempted suicide. Her attempt was unsuccessful, but she suffered damage to the spinal cord that necessitated urgent surgery. In the hospital, when her pregnancy was discovered, the surgery was delayed out of concern for the survival of the foetus until the girl miscarried spontaneously. As a result of the delay in performing surgery on her spinal cord, the victim remains paralysed from the neck down. However, in this case violence against women was not mentioned by any of the involved parties, including the Committee itself. This leads to the first observation. There is a strong tendency in the practice of the Committee to avoid recourse to the language of violence against women if, in the Committee's view, the issue can be addressed appropriately under one of the existing provisions of the CEDAW. In cases 13, 14, and 20, it was not necessary for the Committee to engage in substantive issues because these cases were declared inadmissible. The Committee did not mention violence against women in cases 6, 7, 9, 11, 20, 21, and 24. In many other cases the Committee was able to easily use existing provisions of the CEDAW and, thus, avoided the language of violence against women. The Committee referred to its general recommendations and used the language of violence against women in cases involving issues traditionally associated with violence against women and for which there is no express provision in the CEDAW: domestic violence, honour killings, and coerced sterilization.

For states, the language of violence against women never forms part of their main argument. In all instances where states mentioned violence against women, it was done as a supplementary argument to demonstrate compliance with relevant provisions of the CEDAW and respect for the principle of non-discrimination. Thus, for example, in case 9, the Canadian government affirmed that 'it has acted with due diligence to generally prevent violations under the Convention, and that Canadian governments do act with due diligence to investigate and punish acts of violence against women by individuals, where these acts are brought to their attention'.[65]

The attitude of the Committee in its case law can be interpreted in various ways. However, it is a matter of concern that the Committee does not systematically raise the issue of violence against women in all cases where this would be appropriate because it indicates the Committee's uncertainty about the normative value of the prohibition of violence against women. The Committee prefers recourse to 'harder', more clear-cut provisions when possible and reserves the 'softer' language of violence against women for cases where it is not possible to clearly identify an express provision of the CEDAW. This attitude resembles the one adopted by the CEDAW Committee in General Recommendation 14 on female circumcision. From the point of view of promoting the normative value of the prohibition of violence against women, a more assertive strategy would be to mention violence against women alongside the applicable hard law provisions. The tactic of putting forward some human rights aspects of an issue at the expense of others has its

[65] *Cecilia Kell v. Canada*, Communication No. 19/2008, 26 Apr. 2011, CEDAW/C/51/D/19/2008, para. 8.11 at 12.

benefits. In concrete cases, it can lead to better compliance or a faster acceptance of a new standard. Arguably, the success of the CEDAW's strategy on the issue of violence against women is in large part attributable to this tactic. However, in other contexts this tactic can produce negative side effects. Thus, in the context of the CEDAW Committee's efforts to ensure that all forms of violence against women are recognized as a part of hard human rights law, the changing nature of violence against women and multiplicity of its forms is obscured and some forms of violence against women are privileged over others. As a consequence, the normative relevance of the concept of violence against women as such can be jeopardized: if violence against women is adequately addressed through the existing human rights norms, why should this concept matter at all?

Thus, the jurisprudence of the Committee also oscillates between the use of the language of violence against women as an affirmation of its legally binding character and avoidance of this language out of uncertainty about its consequences when more firmly established provisions are available. This recourse to well-established express provisions by the Committee can be an indication of the less than hard law status of the prohibition of violence against women, contrary to what the Committee affirmed in its general recommendations. As already mentioned, states refer to their programmes, strategies, etc. when addressing violence against women as an argument in favour of their compliance with the CEDAW. Therefore, violence against women is supported by states and recognized as a hard law norm to the extent it fits into or is reflected in the express provisions of the CEDAW. The fate of the forms of violence against women that cannot be easily incorporated into one of the articles of the CEDAW remains uncertain.

4.2.2 Consideration of states' reports

The issue of violence against women was addressed in states' reports and Committee's comments and observations from early on. However, the context and issues addressed varied from country to country. This diversity is linked to the broad nature of the notion of violence against women and simply reflects the fact that different contexts produce different forms of violence. It is also noteworthy that some states followed the language of the Committee in its general recommendations and produced very comprehensive accounts of the situation with regard to violence against women under their jurisdiction. Even more interesting is the approach and language used with regard to violence against women by some states before the adoption of relevant general recommendations. For example, according to the Committee's concluding observations adopted in 1990 with regard to Germany's initial report: 'The federal parliament had been dealing with trafficking in women and efforts were being made to deal with the problems of violence against women, the most serious form of discrimination, through the enactment of laws and the provision of shelter and counselling centres.'[66] The view that

[66] Report of the Committee on the Elimination of Discrimination against Women, 9th session, GA Official Records, 45th session, Supplement No. 38, A/45/38, 1990, para. 59: 13.

violence against women is a form of discrimination appeared officially only in the Committee's General Recommendation 19 adopted in 1992. Also, several states referred to domestic violence and their efforts to combat some forms of sexual violence against women, especially rape, in their reports produced even before the adoption of the Committee's General Recommendation 12 that put the issue of violence against women clearly and expressly on its agenda.[67] Thus, a dialectical relationship between states and the Committee can be observed within the context of states' reporting obligations. The steps taken by the Committee to address the issue of violence against women can be regarded as carefully weighted against the readiness of states to accept the new soft law standards or at least not to openly object to them. Today, the issue of violence against women forms part of all states' reports and is systematically addressed by the Committee in its list of issues and questions to states. In relation to states that provide insufficient information or where the Committee is able to identify particular areas of concern, the Committee requests more information and statistics on measures taken, including the impact of these measures.

The practice emerging in relation to reporting obligations appears at first sight as providing more support to the hard law status of the prohibition of violence against women than the jurisprudence of the Committee. In general, states seem to accept that they have to provide information on their efforts to combat violence against women and respond to related questions of the Committee. Given the general readiness of states to provide information on combating violence against women, can we infer any firm conclusion on the transition of the prohibition of violence against women into hard law? My answer is in the negative for the following reason. As with the pattern that emerged from the analysis of the jurisprudence of the CEDAW Committee, it seems that more attention is needed to precise areas and forms of violence against women that states are ready to discuss in these terms. We can certainly conclude that some forms of violence against women are generally accepted as being prohibited by some provisions of the CEDAW. However, it would be too hasty to conclude that all forms of violence against women and that violence against women as such is subject to the same consensus.

5. Violence against Women: Between Soft and Hard Law?

As already mentioned, there is no single authoritative definition of violence against women. Rather, several very similar definitions exist in four different documents.[68]

[67] See e.g.: Consideration of Reports Submitted by States Parties under Article 18 of the Convention. Second Period Reports of States Parties. Sweden, 26 Mar. 1987, CEDAW/C/13/Add.6: 16, 35, 63–5, 67–9 and CEDAW, Consideration of Reports Submitted by States Parties under Article 18 of the Convention. Initial Reports. Australia, 30 Oct. 1986, CEDAW/C/5/Add.40, pp. 39, 40, 46, 47, and 96.

[68] Section 2.1 of this chapter.

This creates additional difficulties in terms of identifying the status of the prohibition of violence against women in contemporary human rights law.

There is no doubt that from a positivist perspective, the notion of violence against women did not belong to the realm of hard law in the earlier days of the CEDAW. The main argument against classifying the prohibition of violence against women as hard law in contemporary international law is the continuing absence of a convention dealing expressly with this issue at the universal level despite efforts in this direction. Strangely, even positivists have to admit that some specific manifestations of violence against women have become prohibited either through dynamic treaty interpretation or through the formation of custom. However, there is still a lack of agreement at the universal level on the precise contours of violence against women. From the perspective of the relationship between soft law and hard law, the most intriguing aspect is the evolution over time of these elements or particular manifestations of violence against women that, step by step, have become part of recognized hard law. While violence against women, its particular manifestations and precise contours, remains uncertain, its presence and function at the level of international law are undisputed.

What does this strange situation tell us about the nature of the prohibition of violence against women? I suggest that the prohibition of violence against women functions as a passage, as a bridge between discovery and recognition of new forms of suffering and their introduction and integration into hard law. Violence against women as a soft law concept is then not simply an intermediary stage between non-law and hard law that disappears by becoming hard law once sufficient consensus is reached. It functions as a mediating mechanism through which a particular element can be integrated into hard law. If we accept this interpretation of the role played by violence against women, it becomes counterproductive to argue for the adoption of a convention expressly dealing with violence against women. The danger is too great that a convention would narrow down the definition of violence against women, thus preventing the passage into hard law of some forms of violence against women. Ultimately, it could even lead to the destruction of the passage of particular forms of violence against women into human rights law. Therefore, the example of the prohibition of violence against women demonstrates how soft law can function beyond the norm-creating/norm-filling dichotomy.

This chapter's overview of the approach adopted with regard to violence against women at the international level demonstrates the very close dialectical relationship between hard law, soft law, and non-law. Instead of approaching them as binary oppositions, the CEDAW Committee approaches the soft law prohibition of violence against women as an intermediary term that functions as a connecting passage allowing easier access to hard law for newly discovered forms of violence against women. In order to keep this passage open, the Committee adopts a careful attitude and when necessary uses either a softer language of technicalities in regards to reporting obligations, or the available explicit provisions of the CEDAW. Significantly, the CEDAW Committee constantly reminds European and American states parties to the CEDAW about the existence of the two regional conventions dealing with violence against women. It always asks states that belong to one of these regions but have not yet become parties to the relevant convention about their time-line for ratification of this convention. Thus, the Committee acts as a promoter of these regional treaties. Without the input and constant reminders of the CEDAW Committee, the Istanbul Convention would most certainly still be awaiting the ten ratifications required for its entry into force.[69] The fact that it took three years for a convention dealing with violence against women in Europe to get just ten ratifications demonstrates once again the reluctance of states to address this issue internationally in a hard law instrument.[70]

The example of the CEDAW's engagement with the issue of violence against women highlights several important aspects of the hard law/soft law dynamic. The two types of law should not be regarded as completely separate from each other. Soft law can function as a mediating force, as a passage facilitating transition of more specific concepts, or elements, into the realm of hard law. This mediating soft law concept should never become entirely absorbed into hard law. Moreover, its absorption into hard law would interrupt the smooth transition of particular elements into hard law, at least until new soft law that plays a mediating role is introduced. The efficient and continuing function of this mediating soft law is dependent upon the careful and skilful approach of the body that is in charge of the concept.

[69] Art. 75(3) of the Istanbul Convention.

[70] The Istanbul Convention was opened for signature on 11 May 2011 and achieved its tenth ratification on 22 Apr. 2014.

4

Soft Law, Doctrinal Development, and the General Comments of the UN Committee on Economic, Social and Cultural Rights

Mátyás Bódig

1. Introduction

UN treaty bodies in the human rights field (such as the Human Rights Committee or the Committee on the Elimination of Racial Discrimination) regularly publish 'General Comments' or 'General Recommendations' that elaborate on the substantive provisions of the respective human rights treaties.[1] These documents can be usefully analysed as an aspect of the communication and cooperation between states parties and treaty bodies.[2] General Comments are closely associated with the processing of periodic state reports, as they set out general guidance to states parties on the information to be included in state reports. General Comments are auxiliary to treaty obligations, and in themselves not binding on states parties. These features make General Comments paradigmatic examples of soft law in the human rights field. They comfortably fit the criteria typically used in the literature for identifying soft law[3]—including those set out in the Introduction to this volume. While their role and main characteristics may not appear particularly controversial, they can raise difficult theoretical or legal challenges and, as we will see, have the potential to generate considerable doctrinal and political tensions.

This chapter will focus on the General Comments of the UN Committee on Economic, Social and Cultural Rights (CESCR). Although some points made here

[1] See e.g.: Human Rights Committee, *General Comment 6* ('The Right to Life') UN Doc. HRI/GEN/1/Rev.1 at 6 (1994).

[2] The UN Office of the High Commissioner for Human Rights itself characterizes General Comments along these lines. See: <http://www.ohchr.org/EN/HRBodies/Pages/TBGeneralComments.aspx>.

[3] See e.g.: A. Boyle, 'Soft Law in International Law-Making', in *International Law*, ed. M. Evans (Oxford: Oxford University Press, 2010): 128; D. Shelton, 'Law, Non-law and the Problem of "Soft Law"', in *Commitment and Compliance: The Role of Non-binding Norms in the International System*, ed. D. Shelton (Oxford: Oxford University Press, 2003): 10–13; C. Chinkin, 'Normative Development in the International Legal System', in *Commitment and Compliance: The Role of Non-binding Norms in the International System*, ed. D. Shelton (Oxford: Oxford University Press, 2003): 25–31.

are applicable to General Comments across the UN human rights system, CESCR practice will here be analysed in light of challenges specific to the task of implementing the International Covenant on Economic, Social and Cultural Rights (ICESCR).

Even though their manifest function concerns the mere articulation of treaty-based obligations, General Comments are important factors in normative development. General Comments offer the opportunity of securing a foothold within the UN system for more progressive interpretations of human rights norms. As they do not fall under the rigid procedural rules of treaty-making, and are formulated by relatively small expert bodies, they can be more responsive to the ever-shifting challenges of human rights protection. They can trigger gradual changes in the attitudes of key agents (and the states parties in particular) towards human rights problems. CESCR General Comments provide some of the best examples of this dynamic. Due to the deficiencies of the ICESCR (discussed in section 4.2) and the scarcity of relevant domestic jurisprudence,[4] clarifying the content of economic and social rights has always required more than a mere articulation of existing hard law. The CESCR acted as a trailblazer for doctrinal innovations that profoundly shape the parameters for the contemporary interpretations of economic and social rights.

The analysis of soft law in this chapter will have a distinctive focus: the contribution of CESCR soft law to 'doctrinal development'[5] in the human rights field. This means emphasizing the 'doctrinal aspect' of human rights documents: how their content and rationale is captured in terms of normative concepts and principles internal to professional legal discourses. Importantly for us, it is by choosing characteristic normative concepts and principles for the purposes of the documents it issues that a particular body can determine its own 'doctrinal profile'. In this sense, the conceptual arsenal used by the CESCR in its General Comments determines the 'doctrinal profile' of the Committee, hereinafter abbreviated as the 'CESCR doctrine'. In such a context, 'doctrinal development' denotes adjustments in the conceptual arsenal used by human rights bodies necessitated by the changing institutional environment and the shifting challenges of human rights implementation. We will refer to the conceptual devices 'produced' by this development as 'doctrinal constructs' or 'doctrinal devices'. Thus, for example, we can describe the concept of 'minimum core obligation' as a 'doctrinal construct'. From this perspective, the success of doctrinal development at a particular human rights body is measured by

[4] P. Alston, 'Out of the Abyss: The Challenges Confronting the New UN Committee on Economic, Social and Cultural Rights', *Human Rights Quarterly* vol. 9 (1987): 351–2. It must be noted that there has been an encouraging accumulation of domestic jurisprudence on economic and social rights of late: D. Landau, 'The Reality of Social Rights Enforcement', *Harvard International Law Journal* vol. 53 (2012): 189; K. Young, *Constituting Economic and Social Rights* (Oxford: Oxford University Press, 2012).

[5] This is where the present analysis overlaps with my work on the character of doctrinal knowledge and legal scholarship. See: M. Bódig, 'Legal Theory and Legal Doctrinal Scholarship', *Canadian Journal of Law and Jurisprudence* vol. 23 (2010): 494–9; M. Bódig, 'Doctrinal Knowledge, Legal Doctrinal Scholarship and the Problem of Interdisciplinary Engagement', in *Stateless Law: Evolving Boundaries of a Discipline*, ed. H. Dedek and S. van Praagh (Ashgate: Oxford, 2015): 62–4.

its influence on the doctrinal work of other international bodies, the human rights scholarship agenda, the discourse of human rights activism, and ultimately the subsequent development of binding international law.

This chapter progresses from general to specific issues. Section 2 offers a clarification of some additional general points regarding soft law and the inherent qualities of CESCR General Comments. The more specific analysis begins with an exploration of the ways in which the characteristic doctrinal constructs of CESCR soft law are formed. As we will see, the CESCR has made its mark on human rights law primarily by developing a series of obligation-related concepts.[6] Section 3 will single out two of those concepts for more detailed analysis: 'minimum core obligations' and the 'tripartite classification of State obligations' ('respect', 'protect', and 'fulfil'). Importantly, the consideration of these doctrinal devices also aids our understanding of how human rights scholarship influences CESCR soft law. CESCR General Comments have often served as a channel through which conceptual devices developed by human rights scholars have been incorporated into human rights law.

A discussion of the doctrinal constructs of CESCR soft law may yield important insights into normative development in the field of human rights. However, the characteristic dynamics of this development cannot be adequately understood without examining in further depth the political tensions surrounding the doctrinal work of the CESCR. Doctrinal development is not only an intellectual exercise, illustrating the influence exerted by different systematic conceptions of the normative implications of human rights; it is also a political process. As we will see in section 4, in the case of CESCR soft law, the political process is driven by the Committee's own institutional agenda and the characteristic methods of contemporary human rights activism. As a result, CESCR soft law generates a particular kind of doctrinal development that to an extent clashes with the original doctrinal design of the ICESCR. Instead of contributing to the consolidation of successful models of implementing economic and social rights (and thereby focusing on the systemic aspects of ICESCR implementation), the CESCR shifted the emphasis to facilitating the 'naming and shaming' of violators of economic and social rights.[7] It will be argued that this has led to a 'violationist bias' in CESCR soft law. As a result, CESCR General Comments are stretching the institutional competence of the Committee, and raise questions about the very legitimacy of CESCR doctrine. The overall contribution of CESCR General Comments to human rights law will be assessed in light of this issue of legitimacy.

It should be borne in mind that complications regarding the legitimacy and doctrinal plausibility of CESCR doctrine are a particularly pressing concern now

[6] M. Bódig, 'Doctrinal Innovation and State Obligations: The Patterns of Doctrinal Development in the Jurisprudence of the UN Committee on Economic, Social and Cultural Rights', in *Human Rights Protection in Global Politics: Responsibilities of States and Non-state Actors*, ed. D. Karp and K. Mills (Palgrave MacMillan: London, 2015).

[7] Some argue that, when it comes to economic and social rights, human rights activists are only really good at 'naming and shaming'. See: K. Roth, 'Defending Economic, Social and Cultural Rights: Practical Issues Faced by an International Human Rights Organization', *Human Rights Quarterly* vol. 26 (2004): 67.

that the Optional Protocol to the ICESCR has entered into force, marking the conclusion of a decades-long struggle by the Committee to strengthen its monitoring powers. We face more acute questions in terms of the range of normative sources the CESCR can rely on when operating the newly established complaints mechanism. Whether the CESCR will be able and willing to rely on its General Comments in its communications on individual complaints is a pressing issue. However, such questions are set aside in this chapter. With very little CESCR case law available yet,[8] any attempt at an answer would be needlessly speculative. But our analysis is very much motivated by the realization that the changing institutional landscape of CESCR practice renders the next few years hugely important in terms of the future of the Committee, and its soft law in particular.

2. The Character of CESCR General Comments

The conceptual parameters of soft law outlined in the Introduction (and especially the distinction between its norm-filling and norm-creating functions[9]) must be tailored slightly to fit the analytical needs of this chapter.

Three points should be highlighted from the outset which, in my understanding, together constitute an 'institutionally embedded' view of soft law. First, soft law is not binding.[10] Secondly, the quality of being soft law is associated with the instruments issued by an international body, as opposed to the substantive norms they contain.[11] Accordingly, General Comments are 'soft' because they are not binding on states parties (and thus cannot constitute hard law),[12] and have legal quality due to their official character.[13] They come from treaty bodies constituted under international law, and lend themselves to pedigree-based identification. Thirdly, the provisions of soft law are not simply 'norms in prospect': they are already 'practised' in certain ways. Thus, CESCR General Comments already establish the substantive terms under which the Committee will engage with states parties in its procedures (e.g. when formulating Concluding Observations on state reports). Characterizing General Comments as non-binding refers specifically to their normative status in relation to the legal obligations of states parties.

[8] To be more exact, the Committee has so far decided on the merits of one single complaint. This was in a June 2015 case from Spain concerning the right to housing (more specifically the obligation of states parties to provide for effective remedies in foreclosure procedures related to defaulting on mortgage payments). See: *IDG v. Spain*, Communication No. 002/2014, UN Doc. E/C.12/55/D/2/2014.

[9] See the Introduction to this volume.

[10] A. Boyle, 'Some Reflections on the Relationship of Treaties and Soft Law', *International and Comparative Law Quarterly* vol. 48 (1999): 901–2.

[11] See the Introduction to this volume.

[12] This chapter does not advocate a revisionist account of sources in international law. For a recent analysis of the issue of the sources in international law, see: J. d'Aspremont, *Formalism and the Sources of International Law: A Theory of the Ascertainment of Legal Rules* (Oxford: Oxford University Press, 2011).

[13] Boyle (2010): 124.

The 'official' nature of General Comments derives from treaty-based authorization. It is explicitly stipulated in most human rights treaties that treaty monitoring bodies may issue recommendations or General Comments based on the examination of state reports and treaty provisions.[14] The terms of this authorization are a good starting point for clarifying the nature of CESCR General Comments and their role in the human rights system. The relevant ICESCR provision[15] suggests that General Comments are an aspect of communication and cooperation between states parties and treaty bodies. When providing an account of the nature of its own General Comments, the Committee clearly followed this line, depicting them as by-products of its work on state reports:

> The Committee endeavours, through its general comments, to make the experience gained so far through the examination of those reports available for the benefit of all State Parties in order to assist and promote their further implementation of the Covenant; to draw the attention of the States parties to insufficiencies disclosed by a large number of reports, ... and to stimulate the activities of the State Parties, the international organizations and the specialized agencies concerned in achieving progressively and effectively the full realization of the rights recognized in the Covenant.[16]

This account suggests that the General Comments do not have much normative significance outside the work of the CESCR.[17] They simply render CESCR practice more transparent and more directly related to practical issues of implementation. Judged on the terms of their authorization and the Committee's own account of them, CESCR General Comments fit very comfortably into the 'norm-filling' category of soft law.[18] Ostensibly, they have two manifest functions. One is 'hortatory': promoting the implementation of economic and social rights among states parties. The other function is to assist implementation of the Covenant rights—for example, by identifying the challenges states parties tend to face. This could be characterized as an 'obligation-articulating' role:[19] laying out the exact implications of treaty-based obligations for duty-bearers in the context of contemporary challenges.

However, this account (implied by the Committee's own statements) is misleading. A closer consideration of the CESCR General Comments reveals that they

[14] See e.g.: International Covenant on Civil and Political Rights, Art. 40(4).

[15] 'The Economic and Social Council may submit from time to time to the General Assembly reports with recommendations of a general nature and a summary of the information received from the States Parties to the present Covenant and the specialized agencies on the measures taken and the progress made in achieving general observance of the rights recognized in the present Covenant.' International Covenant on Economic, Social and Cultural Rights, Art. 21. As we see, it is actually the ECOSOC that is authorized to issue recommendations. The monitoring powers were delegated to the CESCR by way of Economic and Social Council Resolution 1985/17.

[16] CESCR (1994) Report on the 8th and 9th Session, E/1994/23; UN Doc. E/C.12/1993/19, s. 51.

[17] C. Blake, 'Normative Instruments in International Human Rights Law: Locating the General Comment' (Center for Human Rights and Global Justice Working Paper, NYU School of Law, Nov. 2008) available at <http://chrgj.org/wp-content/uploads/2012/07/blake.pdf>.

[18] See the Introduction to this volume.

[19] This fits into one of the functions of soft law identified in the literature: setting 'mechanisms for authoritative interpretation or amplification of the terms of the treaty'. Boyle (2010): 905.

actually provide a thorough and partisan account of the normative implications of treaty rights. From ideas often originating in academic literature, the Committee has been building an ambitious and expansive conception of state obligations. The General Comments are not descriptive of either current state practice or Committee procedures.[20] They are prescriptive legal instruments that seek to influence professional discourse on human rights and, by implication, normative development. The General Comments do not remain within the boundaries of their manifest 'norm-filling' function. In going beyond a mere interpretation of existing norms and current state practice, they take on the character of 'norm-creating' soft law.

These ventures into 'norm-creation' should not necessarily be considered problematic. This is not only because, in a normative institutional practice of any complexity, maintaining a clean division between either 'norm-filling' or 'norm-creating' soft law is unrealistic. More importantly, the challenge of contributing to the meaningful implementation of human rights cannot really be tackled without at least some ambitions for normative development. Some of the reasons for this follow from the character of international law, while others are explained by the particular features of international human rights law.

Mainstream international law doctrine operates using a rather narrow model for the sources of hard law, seen to revolve around treaty and custom. This is in stark contrast with the ever-broadening activism of international organizations, which produces a huge amount of official documents—many of them structured like legal regulations. (General Comments are paradigmatic examples of this.) Due to the mismatch between the narrow conception of hard law and the breadth of institutional practice, international law lacks the dense web of binding implementation norms so typical of domestic legal systems. This is particularly obvious in the field of economic and social rights. Especially over the past three decades, institutional activity has grown exponentially in the field. In terms of hard law, burgeoning practice is covered by a mere handful of treaty provisions. It would be difficult to achieve anything even approaching complete coverage of important normative issues by simply interpreting the contents of treaty law. Often, the role of treaty bodies (which cannot themselves influence hard law)[21] is to work out the details of contemporary human rights law by producing a vast body of soft law.[22] CESCR General Comments play an important part in this process.

Furthermore, human rights law has a feature that increases the pressure to generate further normative development. The practicability of legal documents is primarily determined by the clarity and specificity of related obligations. Human rights treaties, however, tend to be particularly vague about the exact obligations they generate. (As indicated in section 4.2, the ICESCR is an example of this.)

[20] Blake (2008): 12.

[21] Treaty bodies are not judicial bodies: even when they pass decisions on individual complaints, they do not produce hard law. Their communications on individual complaints constitute a form of advisory opinion.

[22] Soft law can provide the 'detailed rules and technical standards required for implementation of some treaties'. Boyle (1999): 905 and Boyle (2010): 128.

They speak a rhetorically elevated language of rights, and the few provisions they do contain regarding state obligations are not specific enough for the purposes of meaningful implementation. If CESCR General Comments are to provide useful guidance, they must expand on the terms of the treaty obligations.

Of course, this fits a familiar pattern. As the Introduction to this volume points out, we tend to assume that soft law is there to 'push' for more progressive interpretations of human rights.[23] This idea of stimulating normative development through 'expansive' interpretative practice is reflected in the stance of the European Court of Human Rights (ECtHR) on 'evolutive interpretation'[24] and facilitated by the provisions of the Vienna Convention on 'purposive interpretation'.[25] The soft law of the General Comments may here simply be following the lead of the hard law. Dogged textualism with regard to the ICESCR would not do justice to the distinctive features of human rights. We should not forget that international treaties only 'recognize' rather than outright 'create' our human rights. Positive international norms cannot claim to pin down the precise meaning (and exact normative implications) of human rights. This will always remain a matter of contestation, in which the precise language of multilateral international treaties represents a source of guidance more than an ultimate point of reference.

Thus, the questions of whether CESCR soft law stays within the legal mandate of the Committee and of whether it makes a positive contribution to normative development in the human rights field are not without their complexities. The CESCR may have a justification for its distinctive efforts to generate normative development. This chapter seeks to shed light on this issue by assessing the doctrinal work of the Committee and analysing its underlying political dynamics.

3. Two Doctrinal Constructs

This section considers the doctrinal constructs featuring in a series of General Comments. The Committee's doctrinal profile has been determined by a broad variety of doctrinal constructs—not all of them specific to CESCR doctrine. At the very minimum, one must reckon with 'general' and 'specific' obligations, the 'tripartite classification' of state obligations ('respect', 'protect', 'fulfil'), 'minimum core obligations', as well as obligations of 'conduct' and 'outcome', and violations 'through act of commission' or 'through omission'. Here we single out two doctrinal devices for more detailed analysis: the 'tripartite classification' and 'minimum core obligations'. I believe these devices are particularly instructive in terms of ascertaining how soft law can become a device for reconstituting state obligations, and how it reflects the political context of human rights law.

[23] See the Introduction to this volume.
[24] *Tyrer v. United Kingdom* (App. no. 5856/72) (1979–80) 2 EHRR 1, at para. 31.
[25] Vienna Convention on the Law of Treaties, 1969, Art. 31(1).

3.1 Minimum core obligations

'Minimum core obligations' first featured in General Comment 3 on the nature of state obligations.[26] The underlying idea can be traced back to a seminal publication by Philip Alston, later the chairperson of the Committee, in which he suggested that core obligations could be relied on to specify state obligations under the ICESCR.[27]

Alston was not making a statement about economic and social rights in particular: he was discussing a common feature of all rights.[28] The possibility of identifying core obligations was intended to show that economic and social rights are not qualitatively different from civil and political rights. Pointing to core obligations also addressed the sceptical claim that economic and social rights are too indeterminate to lend themselves to meaningful implementation.[29] The idea of core obligations offers an argument to counter this scepticism: the entire range of implications of economic and social rights may not be fully determined, but they each have a core content that can be captured in terms of clear obligations. At least in respect of their minimum content, it is possible to apportion liability for violations of economic and social rights.[30] A further attraction is that shifting emphasis to core obligations brings human rights doctrine into line with the standard practice of human rights activism. Most human rights activists are minimum core campaigners,[31] and are sympathetic to minimalist strategies for human rights that prioritize minimizing goals over lofty ambitions.[32]

Of course, identifying 'minimum core obligations' is not without its challenges. The very idea sits uneasily with the terms in which the obligations of states parties are defined in Article 2(1) of the Covenant.[33] It is hard not to see the reliance on core obligations as an attempt to counterbalance the soft normative language of

[26] CESCR (1990) *General Comment 3* ('The Nature of States Parties Obligations') UN Doc. E/1991/23(SUPP). See: Matthew Craven, *The International Covenant on Economic, Social and Cultural Rights: A Perspective on Its Development* (Oxford: Clarendon Press, 1998): 141.

[27] Alston (1987).

[28] Alston (1987): 352; D. Bilchitz, 'Towards a Reasonable Approach to the Minimum Core: Laying the Foundations for Future Socio-Economic Rights Jurisprudence', *South African Journal of Human Rights* vol. 19 (2003): 13.

[29] See e.g.: O. O'Neill, *Towards Justice and Virtue: A Constructive Account of Practical Reasoning* (Cambridge: Cambridge University Press, 1996): 131–2. For analysis, see: K. Young, 'The Minimum Core of Economic and Social Rights: A Concept in Search of Content', *Yale Journal of International Law* vol. 33 (2008): 173; S. Fredman, *Human Rights Transformed: Positive Rights and Positive Duties* (Oxford: Oxford University Press, 2008): 124.

[30] G. van Bueren, 'Alleviating Poverty through the Constitutional Court', *South African Journal on Human Rights* vol. 15 (1999): 57.

[31] K. Lehmann, 'In Defense of the Constitutional Court: Litigating Socio-Economic Rights and the Myth of the Minimum Core', *American University International Law Review* vol. 22 (2006): 180. See also: Young (2008): 122.

[32] There is strong support for this moderation among human rights scholars. See: C. Scott, 'The Interdependence and Permeability of Human Rights Norms: Towards a Partial Fusion of the International Covenants on Human Rights', *Osgoode Hall Law Journal* vol. 27 (1989): 837; D. Bilchitz, 'Giving Socio-Economic Rights Teeth: The Minimum Core and its Importance', *South African Law Journal* vol. 119 (2002): 500; van Bueren (1999): 57.

[33] 'Each State Party to the present Covenant undertakes to take steps, individually and through international assistance and co-operation, especially economic and technical, to the maximum of its available resources, with a view to achieving progressively the full realization of the rights recognized

'progressive realization', which serves as an argument in itself for the indeterminacy of economic and social rights. By limiting the relativizing force of the principle of 'progressive realization',[34] core obligations establish the presumption that certain forms of privation are definite violations of human rights.[35]

This raises the question of whether including 'minimum core obligations' in General Comments serves to reconstitute state obligations under the Covenant. Unfortunately, the Committee has never explicitly addressed the compatibility of its soft law with the hard law of the ICESCR. Instead, the CESCR settled for amassing a large number of clear examples of core obligations. These examples include securing access to safe and potable water,[36] adopting and implementing a national employment strategy,[37] and monitoring the realization of the right to social security.[38] The doctrinal parameters of the legitimate use of the doctrinal device were never laid out.

As a result, there is chronic uncertainty regarding the exact character of 'minimum core obligations'. Naturally, 'minimum core obligations' cannot completely negate the relativizing force of the progressive realization standard. But what is the result of the somewhat uneasy interaction between the minimum core and Article 2(1)? The progressive realization standard implies that, at different stages of development, economic and social rights may be implemented to a different extent.[39] Is this also reflected in the 'minimum core obligations'? Is the minimum core state-specific or universal?[40] Are there different core obligations for, say, Germany and Niger? Also, what is it about rights that generates core obligations? Is it some sort of 'essential', conceptual connection with underlying values (like 'dignity')? Or should we instead adopt an institutionalist perspective, and focus on some underlying consensus among states parties on minimum standards of good governance? Uncertainty on these points has generated a broad spectrum of different and often incompatible approaches in the academic literature.[41]

This might explain the wide disparity of opinions on the way 'minimum core obligations' feature in CESCR General Comments. The majority view is that early references (e.g. in General Comment 3) were seriously lacking in clarity[42] but others counter that, initially, the concept was well defined and properly related to resource

in the present Covenant by all appropriate means, including particularly the adoption of legislative measures.' ICESCR, Art. 2(1).

[34] Young (2008): 121.

[35] M. Green, 'What We Talk about When We Talk about Indicators: Current Approaches to Human Rights Measurement', *Human Rights Quarterly* vol. 23 (2001): 1073.

[36] CESCR (2000) General Comment 14 ('The Right to the Highest Attainable Standard of Health') UN Doc. E/C.12/2000/4, s. 43.

[37] CESCR (2005) General Comment 18 ('The Right to Work') UN Doc. E/C.12/GC/18, s. 31. Notably, this example seems to integrate the idea of progressive realization into core obligations. Similar, 'adopt and implement a plan of action' type provisions can be found in other General Comments as well, e.g. CESCR (n 36) s. 43(f). But they do not really clarify the exact relationship between the progressive realization standard and core obligations.

[38] CESCR (2007) General Comment 19 ('The Right to Social Security') UN Doc. E/C.12/GC/19, s. 59.

[39] Young (2012): 69. [40] Craven (1998): 141–3. [41] Young (2008): 125.

[42] M. Sepúlveda, *The Nature of the Obligations under the International Covenant on Economic, Social and Cultural Rights* (Cambridge: Intersentia, 2003): 366.

constraints.[43] Some see welcome progress in the trajectory of CESCR doctrine: there is more clarity about core obligations in General Comment 13 (1999) and afterwards.[44] Others argue that an inherent uncertainty persists which the Committee has never tackled. The CESCR 'variously equated the minimum core with a presumptive legal entitlement, a non-derogable obligation, and an obligation of strict liability'.[45] If there was development, it lay in gradually changing the character of the minimum core: it has become a device for the 'technical operationalization' of rights.[46] The minimum core merges increasingly with the idea of obligations requiring immediate performance.[47] Some see here a movement towards a more expansive, less credible, and less coherent understanding of the concept[48]—a deterioration of the quality of CESCR soft law.

Although scholars in general tend to be supportive of the Committee's doctrinal strategy,[49] there are those who question the very viability of 'core obligations'.[50] Karin Lehmann views them as a conceptually and pragmatically misconceived idea that is inimical to principled application.[51] Katherine Young has suggested abandoning the minimum core as a legal concept.[52] Although there are indeed serious issues surrounding the doctrinal plausibility of minimum core obligations in CESCR General Comments, my belief is that the detractors are going too far. The core obligations represent a credible idea and a useful doctrinal innovation that needs to be better embedded in a coherent interpretative strategy. We need to clarify why monitoring the ICESCR makes it necessary to specify 'minimum core obligations'. In other words, there is a need

[43] K. Mechlem, 'Treaty Bodies and the Interpretation of Human Rights', *Vanderbilt Journal of Transnational Law* vol. 42 (2009): 940–1.

[44] Sepúlveda (2003): 368.

[45] Young (2008): 115.

[46] Young (2008): 152. Note how technical some elements on the list of 'minimum core obligations' are in CESCR (n. 36): '(d) To provide essential drugs, as from time to time defined under the WHO Action Programme on Essential Drugs; … (f) To adopt and implement a national public health strategy and plan of action …', s. 43.

[47] See Young (2008): 155.

[48] Mechlem develops this point quite forcefully. In General Comment 15 (2002 ('The Right to Water') UN Doc. E/C.12/2002/11), core obligations are of immediate effect and not subject to progressive realization. However, General Comments 14 (2000), 18 (2005), and 19 (2007) do not include core obligations among immediate obligations. In General Comments 14 and 15, non-compliance cannot be justified, while General Comment 19 allows for a justification of a failure to meet 'minimum core obligations' if it is demonstrated that every effort has been made to make good use of available resources. See: Mechlem (2009): 940–2.

[49] See e.g.: Chinkin (2003): 33–4.

[50] A. Chapman, 'The Status of Efforts to Monitor Economic, Social, and Cultural Rights', in *Economic Rights: Conceptual, Measurement, and Policy Issues*, ed. S. Hertel and L. Minkler (Cambridge: Cambridge University Press, 2007): 154–5. The scepticism was certainly fuelled by the fact that the call to specify 'minimum core obligations' was famously rejected by the South African Constitutional Court. See: *Government of the Republic of South Africa v. Grootboom* 2001 (1) SA 46 (CC), ss 32–3. For commentary, see: A. Sachs, 'Enforcement of Social and Economic Rights', *American University International Law Review* vol. 22 (2007): 673; Fredman (2008): 84; Bilchitz (2002); Bilchitz (2003); Lehmann (2006). On the other hand, in Colombia, the 'vital minimum' doctrine had a huge influence on domestic jurisprudence. See: Landau (2012).

[51] Lehmann (2006): 165–6.

[52] Young's suggestion is that, due to its rhetorical force, the minimum core should be turned into an 'interpretive device for advocacy networks'. Young (2008): 125.

for further doctrinal elaboration and a more politically sensible framing. One crucial step may be integrating the minimum core with other obligations-related concepts in CESCR soft law. This point will become clearer upon consideration of the 'tripartite classification'.

3.2 The tripartite classification

The 'tripartite classification' of state obligations ('respect', 'protect', 'fulfil') began as a pure scholarly invention. (It can be traced back to Henry Shue's seminal book *Basic Rights*.[53]) It has no textual basis in binding international human rights documents, and its principal function appears to be as a framework for a better understanding of the range of human rights obligations. But the tripartite classification also has implications for vexed issues of determinacy and progressive realization. It implies that economic and social rights give rise to negative ('respect') obligations to refrain from depriving right-holders of what they have secured for themselves (in terms of health care, food supplies, etc.). Such obligations are not exposed to the relativizing force of resource constraints.[54]

The attraction of the 'tripartite classification' is strongly linked to its potential to challenge the troublesome distinction between negative and positive rights that proved so damaging to the credibility of economic and social rights.[55] In theoretical terms, the 'tripartite classification' offers a 'two-step' reconstitution of the positive–negative distinction. The first step is a rejection of the idea that rights themselves can be positive or negative. Instead, rights-related obligations may be positive or negative.[56] The second step lies in moving beyond a simple dual categorization of obligations: human rights generate a 'spectrum' of different obligations.[57] The three elements of the 'tripartite classification' are heuristic devices covering 'ranges' within the obligation spectrum. 'Respect' obligations are closer to the negative 'pole', while 'fulfil' obligations cluster closer to the positive 'pole'.

As indicated above, the idea itself, although not its current terminology, can be traced back to academic writing—in particular, Henry Shue's *Basic Rights*. Shue presents a compelling criticism of the categorization of rights as negative and positive, and the analysis develops into a general, tripartite categorization of rights-related obligations: duties to avoid depriving, duties to protect from deprivation, and duties to aid the deprived.[58]

[53] H. Shue, *Basic Rights: Subsistence, Affluence, and U.S. Foreign Policy* (Princeton: Princeton University Press, 1980): 52–60.

[54] Scott (1989): 835; I. E. Koch, *Human Rights as Indivisible Rights: The Protection of Socio-Economic Demands under the European Convention on Human Rights* (Leiden: Martinus Nijhoff, 2009): 15.

[55] E. Palmer, *Judicial Review, Socio-Economic Rights and the Human Rights Act* (Oxford: Hart Publishing, 2007): 22; T. Landman, 'Social Science Methods and Human Rights', in *Methods of Human Rights Research*, ed. F. Coomans, F. Grünfeld, and M. T. Kamminga (Cambridge: Intersentia, 2009): 23.

[56] Theorizing on positive obligations remains eminently plausible. See: Fredman (2008).

[57] Rolf Künnemann, 'A Coherent Approach to Human Rights', *Human Rights Quarterly* vol. 17 (1995): 331; Koch (2009): 16.

[58] Shue (1980): 52–60. For Shue's impact on later theoretical development, see: Fredman (2008): 69.

Shue puts special emphasis on how this categorization applies to economic and social rights, specifying duties not to eliminate a person's only available means of subsistence, to protect people against deprivation of the only available means of subsistence by others, and to provide for the subsistence of those unable to provide for themselves.[59]

It was through Asbjørn Eide's pioneering work that Shue's account was quickly transformed into a doctrinal construct in human rights law. Eide developed and consolidated the current terminology from the early 1980s.[60] Duties to avoid depriving became 'obligations to respect', duties to protect from deprivation became 'obligations to protect', and duties to aid the deprived became 'obligations to fulfil'. His Final Report as Special Rapporteur on the Right to Food[61] played a crucial role in popularizing the tripartite classification.

Importantly, there is no obvious reason why the obligation spectrum should be divided into only three types of obligations. After all, these categories are heuristic devices. In fact, there have been significant attempts to elaborate on the categorization.[62] In 1984, van Hoof argued for including obligations to promote.[63] Eide himself experimented with expanding to four categories (adding a 'duty to facilitate').[64] Steiner and Alston proposed an alternative categorization of five levels of obligations: duties to respect the rights of others; duties to create institutional machinery essential to the realization of rights; duties to protect rights/prevent violations; duties to provide goods and services to satisfy rights; and duties to promote rights.[65] That Eide's original tripartite categorization remains the most influential is largely due to the fact that, under the direct influence of the Maastricht Guidelines,[66] it was 'canonized' in the CESCR General Comments.[67]

The 'tripartite classification' has been an established doctrinal device since the second half of the 1990s in CESCR soft law.[68] First featuring in General Comment

[59] Shue (1980): 53.

[60] *Food as a Human Right*, ed. Asbjørn Eide et al. (Tokyo: The United Nations University, 1984); Asbjørn Eide, 'Economic, Social and Cultural Rights as Human Rights', in *Economic, Social and Cultural Rights*, ed. A. Eide, C. Krause, and A. Rosas (Leiden: Martinus Nijhoff, 2001): 24.

[61] Asbjørn Eide, *The Right to Adequate Food as a Human Right: Final Report Submitted by Asbjørn Eide, Special Raporteur*, UN Doc. E/CN.4/Sub.2/1987/23.

[62] Sepúlveda (2003): 157–64.

[63] G. J. H. van Hoof, 'The Legal Nature of Economic, Social and Cultural Rights: A Rebuttal of Some Traditional Views', in *The Right to Food*, ed. P. Alston and K. Tomasevski (Leiden: Martinus Nijhoff, 1984): 106–8.

[64] A. Eide, *The Realization of Economic, Social and Cultural Rights: The Right to Adequate Food and to be Free from Hunger. Updated Study on the Right to Food*, UN Doc. E/CN.4/Sub.2/1999/12.

[65] H. Steiner and P. Alston, *International Human Rights in Context: Law, Politics, Morals* (Oxford: Oxford University Press, 2000): 180–5.

[66] *The Maastricht Guidelines on Violations of Economic, Social and Cultural Rights* [1997], at s. 6 (available at <http://www1.umn.edu/humanrts/instree/Maastrichtguidelines_.html>). The Maastricht Guidelines were formulated by a group of experts to provide guidance to the interpretation of the ICESCR—elaborating on 'The Limburg Principles on the Implementation of the International Covenant on Economic, Social and Cultural Rights', *Human Rights Quarterly* vol. 9 (1987): 122.

[67] The alternative proposals were not in vain: van Hoof's 'duty to promote', Eide's 'duty to facilitate', and Steiner and Alston's 'duty to provide' found their way into CESCR doctrine. They have become aspects of the 'duty to fulfil' in recent CESCR General Comments. E.g.: CESCR (2007) General Comment 19 ('The Right to Social Security') UN Doc. E/C.12/GC/19, s. 59.

[68] See e.g.: Craven (1998): 107.

12 in 1999,[69] it has become the standard method for capturing the multiplicity of human rights obligations,[70] and popular in quasi-official UN documents.[71] It is widely accepted as applicable to all human rights,[72] and seen by some as the cornerstone of a common doctrinal framework for all human rights bodies.[73]

The 'tripartite classification' is by far the most successful device in CESCR doctrine. For a piece of soft law in international human rights law, it could hardly be more influential. The degree of acceptance is almost surprising[74] considering that, as a doctrinal construct, it is not without its uncertainties. For example, it is difficult to determine whether the relationship between different obligations is static or dynamic. Can 'duties to protect' expand or contract in relation to the 'duty to respect' under changing circumstances?[75] It is not entirely clear why the tripartite classification has fared so much better than 'minimum core obligations' outside CESCR General Comments. Despite appearances, the 'tripartite classification' is not merely a clever way to organize human rights obligations into useful categories. It has a hard edge in doctrinal debates, and facilitates an expansive interpretation of state obligations. (It is no accident that it was a strategic objective for NGOs to include the 'tripartite classification' in the Optional Protocol to the ICESCR.[76])

The similarities of the doctrinal concerns underlying the tripartite classification and 'minimum core obligations' are partly concealed by the fact that the CESCR has failed to integrate the obligations-related concepts. CESCR General Comments use an idiosyncratic distinction: the 'tripartite classification' is used to articulate 'specific obligations', while 'minimum core obligations' feature as a separate,

69 CESCR (1990) General Comment 12 ('The Right to Adequate Food') UN Doc. E/C.12/1999/5.

70 See e.g.: A. E. Yamin, 'Not Just a Tragedy: Access to Medications as a Right under International Law', *Boston University International Law Journal* vol. 21 (2003): 328–9; Louise Bernier, 'International Socio-Economic Human Rights: The Key to Global Health Improvement?', *International Journal of Human Rights* vol. 14 (2010): 259. O. De Schutter, 'The Rights to Everyone to Enjoy the Benefits of Scientific Progress and the Right to Food: From Conflict to Complementarity', *Human Rights Quarterly* vol. 33 (2011): 314–15.

71 Yamin (2003): 352; Office of the United Nations High Commissioner for Human Rights, *Frequently Asked Questions on a Human Rights Based Approach to Development Coordination* (New York: United Nations, 2006): 2.

72 Künnemann (1995): 327–8; S. Leckie, 'Another Step towards Indivisibility: Identifying the Key Features of Violations of Economic, Social and Cultural Rights', *Human Rights Quarterly* vol. 20 (1998): 90–2; S. Fredman, 'New Horizons: Incorporating Socio-economic Rights in a British Bill of Rights', *Public Law* (2010): 303.

73 M. O'Flaherty, 'Towards Integration of United Nations Human Rights Treaty Body Recommendations: The Rights-Based Approach Model', in *Economic, Social and Cultural Rights*, ed. M. A. Baderin and R. McCorquodale (Oxford: Oxford University Press, 2007): 32.

74 Koch is the outlier with her systematic attack on the 'tripartite classification'. See: Koch (2009): 17–27.

75 H. Shue, *Basic Rights: Subsistence, Affluence, and U.S. Foreign Policy* (Princeton: Princeton University Press, 1996); Young (2008): 163.

76 G. E. Türkelli, W. Vandenhole, and A. Vandenbogaerde, 'NGO Impact on Law-Making: The Case of a Complaints Procedure under the International Covenant on Economic, Social and Cultural Rights and the Convention on the Rights of the Child', *Journal of Human Rights Practice* vol. 5 (2013): 18. The proposal did not become part of the Protocol.

stand-alone category. The relationship between the two doctrinal constructs remains to be clarified.[77] Inexplicably, the Committee appears never to have reflected on the fact that the minimum core obligations it identifies clearly fall under the tripartite categorization. Respecting 'the right of everyone to identify with communities' is a 'respect' obligation,[78] while avoiding measures resulting in 'discrimination and unequal treatment in the private and public sectors of disadvantaged and marginalized individuals' is a 'protect' obligation.[79] Interestingly, most of the minimum core obligations in CESCR General Comments, such as 'securing access to safe and potable water',[80] taking action 'to mitigate and alleviate hunger',[81] 'adopting and implementing a national employment strategy',[82] and 'monitoring the realization of the right to social security'[83] are 'fulfil' obligations. The Committee's reluctance to clarify how the 'minimum core obligations' relate to the obligation spectrum makes these obligations appear incompletely articulated, while also rendering the 'tripartite classification' less clearly articulated than it could be.

4. Challenging State Practice

As indicated in section 2, the significance of CESCR doctrine for human rights law cannot be adequately assessed by relying solely on abstract ideas of clarity and doctrinal plausibility. The formation of CESCR soft law is a political process that must be understood as shaped by both political and doctrinal challenges. We need to place the development of CESCR doctrine in its political context.

4.1 Justiciability and violationism

The specific efforts to reconstitute (as opposed to merely articulate) state obligations under the ICESCR is partly driven by the institutional agenda pursued by the Committee. The reform of its monitoring regime (which would establish an individual complaints mechanism) has been a strategic objective for the Committee from the beginning. The CESCR formulated a formal proposal for an Optional Protocol to the ICESCR as early as 1992, and four separate reports on the Protocol were drafted in 1996.[84] The powers of the Human Rights Committee were envisaged as the model for improved and enhanced monitoring for the CESCR.[85]

The undercurrent of this agenda has always been the controversy regarding the justiciability of economic and social rights.[86] A complaint mechanism under

[77] Young (2008): 154.

[78] CESCR (2009) General Comment 21 ('Right of Everyone to Take Part in Cultural Life') UN Doc. E/C.12/GC/21, s. 55(b).

[79] CESCR (n. 37) s. 31(b). [80] CESCR (n. 36) s. 43. [81] CESCR (n. 69) s. 6.

[82] CESCR (n. 37) s. 31. [83] CESCR (n. 38) s. 59. [84] Craven (1998).

[85] Alston (1987) 345; Craven (1998): 56–7.

[86] By 'justiciability', I mean the feasibility of subjecting the implementation of rights to independent judicial or quasi-judicial review. For an overview of the debates on the justiciability of economic and social rights, see: Bódig (2015): 52–4.

the ICESCR is eminently implausible without gaining the upper hand in this debate. The Committee's agenda could not succeed without demonstrating the doctrinal plausibility of subjecting the implementation of economic and social rights to judicial or quasi-judicial review, which is resolutely denied by many governments.[87] General Comments have been explicitly used to flesh out a doctrinal vision that accommodates the Committee's stance on justiciability.[88] The emphasis has shifted markedly towards identifying the aspects of economic and social rights that lend themselves to review procedures. This has meant explicitly arguing that at least some rights in the ICESCR are readily justiciable,[89] as well as showing that economic and social rights give rise to determinate obligations. This explains the pivotal role of 'minimum core obligations' and the 'tripartite classification' in CESCR doctrine: they serve to demonstrate that it is feasible to specify distinct responsibilities for implementing economic and social rights in review processes.

However, the institutional agenda is not the only factor determining the political dynamics here. The Committee has also sought to develop closer cooperation with NGOs,[90] which involved adjusting its doctrinal work to the agenda of mainstream human rights activism. As indicated in section 1, this meant facilitating the 'naming and shaming' of those who breach economic and social rights.[91] Crucially, the CESCR institutional agenda on justiciability and the commitment to bolstering NGO activism have interacted in specific ways within CESCR soft law. The efforts to clarify state obligations focus on improving the possibility of declaring clear violations of economic and social rights.[92] CESCR doctrine has thus taken on a 'violationist' character.

Of course, the ability to define violations is an important test for the clarity of legal obligations anywhere. What makes the focus on violations problematic is that the Committee was not merely articulating the implications of set obligations. As we have seen, CESCR General Comments are not simply manifestations of treaty norms and state practice.[93] The Committee set out to reconstitute state obligations with a view to sharpening and broadening our understanding of violations of economic and social rights. And, in the process, it has moved away from the cooperative model of monitoring that underlies its legal mandate. This unilateralism turns its 'violationism' into 'violationist bias', raising issues about the legitimacy of the Committee's doctrinal work. Is it acceptable for the Committee

[87] M. J. Dennis and D. P. Stewart, 'Justiciability of Economic, Social, and Cultural Rights: Should There be an International Complaints Mechanism to Adjudicate the Rights to Adjudicate the Rights to Food, Water, Housing, and Health?', *American Journal of International Law* vol. 98 (2004): 472–3.

[88] CESCR (1998) General Comment 9 ('The Domestic Application of the Covenant') UN Doc. E/C.12/1998/24, s. 10.

[89] CESCR (n. 26) s. 5. The Committee specifically refers to the justiciability of non-discrimination provisions in ICESCR Arts 3, 7(a)(i), and 10(3), as well as the availability of compulsory and free primary education in Art. 13(2)(a) and the freedom to establish educational institutions in Art. 13(4).

[90] Sepúlveda (2003): 69–70.

[91] Craven (1998): 83.

[92] Dennis and Stewart (2004).

[93] Blake (2008): 27.

to create soft law with the aim of unilaterally imposing normative expectations on states parties?

4.2 The legitimacy of challenging state practice through soft law

It is not very surprising, then, that the doctrinal work of the CESCR is so hotly contested. There is scepticism about the underlying interpretative methods,[94] and the Committee has become embroiled in quarrels with governments.[95] Still, we should not hastily reject CESCR doctrine as originating in a misguided and subversive institutional practice. We must consider whether the Committee, in its attempts to reconstitute state obligations, has reacted to genuine needs to further human rights protection. Perhaps, on occasion, soft law has come to the rescue of flawed hard law. This possibility should not be dismissed on the basis of potentially misguided orthodoxy regarding legal sources and institutional competences.

We need to put the legitimacy challenge facing the Committee into perspective. As we have seen, General Comments carry limited normative force in themselves. States parties do not have enforceable 'minimum core obligations' merely on the basis of CESCR General Comments. Precisely because of the deviations from the terms of the ICESCR and state practice, it is questionable whether CESCR General Comments constitute authoritative interpretations of existing treaty obligations. States parties can always stifle normative developments here by consistent objections,[96] or frustrate the institutional ambitions of the Committee by not ratifying the Optional Protocol to the ICESCR.[97] They are challenged, but never forced.

Of course, it is somewhat unsatisfactory to argue that simply because the Committee has limited institutional capacities, we can overlook ventures beyond its mandate. This would be to underplay the significance to soft law. A better starting point is to acknowledge that fidelity to what states have consented to by ratifying the ICESCR cannot be the sole measure of the legitimacy of doctrinal development. If, as emphasized above, human rights treaties only 'recognize' human rights, positive international norms cannot claim to pin down the exact meaning of human rights. If economic and social rights indeed 'derive from the inherent dignity of the human person',[98] the CESCR, in its claims regarding the concomitant obligations, may be right and states parties wrong. The normative vision underlying the articles of the ICESCR must be open to contestation. It is a distinct possibility that the ICESCR, as we find it today, may not be fit for purpose in the twenty-first century.

[94] Mechlem (2009); M. Odello and F. Seatzu, *The UN Committee on Economic, Social and Cultural Rights: The Law, Process and Practice* (Oxford: Routledge, 2013): 34.

[95] E. Bates, 'The United Kingdom and the International Covenant on Economic, Social and Cultural Rights', in *Economic, Social and Cultural Rights*, ed. M. A. Baderin and R. McCorquodale (Oxford: Oxford University Press, 2007): 271.

[96] Blake (2008): 34.

[97] In over six years, of the 165 parties to the ICESCR, only 47 have become signatories of the Optional Protocol, and 21 have become parties to it (as of Mar. 2016).

[98] ICESCR Preamble.

As a redraft does not seem feasible in the foreseeable future, doctrinal development by way of soft law may be the only practicable way of getting right the character of economic and social rights in international law.

There is considerable force to this line of argument: the ICESCR (as a legal document) indeed suffers from a number of deficiencies. The Covenant's open 'redistributionism'[99] and its emphasis on trade union activism derive from the aspirations of the labour movement in the first half of the twentieth century to build a model for the welfare state.[100] Also, the text of the Covenant reflects an unfortunate mixture of a minimalist and maximalist agenda in terms of economic and social rights.[101] It has been a genuine worry that the Covenant in fact misconstrues the character of economic and social rights. The drafters made a mistake when capturing the nature of state obligations in Article 2(1) in a way that gives licence to postpone any meaningful implementation. There may be a need to establish international standards that are consciously pitched against the original doctrinal design of the Covenant. Soft law may then offer a framework for consolidating such international standards. Precisely because they challenge state practice without forcing states parties, CESCR General Comments may play a crucial role in setting the course for much-needed normative development. Seen in this light, the doctrinal work of the CESCR may be considered admirable: it has done well in bringing the ICESCR into the twenty-first century. Moreover, it has broadened the range of actors playing a role in normative development. CESCR General Comments have provided an avenue for human rights scholars and NGOs to influence normative development.[102]

4.3 Rethinking the formation of CESCR soft law

In light of these considerations, the key question regarding legitimacy may not be whether the Committee has never gone beyond its substantive remit, but whether its doctrinal work reflects a plausible understanding of the character and significance of economic and social rights, and whether it has the potential to nudge state practice towards better implementation. Has the Committee successfully balanced the need to repair some of the deficiencies of the ICESCR with the importance of not blatantly flouting the treaty provisions that the states parties have signed up to? Has the Committee managed to outline where state practice can reasonably go in terms of economic and social rights in the twenty-first century?

[99] Craven (1998): 157–8.

[100] Craven (1998): 138; Palmer (2007): 8; C. Tomuschat, 'Human Rights in a World-Wide Framework: Some Current Issues', *Zeitschrift für auslandisches öffentliches Recht und Völkerrecht* vol. 45 (1985): 566.

[101] Art. 11(1) of the ICESCR makes the continuous (!) improvement of living conditions a right of everyone (that is, even of the well-off citizens of the richest countries). On the other hand, Art. 14 settles for an obligation to introduce a detailed plan (!) to implement compulsory primary education for countries that were not able to implement it before acceding to the ICESCR.

[102] Blake (2008): 2; Sepúlveda (2003): 69–70.

Assessed in these terms, the record of CESCR General Comments is clearly positive but not without problems. The most obvious defect in terms of striking the right balance between the ambition to improve human rights protection and the need to show due respect for treaty law is that the Committee has failed to ensure the coherence and clarity of its doctrinal work, as seen in the analysis of doctrinal constructs in section 3. The uncertainty surrounding some of the Committee's doctrinal constructs compromises the credibility of CESCR doctrine and weakens its ability to influence the course of normative development. There is a need for much better integration of obligation-related concepts in CESCR soft law.

The violationist bias of the Committee has an even more detrimental impact on CESCR soft law. It has steered the Committee towards 'unilateralism' when it comes to specifying the normative implications of human rights. The 'minimum core' that, fairly or unfairly, has become the symbolic manifestation of the Committee's violationist bias is a fitting example. The problem is not that it is implausible to claim that economic and social rights give rise to core obligations. The trouble is that the CESCR is not particularly well positioned to specify them unilaterally. Issuing General Comments is an aspect of the communication and cooperation between the CESCR and states parties, a view matched by the Committee's own description.[103] If this is true, the Committee should have chosen to develop its conception of core obligations more directly via its communications with states parties through state reports.[104] Concrete obligations could be presented as implications of more successful models of implementation.[105] This would still allow for challenging state practice and setting the agenda for normative development, but CESCR soft law could arise from a more explicitly dialogical process and move away from the unilateralism that the Committee's violationist approach currently entails. The result would be a more institutionalist understanding of minimum core obligations:[106] that they are specified as part of the process of key actors developing a shared understanding of the normative implications of implementing human rights.

This more dialogical model of doctrinal development looks more feasible if we realize that it is not only the CESCR that faces legitimacy challenges here. Joining human rights mechanisms makes sense for states parties partly because it addresses aspects of their legitimacy that they cannot address through domestic legitimizing processes. Participation in international cooperation (e.g. international trade) becomes troublesome if they struggle to get their practices of governance accepted by the international community (and even the global public). This partly explains why states ratify human rights treaties in the first place.[107] Monitoring by treaty

[103] CESCR (n. 16) para. 51.

[104] Actually the CESCR has claimed that it derives core obligations from its work on State Reports. See: CESCR (n. 26) s. 10. But this does not seem to bear out in later General Comments.

[105] This was Philip Alston's original suggestion. See: P. Alston, 'The Committee on Economic, Social and Cultural Rights', in *The United Nations and Human Rights: A Critical Appraisal*, ed. P. Alston (Oxford: Oxford University Press, 1992): 491.

[106] Young (2010): 125.

[107] O. Hathaway, 'Why Do Countries Commit to Human Rights Treaties?', *Journal of Conflict Resolution* vol. 51 (2007): 613.

bodies is predicated on the responsibility of states parties towards the international community.[108] This has implications for the appropriate attitude of states parties towards doctrinal development in soft law.

Once again, reflecting on core obligations helps to substantiate this point. State obligations under the ICESCR are indeed subject to a 'progressive realization' standard. Still, for each state party, there is a certain level below which the lack of implementation efforts calls into question the very commitment that ratifying the Covenant entails. There is no reliable way of determining this 'level' in the abstract. Sustained communication between monitoring bodies and states parties offers the best chance of filling the idea of meaningful implementation with more concrete content. If framed appropriately, specific examples of 'minimum core obligations' (and a more nuanced understanding of the obligations to 'respect', 'protect', and 'fulfil', for that matter) may be considered products of this communication process from the perspective of states parties.

5. Conclusion

This chapter has argued that CESCR General Comments play the role of both 'norm-filling' (obligation-articulating) and 'norm-creating' soft law. The analysis of specific doctrinal constructs developed by the CESCR suggests that the CESCR has been working on at least partly reconstituting (as opposed to merely clarifying) state obligations under the ICESCR. CESCR General Comments stretch the institutional competence of the Committee, and expose it to political and even doctrinal criticism.

This does not mean that the Committee's doctrinal innovations are without justification. The overall doctrinal record of the Committee is positive. CESCR soft law holds the promise of a more balanced development of human rights law, and represents a move towards broadening the range of agents contributing to normative development in human rights law. The CESCR deserves credit for using its General Comments to 'paper over' some of the drafting deficiencies of the ICESCR. Importantly, the Committee has sought to achieve this by channelling concepts and ideas from human rights scholarship into its soft law. The CESCR has also aligned its interpretative practices with mainstream human rights activism, offering a more prominent role to human rights activists in setting the agenda for the protection of economic and social rights.[109]

[108] This is, of course, a vision of the relationship between sovereignty and responsibility that underlies the UN documents on 'Responsibility to Protect' (R2P). E.g.: *World Summit Outcome* (2005) GA Res. A/RES/60/1 (24 Oct. 2005), ss 138–9.

[109] The Committee cooperates with a range of NGOs, and the profile of economic and social rights has indeed been raised among human rights activists. See: Sepúlveda (2003): 69–70. An NGO coalition was assisting the Committee in its drive for the Optional Protocol to the ICESCR. See: Türkelli, Vandenhole, and Vandenbogaerde (2013).

However, the time may be ripe for reconsidering the direction of doctrinal development in CESCR General Comments. CESCR soft law has some unappealing substantive features. Its doctrinal credibility is compromised by the uncertainty regarding how the different obligations-related concepts used in General Comments (like 'minimum core obligations' and obligations of 'respect', 'protect', and 'fulfil') relate to one another. Even more importantly, the CESCR has steered its General Comments towards a more adversarial stance in relation to states parties.[110] The idea that the best hope for improved implementation of human rights lies with expert bodies unilaterally imposing normative expectations on states parties has shown its limitations over the past couple of decades.[111] The chapter has argued that the doctrinal constructs of the CESCR (and 'minimum core obligations' in particular) could benefit from being embedded within a more 'dialogical' model of monitoring.

Human rights law, like any law, requires continuous normative development. It must be adjusted to the shifting challenges of human rights protection. However, such adjustments do not make a lasting positive impact on the quality of the law without adequate doctrinal groundwork—without developing the conceptual arsenal for formulating human rights norms and articulating their content. One aim of this chapter has been to show that soft law has formidable potential in providing this doctrinal groundwork in human rights law. Soft law can play the leading role in elaborating principles and conceptual constructs capable of setting the course for the development of hard law.

[110] Craven (1998): 83.

[111] We have seen how this unilateralism created political tensions around the practice of the European Court of Human Rights. See: High Level Conference on the Future of the European Court of Human Rights, *Brighton Declaration*, available at <http://www.echr.coe.int/Documents/2012_Brighton_FinalDeclaration_ENG.pdf>.

5

The Role and Use of Soft Law Instruments in the African Human Rights System

Debra Long and Rachel Murray

1. Introduction

The proliferation and multifaceted nature of soft law within the human rights field, as noted in the Introduction to this volume, is nowhere more evident than in the work of the African Commission on Human and Peoples' Rights (African Commission).

The African Commission is the primary regional body mandated to monitor implementation of and compliance with the rights set out under the African Charter on Human and Peoples' Rights (African Charter).[1] Soft law and soft law instruments are prevalent within the African human rights system and are arguably an inherent part of it. The African Commission is expressly mandated by the African Charter to take into account a range of binding and non-binding instruments when carrying out its functions.[2] In addition it has established a number of different procedures and activities which generate a range of outputs that are arguably soft law and soft law instruments.

These outputs of the African Commission have played an important role in developing the human rights framework within the region and have 'potentially persuasive normative value'.[3] They also reflect the variety of reasons identified in the Introduction to this book for which soft law may be developed, and the diverse types of instruments that in a broad interpretation may be categorized as 'soft law instruments' but which may have very different persuasive force or purpose in practice.[4]

[1] Art. 45 of the African Charter on Human and Peoples' Rights.

[2] Arts 60 and 61 of the African Charter on Human and Peoples' Rights states that the applicable principles the African Commission shall draw inspiration from and take into consideration include non-binding instruments from the African and UN human rights systems, as well as African practices and customs. This reference to non-binding instruments and concepts is unusual. See also: R. Murray, *The African Commission on Human and Peoples' Rights & International Law* (Portland: Hart Publishing, 2000): 25.

[3] F. Viljoen, *International Human Rights in Africa* (Oxford: Oxford University Press, 2nd edn, 2012): 213.

[4] See also: R. Baxter, 'International Law in Her Infinite Variety', *International and Comparative Legal Quarterly* (*ICLQ*) vol. 29 (1980): 549–66; A. Boyle, 'Some Reflections on the Relationship between Treaties and Soft Law', *ICLQ* vol. 48 (1999): 901–9; C. Chinkin, 'Normative Development in the International Legal System', in *Commitment and Compliance: The Role of Non-binding Norms in the International Legal System*, ed. D. Shelton (Oxford: Oxford University Press, 2000): 30–4; D. Shelton,

It is beyond the scope of this contribution and book to look in detail at all of the different types of soft law and soft law instruments emanating from the African Commission. Therefore this chapter looks in particular at the thematic instruments that have been adopted by the African Commission to elaborate on states' obligations in respect of particular rights. These instruments are designed to guide and modify state behaviour by enunciating principles and measures required to implement and comply with specific rights. Consequently they form an important body of soft law within the human rights framework of the African Commission and have the potential to play a significant role in influencing policy and practice both at the national and regional levels.

This chapter draws on a four-year research project conducted by the authors that examined in what contexts soft law instruments of the African Commission are used in practice and what factors have an influence on their use and implementation.[5] It uses as a case study the *Guidelines and Measures for the Prohibition and Prevention of Torture, Cruel, Inhuman or Degrading Treatment or Punishment in Africa* (Robben Island Guidelines). By tracking how the Robben Island Guidelines have been used in practice, trends in the use of thematic instruments of the African Commission generally can be observed and factors that influence their use in practice can be identified.

Therefore section 2 considers the prevalence and role of soft law instruments within the work of the African Commission. In particular it considers the reasons and process for the development of thematic instruments adopted by the African Commission. Then, using the Robben Island Guidelines as a case study, section 3 examines observable trends in their use both at the national and regional levels. Lastly, the contribution considers the key factors that have an influence on the degree of traction these thematic soft law instruments can gain.

2. The Role of Soft Law within the African Commission on Human and Peoples' Rights

The African Commission derives its mandate from Article 45 of the African Charter, which sets out the express functions of the Commission to promote, protect, and interpret the rights contained in the African Charter. From the outset soft law is given prominence within the functions and outputs of the African Commission; for example Article 45 states that the Commission is to:

> 1. … a) give its views or make recommendations to Governments.
> b) to formulate and lay down, principles and rules aimed at solving legal problems relating to human and peoples' rights and fundamental freedoms upon which African Governments may base their legislation….

'Law, Non-law and the Problem of Soft Law', in *Commitment and Compliance: The Role of Non-binding Norms in the International Legal System*, ed. D. Shelton (Oxford: Oxford University Press, 2000): 10–13.

[5] This research project was funded by the Arts and Humanities Research Council of the UK. The research project ran from Oct. 2008 to 2012. The research documents produced under the project are available at: <http://www.bris.ac.uk/law/research/centres-themes/hric/projects/softlawrigproject/>.

3. Interpret all the provisions of the present Charter at the request of a State Party, an institution of the OAU or an African Organisation recognised by the OAU....[6]

The African Commission has therefore been established as a monitoring body with quasi-judicial, advisory, and investigative powers. It can be inferred from the references to 'views', 'recommendations', 'principles', and 'rules' in Article 45 that a fundamental aspect of the mandate of the African Commission is to develop soft law, and/or soft law instruments, in order to promote human and peoples' rights and assist states to implement their obligations under the African Charter.

In interpreting its mandate the African Commission has established a range of procedures and functions such as the consideration of periodic state reports, missions to countries, the adoption of resolutions on country specific issues; the adoption of thematic resolutions; General Comments on thematic issues; and the consideration of individual and state communications, which generate a significant number of views, observations, recommendations, guidelines, and rules, which are arguably soft law or soft law instruments.[7]

These instruments of the African Commission can be regarded as 'secondary soft law' as described by Shelton,[8] because they emanate from a treaty body and not states themselves. As will be explored in this chapter the institutional context within which these instruments have been developed has a significant impact on their role and use in practice.

Over the years the African Commission has adopted a number of thematic instruments, usually in the form of 'principles' and/or 'guidelines', such as the *Guidelines on the Conditions of Arrest, Police Custody and Pre-Trial Detention in Africa*;[9] *Guidelines and Principles on Economic, Social and Cultural Rights in the African Charter on Human and Peoples' Rights*;[10] *Principles and Guidelines on the Right to a Fair Trial and Legal Assistance in Africa*;[11] and *Guidelines and Measures for the Prohibition and Prevention of Torture, Cruel, Inhuman or Degrading Treatment or Punishment in Africa* (Robben Island Guidelines).[12] In addition the African Commission has also adopted the *Declaration of Principles on Freedom of Expression in Africa*,[13] which can be regarded as falling within this category of soft law instruments of the African Commission.

See also: R. Murray and D. Long, *The Implementation of the Findings of the African Commission on Human and Peoples' Rights* (Cambridge: Cambridge University Press, 2015).

[6] Art. 45 of the African Charter.

[7] The legal status of the African Commission's decisions on individual communications is ambiguous. The African Commission sometimes seeks to argue that its decisions are legally binding on states. This is supported by some commentators who assert that the adoption of the report of the African Commission which includes its decisions on individual communications by the AU has a 'hardening effect', see e.g.: Viljoen (2012): 339; F. Viljoen and L. Louw, 'The Status of the Findings of the African Commission', *Journal of African Law* vol. 48 (2004): 18–19. However cf. Murray and Long (2015): 56–8.

[8] Shelton (2000): 451. See also: Chinkin in Shelton (2000): 29.

[9] Adopted on 9 Mar. 2015. <http://www.achpr.org/instruments/guidelines_arrest_detention/>.

[10] Adopted on 24 Oct. 2011. <http://www.achpr.org/instruments/economic-social-cultural/>.

[11] Adopted on 29 May 2003. <http://www.achpr.org/instruments/principles-guidelines-right-fair-trial/>.

[12] Adopted on 23 Oct. 2002. <http://www.achpr.org/instruments/robben-island-guidelines-2008/>.

[13] Adopted on 23 Oct. 2002. <http://www.achpr.org/sessions/32nd/resolutions/62/>.

These instruments are all expressly categorized as soft law instruments by the African Commission itself,[14] and have been described as playing 'a role similar to that of General Comments adopted by UN human rights treaty bodies'.[15] In a further development of its interpretative function in 2012 the African Commission adopted its first 'General Comment' on the Protocol to the African Charter on General Comments on Article 14(1)(d) and (e) of the Protocol to the African Charter on Human and Peoples' Rights on the Rights of Women in Africa,[16] which was followed in 2014 by a second General Comment on the same Protocol.[17] With these precedents there are indications that other General Comments in relation to other rights contained within the African Charter will be developed.[18]

Although the rights addressed by these thematic instruments vary they have a common primary purpose. These instruments have been adopted by the African Commission as a means to fulfil its mandate as set out in Article 45(1)(b) of the African Charter 'to formulate and lay down, principles and rules aimed at solving legal problems relating to human and peoples' rights and fundamental freedoms upon which African Governments may base their legislation ...'.

Generally the intention is not to use these instruments to lead towards a 'hardening' of them in the form of a legally binding instrument, instead they are used to elaborate and strengthen the human rights framework within the region. In other words they are useful additions to the human rights 'armoury' which the African Commission, and others working in the field of human rights, can draw upon to encourage states to comply with their human rights obligations. Therefore these soft law instruments can be said to have a 'norm-filling' purpose as described in the Introduction to this book.[19] In addition some of these instruments also provide evidence of the existence of hard law obligations.[20] As Shelton notes, some soft law can have normative content and the soft law instruments of the African Commission are evidence of this;[21] for example numerous provisions of the Robben Island Guidelines reflect obligations contained in the UN Convention against Torture,[22] as well as those in the International Covenant on Civil and Political Rights.[23]

[14] See the list of legal instruments on the African Commission's website at <http://www.achpr.org/instruments/>.

[15] Viljoen (2012): 378.

[16] General Comments on Article 14(1)(d) and (e) of the Protocol to the African Charter on Human and Peoples' Rights on the Rights of Women in Africa. <http://www.achpr.org/instruments/general-comments-rights-women/>.

[17] General Comment No. 2 on Article 14.1(a), (b), (c), and (f) and Article 14.2(a) and (c) of the Protocol to the African Charter on Human and Peoples' Rights on the Rights of Women in Africa. <http://www.achpr.org/instruments/general-comment-two-rights-women/>.

[18] African Commission's Committee for the Prevention of Torture in Africa, 'Concept Paper on the Development of a General Comment on Article 5 of the African Charter on Human and Peoples' Rights' (13 May 2015).

[19] See also: Murray and Long (2015): 58–61; Shelton (2000): 14; Chinkin in Shelton (2000): 30; Viljoen (2012): 379–80.

[20] Chinkin in Shelton (2000): 30–1.

[21] Shelton (2000): 4.

[22] See e.g.: Guidelines 4, 6, 7, 9, 11, 12, 15, 16, 18, 19, 29, and 50 of the Robben Island Guidelines.

[23] See e.g.: Guidelines 4, 9, 10, 20, 25, 26, 27, 32, 35, 36, and 50 of the Robben Island Guidelines.

Typically these thematic instruments have been developed at the instigation of civil society organizations (CSOs) in order to highlight and advance a particular area of focus at the regional level.[24] The influence and role of CSOs in the work of the African Commission has been well documented by commentators over the years.[25] The impact this reliance on CSOs has on the level of traction these thematic instruments gain at the regional and national levels is discussed further in section 4.

CSOs have instigated the development of these thematic instruments for a number of strategic reasons. They have been encouraged as a means to influence state behaviour by articulating measures required to implement their obligations in relation to particular rights.

The thematic instruments have been developed very deliberately and strategically in a 'soft law' form rather than a binding one. As Shelton notes, the soft law form may be used 'when there are concerns about the possibility of non-compliance either because of domestic political opposition, lack of ability of capacity to comply, uncertainty about whether compliance can be measured, or disagreement with aspects of the proposed norm'.[26] Soft law may also allow for more active participation of non-state actors and can be adopted or amended more rapidly because it is non-binding.[27] Therefore developing a thematic instrument in a 'soft law form' can be an expedient and pragmatic means to enunciate what measures states must take to implement their obligations. Consequently, these thematic instruments can be a useful tool to support and encourage implementation at the national level.[28]

The development of thematic instruments has also been used by CSOs as a device to strengthen the strategic approach and procedures of the African Commission itself in relation to a particular thematic issue. The aim being that these instruments can be used by the African Commission through its various procedures, such as the state reporting system, missions to countries, and the communications procedure, to strengthen the quality of its dialogue with and advice to states on particular human rights issues.

The African Commission has also established thematic 'Special Mechanisms' consisting of rapporteurs, working groups, and committees, as a means to provide a particular focus and focal point within the Commission in relation to specific rights.

[24] E.g. the development of the Declaration on Freedom of Expression and Access to Information was led by Art. 19, the Robben Island Guidelines were developed at the instigation of the Association for the Prevention of Torture (APT), the drafting of the Model Law on Freedom of Information was led by the Human Rights Centre of the University of Pretoria, and the were led by the African Policing Civilian Oversight Forum (APCOF) and the Open Society Justice Initiative (OSJI).

[25] See e.g.: Viljoen (2012): 383–8; R. Murray, 'Special Rapporteur in the African System', in *The African Charter on Human and Peoples' Rights*, ed. M. Evans and R. Murray (Cambridge: Cambridge University Press, 2nd edn, 2008): 373–5; N. Mbelle, 'The Role of Non-governmental Organisations and National Human Rights Institutions at the African Commission', in Evans and Murray (2008): 289–310; J. Harrington, 'Special Rapporteurs of the African Commission on Human and Peoples' Rights', *African Law Journal* vol. 1 (2001): 251; Murray (2000): 95–6.

[26] Shelton (2000): 12.

[27] Shelton (2000): 13.

[28] Murray and Long (2015): 77; Viljoen and Louw (2004): 13; O. C. Okafor, *The African Human Rights System: Activist Forces and International Institutions* (Cambridge: Cambridge University Press, 2007): 80.

Again the creation of these procedures has been at the instigation of CSOs, therefore not surprisingly the thematic instruments are often linked to particular themes that fall under the mandate of these Special Mechanisms. For example the *Guidelines on the Conditions of Arrest, Police Custody, and Pre-Trial Detention in Africa* were developed in cooperation with the Special Rapporteur on Prisons and Conditions of Detention in Africa; and the *Declaration of Principles on Freedom of Expression in Africa* and the Model Law for African States on Access to Information support the work of the Special Rapporteur on Freedom of Expression and Access to Information.

In this regard the Robben Island Guidelines are a particularly interesting example as they directly brought about the establishment of a Special Mechanism of the African Commission with a focus on the prevention of torture and, rather unusually for a soft law instrument, an express mandate to promote and monitor the implementation of the Guidelines themselves.[29] In October 2002, the African Commission passed a resolution adopting the Robben Island Guidelines and which also called for the establishment of a Special Mechanism, the 'Follow-up Committee on the Robben Island Guidelines' (Follow-up Committee). The mandate of the Follow-up Committee was expressed as follows:

- to organise, with the support of interested partners, seminars to disseminate the Robben Island Guidelines to national and regional stakeholders;
- to develop and propose to the African Commission strategies to promote and implement the Robben Island Guidelines at the national and regional levels;
- to promote and facilitate the implementation of the Robben Island Guidelines within member states; and
- to make a progress report to the African Commission at each ordinary session.[30]

The close nexus between the Robben Island Guidelines and the mandate of this Special Mechanism is evident in the wording of this resolution. In 2009 the name of the committee was changed to the 'Committee for the Prevention of Torture in Africa' (CPTA), in order to identify the Committee more clearly with the issue of torture, although its mandate and its express link to the Robben Island Guidelines remains the same.[31]

The creation of this Special Mechanism was a deliberate strategy of the main CSO behind the development of the Robben Island Guidelines, as means by which

[29] African Commission Resolution 61: Resolution on Guidelines and Measures for the Prohibition and Prevention of Torture, Cruel, Inhuman or Degrading Treatment or Punishment in Africa, adopted in Oct. 2002. For more information on the creation of the Follow-up Committee: D. Long and R. Murray, 'Ten Years of the Robben Island Guidelines and Prevention of Torture in Africa: For What Purpose?', *African Human Rights Law Journal* vol. 12 (2012): 311–47.

[30] Art. 3 of the Resolution on Guidelines and Measures for the Prohibition and Prevention of Torture, Cruel, Inhuman or Degrading Treatment or Punishment in Africa (Robben Island Guidelines, 2002).

[31] African Commission's Resolution on the Change of Name of the Robben Island Guidelines Follow-Up Committee to the 'Committee for the Prevention of Torture in Africa' and the Reappointment of the Chairperson and Members of the Committee, adopted on 25 Nov. 2009; Long and Murray (2012): 338–9.

to try and ensure the Guidelines gained traction at the national and regional levels after their adoption by the African Commission.[32] It was anticipated that creating a specific focal point within the Commission for the Guidelines would have a number of benefits. First it was hoped that having a Special Procedure as an 'advocate' for the Guidelines would raise their visibility within the Commission's procedures and inform the approach of the Commission to issues relating to torture and other ill-treatment. It was also expected that the Committee could be a conduit for activities that would promote the implementation of the Guidelines at the national level.

This leads us on to consider briefly the drafting process for these thematic instruments. Until recently these instruments were typically drafted in workshops involving representatives from the African Commission, CSOs, and other experts on the issue. The Robben Island Guidelines for example were finalized in a three-day expert workshop held in South Africa. The workshop was co-chaired by the African Commission and the APT, and involved representatives from CSOs, the police, and other experts.[33] Until recently therefore state representatives have not been involved in the drafting process for these thematic instruments.

However, there does appear to be a change in approach to the development of thematic instruments at the African Commission. The Guidelines on Conditions of Police Custody and Pre-trial Detention in Africa have emerged from a drafting process that have been more inclusive and engaged a wider range of stakeholders within the region.[34] For example drafts of this instrument were posted on the website of the African Commission with a call for comments, and regional meetings were held in order for input to be provided from more stakeholders, including state representatives. This change in approach may be attributed partly as a response to perceived limitations to the level of traction and influence that previous instruments such as the Robben Island Guidelines have at the regional and national levels, which was to some extent attributed to the lack of inclusivity and visibility generated from the outset of their development.

3. Trends in the Use of Thematic Instruments of the African Commission

This section draws on the conclusions of a four-year research project by the authors which used the Robben Island Guidelines as a case study to identify how soft law instruments of the African Commission are used in practice at the regional and national levels. The Robben Island Guidelines intended to elaborate states'

[32] Long and Murray (2012): 315–16, 333, and 339. See also: Murray and Long (2015): 73.

[33] For a detailed examination of the text of the Robben Island Guidelines: Long and Murray (2012): 327–31.

[34] Invitation to Experts Meeting on the Development of Guidelines on Pre-Trial Detention, <http://www.achpr.org/news/2013/03/d78/>. The drafting approach of these Guidelines were influenced by the development of other documents such the Model Law for African States on Access to Information, which had a more inclusive and transparent drafting process.

obligations in relation to Article 5 of the African Charter which, among other issues, prohibits torture and other ill-treatment.[35] The Robben Island Guidelines make an interesting case study for a number of reasons: they exemplify the dual purpose of the thematic instruments of the African Commission, namely to influence not only state practice but that of the African Commission itself; their drafting process illustrates the role of CSOs in the development of thematic instruments; they led to the creation of a Special Mechanism with a specific mandate to promote their implementation; and there is some evidence they have been used in practice at the national and regional levels.

In order to examine the use of the Robben Island Guidelines in practice, the research methodology included a review of all relevant instruments of the African Commission, other African Union organs, and the UN in order to see what instruments have been referenced by these bodies and in what context. A series of semi-structured interviews were undertaken with stakeholders,[36] and a number of high-level seminars and workshops were held to explore related themes.[37]

By tracing in depth the use of one thematic instrument in practice the authors were able to identify some notable trends in the use of these soft law instruments generally, as well as factors that influence their use in practice.

3.1 Trends at the national level

The overall objective for the adoption of thematic instruments by the African Commission is for them to be used at the national level to assist states to implement and comply with their obligations in respect of the rights addressed by the instruments, and also for them to be used to monitor the level of state compliance with these obligations. In order to achieve these objectives these instruments have a number of potential uses and 'users' at the national level.

Thematic instruments of the African Commission have the potential to be used in a range of advocacy initiatives and to initiate national discussions on the particular issue that they address. In relation to the Robben Island Guidelines these have been used in various advocacy initiatives, including in training programmes

[35] Art. 5 of the African Charter states, 'Every individual shall have the right to the respect of the dignity inherent in a human being and to the recognition of his legal status. All forms of exploitation and degradation of man, particularly slavery, slave trade, torture, cruel, inhuman or degrading punishment and treatment shall be prohibited.'

[36] Research trips where undertaken to Egypt, Ethiopia, The Gambia, South Africa, Tanzania, and Uganda. In addition participants from Botswana, Cameroon, Kenya, Nigeria, Rwanda, and South Sudan took part in project seminars. <http://www.bris.ac.uk/law/research/centres-themes/hric/projects/softlawrigproject/>.

[37] The following seminars and workshops were organized under the project: 2009, a seminar on 'Follow-Up and Implementation of Decisions by Human Rights Treaty Bodies', held in Bristol; 2010, a workshop for East African national human rights institutions on the implementation of torture prevention standards, held in Nairobi, Kenya; 2011, a seminar on the 'Implementation of UN Treaty Body Concluding Observations: The Role of National and Regional Mechanisms in Europe', held in Bristol, and a seminar on 'Identifying National Mechanisms to Follow up and Implement Decisions of the African Commission', held in Addis Ababa, Ethiopia; 2012, a seminar on 'The Strategic Use of Soft Law Human Rights Documents', held in Bristol, and a seminar on 'AU Follow up to Decisions of

on the prohibition and prevention of torture,[38] and the drafting of national legislation criminalizing torture. For example the Robben Island Guidelines were used as a resource in Uganda by the Uganda Human Rights Commission, APT, and national CSOs, when drafting text for a Bill on the prohibition and prevention of torture, and in Burundi by FIACAT, an international NGO, when drafting text on the criminalization of torture. One of the most visible uses of the Robben Island Guidelines can be found in the 2011 draft anti-torture Bill of Liberia, which specifically references the Robben Island Guidelines in its Preamble.[39] In these initiatives the Guidelines were perceived to be a useful tool for advocacy as they could be used 'as a platform for continuously challenging States and other stakeholders to take action to prevent torture'.[40] This was seen to be important 'because it is almost like a renewed focus on various human rights and particular human rights standards'.[41]

Therefore the Robben Island Guidelines have been used directly in national activities on torture and other ill-treatment, partly because they could act as a 'bridge' between obligations contained in treaties and action required to implement these on the ground. As one person noted, 'if the binding treaties have set the obligation to prohibit and prevent torture and also to respond to the needs of victims it is a set obligation so how then to reach the other side of the river? The Robben Island Guidelines act as this kind of bridge.'[42] In other words, soft law instruments such as the Robben Island Guidelines can articulate and encourage practical measures to be taken at the national level to implement obligations contained in binding instruments.

However, notwithstanding the instances where the Robben Island Guidelines have been used at the national level, the Guidelines have, to date, been used only to a very limited extent by national actors in practice. It can be observed that most relevant national stakeholders, such as state representatives, law enforcement officials, and CSOs, are largely unaware of the existence of the Guidelines and/or lack knowledge of their content in order to apply them in their work in any meaningful way.[43]

the African Commission', held in Addis Ababa, Ethiopia. For more information see: <http://www.bris.ac.uk/law/research/centres-themes/hric/projects/softlawrigproject/>.

[38] E.g.: the Robben Island Guidelines have been used in training undertaken between 2010 and 2014 in Burundi, Kenya, Mozambique, Rwanda, South Africa, and Uganda, as part of the Article 5 Initiative partnership, see <http://www.bris.ac.uk/law/research/centres-themes/hric/projects/article5initiative/>; in 2008 a regional training and sensitization workshop in Nigeria for heads of police and prisons within West African states: 'Report of Activities by Commissioner Dupe Atoki delivered at the 43rd ordinary session of the African Commission': 2; and in 2008 training on the Robben Island Guidelines was organized by the Liberian Police Force and the African Commission, see also: J. B. Niyizurugero and G. P. Lessène, 'The Robben Island Guidelines: An Essential Tool for the Prevention of Torture in Africa', *Essex Human Rights Review* vol. 6 (2010): 80.

[39] A copy of the Act is available at: <http://www.apt.ch/content/files/npm/africa/Liberia1.pdf>.

[40] ACHPR, APR, UNOHCHR, 'Robben Island Guidelines for the Prohibition and Prevention of Torture in Africa: Practical Guide for Implementation' (2008).

[41] Interview with Amanda Dissel, Human Rights Consultant, 2010.

[42] Interview with Jean-Baptiste Niyizurugero, Africa Programme Officer for the Association for the Prevention of Torture, 2010.

[43] Murray and Long (2015): 75.

Overall two prevailing trends can be observed in relation to the use of soft law thematic instruments of the African Commission at the national level. First, within domestic litigation binding national instruments are, perhaps unsurprisingly, predominantly the first choice for litigators due to perceptions that they carry more legal 'weight' and force, as well as relevance to the national context.[44] In addition there is a general lack of knowledge of the existence and content of the instruments emanating from the African Commission.[45]

The second trend that can be observed is that while on the one hand it is often claimed that the merit and relevance of regional instruments comes from the fact that they emanate from the African system, and therefore can cut across concerns and arguments that they are 'foreign' impositions that do not take into account the regional context,[46] in practice this has not translated into soft law instruments, such as the Robben Island Guidelines, being preferred over international soft law instruments on the same topic. In fact, apart from in litigation, there is evidence that there is a marked preference to use international instruments, binding or otherwise, at the national level.[47] A number of reasons can be advanced for this preference.

First, as noted above key stakeholders are simply not aware of the range of existing regional instruments. Most people we interviewed had not heard of the Robben Island Guidelines nor were familiar with other instruments and decisions of the African Commission. Furthermore, the African Commission has not developed as much jurisprudence or authoritative interpretation of obligations as the UN human rights mechanisms. Many stakeholders feel better able to access the international standards and mechanisms and/or have received training on the international standards and human rights system.[48] Therefore overall the UN instruments are generally better known and more visible.

There is also a prevailing perception of the African Commission as a weaker body than the UN human rights bodies. Thus a preference to use the instruments from the UN bodies arises out of a perception that these carry more weight and can apply

[44] See e.g.: M. Killander and H. Adjolohoun, *International Law and Domestic Litigation in Africa* (Pretoria: Pretoria University Press, 2010); T. Maluwa, 'International Law as an Aid in the Interpretation and Application of Law in Municipal Legal Systems', in *The Judiciary in Africa*, ed. B. Ajibola and D. van Zyl (Cape Town: Juta, 1998): 47–63; Viljoen (2012): 527–43; Murray and Long (2015): 75–6.

[45] See e.g.: HRIC report, 'Workshop for East African National Human Rights Institutions on the Implementation of Torture Prevention Standards' (18–19 Oct. 2010): 18–20, available at: <http://www.bris.ac.uk/law/research/centres-themes/hric/projects/softlawrigproject/>; HRIC project report 'Summary and Recommendations from an Expert Seminar on identifying National Mechanisms to Follow up and Implement Decisions of the African Commission on Human and Peoples' Rights' (11 Nov. 2011): 2–3, available at: <http://www.bris.ac.uk/law/research/centres-themes/hric/projects/softlawrigproject/>.

[46] See e.g.: B. Niyizurugero and G. P. Lessène, 'The Robben Island Guidelines: An Essential Tool for the Prevention of Torture in Africa', *Preventing Torture in the 21st Century: Monitoring in Europe Two Decades on, Monitoring Globally Two Years on, Essex Human Rights Review*, Special Issue (2010): Part II, 113. For more information on this issue see also: Murray and Long (2015): 77; Long and Murray (2012): 314–15.

[47] Murray and Long (2015): 77–8.

[48] HRIC report, 'Workshop for East African National Human Rights Institutions on the Implementation of Torture Prevention Standards' (18–19 Oct. 2010): 20.

more pressure on states, or that the international arena provides more of a platform to raise awareness at home on a particular issue.[49]

Lastly, it was observed that those actors who were aware of the Robben Island Guidelines nevertheless sometimes chose to use relevant international non-binding instruments instead because these were considered to be more detailed, and therefore strategically useful, than the Robben Island Guidelines.[50] This indicates that the content of soft law instruments is a determinant of its actual use in practice.

3.2 Trends at the regional level

The thematic instruments of the African Commission are notable as they are intended not only to influence state behaviour and modify national policy but also to influence the strategy and policy of the African Commission itself in respect of a particular issue. Therefore one of the primary reasons for CSOs to push for the development and adoption of thematic instruments by the African Commission is advocacy at the regional level as well as the national.

The African Commission has established a number of procedures and mechanisms which provide a platform for its instruments and decisions to be used by states and other actors and within which it would be natural to expect the African Commission to use its thematic instruments itself.

The Robben Island Guidelines are one of the few instruments that Commissioners have made an express reference to during the periodic state reporting procedure. For example during the oral examination of state parties reports, until recently, it has been standard practice for the African Commission to request the state concerned to report on any measures taken to implement the Robben Island Guidelines. The African Commission has referenced the Robben Island Guidelines in its concluding observations and recommendations on state reports, and it is arguable that this may have helped to give a certain visibility to the Guidelines. For example the African Commission has called for officials to be made aware of and trained on the Guidelines and requested their dissemination,[51] or for the Robben Island Guidelines to be implemented or 'incorporated into national legislation'.[52] One of

[49] See e.g.: HRIC report, 'Workshop for East African National Human Rights Institutions on the Implementation of Torture Prevention Standards' (18–19 Oct. 2010): 11.

[50] See e.g.: HRIC report 'Workshop for East African National Human Rights Institutions on the Implementation of Torture Prevention Standards' (18–19 Oct. 2010): 18.

[51] 'Concluding Observations and Recommendations on the Seventh and Eighth Periodic Reports of Arab Republic of Egypt' (2005) para. 28; 'Concluding Observations and Recommendations on the Periodic Report of the Great Socialist People's Republic of Libyan Arab Jamahiriya' (2006) para. 20; 'Concluding Observations and Recommendations on the Ninth and Tenth Periodic Reports of the Republic of Rwanda 2010' para. 20; 'Concluding Observations and Recommendations on the Third Periodic Report of the Republic of Sudan' (2009) paras 37 and 58.

[52] 'Concluding Observations and Recommendations on the Consolidated 2nd to 10th Periodic Report of United Republic of Tanzania' (2008) para. 40; 'Concluding Observations and Recommendations on the Periodic Report of the Great Socialist People's Republic of Libyan Arab Jamahiriya' (2006) para. 20; 'Concluding Observations and Recommendations on the Third Periodic Report of Uganda' (2009) Part V (e); 'Concluding Observations and Recommendations on the

the reasons for this evident use of the Robben Island Guidelines during this procedure is we suggest the existence of a Special Mechanism with the specific mandate to promote the Guidelines. This has ensured that the particular Commissioner who is the Chair of the Special Mechanism for the Robben Island Guidelines routinely asks questions relating to this mandate during the state reporting process.

However, during the state reporting procedure other actors in particular reporting states are not using these Guidelines, or indeed other instruments and decisions of the African Commission in their reports. Thus, most state reports to date have not mentioned these Guidelines in their reports. On the rare occasion where a state has referred to the Guidelines this has been in a cursory way, for example noting that the members of the Special Mechanism linked to the Guidelines had visited the country in order to carry out promotional activities.[53] Furthermore, although the African Commission has requested states to comment on measures taken to implement the Robben Island Guidelines, this practice has not translated into these Guidelines being used in any substantive way during this process and the exchange is largely superficial with little obvious impact. Notably at the 56th Ordinary Session of the African Commission held between 21 April and 7 May 2015, during the oral examination of the state report from the Federal Republic of Nigeria, the Chair of the Committee for the Prevention of Torture in Africa asked more direct questions on measures taken to prohibit and prevent torture. Therefore this may indicate that the approach of the African Commission may be changing in favour of more targeted questions in relation to specific measures taken to implement Article 5 of the African Charter on the prohibition and prevention of torture.

When turning to look at the other procedures of the African Commission the use of the Robben Island Guidelines, and other instruments, is just as, and in some instances more, limited and superficial than in the state reporting process. For example, the African Commission has established a procedure for considering communications (cases) from states and individuals (although in practice the state communication procedure is rarely used). In respect to allegations of violations of torture and other ill-treatment, the communications procedure has been one of the main avenues for individuals to raise concerns before the African Commission. The communications procedure has also enabled the African Commission to interpret the obligations contained within the African Charter.[54] Therefore, it would be reasonable to assume that the Robben Island Guidelines, as the principal document of the African Commission which interprets the obligation in Article 5, have been used within this procedure. However, an examination of over seventy individual

Republic of Tunisia' (2007) para. 29; 'Concluding Observations and Recommendations on the Seventh and Eighth Periodic Reports of Arab Republic of Egypt' (2005) para. 28.

[53] 'Fourth Periodic Report of Uganda to the African Commission on Human and Peoples' Rights' (2010–12): 12.

[54] For further details of the African Commission's decisions on communications see: the *African Human Rights Law Reports* compiled by the Centre for Human Rights, University of Pretoria, available at: <http://www.chr.up.ac.za/index.php/publications/ahrlr.html>.

communications involving aspects of torture and other ill-treatment since the adoption of the Robben Island Guidelines in 2002 reveals that, at the time of writing, only five refer to them expressly.[55] Within these cases the Robben Island Guidelines have been used at times as evidence of the existence of an obligation under international human rights law. For example in *Abdel Hadi, Ali Radi & Others v. Republic of Sudan* the Commission stated that '... As outlined in the Commission's Robben Island Guidelines, States Parties are under an obligation to put in place certain procedural safeguards in order to prevent detainees from being subjected to abuse.'[56] In particular the Commission held that '[it] has established in its Principles and Guidelines on the Right to a fair Trial and Legal Assistance in Africa and in the Robben Island Guidelines that anyone who is arrested shall be informed, at the time of arrest, of the reasons for his/her arrest and shall be promptly informed, in a language he/she understands, of any charges against him/her'.[57]

Similarly, in *Egyptian Initiative for Personal Rights and Interights v. The Arab Republic of Egypt*, the Commission used the Robben Island Guidelines to show the existence, inter alia, of the right of detainees to an independent medical examination.[58] These references perhaps demonstrate one of the roles for soft law instruments identified by Chinkin, namely that they can be used as evidence of the existence of hard law obligations.[59]

The limited use of the African Commission's thematic instruments in the communications process is again symptomatic of a general lack of knowledge of these instruments at the national level. Yet, the limited use by the African Commission of its own thematic instruments is perhaps more striking and indicative of more fundamental problems with this procedure. Although commentators have noted an improvement in the communications procedure over the years,[60] nevertheless this process is still regarded as characterized by an inconsistent and contradictory approach in need of further strengthening.[61] Thus, the general lack of reference to relevant instruments is symptomatic of a lack of detail and reasoning within the analysis of the merits of communications that has, until recently, typified the decisions on individual communications. Notably where the Robben Island Guidelines have been referenced this has frequently been as a result of the litigant using them rather than as a result of the African Commission taking the initiative to do so.[62] Thus, the African Commission

[55] See: case 245/02 *Zimbabwe Human Rights NGO Forum v. Zimbabwe*, 2006, para. 208; case 262/02 *Mouvement ivoirien des droits humains (MIDH)/Cote d'Ivoire*, 2008, para. 96; case 334/06 *Egyptian Initiative for Personal Rights and Interights v. Arab Republic of Egypt*, 2011, paras 109, 112, 174, 179, 184; case 288/04 *Gabriel Shumba v. Zimbabwe*, 2012, paras 145, 147; case 368/09 *Abdel Hadi, Ali Radi & others v. Republic of Sudan*, 2014, para. 75.

[56] Case 368/09 *Abdel Hadi, Ali Radi & others v. Republic of Sudan*, 2014, para. 75.

[57] Case 368/09 *Abdel Hadi, Ali Radi & others v. Republic of Sudan*, 2014, para. 82.

[58] *Egyptian Initiative for Personal Rights and Interights v. Arab Republic of Egypt*, paras 174–5.

[59] Chinkin in Shelton (2000): 30–1.

[60] F. Viljoen, 'Communications under the African Charter: Procedure and Admissibility', in Evans and Murray (2008): 77; Viljoen (2012): 336–9.

[61] Viljoen and Louw (2004): 15; Murray and Long (2015): 57–8, 120, and 125.

[62] See e.g.: case 245/02 *Zimbabwe Human Rights NGO Forum v. Zimbabwe*, 2006; and case 368/09 *Abdel Hadi, Ali Radi & others v. Republic of Sudan*, 2014.

has a poor record of using its own instruments in a strategic and interpretative way to strengthen its consideration and reasoning on individual communications.

Turning to look at in-country activities, that is promotional and fact-finding missions to states, here it can be observed that the Robben Island Guidelines, and other instruments, have been referenced in a few mission reports of the Commissioners and there is evidence that the Commissioners do use them in their dialogue with states at the national level. However, the reference to the Robben Island Guidelines in the mission reports is relatively passive and is frequently noted simply in terms of recommending them to the attention of various officials.[63] Thus, the Guidelines do not appear to have been used in any substantive way by Commissioners during their missions.

Some visibility for the Robben Island Guidelines has been generated at the national level by members of the Committee linked to these Guidelines undertaking promotional visits or being involved in training activities. However, notwithstanding these initiatives, the Committee has, to date, had limited impact on raising the profile of the Robben Island Guidelines to any great extent. One of the primary reasons for this, according to the Committee, is that it has lacked the necessary resources to carry out its mandate.[64] This has resulted in it only being able to carry out a few missions to states and being unable to systematically implement and develop its mandate. However, although a lack of resources may be one factor, we would also contend that the Committee has, until recently, failed to demonstrate creativity in the delivery of its mandate to think strategically in order to overcome these obstacles and demonstrate ownership over the Guidelines.[65] However, there is evidence that the Committee is attempting to overcome some of these difficulties and in 2015 the Committee commenced the process of developing a series of General Comments to elaborate states' obligations under Article 5 of the African Charter to prohibit and prevent torture and other ill-treatment.[66]

In summary, the most noticeable trend at the regional level is the limited use of the thematic instruments by states, CSOs, and perhaps most remarkably by the African Commission itself. There is a notable failure by the African Commission to use its own instruments to any great extent when carrying out its broad promotional mandate. With the limited use of the Robben Island Guidelines, and other instruments, by the African Commission itself in its various procedures it is unsurprising that there is a lack of knowledge of these instruments at the national level.

[63] See e.g.: 'Report of the Fact-Finding Mission to Zimbabwe' (2002): 16; 'Report of the Promotional Mission to the Republic of Botswana' (2006): 38; 'Report of the Promotional Mission to the Seychelles' (2004): 26; 'Report of the Promotional Mission to Lesotho' (2006) paras 46, 81, and 153; 'Report of the Promotional Mission to Mauritius' (2006) paras 58 and 127.

[64] Long and Murray (2012): 343–4; '19th Activity Report of the African Commission on Human and Peoples' Rights' (2005) para. 46; '20th Activity Report of the African Commission on Human and Peoples' Rights' (2006) para. 39.

[65] Long and Murray (2012): 346.

[66] Committee on the Prevention of Torture, 'Concept Paper on the Development of a General Comment on Article 5 of the African Charter on Human and Peoples' Rights' (African Commission, 13 May 2015).

4. Factors that Impact on the Use of Thematic Instruments of the African Commission

Thus it can be observed that the Robben Island Guidelines, and other thematic instruments of the African Commission, are being used at the national and regional levels but not necessarily consistently or extensively. Although there would appear to be a marked preference to use binding instruments in litigation, the legal status of an instrument does not appear to be the primary factor in determining its use; rather other factors can be identified that are more significant.

4.1 Ownership

First, we would assert that creating a sense of 'ownership' over an instrument at the outset is important in influencing the extent to which it is subsequently used. Instruments need to be 'nurtured' in order to gain traction. Ownership can be created and demonstrated in a number of ways and be exercised by a range of actors. Ownership can be created through an inclusive, comprehensive, multi-stakeholder drafting process and demonstrated through the subsequent use by the adopting body such as the African Commission.[67] Ownership can also be exercised by states and CSOs through the use of soft law instruments in their activities. However, the African Commission has a poor record of taking 'ownership' over its instruments and this has a detrimental effect on the subsequent traction these instruments have gained. As has been noted the African Commission has a history of over-reliance on CSOs for its strategic development.[68] The experience of the Robben Island Guidelines demonstrates that without a CSO partner providing strategic guidance and resources the African Commission has been unlikely to commit to and utilize an instrument or Special Mechanism. Unfortunately, the failure of the African Commission itself to exercise ownership over the Robben Island Guidelines and use them in a systematic way has had a detrimental impact on their visibility and perceived value among national stakeholders.

A further crucial factor in the development of 'ownership' for any instrument, binding or non-binding, is the drafting process from which it emanates.[69] The Robben Island Guidelines are a good case in point. The Guidelines were the idea of a CSO who worked with the African Commission and a few select experts in a small drafting workshop to develop a text that was subsequently adopted by the Commission.[70] At the time of drafting the Robben Island Guidelines there was no precedent for wider more inclusive consultations at the regional, sub-regional, and national levels prior to the development of a standard-setting instrument.

[67] M. Barelli, 'The Role of Soft Law in the International Legal System: The Case of the United Nations Declaration on the Rights of Indigenous Peoples', *ICLQ* vol. 58 (2009): 957–83 at 970.

[68] Murray in Evans and Murray (2008): 374.

[69] Barelli (2009): 970.

[70] For more information about the background to the drafting of the Robben Island Guidelines see: Long and Murray (2012).

Unfortunately, the limited range of actors involved in the drafting of the Robben Island Guidelines has arguably hindered the number of potential initial 'promoters' of the instrument and consequently growth of a wider sense of ownership being exercised over the Guidelines at the national level by governments, NHRIs, and civil society organizations.

In recent years, drawing on the experience of instruments such as the Robben Island Guidelines, it would appear that there is now a reconsidered strategy for developing standard-setting instruments. Recent documents adopted by the African Commission, such as the 2015 'Guidelines on Conditions of Arrest, Police Custody and Pre-trial Detention in Africa', have emerged from drafting processes that have engaged more stakeholders within the region.[71] The anticipation is that more inclusive drafting processes will help to raise the visibility of the instruments, increase knowledge of the instruments, and create a sense of 'ownership' over the texts, thereby increasing the likelihood that these instruments will be used by relevant stakeholders in practice.

However, there are earlier indications that even with the inclusive process and broad range of consultations that took place around the drafting of the Guidelines on Conditions of Arrest, Police Custody, and Pre-trial Detention in Africa, traction at the national level requires an organization or institution to actively promote and push for the thematic instrument to be implemented on the ground.[72]

These experiences appear to support the argument advanced by Shelton, namely that 'the institutional structure and processes supporting the substantive norms are significant factors in compliance',[73] and that it is 'the synergy between human rights bodies created by inter-governmental organisations and non-governmental organisations that leads to greater compliance'.[74]

Therefore it is proposed that for soft law instruments to gain a greater degree of traction at the national level, 'active ownership' must be demonstrated both at the regional and national levels.

4.2 The importance of clarity

Various commentators have noted that there can be a wide variety of reasons for creating soft law instruments and they can take many forms.[75] It can be observed that the level of specificity of a soft law instrument has a significant impact on the extent to which it is used and perceived to be useful, and that it must be seen to have 'added value'.

[71] Invitation to Experts Meeting on the Development of Guidelines on Pre-Trial Detention, <http://www.achpr.org/news/2013/03/d78/>.

[72] Interview with civil society representative, Apr. 2015.

[73] Shelton (2000): 460. [74] Shelton (2000): 462.

[75] See e.g.: M. Bareli (2009): 957; A. Boyle and C. Chinkin, *The Making of International Law* (Oxford: Oxford University Press, 2007): 211–12; C. Chinkin, 'The Challenge of Soft Law: Development and Change in International Law', *ICLQ* vol. 38 (1989): 850–66; Chinkin in Shelton (2000): 26–37; Shelton (2000): 10–13.

For example, the Robben Island Guidelines were intended to elaborate on the general obligation to prohibit torture and other ill-treatment contained in Article 5 of the Charter. As noted in section 3, there are a few instances where the Robben Island Guidelines had been used by stakeholders, for example in discussions on the development of national law to criminalize torture; in a handful of cases before the African Commission; and also as a means to create a platform for dialogue around the ratification of the Optional Protocol to the UN Convention against Torture within African States.

However, many stakeholders appeared to be unclear of the 'added value' of the Robben Island Guidelines and consequently how they could be used to assist their work. We identified a number of reasons for this: first, although the provisions of the Robben Island Guidelines do elaborate on the obligations contained in Article 5 of the African Charter, they do not necessarily 'fill a gap' generally as many of their provisions restate or paraphrase obligations and standards found in UN instruments. Secondly, linked to this, some of the provisions of the Robben Island Guidelines are vaguely worded or extremely broad and are not as specific as those found in related UN instruments. Therefore many stakeholders who were aware of the Guidelines nevertheless made a strategic decision to use other soft law instruments because they are more specific. As Shelton notes, '[a]mbiguity and openendedness of international standards can limit efforts to secure compliance'.[76]

However, despite the limited traction the Robben Island Guidelines has gained, it is arguable that they have already served an important, perhaps their primary, purpose namely the establishment of a Special Mechanism with a mandate to promote the prohibition and prevention of torture and other ill-treatment at the national and regional level. Although the Robben Island Guidelines can have a role in initiating and strengthening dialogue with states and other actors, or as evidence of the existence of a particular right, perhaps there are misplaced expectations on what their role should be? The Robben Island Guidelines are not as detailed as other thematic instruments adopted by the African Commission therefore it is perhaps unreasonable to expect them to be used in the same contexts and to the same degree. Thus the purpose for and subsequent use of thematic instruments within the African human rights system may vary and not always be as simple as 'filling a gap' within the normative framework. Consequently, the thematic instruments of the African Commission are illustrative of the diversity and multifaceted nature of instruments that can be categorized as 'soft law instruments'—they may carry the same label but have very different purposes and uses. It is also perhaps indicative of the problems that can arise when there is a lack of clarity around the purpose and content of a soft law instrument.

4.3 The institutional context

Some commentators have noted that the respect accorded to the institution generating soft law instruments is an important factor in their subsequent use and

[76] Shelton (2000): 14.

implementation.[77] As noted, it has been observed that many stakeholders prefer to use the mechanisms and instruments of the UN human rights system over the African Commission. One of the reasons that can be identified for this is that the international instruments have a much higher profile and arguably therefore a greater persuasive force than instruments emanating from the African Commission. This is perhaps inevitable because the international nature and scope of these instruments means that more has been written on them and this international profile creates a greater awareness across regions and nationally.

In addition the level of ownership demonstrated over a finding by the adopting body has a crucial role to play in its subsequent use by other actors. The UN human rights bodies and other mechanisms have a better record of making reference to their own instruments and decisions within their activities. Unfortunately, the failure of the African Commission to make use of its own instruments in a systematic and comprehensive way has had a number of consequences. First, it has had an impact on the level of visibility of its instruments, and its work generally, thus stakeholders are unaware of instruments that could be useful to their work. Secondly, linked to the above, it has impacted on the perceived legitimacy and utility of its instruments: if the adopting body itself does not use its own instruments can others be expected to?

5. Conclusion

In the Introduction to this book a question was posed whether the importance of soft law was waning. Certainly in the African human rights system there is no evidence to this effect, and there is still an apparent appetite to develop soft law instruments. This is demonstrated by the adoption in 2015 of the Principles and Guidelines on Pre-trial Detention and plans to develop further General Comments. Soft law instruments are very prominent within the output of the African Commission. Perhaps this is not surprising in light of the status of the African Commission as a quasi-judicial and monitoring body.

However, notwithstanding the prevalence of soft law instruments within the work of the African Commission, issues relating to a lack of implementation continue to dominate discussions on the effectiveness of the African human rights system as a whole. Clearly there would appear to be a problem with the degree of traction that these soft law instruments have at the national and regional levels.

It would appear, however, that the limited traction these soft law instruments enjoy to date cannot be attributed principally to their actual or perceived status as 'soft law' instruments. Rather there are other factors that are more significant in determining the degree to which these instruments will be used in practice and therefore the degree of influence they will assert. Issues such as the inclusivity of the

[77] F. Viljoen and L. Louw, 'State Compliance with the Recommendations of the African Commission on Human and Peoples' Rights', *AJIL* vol. 101 (2007): 1–34 at 13; Shelton (2000): 15.

drafting process, their content and perceived purpose, are all significant factors that impact on the level of 'uptake' these instruments enjoy once adopted by the African Commission. Perhaps most striking of all is the extent to which demonstrable 'ownership' is important in determining the degree of traction that an instrument can obtain. Ownership can be demonstrated by a range of national actors such as CSOs and NHRIs, and of course ideally states. However, without the African Commission demonstrating ownership over its own soft law instruments, by using them in a strategic and visible way in its procedures, these instruments may continue to face problems gaining legitimacy and traction at the national level.

6

The Copenhagen Process

Some Reflections Concerning Soft Law

Bruce 'Ossie' Oswald[*]

1. Introduction

On 19 October 2012, the 'Copenhagen Process on the Handling of Detainees in International Military Operations' ('The Copenhagen Process') was concluded with seventeen states welcoming the Copenhagen Process Principles and Guidelines ('Principles and Guidelines'). The objective of the Process was to reach consensus among states and relevant international organizations on the international legal regimes applicable to the taking and handling of detainees in military operations; and for states to agree upon generally acceptable principles, rules, and standards for the treatment of detainees. The Principles and Guidelines apply to detention of individuals deprived of their liberty for reasons related to an international military operation (including non-international armed conflicts and peace operations, but excluding international armed conflict and law enforcement operations). They do not seek to create new legal obligations but to guide the implementation of existing obligations by facilitating a common approach to address the humane treatment of detainees while ensuring the effectiveness of international military operations. The Principles and Guidelines are accompanied by a commentary, which is the sole responsibility of the Chairman of the Process. In other words, the commentary is the Chairman's interpretation concerning the meaning, and in some cases the applicability, of the substantive provisions found in the Principles and Guidelines.

The primary purpose of this chapter is to use the Copenhagen Process and the ensuing Principles and Guidelines to show how soft law was and is developed in the context of one aspect of military operations—detention. First, however, a few words about the background to the Copenhagen Process and the evolution of the Principles and Guidelines are necessary.[1]

* Bruce 'Ossie' Oswald is grateful to Ms Skye Chapman for her research assistance, and Ms Natasha Robbins, Ms Zoe Hough, and Ms Sophie Parr for their editing. He is also grateful to Professor Gerry Simpson and Ambassador Thomas Winkler for their comments in relation to earlier versions of this chapter. The views expressed in this chapter do not necessarily reflect those of any government or institution.

[1] For more detail of the Copenhagen Process and the Principles and Guidelines, see e.g.: B. Oswald and T. Winkler, 'The Copenhagen Process: Principles and Guidelines on the Handling of Detainees in International Military Operations', *Nordic Journal of International Law* vol. 83 (2014): 128–67.

2. Background

The Danish Ministry of Foreign Affairs led and chaired the Copenhagen Process. Denmark's interest in the taking and handling of detainees can be traced to its presidency of the UN Security Council in mid-2006 when it prepared a paper concerning the role of UN forces exercising detention powers during UN peace operations where local authorities are unwilling or unable to maintain law and order.[2] The Danish government was also concerned with the legal, political, diplomatic, and practical issues that arise when its military forces take detainees in military operations such as those conducted in Afghanistan.

The start of the Copenhagen Process may be traced to December 2006 when the Danish Ministry of Foreign Affairs hosted a small number of legal and diplomatic experts to participate in a round table meeting in Copenhagen. At that meeting the political, legal, and practical problems relating to dealing with the taking and handling of detainees in military operations were discussed. Following that round table the Danish government decided to host a 'by invitation conference' in 2007. Those invited to the 2007 conference included representatives of states, the United Nations, regional organizations, and the ICRC. The discussions during the conference led the Danish government to conclude that there was sufficient international support to develop a common platform of principles and rules for dealing with detainees.

The development of that platform was further considered in a 2008 seminar again hosted by the Danish Ministry of Foreign Affairs. That seminar focused on the best practices of states, international, and regional organizations in the taking and handling of detainees. Reflections on the discussions held during the 2007 conference and the 2008 seminar led the Danish Ministry of Foreign Affairs to issue a non-paper concerning detention. The non-paper provided the foundation for discussions at the 2009 conference, which was again hosted by the Danish Ministry of Foreign Affairs. During that conference there was broad agreement amongst the participants that 'the challenge is not the elaboration of new rules on detention, but to reach [a] common understanding of the specific content of the existing legal framework'.[3]

Following that conference, the Danish Ministry of Foreign Affairs developed a draft Declaration of guiding principles to apply to detention in military operations and circulated the draft with states, the UN, regional organizations, and the ICRC. After receiving comments concerning that draft Declaration a revised document entitled the 'Copenhagen Process Rules and Guidelines' was again circulated. The comments received from those consultations informed the content of another revised draft of rules and guidelines, which set the basis for negotiating the text of a

[2] Letter dated 7 June 2006 from the Permanent Representative of Denmark to the United Nations addressed to the Secretary General, UN Doc. S/2006/367 (2006).

[3] T. Winkler, 'The Copenhagen Process on Detainees: A Necessity', *Nordic Journal of International Law* vol. 78, (2009): 489–98 at 492.

common platform at another conference hosted by the Danish Ministry of Foreign Affairs in October 2012. At the end of the 2012 Conference the chairperson:

> noted that the delegations from Argentina, Australia, Canada, China, Denmark, France, Finland, Germany, Malaysia, the Netherlands, Norway, South Africa, Sweden, Uganda, United Kingdom and the United States of America welcomed the Copenhagen Process Principles and Guidelines. By welcoming the Principles and Guidelines participants agreed that the Principles and Guidelines accurately reflect the discussions held during the final conference, and that the Principles and Guidelines are an expression of a global approach to the issue of detention.[4]

Two states attending the 2012 conference caveated their recognition of the Principles and Guidelines. The Russian Federation:

> *welcomed* the conclusion of … [the Process] and *took note* of … [the Principles and Guidelines]. The Russian Federation further indicated that the Copenhagen Process could contribute more to the safeguarding of the humane treatment of detainees by placing greater emphasis on their inherent rights, which derive from international human rights law and international humanitarian law.[5]

Sweden stated that its 'interpretation of the reference to international law in Principle 16 is that this also includes human rights law and that Sweden would have preferred if this had been stated explicitly in Principle 16'.[6]

A number of factors gave rise to the Process and the desire to reach agreement on a common approach for dealing with detainees during military operations. At the strategic and operational level the broad factors included: the need to identify the relevant law and practice to the taking and handling of detainees; the matters that should be taken into account in seeking to ensure both the humane treatment of detainees and the effectiveness of international military operations; litigation concerning the lawfulness and treatment of detainees; diplomatic, political, and operational concerns arising from different standards of treatment by contingents serving in coalition operations; and the applicability of both International Humanitarian Law (IHL) and International Human Rights Law (IHRL) to detention operations.[7] At a more practical and tactical level there are a number of matters that the Process

[4] Oswald and Winkler (2014): 145–6.

[5] Oswald and Winkler (2014): 146.

[6] Oswald and Winkler (2014): 146.

[7] There has been considerable academic and practitioner engagement concerning the need to develop legal norms to deal with detention across the spectrum of military operations, see e.g.: B. Oswald, 'Detention of Civilians on Military Operations: Reasons for and Challenges to Developing a Special Law of Detention', *Melbourne University Law Review* vol. 32 (2008): 524–53 at 534; T. Winkler, 'The Copenhagen Process on Detainees: A Necessity', *Nordic Journal of International Law* vol. 78 (2009): 489–98; J. Bellinger III and V. Padmanabhan, 'Detention Operations in Contemporary Conflicts: Four Challenges for the Geneva Conventions and Existing Law', *American Journal of International Law* vol. 105 (2011): 201–43; ICRC, 'International Humanitarian Law and the Challenges of Contemporary Armed Conflicts' (31st International Conference of the Red Cross and Red Crescent, 2011); R. Chesney and J. Goldsmith, 'Terrorism and the Convergence of Criminal and Military Detention Models', *Stanford Law Review* vol. 60 (2008): 1079–134; R. Goodman, 'The Detention of Civilians in Armed Conflict', *American Journal of International Law* vol. 103 (2009): 48–74; M. J. Matheson, 'Continuity and Change in the Law of War: 1975 to 2005: Detainees and POWS', *George Washington International Law Review* vol. 38 (2006): 543–50.

sought to address. Some of those matters concerned: whether a person stopped temporarily (e.g. at a checkpoint) should be considered a 'detainee'; the circumstances in which physical force may be used against a detained person (e.g. if the person is resisting detention); the right of detainees to complain about their treatment and conditions of detention, and the obligation to review such complaints if based on credible information; and the obligations of a detaining authority to monitor the treatment of a detainee that the authority has transferred to the host state.

At the conclusion of the Process about twenty-five states, the UN, African Union (AU), North Atlantic Treaty Organization (NATO), European Union (EU), and the ICRC had participated in the Copenhagen Process seminars and conferences. A number of other states and civil society bodies were also consulted by the Danish Ministry of Foreign Affairs during the five-year life of the Process. Denmark's lead, and the contribution to varying extents by a number of states, international organizations, and civil society, provides a reason to consider the relevance and importance of such activism in the development of IHL.

3. Activism in International Humanitarian Law

Commencing a review of the activism in IHL beginning with the middle of the seventeenth century, as the respected IHL historian Geoffrey Best does, it becomes immediately apparent that early developments in IHL were not binding and 'owed nothing to the letter of treaty law, [and] everything to the spirit of culture'.[8] Best further reminds us that '[o]fficers and gentleman stuck to ... [the laws and customs of war] because their religion and mores impelled them to, not because their governments had signed treaties guaranteeing that they would'.[9] The codification of IHL only commenced in the 1860s with the efforts of individuals such as Francis Lieber,[10] international organizations such as the Institute of International Law,[11] the International Movement of the Red Cross,[12] and states working with commissions.[13] After the First World War the only codification of IHL to take place was in relation to the 1925 Geneva Protocol for the Prohibition of the Use in War of Asphyxiating, Poisonous or other Gases, and of Bacteriological Methods of Warfare.[14] At the close of the Second World War the ICRC undertook the challenge

[8] G. Best, *War and Law Since 1945* (Oxford: Oxford University Press, 1994): 40.

[9] Best (1994): 40.

[10] *Instructions for the Government of the Armies of the United States in the Field*, General Order No. 100 promulgated on 24 Apr. 1863 by Abraham Lincoln, as prepared by Francis Lieber (generally referred to as the 'Lieber Code'), <http://ecclesia.org/forum/library/Lieber_Code.pdf>.

[11] *The Laws of War on Land*, Oxford (9 Sept. 1880), <http://www.gwpda.org/1914m/land1880.html>.

[12] See e.g.: Convention for the Amelioration of the Condition of the Wounded Armies in the Field (Red Cross Convention) (22 Aug. 1864), <http://avalon.law.yale.edu/19th_century/geneva04.asp>.

[13] Declaration of St Petersburg (29 Nov. 1868), <http://avalon.law.yale.edu/19th_century/decpeter.asp>.

[14] Geneva Protocol for the Prohibition of the Use in War of Asphyxiating, Poisonous or other Gases, and of Bacteriological Methods of Warfare, 17 June 1925, <http://avalon.law.yale.edu/20th_century/geneva01.asp>.

of reviewing existing IHL and submitted what would become the four Geneva Conventions[15] to states for further negotiations. Throughout the 1960s and 1970s the ICRC and the UN worked together to bring states to the table to settle on the two Additional Protocols to the Geneva Conventions.[16]

The ICRC, in its capacity as the guardian of IHL, has remained engaged with developing and clarifying IHL. Examples of its engagement include its customary international law study concerning international humanitarian law,[17] the interpretative guidance concerning direct participation in hostilities,[18] the law of occupation,[19] and, more recently, compliance and detention.[20] ICRC lawyers, for example Jelena Pejic, have also on occasions written in their private capacity about a specific area of IHL, which in due course has been accepted by the ICRC as its institutional view.[21]

Courts and tribunals have also contributed to the development of IHL in a number of ways. The Nuremberg Tribunal and the Japanese war crimes tribunals developed laws concerning such matters as command responsibility, treatment of prisoners of war, military necessity, hostage taking, and reprisals.[22] More recently, the International Court of Justice has dealt with the law of military occupation and

[15] Geneva Convention Relative to the Amelioration of the Condition of the Wounded and Sick in Armed Forces in the Field, opened for signature 12 Aug. 1949, 75 UNTS 31 (entered into force 21 Oct. 1950) (Geneva Convention I); Geneva Convention Relative to the Amelioration of the Condition of Wounded, Sick and Shipwrecked Members of Armed Forces at Sea, opened for signature 12 Aug. 1949, 75 UNTS 85 (entered into force 21 Oct. 1950) (Geneva Convention II); Geneva Convention Relative to the Treatment of Prisoners of War, opened for signature 12 Aug. 1949, 75 UNTS 135 (entered into force 21 Oct. 1950) (Geneva Convention III); and Geneva Convention Relative to the Protection of Civilian Persons in Time of War, opened for signature 12 Aug. 1949, 75 UNTS 287 (entered into force 21 Oct. 1950) (Geneva Convention IV). The ICRC also wrote commentaries to the four Conventions and those commentaries remain influential in understanding and interpreting the Conventions. The ICRC is currently engaged in updating those commentaries.

[16] Protocol Additional to the Geneva Conventions of 12 August 1949, and Relating to the Protection of Victims of International Armed Conflicts, opened for signature 8 June 1977, 1125 UNTS 609 (entered into force 7 Dec. 1978) (Additional Protocol I) and Protocol Additional to the Geneva Conventions of 12 August 1949, and Relating to the Protection of Victims of Non-International Armed Conflicts, opened for signature 8 June 1977, 1125 UNTS 609 (entered into force 7 Dec. 1978) (Additional Protocol II).

[17] *Customary International Humanitarian Law*, ed. J. M. Henckaerts and L. Doswald-Beck, vols. 1–3 (ICRC, 2005) and updated periodically, <https://www.icrc.org/en/war-and-law/treaties-customary-law/customary-law>.

[18] Report prepared and edited by T. Ferraro, 'Expert Meeting, Occupation and Other forms of Administration of Foreign Territory' (ICRC, 2012).

[19] N. Melzer, 'Interpretive Guidance on the Notion of Direct Participation in Hostilities: Under International Humanitarian Law' (ICRC, Geneva, 1 July 2009).

[20] ICRC, 'International Humanitarian Law and the Challenges of Contemporary Armed Conflicts', 31st International Conference of the Red Cross and Red Crescent (2011). See also: 'Strengthening Compliance with International Humanitarian Law (IHL): The Work of the ICRC and Swiss Government' (updated 10 July 2014); ICRC, 'Strengthening Legal Protection for Persons Deprived of their Liberty in Relation to Non-international Armed Conflict, Regional Consultations 2012–13' (ICRC, Background Paper, 2013).

[21] J. Pejic, 'IHL and the Challenges of Contemporary Armed Conflicts' presented to the 30th International Conference of the Red Cross and the Red Crescent, Annex 1 (ICRC Report, 2007).

[22] See e.g.: United States, Military Tribunal at Nuremberg, List (Hostages Trial) (Judgment) (19 Feb. 1948).

the application of IHRL and IHL during armed conflicts.[23] International criminal tribunals, such as the International Criminal Tribunal for the Former Yugoslavia and the International Criminal Court, have added to understandings of such crimes as rape during armed conflicts, targeting, the treatment of detainees, and the use of child soldiers.[24] The European Court of Human Rights has also contributed to the way that states subject to its jurisdiction must deal with detainees captured during armed conflict and the obligation to investigate deaths of detainees during armed conflicts.[25] On a number of occasions, particularly in the United States[26] and in the United Kingdom,[27] national courts have also issued judgments concerning the status and treatment of detainees.

The UN has been active in developing and reinforcing IHL norms in a number of contexts. The Secretary General's Bulletin on Observance by United Nations Forces of International Humanitarian Law,[28] the Security Council's cross-cutting resolutions concerning the protection of civilians in armed conflict,[29] Human Rights Committee investigations concerning such matters as the use of force in armed conflicts,[30] and Reports of Special Rapporteurs[31] are some examples of the role taken by UN organs in developing IHL.

[23] See e.g.: 'Legality of the Threat or Use of Nuclear Weapons' (Advisory Opinion) (ICJ Reports, 2006): 226–67; 'Legal Consequences of the Construction of a Wall in the Occupied Palestinian Territory' (Advisory Opinion) (ICJ Reports, 2004): 136–203; 'Armed Activities on the Territory of the Congo (Democratic Republic of Congo v Uganda) (Judgment)' (ICJ Reports, 2005): 168–283.

[24] See e.g.: ICTY cases: *Prosecutor v. Karadžić and Mladić* (Initial Indictment and Review of the Indictments) IT-95-5/18-1 (25 Nov. 1995); *Prosecutor v. Tihomir Blaškić* (Judgment) IT-95-14-T (3 Mar. 2000); *Prosecutor v. Kordić and Mario Erkez* (Judgment) IT-95-14/2-T (26 Feb. 2001); *Prosecutor v. Mucic* et al. *('Celebici')* (Judgment) IT-96-21 (16 Nov. 1998). ICC case: *The Prosecutor v. Thomas Lubanga Dyilo* ICC-01/04-01/06 (14 Mar. 2012).

[25] See e.g.: *Al-Saadoon & Mufdhi v. United Kingdom* (App. no. 61498/08) ECHR 2010; *Agim Behrami and Bekir Behrami v. France* (App. no. 71412/01) ECHR 2007; *Ruzdhi Saramati v. France, Germany and Norway* (App. no. 78166/01) ECHR 2007; *Al-Jedda v. The United Kingdom* (App. no. 27201/08) ECHR 2011; *El-Masri v. The Former Yugoslav Republic of Macedonia* (App. no. 9630/09) ECHR 2012.

[26] See e.g.: *Hamdi v. Rumsfeld* 542 US 507 (2004); *Hamdan v. Rumsfeld* 548 US 557 (2006); *Boumediene v. Bush* 533 US (2008); *Munaf v. Green (SC); Gherebi v. Obama*, 609 F. Supp. 2d 43 (DDC 2009); *Handily v. Obama*, 616 F. Supp. 2d 63 (DDC 2009); *Awad v. Obama*, 608 F. 3rd 1 (DC Cir. 2010).

[27] See e.g.: *Secretary of State for Foreign and Commonwealth Affairs and another (Appellants) v. Yunus Rahmatullah (Respondent), Secretary of State for Foreign and Commonwealth Affairs and another (Respondents) v. Yunus Rahmatullah* (Appellant) [2012] UKSC 48; *R (on the Application of Maya Evans) v. Secretary of State for Defence* [2010] EWCH 1445; *R (on the Application of Al Jedda) (FC) v. Secretary of State for Defence* [2007] UKHL 58; and *Serdar Mohammed v. Ministry of Defence* [2014] EWHC 1369 (QB).

[28] UNSG, Secretary-General's Bulletin on Observance by United Nations Forces of International Humanitarian Law, UN Doc. ST/SGB/1999/13 (6 Aug. 1999).

[29] See e.g.: SC Res. 1674, UN Doc. S/RES/1674 (28 Apr. 2006) on the protection of civilians in armed conflict; SC Res. 2143, UN Doc S/RES/2143 (7 Mar. 2014) on children in armed conflict.

[30] See e.g.: Office of the High Commissioner for Human Rights, 'Investigations into Violations of International Humanitarian Law in the Context of Attacks and Clashes between the Communist Party of Nepal (Maoists) and Government Security Forces: Findings and Recommendations' (Jan.–Mar. 2006); Human Rights in Palestine and Other Occupied Arab Territories, Report of the UN Fact-Finding Mission on the Gaza Conflict, Human Rights Council, UN Doc. A/HRC/12/48 (25 Sept. 2009).

[31] See e.g.: Situation of Detainees at Guantánamo Bay, Report of the Chairperson-Rapporteur of the Working Group on Arbitrary Detention, L. Zerrougui, Special Rapporteur on the independence

A number of military forces have issued manuals, handbooks, doctrines, standard operating procedures, and codes of conduct to set limits for the behaviour of their personnel during military operations. Examples include the United Kingdom Ministry of Defence's manual on the laws of armed conflict;[32] the United States operations law handbook;[33] and the Australian Defence Force doctrine concerning the laws of armed conflict.[34] These documents published by military forces take a national, legal, and policy approach to the application of IHL.

More recently there has been a considerable amount of IHL activism by experts and academics. For example, the *San Remo Manual on the Law of Non-international Armed Conflict*,[35] the *Manual on the International Law Applicable to Air and Missile Warfare*,[36] and the *Tallinn Manual on the International Law Applicable to Cyber Warfare*[37] were drafted by experts acting in their private capacity.[38] Academics have also undertaken detailed analysis of IHL and military law more generally so as to develop 'black letter rules' that are accompanied by commentary.[39]

Civil society has increasingly become involved in developing IHL. For example, the drafting of the Ottawa Convention[40] owes much to the involvement of the International Campaign to Ban Landmines coalition.[41] Non-government organizations (NGOs), such as Geneva Call and Human Rights First, have also taken the lead in pushing the boundaries of IHL. Geneva Call's work with non-state armed actors is a particularly good example of an organization working towards ensuring that IHL norms are adopted by non-state armed actors.[42] The *Draft Lucens Guidelines for Protecting Schools and Universities from Military Use during*

of judges and lawyers; L. Despouy, the Special Rapporteur on torture and other cruel, inhuman, or degrading treatment or punishment; M. Nowak and A. Jahangir, the Special Rapporteur on freedom of religion or belief; P. Hunt, the Special Rapporteur on the right of everyone to the enjoyment of the highest attainable standard of physical and mental health, UN Doc. E/CN.4/2006/120 (15 Feb. 2006); P. Alston, *Report of the Special Rapporteur on Extrajudicial, Summary or Arbitrary Executions: Study on Targeted Killings*, A/HRC/14/24 Add. 6 (28 May 2010).

32 Ministry of Defence (United Kingdom), *The Manual of the Laws of Armed Conflict* (2006).

33 The Judge Advocate General, *Operational Law Handbook* (2013). This document is updated yearly.

34 Australian Defence Force, *The Laws of Armed Conflict* (2006).

35 *San Remo Manual on International Law Applicable to Armed Conflicts at Sea*, ed. L. Doswald-Beck (International Institute of Humanitarian Law, 1995).

36 Program on Humanitarian Policy and Conflict Research at Harvard University, 'Manual on International Law Applicable to Air and Missile Warfare' (Bern, 2009).

37 *Tallinn Manual on the International Law Applicable to Cyber Warfare*, ed. M. Schmitt (Cambridge: Cambridge University Press, 2013).

38 For a more detailed discussion about those Manuals, see e.g.: Peter Vedel Kessing's chapter in this volume, sections 3.2, 3.5, 3.7, and 4.2.

39 See e.g.: *The Handbook of Humanitarian Law in Armed Conflicts*, ed. D. Fleck (Oxford: Oxford University Press, 3rd edn, 2013).

40 Convention on the Prohibition of the Use, Stockpiling, Production and Transfer of Anti-Personnel Mines and on Their Destruction (18 Sept. 1997), <http://www.un.org/Depts/mine/UNDocs/ban_trty.htm>.

41 International Campaign to Prevent Landmines, <http://www.icbl.org/en-gb/home.aspx>.

42 See e.g.: Deed of Commitment developed by Geneva Call that permits non-state armed actors to respect specific IHL principles, rules, and standards, <http://www.genevacall.org/how-we-work/deed-of-commitment/>.

Armed Conflict[43] are a more recent example of how both international organizations (e.g. UNICEF and UNESCO) and NGOs (e.g. Human Rights Watch) have come together to develop norms for both states and non-state actors to apply when engaged in armed conflicts.

Finally, non-state armed actors are also engaged in developing and reinforcing normative frameworks, which they 'require' their members to apply. From the late 1920s until the late 1940s the Workers' and Peasants' Army/the People's Liberation Army—China issued a number of codes of conduct to its military forces.[44] More recently, in May 2011, the Libyan National Transitional Council issued guidelines to its armed forces in relation to respecting IHL.[45]

For the purposes of this chapter there are four important points to be made about the activism described here. The first is that the process for creating, developing, advocating, and negotiating principles, rules, and standards relevant to IHL has involved a wide variety of formal and informal structures. The term 'formal structures' as used here refers to those exclusively dominated by states, including international organizations and international tribunals engaged in creating or developing norms. On the other hand, 'informal structures' focus on the engagement of, for example, academics, non-state armed actors, and civil society in creating or developing norms. The four Geneva Conventions and the two Additional Protocols, the Security Council engagement in dealing with IHL matters, and judgments of international tribunals such as the ICJ and the ICC are all examples of formal structures. The development of the Tallin Manual is an example of an informal structure.[46]

Second, not only have the processes varied, but so have the forms of IHL norm-creation and development. Some of the forms include treaties, customary law, interpretative guidelines, UN resolutions, military manuals, and non-government advocacy endeavours. Some of those forms constitute legal obligations and others do not. As explained by Sir Daniel Bethlehem, the text of treaties, principles of customary international law, binding decisions of the UN Security Council, and binding decisions of other international organizations create legal obligations.[47] Other documents, resolutions, and observations made by state representatives 'go to the possible content of customary international law or to questions of treaty

[43] Developed by the Global Coalition to Protect Education from Attack (8 July 2013).

[44] International Committee of the Red Cross, 'A Collection of Codes of Conduct Issued by Armed Groups', *International Review of the Red Cross* vol. 93 (2011): 483–501 at 487–8.

[45] International Committee of the Red Cross, 'A Collection of Codes of Conduct Issued by Armed Groups', *International Review of the Red Cross* vol. 93 (2011): 483–501 at 497–501. For a more detailed discussion concerning the typology of commitments of non-state armed actors with IHL, see e.g.: S. Sivakumaran, 'Lessons for the Law of Armed Conflict from Commitments of Armed Groups: Identification of Legitimate Targets and Prisoners of War', *International Review of the Red* Cross vol. 93 (2011): 463–82.

[46] For an interesting discussion concerning the development of international law through formal and informal mechanisms, see e.g.: J. Pauwelyn, R. Wessel, and J. Wouters, 'When Structures Become Shackles: Stagnation and Dynamics in International Law Making', *European Journal of International Law* vol. 25 (2014): 733–63.

[47] D. Bethlehem, 'The Secret Life of International Law', *Cambridge Journal of International and Comparative Law* vol. 23 (2012): 23–36 at 26.

interpretation. In other words, they are evidence of law rather than dispositive statements of what the law actually is'.[48]

Third, linked to the question of process and form is the matter of legitimacy.[49] At one level, it might be argued that any discussion about the legitimacy of the process and form chosen will depend on the subject matter, who is involved, and what the stakeholders are seeking to achieve. Thus, if the subject matter is technical, and, for example, it involves a state wishing to interpret provisions in a particular manner for its armed forces to apply, the debate concerning legitimacy of process and form is likely to be much more limited and relatively uncontroversial. At another more general level, that of the overarching principle of humanitarianism versus achieving the military mission, the process and form are likely to be much more controversial if there is a belief that either humanitarianism has been privileged far too greatly or that far too much emphasis has been paid to military effectiveness.

Fourth, not all the activism has been IHL-centric. Some of the activism has sought to address the role that IHRL has in military operations such as non-international armed conflict. There has been an ever-growing debate since the ICJ Advisory Opinion in the *Nuclear Weapons Case* about the relationship between IHL and IHRL in armed conflict. That debate has taken a number of perspectives including: IHL and IHRL are mutually exclusive and do not apply concurrently; IHL and IHRL are complementary; and IHL and IHRL converge in certain matters. There has also been activism in the form of international criminal law with various tribunals and courts (such as the International Criminal Tribunal for the Former Yugoslavia and the International Criminal Court) opining on the application of IHL in the context of international criminal law.[50]

The Copenhagen Process brings into sharp focus all four points. As a process, because it was state led, and privileged state and international organization participation, it is the only example of states creating and developing IHL norms without an institutional anchor such as the ICRC or the UN in albeit a narrow area of IHL—detention. As such, it is a stark example of a counter prevailing trend that has been commented upon by Professors Mike Schmitt and Sean Watts. They have recently written about the decline in states taking responsibility for the process of developing IHL and have lamented the consequences of the trend of 'states ceding control over the content, interpretation, and development of IHL to others'.[51] The Copenhagen Process therefore not only brought norm formalization but also norm interpretation firmly back into the hands of states. As a matter of form, using Sir Daniel's typology, the individual articles contained in the Copenhagen Principles and Guidelines are dispositive statements of the law in relation to the subject

[48] Bethlehem (2012): 28.

[49] For a more detailed discussion of legitimacy in the context of international law-making, see e.g.: A. Boyle and C. Chinkin, *The Making of International Law* (Oxford: Oxford University Press, 2007): 24–8.

[50] For a more detailed discussion concerning the interaction between IHL and IHRL, see e.g.: Peter Vedel Kessing's chapter in this volume, sections 2.2 and 4.4.

[51] M. Schmitt and S. Watts, 'The Decline of International Humanitarian Law Opinio Juris and the Law of Cyber Warfare', *Texas International Law Journal* vol. 50 (2014): 189–231 at 230.

matters they cover, which go to interpreting treaties or identifying the content of customary international law rather than creating legal obligations. In regard to the matter of legitimacy—regardless of whether a broad or a narrow approach is taken in determining legitimacy it is without doubt that the Copenhagen Process cannot be described as unlawful—clearly, it is lawful for states to develop international law. More specifically, the Principles and Guidelines add to the legitimacy of clarifying and developing detention norms because they are based on state consent; and they seek to balance both military requirements and humanitarianism without privileging one to the complete detriment of the other.

Finally, the Process and the final form of the Principles and Guidelines demonstrate that it is almost impossible in practical terms to ignore the application of either IHL or IHRL in a matter like detention in military operations. The Process did not however settle the debate as to the precise relationship between those two areas of law.

4. The Status of the Principles and Guidelines

Starting with the preamble, it is clear that the Principles and Guidelines do not seek 'to create new legal obligations or authorizations under international law'.[52] The focus of participants during the final meeting was to 'develop principles to guide the implementation of the existing obligations with respect to detention in military operations; by facilitating a common approach ... [that] contribute[s] to ensuring the humane treatment of detainees and the effectiveness of international operations'.[53] Further, as reinforced both in the Preamble and paragraph 16: the Principles and Guidelines 'do not affect the applicability of international law to military operations conducted by States, or international organisations; the obligations of their personnel to respect such law, or the applicability of international and national law to non-state actors'.[54]

So, if the Principles and Guidelines do not create new obligations or authorizations, nor change existing legal obligations with respect to detention, nor affect the applicability of international law either on the international or national plane—what normative value do they have? Might they be considered 'soft law'?

While this is not the place to engage in a lengthy discussion about soft law and the various controversies that surround its existence and application,[55] it

[52] Principles and Guidelines, Preamble, para. II.

[53] Principles and Guidelines, Preamble, para. II.

[54] Principles and Guidelines, Preamble, para. 16 and the Preamble XI.

[55] See e.g.: K. W. Abbott and D. Snidal, 'Hard and Soft Law in International Governance', *International Organization* vol. 54 (200): 421–56; L. Blutman, 'In the Trap of a Legal Metaphor: International Soft Law', *International and Comparative Law Quarterly* vol. 59 (2010): 605–24; C. Chinkin, 'The Challenge of Soft Law: Development and Change in International Law', *International and Comparative Law Quarterly* vol. 38 (1989): 850–66; J. Ellis, 'Shades of Grey: Soft Law and the Validity of Public International Law', *Leiden Journal of International Law* vol. 25 (2012): 313–34; T. Gruchalla-Wesierski, 'A Framework for Understanding "Soft Law"', *McGill Law Journal* vol. 30 (1984): 37–88; J. Klabbers, 'The Undesirability of Soft Law', *Nordic Journal of International Law*

is nonetheless appropriate to make some comments concerning its relevance in understanding and applying the Principles and Guidelines. First, there is a general consensus that international law is either binding or non-binding. Binding law, or 'rules of international law', are found in treaties and custom. Second, if norms are not binding, then what are they? Some refer to them as soft law and as such the term has a range of meanings, including a convenient way of describing a variety of non-legally binding instruments, interpretative guidance, codes of conduct, and 'non-treaty agreements between states or between states and other entities that lack capacity to conclude treaties'.[56] Third, 'soft law mechanisms are broadly those that do not involve formal legal obligations or legal processes, but nevertheless represent a shared understanding or consensus about procedure or behaviour among the parties'.[57] One must conclude therefore that because states participating in the final Copenhagen conference stated that the Principles and Guidelines were not seeking 'to create new legal obligations or authorizations under international law[58] ... [and that the Principles and Guidelines] do not affect the applicability of international law',[59] they are non-binding and therefore fit within the general understanding of being soft law.[60] That view is further reinforced by the fact that the Principles and Guidelines were 'welcomed' by states—thus using weaker language—rather than, for example, using stronger language such as 'adopted' or 'ratified' by states. In view of this it is perhaps most appropriate to consider the Principles and Guidelines to be soft law in the sense that they are contained in a 'written international instrument which ... [is] non-binding at the time of adoption, but create[s] particular expectations of future behaviour and ... [is] likely to have political [or diplomatic] ... effect'.[61] Finally, it is important to point out that for some legal advisers working for states in the armed forces or government departments the Principles and Guidelines would be simply described in terms of being a policy and therefore there would be no debate as to whether the document and its contents are soft law.[62]

vol. 67 (1998): 381–91; J. Klabbers, 'Reflections on Soft International Law in a Privatized World', *Finnish Yearbook of International Law* vol. 16 (2005): 1–15; C. Ku and P. F Diehl, 'Filling in the Gaps: Extrasystemic Mechanisms for Addressing Imbalances between the International Legal Operating System and the Normative System', *Global Governance* vol. 12 (2006): 161–83; T. Meyer, 'Soft Law as Delegation', *Fordham International Law Journal* vol. 32 (2008): 888–942; G. C. Shaffer and M. A. Pollack, 'Hard Versus Soft Law in International Security', *Boston College Law Review* vol. 52 (2001): 1147–242; and P. Weil, 'Towards Relative Normativity in International Law?', *American Journal of International Law* vol. 77 (1983): 413–42.

56 Boyle and Chinkin (2007): 212–13.

57 Ku and Diehl (2006): 177.

58 Principles and Guidelines, Preamble para. II.

59 Principles and Guidelines, Preamble XI.

60 For a more detailed discussion about the effect of combining binding and non-binding norms, see e.g.: Weil (1983): 413–42.

61 Villeneuve in this volume.

62 That is not to say that legal advisers working for armed forces or governments are acting in bad faith if they refer to the Principles and Guidelines as policy but rather to recognize that both policy and law would be considered systematically in the sense of being properly considered and openly dealt with in the decision-making process. See e.g.: R. Higgins, *Problems and Processes: International Law and How We Use It* (Oxford: Oxford University Press, 1994): 5.

For such lawyers the issue is not that the norms are binding, it is the fact that the instrument in which the norms are contained is non-binding.

Accepting that the Principles and Guidelines might be described as soft law, they are instructive as a case study in two ways: (1) the process used by states to develop soft law; and (2) as an example of developing substantive norms to engage with a serious concern for states—dealing with detainees.

As a case study in how states develop soft law the Principles and Guidelines are useful for four reasons. First, the Principles and Guidelines were 'welcomed' via a process that was primarily state led in the sense that they were not negotiated with the broader international non-government community. That fact is noteworthy because it raises the issue of whether developing soft law must have wide international community involvement to enhance the legitimacy of both the process and the values that a particular set of soft law norms seek to reflect. As stated, IHL continues to develop through a variety of means and methods. The government of Denmark's focus on limiting the formal Copenhagen Process meetings to invited states and international organizations was a calculated decision to ensure that participants could be open and robust about their experiences in the taking and handling of detainees during military operations, and that they would be willing to think and share their concerns about the legal, policy, diplomatic, and military issues surrounding military detention operations. States were able to discuss in a relatively open manner their practical experiences derived from military operations in such places as Afghanistan and Iraq; the lessons they learned in relation to matters such as allocating resources to handling detainees; and the political and legal risks of getting detention 'wrong'. Inviting international organizations such as the UN, the AU, and the ICRC as observers added to the sense of learning from experiences in other contexts, such as UN peace operations or military detentions operations conducted in a variety of contexts. While NGOs were not invited to any of the formal seminars or conferences, they were updated about developments during the Process by the Danish Ministry of Foreign Affairs.[63]

[63] See e.g.: T. Winkler, *Transfer of Detainees*, address at the International Institute of Humanitarian Law 33rd Round Table on Current Issues of International Humanitarian Law, 'Global Violence: Consequences and Responses' (San Remo, 9–11 Sept. 2010). Denmark conducted public briefings on the Process at the San Remo Round Tables in 2008 and 2010, at the Bruges Colloquium in 2008, at a side-event during the UN General Assembly in 2008, and at the 31st Conference Red Cross and Red Crescent. Furthermore, the Process has been discussed at a number of academic conferences, including at the London School of Economics in 2009 and the University of Wollongong in 2011. See e.g.: T. Winkler, *The Copenhagen Process on the Handling of Detainees in International Military Operations*, address at the International Institute of Humanitarian Law 31st Round Table on Current Issues of International Humanitarian Law, Human Rights and Peace Operations (San Remo, 4–6 Sept. 2008); T. Winkler, *The Copenhagen Process on the Handling of Detainees in International Military Operations*, address at the 9th Bruges Colloquium, Transfers of Persons in Situations of Armed Conflict (Brussels, 16–17 Oct. 2009); C. Droege and L. Arimatsu, 'Conference on the European Convention on Human Rights and International Humanitarian Law: Conference Report', *Yearbook of International Humanitarian Law* vol. 12 (2009): 435–49. The last engagement with civil society occurred in Oct. 2012 when the Ministry hosted a round table discussion with civil society to inform them about the government of Denmark's negotiations at the final conference. Those attending the round table included Amnesty International, Danish Society of the Red Cross, Human Rights First, and Danish academia.

It might be concluded that the decision to have a process that was both state led and state focused was appropriate for dealing with a serious matter—detention on military operations—because it provided a focal point for states to determine legal and behavioural norms. The chance of voluntary compliance therefore increases because those applying the norms negotiated them. Allowing states to robustly engage in addressing challenges and tensions arising from dealing with detainees also meant that the final version of the Principles and Guidelines was not divorced from state behaviour or interests. Furthermore, a process that focuses on the will of states has an added benefit in creating norms because it reinforces the margins of their opinion and practice. The Process therefore should be seen as a means by which a state-led and state-focused process represents law generating in an area of law and practice in which state interests are ultimately very high.

Second, it is worth considering the extent to which the legal matter that is subject to soft law development affects the approach states adopt. Considering the fact that taking and handling detainees is a legitimate aspect of military operations it is important to ask why detention principles and guidelines for non-international armed conflicts and peace operations were not settled by states much earlier. There is no doubt that some of the impetus for engaging in the Copenhagen Process arose from the fact that a number of states who were participating in the Copenhagen Process had dealt with, or were dealing with, litigation arising from their detention operations.[64] It is also likely that after more than a decade of armed conflict in Afghanistan and Iraq the practices of states in taking and handling detainees had evolved to a point where participants felt the time was ripe to articulate a 'common approach that ... should contribute to ensuring the humane treatment of detainees and the effectiveness of international military operations'.[65] The importance of the practice of states in dealing with detainees was also reflected by the statement in the preamble: '[p]articipants were ... inspired by the good practices that States and organisations have developed in international military operations.'[66] A five-year process might therefore have benefited states by giving them ample time to understand the scope of the litigation issues, the extent of their practices, and the lessons learned. In other words, the Process timeline adopted proved to be appropriate considering that the subject of detention in military operations turned out to be a highly contentious matter for some states.

Third, is the extent to which the Process permitted states to engage with developing a better understanding of the interaction between IHL and IHRL in identifying norms for dealing with detainees. From the very start of the Process in 2007 there were debates concerning the application of both IHL and IHRL to detention operations. The Process facilitated those debates by permitting participants

[64] See e.g.: Canada: *Amnesty International, Canada v. Canada (Minister of National Defence)* [2007] C. 1147 (Can.); Denmark: Case No. 180/2011 *Ghousouallah Tarin v. Ministry of Defense*; Iraq: Cases No. B3421-11 *Brak and others v. Ministry of Defense*; B397-12, *Shahel and others v. Ministry of Defense*; B1162-12, *Al Saadoun and others v. Ministry of Defense*; B3534-12, *Albarrak and others v. Ministry of Defense*; and B420-13, *Abdullah and others v. Ministry of Defense*.

[65] Principles and Guidelines, Preamble II.

[66] Principles and Guidelines, Preamble VI.

to, among other things, exchange views through table top exercises where issues relating to detention were 'war gamed', and provide comments on the approaches taken in the non-papers and draft versions of the Principles and Guidelines circulated by the Chair of the Process. The issue throughout was not that IHL or IHRL did not apply, but determining what the precise relationship between IHL and IHRL in the context of detention is. Notwithstanding the fact that participants recognized the 'challenges of agreeing upon a precise description of the interaction between international human rights law and international humanitarian law'[67] the settled Principles and Guidelines took both areas of law into account. For example, the provisions concerning non-discrimination,[68] the requirement to release,[69] and the need to promptly inform[70] are found in both IHL and IHRL. The Process did facilitate a compromise at the last conference—that is to restrict the final document to applying only to non-international armed conflicts and peace operations and not law enforcement operations such as counter-piracy. This compromise was precisely because of the belief of participants and civil society that law enforcement operations should be dominated by IHRL. The fact that the Process facilitated both broad and narrow discussions concerning the application of IHL and IHRL principles, rules, and standards concerning detention in military operations might therefore be seen as benefiting the overall understanding of the role that IHL and IHRL have in regard to detention in military operations.

Fourth, there is the issue of the Danish Ministry of Foreign Affairs acting as a norm negotiator or incubator in developing the Principles and Guidelines. By leading and hosting the Copenhagen Process, developing the drafts of the Principles and Guidelines, and taking sole responsibility for the commentary that accompanied the Principles and Guidelines the Ministry of Foreign Affairs clearly played an important role in negotiating and developing both the process and substance of the Process and Principles and Guidelines. It is necessary to distinguish the Ministry's role as a norm negotiator from that of a normative intermediary. The Ministry did not play a normative intermediary role in the sense of 'seeking to promote observance of a norm, ... [where the issue of] a particular compliance shortcoming of a state ... [was at issue so as to] induce compliance through a hands on process of communication and persuasion with relevant decision makers'.[71]

From a substantive 'soft law' perspective there are six observations that might be made concerning the content of the Principles and Guidelines. First, substantively the Principles and Guidelines document is not law. While it is true that it has a number of hard law or binding norms (e.g. the prohibition against torture),[72] it does not purport to alter the treaty or customary law obligations that states have. Even where the Principles and Guidelines use norm binding words such as 'will' or 'must' the emphasis in the Preamble and Principle 16 on the fact that the document does

[67] Principles and Guidelines, Preamble IV.

[68] Principles and Guidelines, Principle 2.

[69] Principles and Guidelines, Principle 3.

[70] Principles and Guidelines, Principle 7.

[71] S. Ratner, 'Does International Law Matter in Preventing Ethnic Conflict?', *NYU Journal of International Law and Policy* vol. 32 (2000): 591–724 at 668.

[72] Principles and Guidelines, Principle 2.

not affect the applicability of international law reinforces the soft law nature of the document. Thus it is important to distinguish, in the context of the Principles and Guidelines, between the fact that some of the principles are clearly binding principles as a matter of international law (e.g. the prohibition against torture), and some are norms that are not binding such as 'where practicable, the detainee's family is to be notified of the deprivation of liberty, release or transfer of a detainee'[73] but that the document in which they are contained is a soft law document. Put another way: the document is soft law and the Principles and Guidelines are evidence of law and sometimes policy or practice.

Second, the fact that they describe a shared understanding of how legal norms are to apply in the narrow context of taking and handling detainees in non-armed conflicts and peace operations provides greater clarity about dealing with detainees from the moment they are detained, or have their movement restricted, until their release or their transfer to another entity, such as the host nation. The Principles and Guidelines also address substantive issues such as the meaning of detention, the humane treatment to be afforded to detainees (including the use of force against detainees and the conditions for detention), the release of detainees, providing detainees with contact with the outside world, notifications concerning detention, dealing with complaints by detainees, the reviews to be conducted if a detainee is to be held in ongoing detention, and the transfer of detainees. The clarity concerning the phases of detention and the treatment of detainees, which does not exist in any other normative framework concerning detention in non-international armed conflicts and peace operations, contributes to filling a normative lacuna. Further, because of that normative lacuna the Principles and Guidelines provide a useful framework to assist military forces with a common starting point to develop their orders and standard operating procedures for dealing with detainees. That common starting point or platform is also useful in coalition or multinational operations when states engaged in such operations might have differing hard law obligations.

Third, the fact that the Principles and Guidelines take existing legal principles and rules—such as the obligation of humane treatment and the prohibition against torture[74]—and apply them by analogy[75] to peace operations reinforces the application of those principles and rules in other military operations that might not be viewed as either armed conflicts or law enforcement. Taking binding norms by analogy and putting them to work in a non-binding document such as the Principles and Guidelines reinforces the interaction that can exist between hard and soft law. The former informs the latter and vice versa. The Principles and Guidelines also develop norms by, for example, providing that detaining authorities 'should develop and implement standard operating procedures and other relevant guidance regarding the handling of detainees'.[76] That norm development is important

[73] Principles and Guidelines, Principle 11. [74] Principles and Guidelines, Principle 2.

[75] For a more detailed explanation of the methodology used by lawyers to develop law by analogy see e.g.: International Law Commission, Report of the Study Group on Fragmentation of International Law: Difficulties Arising from Diversification and Expansion of International Law, UN Doc. A/CN.4/L.628 (2006) para. 36.

[76] Principles and Guidelines, Principle 5.

because it recognizes the nexus between doctrine and training on the one hand, and the humane treatment of detainees during operations. The articulation of shifting legal principles and rules by analogy, and developing norms, is an example of how the Principles and Guidelines might therefore be viewed as progressively developing law.

Another way of looking at norm development in the context of the Principles and Guidelines is to consider that they are both norm-filling and norm-creating. By way of example, the fact that the Principles and Guidelines recognize that security detainees (i.e. a person detained because there is a reasonable belief that he or she is a 'security threat')[77] might be taken during non-international armed conflict is norm-filling—in the sense that such detention is not prohibited under the broad terms of Article 4 of AP II. However, it might be argued that the Principles and Guidelines are norm-creating in the sense that they take the category of security detainee as applicable to those who might be detained for security reasons during peace operations. The norm development role played by the Principles and Guidelines might therefore be seen as 'operationalizing' certain norms in the context of both non-international armed conflicts and peace operations.

Fourth, some of the Principles and Guidelines address matters not dealt with in any other normative framework but which nonetheless exist in practice. For example, the distinction between security detainees and criminal detainees (i.e. a person detained on suspicion of attempting to commit, or having committed a criminal offence)—two categories of detainees that have been taken in many military operations—and the rights concerning the review of ongoing detention[78] is not addressed in any international law treaty or in customary international law that relates to peace operations that are not categorized as armed conflicts. That distinction reaffirms that states participating in the Process believed that both security and criminal detentions are valid forms of detention. Furthermore, participating states also accepted that in the context of security detainees there are legal norms applicable, such as prompt initial review, and having the decision reviewed periodically by an impartial and objective authority.[79] In the case of criminal detainees the Principles and Guidelines accept that it is appropriate to transfer such detainees to an appropriate authority, or to have proceedings initiated against them. If the transfer or initiation of proceedings is not possible in a reasonable time then 'the decision to detain is to be reconsidered in accordance with applicable law'.[80] Principle 13 demonstrates how the Principles and Guidelines give effect to practice, the taking of both security and criminal detainees, while at the same time ensuring that the time of detention and subsequent ongoing detention are governed by appropriate norms. The blending of practice and norms therefore value-adds to the development of both policy and law.

[77] Principles and Guidelines, Commentary 12.1. The notion of a security detainee is derived from Geneva Convention IV, Arts 42 and 78. Other terms used for such detention include 'administrative', 'preventative', or 'operational detention'.

[78] Principles and Guidelines, Principles 12–13.

[79] Principles and Guidelines, Principle 12.

[80] Principles and Guidelines, Principle 13.

Fifth, it has been noted that 'states and non-state actors increasingly use soft law not to "progressively develop" existing hard law, but to undermine it'.[81] Such a view about the 'antagonistic'[82] nature of soft law assumes that states and non-state actors are acting in bad faith. It also assumes that the notion of hard and soft norms is a binary phenomenon and fails to recognize that the interpretation of norms, whether they be hard or soft, 'comes in degrees'.[83] As described by Ratner, states use all norms in international law with such flexibility in mind so as to determine interpretations based on factors such as who developed the norms, the level of precision expected of the norm, and the control mechanisms involved in making the norms effective.[84] A more optimistic view is that soft law 'in its various forms can of course be abused, but so can most legal forms, and ... [soft law] has generally been more helpful to the process of international law-making than it has been objectionable. It is simply another tool in the professional lawyer's armoury'.[85] The Principles and Guidelines having been inspired by good practices and lessons learned and '[f]ounded on the legal principles that all persons who are detained or whose liberty is being restricted must be treated humanely, that any detention must be conducted in accordance with applicable law, on the policy principle that legal authority to detain should be exercised in a prudent manner'[86] should allay concerns about the bad faith of states or their antagonistic nature.

Sixth, the fact that states were unable to settle on the precise relationship between IHL and IHRL in the context of detention operations in non-international armed conflicts and peace operations reinforces the general view that some states are hesitant to meld the two branches of law together—at least in relation to military operations. In the end perhaps some states felt that since IHL and IHRL 'have different presumptions about the context of detention, they have different, specific, but contradictory rules'.[87] From a state perspective this is important to understand as it demonstrates a tension that exists in recognizing the precise reach of IHRL in armed conflict situations and peace operations when, for some states, the belief is that IHL is the appropriate legal regime to deal with the competing needs of humanitarianism and achieving the military mission.

4.1 Some post-Copenhagen Process developments

So, post-Copenhagen Process, have the Principles and Guidelines gained any traction among states or international organizations so as to indicate their normative

[81] Shaffer and Pollack (2001): 1159–60. [82] Shaffer and Pollack (2001): 1159–60.

[83] S. Ratner, 'Jus ad Bellum and Jus in Bello after September 11', *American Journal of International Law* vol. 96 (2002): 905–21 at 914.

[84] Ratner (2002): 914.

[85] A. F. Boyle, 'Reflections on the Relationship of Treaties and Soft Law', *International and Comparative Law Quarterly* vol. 48 (1999): 901–13.

[86] Principles and Guidelines, Preamble VIII.

[87] Bellinger and Padmanabhan (2011): 210. See also: B. Oswald, 'Detention of Civilians on Military Operations: Reasons for and Challenges to Developing a Special Law of Detention', *Melbourne University Law Review* vol. 32 (2008): 524–53.

standing? As a starting point, no state or international organization has announced that it is applying the Principles and Guidelines. That is hardly surprising considering that detention policies and standard operating procedures are usually classified and therefore not disseminated to the public. However, it is clear from the ICRC report of 2013, concerning regional consultations on persons deprived of their liberty, that the Principles and Guidelines were referred to by states in a number of contexts such as developing further guidance regarding detention, reviews of detention, and non-refoulement.[88] The UK High Court has also made reference to them in relation to the lawfulness of detention in non-international armed conflicts in the *Serdar Mohammed* case.[89] In that case the Court concluded that notwithstanding the UK Ministry of Defence's argument that the power to detain exists as a matter of customary law as evidenced by the Principles and Guidelines, the fact was that the Principles and Guidelines are not law.[90] The Court relied on the chairperson's commentary concerning Principle 16 to reach that conclusion.[91] In the recent European Court of Human Rights (ECHR) decision of *Hassan*, the Court made no reference to the Principles and Guidelines but that is not surprising because in that case their application was not raised by the UK.[92] In view of this it might be concluded that the status of the Principles and Guidelines remains very much a matter of soft law.

5. Conclusion

In reflecting broadly about the Copenhagen Process and the resulting Principles and Guidelines it must be hoped that they will add to the humanitarian protections of detainees by promoting, clarifying, and promulgating legal norms. That hope stems from accepting that because the Process was state-centric it was effective in taking good practices and lessons learned and applying them to best mitigate the tension that arises both in ensuring the humane treatment of detainees and ensuring military effectiveness in achieving the mission.

Further, it is clear that IHL has developed since at least the nineteenth century through the interaction of different processes. It is worth noting though that the Copenhagen Process appears to be a rare example of a state-centric approach to developing IHL norms for a specific type of activity—dealing with detainees.

[88] ICRC, Strengthening International Humanitarian Law Protecting Persons Deprived of their Liberty: Synthesis Report from Regional Consultations of Government Experts (ICRC, Nov. 2013).

[89] *Serdar Mohammed v. Ministry of Defence and Mohammed Qasim, Mohammed Nazim and Abdullah and Secretary of State for Defence* [2014] EWHC 1369 (QB). See also *Serdar Mohammed & others and Secretary of State for Defence; Yunus Rahmatullah & Iraqi Civilian Claimants and Ministry of Defence and Foreign and Commonwealth Office* [2015] EWCA Civ. 843.

[90] *Serdar Mohammed v. Ministry of Defence and Mohammed Qasim, Mohammed Nazim and Abdullah and Secretary of State for Defence* [2014] EWHC 1369 (QB), para. 262.

[91] *Serdar Mohammed v. Ministry of Defence and Mohammed Qasim, Mohammed Nazim and Abdullah and Secretary of State for Defence* [2014] EWHC 1369 (QB), para. 265.

[92] *Case of Hassan v. The United Kingdom*, 16 Sept. 2014, App. no. 29750/09.

The Process might therefore be seen as an example of recognizing that the balance between engaging communities narrowly rather than broadly is not just about seeking an acceptance of the norms settled on but also permitting relevant stakeholders an opportunity to craft norms that suit the circumstances as they perceive them to be and to get a consensus that clarifies the application of existing norms.

As for the substantive provisions found in the Principles and Guidelines, it is clear that the states that welcomed them did not intend for them to be binding. It nevertheless remains to be seen the extent to which they will give rise to legal consequences. It might, for example, be the case that a court or tribunal adopts some or all the Principles and Guidelines to fill a perceived or actual gap in relation to standards of treatment of detainees in peace operations, or that the Security Council refers to them in a resolution thus giving the Principles and Guidelines a firmer degree of hardness as norms.

7

The Use of Soft Law in Regulating Armed Conflict

From *Jus in Bello* to 'Soft Law *in Bello*'?

Peter Vedel Kessing

1. Introduction

Historically, soft law has not played a major role in regulating situations of armed conflict. Armed conflict has—contrary to the human rights field—almost exclusively been regulated by hard law instruments. However, this has changed within the last two decades, with new standards targeting situations of armed conflict increasingly being elaborated in soft law instruments.

This chapter explores and discusses the new trend of regulating armed conflict with soft law instruments and more specifically assesses whether international human rights norms are reflected in recent soft law instruments.

The existing hard law regulating armed conflict, particularly non-international armed conflict, is outdated and in many respects inadequate. It basically consists of: the four Geneva Conventions (GC) from 1949; the two Additional Protocols (AP) from 1977; the Hague Conventions I–XIII on Means and Methods of Warfare from 1907; and the more recent weapon conventions.[1]

Even though there is a great need for new rules to regulate present-day armed conflicts, particularly non-international armed conflicts, states have been cautious in adopting new international binding rules. When states negotiated and adopted the two Additional Protocols to the Geneva Conventions in 1977, there were major disagreements between states on the need for new international rules and on the scope, content, and precise formulation of the rules. Finally, a compromise was reached leading to the two APs, which in a certain (small) number of areas clarify and to some extent broaden the existing rules in the four GCs. This outcome has

[1] 1972 Biological Weapons Convention; the 1980 Convention on Conventional Weapons; the 1993 Convention on Chemical Weapons; the 1997 Ottawa Convention on Anti-Personnel Mines; the 2003 CCW Protocol (V) on Explosive Remnants of War; and the 2008 Convention on Cluster Munitions.

been described by many commentators as disappointing, or even a failure. As one commentator has noted:

> Not counting the ICRC preparatory conferences of experts and the UN debates, the 1974 Diplomatic Conference consumed approximately 7,000 pounds of paper and produced some 4.5 million pages of reports, amendments, summary records, and the like. From all of this, there was little progress on specific legal issues. The future is particularly murky for this exercise of reaffirmation and development of the law of armed conflict. 1974 may have been a bad time to have tried to develop this law. Then again, when has there ever been a good time?[2]

In any event, it is a fact that a number of states often involved in or affected by armed conflict have refrained from ratifying the APs, including the United States, Israel, Iran, Pakistan, India, and Turkey. Based on this experience, the International Committee of the Red Cross (ICRC) and a number of states have been reluctant to initiate new diplomatic processes to negotiate international humanitarian law (IHL).[3]

Instead, other legal sources and norms—most pertinently customary international humanitarian law (CIHL) and international human rights law (IHRL)—have played an increasingly important role in regulating armed conflict and thereby to some extent filling the norm gap in IHL hard law.[4]

This development has led to legal as well as operational challenges for the military at large and the ordinary soldier in particular. In relation to CIHL there is no general international consensus on which IHL norms have crystallized into customary international law. The vast majority of hard law rules in the Geneva and Hague Conventions, particularly those governing the conduct of hostilities, are only applicable in international armed conflict and it is strongly debated whether some or all of these rules are applicable in non-international armed conflict as CIHL.

In relation to IHRL, however, the challenges are much more overwhelming and fundamental since there are crucial differences between the legal standards in IHL and in IHRL. IHL is developed for armed conflict and IHRL basically for peacetime situations. Thus, all IHL norms express a delicate balance between military necessity and humanity. On the contrary, military necessity is not reflected in IHRL norms. As a consequence, IHRL norms are more restrictive than IHL in allowing states to use force, often leading to a stronger legal protection of the

[2] D. P. Forsythe, 'The 1974 Diplomatic Conference on Humanitarian Law: Some Observations', *American Journal of International Law* vol. 69 (Jan. 1975): 77–91.

[3] One exception could be the pending ICRC initiative on establishing new hard law norms on detention in NIAC. See the ICRC, Background Document, 'Strengthening International Humanitarian Law Protecting Persons Deprived of Their Liberty' (Apr. 2015). However, the ultimate outcome of this process will apparently be 'just' a non-legally binding soft law document, see para. 8 in the resolution on 'Strengthening international humanitarian law—protecting persons deprived of their liberty', adopted at the 32nd International Conference of the Red Cross 8–10 Dec. 2015.

[4] For a thorough discussion of the two competing ways (CIHL and IHRL) of filling the norm gap in IHL in NIAC: W. Abresch, 'A Human Rights Law of Internal Armed Conflict: The European Court of Human Rights in Chechnya', *European Journal of International Law* vol. 16 (2005): 741–67.

individual, for instance in relation to the right to life, the right to liberty, and the right to freedom from torture.

In parallel with this development and the increasing influence of alternative hard law norms in the form of CIHL and IHRL, a number of soft law instruments regulating certain aspects of international armed conflict and non-international armed conflict have been elaborated by various stakeholders within the last twenty years, for example concerning sea warfare, air and missile warfare, and cyber warfare. These soft law instruments often draw on and reflect CIHL and IHRL norms.

While it is uncontroversial that CIHL is applicable to and regulates situations of armed conflict, the question of whether IHLR is applicable in armed conflict is much more contentious. CIHL is a very old and well-established legal source in armed conflict pre-dating treaty law, that is, the Hague and Geneva Conventions. However, whether and to what extent IHRL norms are applicable in situations of armed conflict is a much more recent and contemporary question.

Therefore, this chapter first explores, in section 2, the extent to which IHRL is applicable in times of armed conflict, and how different and sometimes conflicting norms in IHL and IHRL interrelate.

Section 3 provides a brief overview of the most important *jus in bello* soft law instruments that have been adopted over the last twenty years. For each instrument, it will discuss who has been responsible for elaborating and adopting the instrument; the purported legal status of the instrument; and whether IHRL norms have been incorporated or reflected in the instrument.

Section 4 discusses some of the consequences of the new trend of regulating armed conflict through soft law. Finally, section 5 contains some concluding observations.

2. Application of IHRL in Times of Armed Conflict and the Interrelationship with IHL

2.1 Is IHRL applicable in times of armed conflict?

Legal and jurisprudential developments over the past decade have clearly confirmed the concurrent application of IHL and IHRL in times of armed conflict. This has been firmly established by the International Court of Justice (ICJ) in several cases and by international and regional human rights monitoring bodies, including the UN Human Rights Committee, the European Court of Human Rights, and the Inter-American Court of Human Rights.[5] In addition, many states and international organizations have expressed the same view. Until recently there were doubts regarding the US position, but the USA confirmed during the UN Human Rights

[5] See section 2.2 of this chapter for the references.

Committee's examination in 2014 that IHRL continues to be applicable in armed conflict:

> With respect to the application of the Covenant [the ICCPR] and the international law of armed conflict (also referred to as international humanitarian law or 'IHL'), the United States has not taken the position that the Covenant does not apply 'in time of war'. Indeed, a time of war does not suspend the operation of the Covenant to matters within its scope of application.[6]

This position was reiterated by the USA with regard to the UN Torture Convention (UN CAT) during the UN Torture Committee's examination of the USA in December 2014. In its Concluding Observations, the committee welcomed

> the firm and principled position adopted by the State party with regard to the applicability of the Convention [UN CAT] during armed conflict, and its statement that a time of war does not suspend the operation of the Convention, which continues to apply even when the State is engaged in an armed conflict.[7]

International organs like the UN Security Council have also repeatedly stated that human rights apply during armed conflict. This was particularly highlighted in a number of resolutions on the protection of civilians during armed conflict, where the Council '[d]emand[ed] that parties to armed conflict comply strictly with the obligations applicable to them under international humanitarian law, human rights and refugee law'.[8] Similarly, the Security Council stressed in 2014 in relation to the armed conflict in Syria that 'All parties to the conflict, in particular the Syrian authorities, must comply with their obligations under international humanitarian law and international human rights law.'[9]

The UN Human Rights Council (UN HRC) has also in a number of resolutions dealt with IHRL and IHL as complementary, stressing that 'human rights law and international humanitarian law are complementary and mutually reinforcing'.[10]

Finally, over roughly the past decade, international organizations such as the UN, EU, and OSCE have established a large number of commissions of inquiry with the mandate to investigate possible violations of IHL and IHRL in times of armed conflict. The UN HRC decided in late August 2011 to establish an international commission of inquiry on Syria to 'investigate all alleged violations of international human rights law since March 2011 in the Syrian Arab Republic'.[11] There

[6] 'Fourth Periodic Report of the US to the UN Human Rights Committee concerning the ICCPR' (30 Dec. 2011), paras 506 and 507.

[7] UN CAT, 'Concluding Observations on the Combined Third to Fifth Periodic Reports of the United States of America' (19 Dec. 2014), para. 6.

[8] UN Security Council, Resolution 1894, 11 Sept. 2009. Likewise see: Resolution 1674 (2006), S/Res/1674 (2006), 28 Apr. 2006, para. 26 and Resolution 1738 (2006), S/Res/1738 (2006), 23 Dec. 2006, para. 9.

[9] UN Security Council, Resolution 2165, 14 July 2014, op. para. 1.

[10] UN Human Rights Commission, Protection of the Human Rights of Civilians in Armed Conflict, E/CN.4/2005/L.82, 15 Apr. 2005.

[11] Independent International Commission of Inquiry on The Syrian Arab Republic, UNHCR, 2015, <http://www.ohchr.org/en/hrbodies/hrc/iicisyria/pages/independentinternationalcommission.aspx>.

is evidently an ongoing non-international armed conflict in Syria—a conflict that can be said to have started in spring and summer 2011 with unrest and widespread fighting—and it is remarkable that the UN HRC did *not* mention in the resolution that violations of IHL should be investigated. In 2014, the UN HRC decided to set up a commission of inquiry to investigate the war between Israel and Gaza. The UN HRC stated that the Commission of Inquiry shall 'investigate all violations of international humanitarian law and international human rights law'.[12]

In conclusion, there is overwhelming evidence that IHRL is applicable in times of armed conflict. The question is rather: in the event of conflicting norms between IHL and IHRL, which standards prevail? The problem is, as mentioned in section 1, that the protection of individuals is often much stronger and more far-reaching in IHRL than in IHL. An illustration of this is the protection of life. While IHRL generally requires that states only use lethal force against individuals as a last resort,[13] IHL generally authorizes states to use lethal force as a first resort against enemy combatants and civilians taking direct part in hostilities. Hence, a soldier killing an individual during armed hostilities might be legal if assessed pursuant to IHL, but illegal if assessed according to IHRL. Therefore, it is of crucial importance to resolve the issue of how the two bodies of law should interact.

2.2 How can different and sometimes conflicting norms in IHL and IHRL interact?

As already mentioned, the International Court of Justice has examined the status of human rights in times of international armed conflict[14] and occupation[15] and found that IHRL continues to apply in these situations. As regards the interaction between international humanitarian law and human rights law in times of international armed conflict (the *Congo* case) and occupation (the *Wall* case) the Court has, at a general level, stated that international humanitarian law and human rights law may interact in three possible ways: 'Some rights may be exclusively matters of international humanitarian law; others may be exclusively matters of human rights law; yet others may be matters of both these branches of international law.' More specifically, concerning the right to life under international armed conflict, the ICJ found in the 1996 *Nuclear Weapons* case that the test of what is an arbitrary deprivation of life is to be determined by the applicable *lex specialis*, namely, the law applicable in (international) armed conflict, which is designed to regulate the conduct of hostilities.

[12] 'Council President appoints Members of Commission of Inquiry under HRC resolution S-21/1', UNHCR, Aug. 2014, <http://www.ohchr.org/en/NewsEvents/Pages/DisplayNews.aspx?NewsID=14934&LangID=E>.

[13] More specifically, it must be absolutely necessary to use lethal force in order to protect other individuals against an imminent threat to life and that other less intrusive powers, e.g. arrest or warning shots, are perceived to be inefficient in the situation; see e.g.: Art. 2 in the ICCPR and the ECHR.

[14] ICJ, 'Legality of the Threat or Use of Nuclear Weapons in Armed Conflict' (8 July 1996), para. 25; and 'Case Concerning Armed Activities on the Territory of the Congo' (19 Dec. 2005), para. 220.

[15] ICJ, 'Legal Consequences of the Construction of a Wall in the Occupied Palestinian Territory' (9 June 2004), para. 106.

Human rights bodies have also reviewed this issue. In 2001, the UN HRC established in a General Comment that the ICCPR also applies in situations of armed conflict and found that the two spheres of law are complementary rather than mutually exclusive. It went on to state that with respect to 'certain Covenant rights, more specific rules of international humanitarian law may be especially relevant for the purposes of interpreting the Covenant rights'.[16]

The European Court of Human Rights considered the issue on the interaction between IHL and IHRL in times of international armed conflict for the first time in the case *Hassan v. UK* in September 2014.[17] The case concerned the UK detention of an Iraqi national in Iraq in April 2003, in a period when there were still major combat operations—that is, an active IAC.[18]

The UK government contended, among other things, that IHLR, and more specifically Article 5 on detention in the European Convention on Human Rights (ECHR), is 'displaced by international humanitarian law as *lex specialis*, or modified so as to incorporate or allow for the capture and detention of actual or suspected combatants in accordance with the Third and/or Fourth Geneva Conventions, such that there was no breach by the United Kingdom with respect to the capture and detention [of the applicant]'.[19]

The Court did not accept this view. It stated:

> ... Consistently with the case-law of the International Court of Justice, the Court considers that, even in situations of international armed conflict, the safeguards under the Convention continue to apply, albeit interpreted against the background of the provisions of international humanitarian law.[20]

Accordingly, ECHR obligations are not displaced under international armed conflict, but must be interpreted against the 'background' of standards in IHL. Thus, IHL functions as *lex specialis* in international armed conflict in the sense that it elaborates on and suggest modes of application of the broad and general standards in IHRL (general law) in a particular situation. This does not mean that IHRL is displaced.[21]

In line with this view, the Court held that some of the detention review guarantees found in Articles 5(2) and (4) in the ECHR are still applicable when individuals are detained during international armed conflicts. The detention must be reviewed by a 'competent body' which 'should provide sufficient guarantees of impartiality and fair procedure to protect against arbitrariness. Moreover, the first review should take place shortly after the person is taken into detention, with subsequent reviews at frequent intervals.'[22]

[16] UN Human Rights Committee, General Comment No. 29.

[17] ECHR, *Hassan v. United Kingdom*, App. no. 29750/09, 16 Sept. 2014.

[18] Major combat operations ended 1 May 2003, see: ECHR, *Hassan v. United Kingdom*, App. no. 29750/09, 16 Sept. 2014, para. 9.

[19] ECHR, *Hassan v. United Kingdom*, App. no. 29750/09, 16 Sept. 2014, para. 88.

[20] ECHR, *Hassan v. United Kingdom*, App. no. 29750/09, 16 Sept. 2014, para. 104.

[21] On the function and scope of the *lex specialis* principle, see e.g.: the International Law Commission Study Group on Fragmentation, Koskenniemi, A/CN.4/L.682, 13 Apr. 2006.

[22] ECHR, *Hassan v. United Kingdom*, App. no. 29750/09, 16 Sept. 2014, para. 106.

These detention review guarantees are not found in IHL standards on detention/internment, and particularly not for prisoners of war who, under IHL, can be detained for the duration of hostilities without any form of review.[23]

In situations of non-international armed conflict, it is more difficult to argue that a possible norm conflict between IHL and IHRL should be settled on the basis of the *lex specialis* principle. Non-international armed conflict is only regulated in treaty law in common Article 3 of the four GCs and in Additional Protocol II (AP II), if it is applicable. Hence, IHL does not provide detailed and precise regulations in non-international armed conflict that can inform standards in IHRL. Furthermore, it is stressed—admittedly in rather ambiguous terms—in the preamble to AP II that human rights are applicable and must be taken into consideration in times of non-international armed conflict.[24]

The European Court of Human Rights (ECtHR) has also decided a number of cases concerning non-international armed conflict, but the Court has never directly in its reasoning referred to standards in IHL. On the contrary, the Court seems to decide such cases strictly on the basis of the ECHR and does not resort to IHL when interpreting ECHR standards, for example the meaning of the right to life in Article 2.[25] In line with this the Court stated in 2014, in the aforementioned case *Hassan v. UK*, that:

> It can only be in cases of international armed conflict, where the taking of prisoners of war and the detention of civilians who pose a threat to security are accepted features of international humanitarian law, that Article 5 could be interpreted as permitting the exercise of such broad powers.[26]

The UN Office of the High Commissioner for Human Rights has likewise argued that IHRL, and more specifically the right to life, should be considered the *lex specialis* in times of non-international armed conflict in cases of inconsistency or even conflict with standards in IHL:

> Some have interpreted—by analogy with international armed conflicts—that international humanitarian law permits the authorities to shoot to kill [a fighter in non-international armed conflict]. Under international human rights law, a person must be arrested and a graduated use of force must be employed. In this case, taking into account the extent of Government control (if any) over the place where the killing occurs, international human rights law should be considered as the *lex specialis*.[27]

[23] Pursuant to IHL, civilians can be detained for 'imperative reasons of security'. For detention review standards in IHL see: Arts 43 and 78(2) in the fourth GC. For more details see: Peter Vedel Kessing, 'Security Detention in Peace Operations', in *Searching for a 'Principle of Humanity' in International Humanitarian Law*, ed. K. M. Larsen, C. G. Cooper, and G. Nystuen (Cambridge: Cambridge University Press, 2013): 272–304.

[24] 'Recalling furthermore that international instruments relating to human rights offer a basic protection to the human person.'

[25] Nevertheless, the Court does take into consideration the difficult factual situation in an armed conflict and seems to apply a less strict proportionality test. See e.g.: ECtHR, *Özkan v. Turkey*, 6 Apr. 2004, paras 305–6.

[26] ECtHR, *Özkan v. Turkey*, 6 Apr. 2004, paras 305–6.

[27] UN Human Rights Office of the High Commissioner, 'International Legal Protection of Human Rights in Armed Conflict' (New York and Geneva, 2011): 67.

Contrary to this position, the Inter-American Court of Human Rights has applied IHL standards when considering human rights complaints in times of non-international armed conflict:

[D]uring such situations of *internal hostilities*, the Commission has received from Colombia and other OAS member States numerous complaints alleging serious violations of the fundamental rights guaranteed in the American Convention and Declaration arising out of the conduct of military operations by State security forces and its other agents. In order to properly judge the specific claims raised in such petitions, *the Commission has found it necessary at times either to directly apply rules of international humanitarian law, i.e. the law of armed conflict, or to inform its interpretations of relevant provisions of the American Convention by reference to these rules.*[28]

The role of IHRL under armed conflict and the relationship with standards in IHL has also been much debated among scholars, with little resulting consensus.[29]

In summary, there is clearly widespread agreement among judicial review bodies and among states and international organizations regarding the fact that IHRL continues to be applicable and plays an increasingly important role during armed conflict, particularly in non-international armed conflict. On the other hand, it is equally evident that there is little consensus among international complaints bodies, states, international organizations, and scholars on how the different and sometimes conflicting norms in IHL and IHRL can and should interrelate in international and non-international armed conflict. Nevertheless, it can hardly be disputed that IHRL is a relevant legal source in armed conflict and that any new legal instrument—hard law or soft law—dealing with situations of armed conflict and regulating behaviour in armed conflict—no matter what subject matter—would have to reflect international human rights norms, or at the very least to take IHRL into consideration. This is, however, not always the situation in relation to the new soft law instruments concerning IHL, as we shall see in section 3. On the contrary, IHRL norms are often excluded in these new instruments.

[28] 'Third Report on the Human Rights Situation in Colombia', OEA/Ser.L/V/II.102 Doc. 9 rev. 1, 26 Feb. 1999, ch. IV (emphases added). The IACHR has not dealt with situations of international armed conflicts.

[29] See e.g.: G. Oberleitner, *Human Rights in Armed Conflict* (Cambridge: Cambridge University Press, 2015); F. J. Hampson, 'The Relationship between International Humanitarian Law and International Human Rights Law', in *Routledge Handbook of International Human Rights Law*, ed. S. Sheeran and N. Rodley (London: Routledge, 2013); O. A. Hathaway et al., 'Which Law Governs during Armed Conflict? The Relationship between International Humanitarian Law and Human Rights Law', *Minnesota Law Review* vol. 96 (2012): 1883–943; Hans-Joachim Heintze, 'On the Relationship between Human Rights Law Protection and International Humanitarian Law', *International Review of the Red Cross* vol. 86 (Dec. 2004); D. Kretzmer, 'Targeted Killing of Suspected Terrorists: Extra Judicial Executions or Legitimate Means of Defence?', *European Journal of International Law* vol. 16 (2005).

3. Overview of Soft Law Documents Regulating Situations of Armed Conflict (*Jus in Bello*)

During the last years, a number of soft law instruments in the form of manuals, studies, and guidelines seeking to regulate situations of armed conflict have been elaborated. These instruments have been developed by different actors, including the ICRC, small groups of experts, small groups of states, and a combination of experts and states.[30]

The question can rightly be asked whether all of these documents qualify as soft law instruments. It is a fact, however, that these documents formulate rules that have a certain degree of traction. The documents are often referred to by states and in international fora. Most of the documents are included in handbooks and compendiums on the most important legal instruments that pertain to armed conflicts and are referred to in national military manuals and in military training materials.[31] In that sense, they reflect standards which arguably have an impact on regulating situations of armed conflicts. Hence, it can hardly be disputed that these documents formulate rules that are in the process of incubation, that is, emerging rules of international law (see Chapter 1 on the definition of soft law for the purpose of this volume).

In this regard, it should be mentioned that international and regional organizations such as the UN, NATO, and the EU have also adopted operational policy documents concerning situations of armed conflict.[32] These documents clearly regulate the behaviour of UN-, NATO-, and EU-led military armed forces in times of armed conflict. They are, however, internal operational policy documents, binding only for the organizations and member states contributing troops to the organizations.[33] Therefore, they cannot qualify as soft law documents.

This section provides a brief overview of the most important soft law instruments applicable in situations of armed conflict (*jus in bello*).[34] It is not our intention to discuss the content and substance of each soft law instrument in detail. Rather, the description of each soft law instrument will focus on the following three questions:

[30] This chapter will not consider the use of soft law in relation to *jus ad bellum* even though soft law arguably has played a significant role in relation to *jus ad bellum*, see e.g.: the UN Declarations on Friendly Relations among States and Emerging New Norms on Responsibility to Protect (R2P).

[31] See e.g.: A. Roberts and R. Guelff, *Documents on the Laws of War* (Oxford: Oxford University Press, 3rd edn, 2004); J. Wouters and P. De Man, *Humanitarian and Security Law: A Compendium of International and European Instruments* (Cambridge: Intersentia, 2012).

[32] See e.g.: UN Secretary-General's Bulletin on Observance by the United Nations Forces of International Humanitarian Law from 1999; NATO Standardization Agreements (STANAG); and the European Union Concept for EU-led Military Operations and Missions (EEAS, 17107/14, Brussels, 19 Dec. 2014) and for the use of Non-Lethal Capabilities in EU-led CSDP Military Operations and Missions (EEAS, 7674/15, Brussels, 30 Mar. 2015).

[33] With regard to the EU, these EU operational policy documents are also binding on member states when they are implementing EU law—e.g. in third states.

[34] There are undoubtedly other soft law instruments regulating armed conflict, but these are the most well-known and often referred-to instruments.

Firstly, who has been responsible for drafting and adopting the instrument? Secondly, what is the purported legal nature of the instrument as claimed in the instrument; that is, is it a 'real' soft law document or does it claim to reflect hard law obligations, for example customary international law? Thirdly, have international human rights standards been incorporated or reflected in the soft law instrument?

3.1 The International Institute of Humanitarian Law, *Manual on International Law Applicable to Armed Conflicts at Sea*, San Remo, 1994

The San Remo Manual[35] was prepared during the period 1988–94 by a group of legal and naval experts participating in their personal capacity in a series of Round Tables convened by the International Institute of Humanitarian Law.[36] The ICRC supported the project and played a major role throughout. Apart from co-organizing the meetings held in Geneva, it offered its advice to the Institute throughout the process, coordinated the drafting work, and helped contribute to the administrative and secretarial work. The ICRC also convened three meetings of the rapporteurs, whose reports were the basis of discussion in the annual meetings, in order to organize the drafting of the explanations to the manual.[37]

The purpose of the San Remo Manual was to draw up a statement of contemporary international law applicable to international armed conflicts at sea. Pursuant to the ICRC, the manual includes a few provisions that might be considered progressive developments in the law. However, most of its provisions are considered to state the law that is currently applicable, that is, as an expression of customary international law.[38]

There are no references to human rights norms and human rights do not seem to have been reflected in the Manual. It is mentioned in the introduction to the Manual that: 'Although this Manual does not deal with human rights law as such, it should be noted that such law continues to apply, subject to any derogations made under applicable treaties.'[39]

[35] The Manual can be found here: <https://www.icrc.org/eng/resources/documents/misc/57jmsu.htm>.

[36] The International Institute of Humanitarian Law is an independent, non-profit humanitarian organization founded in 1970. The main purpose of the Institute is to promote IHL, particularly through training, organizing international seminars, and undertaking research.

[37] L. Doswald-Beck, 'San Remo Manual on International Law Applicable to Armed Conflicts at Sea', *International Review of the Red Cross* vol. 31 (Dec. 1995): 1.

[38] See the ICRCs description of the Manual here: <https://www.icrc.org/applic/ihl/ihl.nsf/INTRO/560?OpenDocument>.

[39] ICRC Description of the San Remo Manual, <https://www.icrc.org/applic/ihl/ihl.nsf/INTRO/560?OpenDocument>.

3.2 The ICRC study on *Customary International Humanitarian Law*, 2005

Following the successful completion of the San Remo Manual on International Law applicable to Armed Conflicts at Sea in 1994, the ICRC decided in its own capacity in 1996 to embark on a major study to identify rules of CIHL.[40]

The study was organized and controlled by ICRC in consultation with a large group of experts from around the world. The ICRC spent nearly ten years on research and consultations involving more than 150 governmental and academic experts before releasing the study in 2005.

It was the explicit purpose of the study to identify applicable customary international law in international and non-international armed conflict. This raises the question of whether it can be perceived as a 'real' soft law instrument. However, some states, including the USA, clearly disagree with some of the findings in the study and would probably qualify the document as a soft law document.[41]

It is stated in the study that IHRL has been included where relevant. This was because 'IHRL continues to apply during armed conflicts, as indicated by the express terms of the human rights treaties themselves' and 'confirmed on numerous occasions by the treaty bodies that have analysed State behaviour, including during armed conflict, and by the International Court of Justice'.[42] Furthermore, an analysis of the 161 identified rules in the study—and in particular the commentary to the rules—clearly indicates that human rights standards have been reflected and taken into consideration, particularly with regard to the rules in chapter 32 on fundamental guarantees.[43]

3.3 The International Institute of Humanitarian Law, *The Manual on the Law of Non-International Armed Conflicts*, San Remo, 2006

This Manual[44] was prepared for the San Remo International Institute of Humanitarian Law by a small group of experts.[45] The ICRC was invited as an observer.

The Manual is a guide for behaviour during non-international armed conflict. According to the drafting committee, 'while not a comprehensive restatement of

[40] ICRC, *Customary International Humanitarian Law*, vols 1 and 2, ed. Jean-Marie Henckarts and Louise Doswald-Beck (2005), <https://www.icrc.org/eng/assets/files/other/customary-international-humanitarian-extract-i-icrc-eng.pdf>.

[41] See e.g.: J. M. Henckaerts, 'Customary International Humanitarian Law: A Response to US Comments', *International Review of the Red Cross* vol. 89 (June 2007).

[42] J. M. Henckaerts, 'Customary International Humanitarian Law: A Response to US Comments', *International Review of the Red Cross* vol. 89 (June 2007), Introduction xxxvii.

[43] It is explicitly mentioned in the introduction to the chapter on page 299 that 'references to human rights law instruments, documents, and case law have been included (IHRL)' and there are a large number of references to IHRL throughout the chapter.

[44] The Manual can be found here: <http://www.iihl.org/wp-content/uploads/2015/12/Manual-on-the-Extract-of-NIAC.pdf>.

[45] The drafting Committee consisted of Yoram Dinstein, Charles Garraway, and Michael Schmitt.

law applicable in such conflicts, it nevertheless reflects the key principles contained in that law'.[46]

Human rights norms are not incorporated or reflected in the Manual. The Manual uses the same phrase as the San Remo Manual on International Law applicable to Armed Conflicts at Sea from 1994: 'Although this Manual does not deal with human rights law as such, it should be noted that such law continues to apply, subject to any derogations made under applicable treaties.'[47]

3.4 The ICRC and Switzerland, *The Montreux Document on Pertinent International Legal Obligations and Good Practices for States Related to Operations of Private Military Companies during Armed Conflict*, 2008

The Montreux Document on Private Military Companies was the result of an international process launched by the Government of Switzerland and the ICRC.[48] The Montreux Document was accepted by consensus on 17 September 2008 by seventeen states.[49]

States and international organizations can 'join' the Montreux Document. Its preface reads: 'The participating States invite other States and international organizations to communicate their support for this document to the Federal Department of Foreign Affairs of Switzerland'. As of April 2015, fifty-two states and three international organizations have 'joined' the Document and the number of supporting states is growing steadily.[50] In December 2014, the 'Montreux Document Forum' was established as a platform to share good practices and discuss challenges regarding the regulation of private military security companies (PMSCs). It gathers all participants to the Montreux Document and is currently co-chaired by the Swiss Ministry of Foreign Affairs and the ICRC, with the support of the Geneva Centre for the Democratic Control of Armed Forces (DCAF) acting as the Secretariat.

The Document is not legally binding but rather contains a compilation of relevant international legal obligations and good practices. As mentioned in the Document, it does not seek to establish new regulation but simply to provide guidance on a number of difficult and unclear legal and practical points, on the basis of existing international law.

[46] The International Institute of Humanitarian Law, *The Manual on the Law of Non-International Armed Conflicts* (San Remo, 2006): 2.

[47] The International Institute of Humanitarian Law, *The Manual on the Law of Non-International Armed Conflicts* (San Remo, 2006): 3.

[48] The Montreux document can be found here: <https://www.icrc.org/eng/assets/files/other/icrc_002_0996.pdf>.

[49] Namely Afghanistan, Angola, Australia, Austria, Canada, China, France, Germany, Iraq, Poland, Sierra Leone, South Africa, Sweden, Switzerland, the United Kingdom of Great Britain and Northern Ireland, Ukraine, and the United States of America.

[50] Swiss Federal Department of Foreign Affairs, 'Participating States of the Montreux Document', <https://www.eda.admin.ch/eda/en/fdfa/foreign-policy/international-law/international-humanitarian-law/private-military-security-companies/participating-states.html>.

IHRL plays an important and integral part in the document. The purpose of the Montreux Document, as described by ICRC, is to promote respect for international humanitarian law and human rights law whenever private military and security companies are present in armed conflicts. The Document recalls existing legal obligations of states and PMSCs and their personnel under IHL and IHRL and customary international law and provides states with recommendations regarding good practices to promote compliance with international humanitarian law and human rights law during armed conflict.[51]

3.5 ICRC, *Interpretative Guidance on the Notion of Direct Participation in Hostilities*, February 2009

The Interpretive Guidance is an expression solely of the ICRC's views.[52] A group of eminent legal experts were consulted during the process, but the positions enunciated are the ICRC's alone.

It is explained in the introduction to the Guidance paper that the document is not and cannot be a text of a legally binding nature. Only state agreements (treaties) or state practice followed out of a sense of legal obligation on a certain issue (custom) can produce binding law. Hence, the paper does not purport to change the law, but provides an interpretation of the notion of direct participation in hostilities within existing legal parameters.

IHRL standards are not reflected in the Guidance paper as the paper solely relates to international humanitarian law and the interpretation of the notion of direct participation in hostilities.

3.6 Humanitarian Policy and Conflict Research (HPCR), *Manual on International Law Applicable to Air and Missile Warfare*, 15 May 2009

This Manual[53] was elaborated by a group of experts under the guidance of HPCR's Senior Academic Adviser, Professor Dr Yoram Dinstein.[54] The ICRC was invited to participate as an observer.

[51] Swiss Federal Department of Foreign Affairs, 'Participating States of the Montreux Document', <https://www.eda.admin.ch/eda/en/fdfa/foreign-policy/international-law/international-humanitarian-law/private-military-security-companies/participating-states.html>.

[52] The Interpretative Guidance Paper can be found here: <https://www.icrc.org/eng/assets/files/other/icrc-002-0990.pdf>.

[53] The Manual can be found here: <http://ihlresearch.org/amw/Commentary%20on%20the%20HPCR%20Manual.pdf>. The Program on Humanitarian Policy and Conflict Research is a research and policy programme that provides technical assistance and information support for international organizations engaged in humanitarian action and conflict transformation. The Program was established in August 2000 as a collaborative effort of the Harvard School of Public Health (HSPH), the Executive Office of the United Nations Secretary-General, and the Swiss Federal Department of Foreign Affairs, with the governments of Switzerland and Sweden serving as its core donors.

[54] The document was drafted by Arne Willy Dahl, Bruno Demeyere, Yoram Dinstein (Chair), Wolff Heintschel von Heinegg, Jean-François Queguiner, and Michael N. Schmitt.

As a follow-on to the Manual's publication, a team of experts—all of whom were involved in the drafting of the Manual—were made available to deliver two- or three-day tailored courses to groups of military professionals (either operators or military lawyers).[55] Such training courses are organized by the Geneva Centre for Security Policy. It is stated on the Centre's webpage that the Centre will be 'delighted to hear from any nations or institutions that are considering taking advantage of the courses'.[56]

The Manual does not have binding force but nevertheless seeks to 'present a methodical restatement of existing international law on air and missile warfare, based on the general practice of States accepted as law (*opinio juris*) and treaties in force'.[57] It is emphasized in the introduction to the document that no attempt has been made to 'be innovative or to come up with a *lex ferenda* (however desirable this may appear to be): the sole aim has been to systematically capture in the text the *lex lata* as it is.'

Nevertheless, it is also stated in the introduction that: 'From the onset of the Project, it was perceived that—if the *HPCR Manual* is to have any impact in the world of reality—it cannot be finalized without prior consultations with Governments.'[58] While the HPCR did not seek the endorsement of governments for the Manual, it believes that their views as to the applicable law are indispensable to the elaboration of both the Black-letter Rules and the Commentary. Participating government representatives provided many critical comments and observations. These were subsequently reviewed by the Group of Experts, leading to a considerable revision of the HPCR Manual.

There might arguably be a conflict—or at least a potential conflict—between, on the one hand, 'stating the *lex lata* law as it is' and, on the other hand, consulting with selected states with a view to ensuring that the identified law is acceptable to them.

The Manual is mainly applicable in international armed conflicts. However, some rules are also found to be applicable in non-international armed conflict. It is indicated in the commentary to the Manual—on a section-by-section or rule-by-rule basis—whether the same or similar rules are also applicable in non-international armed conflict.

Human rights norms are almost entirely excluded from the Manual. It is explained in the introduction to the Manual that 'there was discussion of human rights'law without agreement. Most members of the Group of Experts believe that

55 Geneva Centre for Security Policy, 'Emerging Security Challenges Programme', <http://www.gcsp.ch/Emerging-Security-Challenges/AMPLE>.

56 A two-day training course on the Manual was organized in Denmark in spring 2014 for, inter alia, military lawyers and operators.

57 Program on Humanitarian Policy and Conflict Research, 'Commentary on the HPCR Manual on International Law Applicable to Air and Missile Warfare' (Published paper, Mar. 2010): 2.

58 The following states were consulted during the drafting process: Belgium, Brazil, Canada, Democratic Republic of Congo, People's Republic of China, Denmark, Egypt, France, India, Italy, Japan, Jordan, Republic of Korea, Mexico, Netherlands, Nigeria, Norway, Pakistan, Russian Federation, Saudi Arabia, Spain, Sweden, Switzerland, United Kingdom, and United States.

it has only minimal bearing on air and missile warfare in international armed conflicts because the law of armed conflict is *lex specialis*.'[59] However, IHRL might play a role in situations of international armed conflict, as stated by the European Court of Human Rights in *Hassan v. UK* in 2014: '… consistently with the case-law of the International Court of Justice, the Court considers that, even in situations of international armed conflict, the safeguards under the Convention continue to apply, albeit interpreted against the background of the provisions of international humanitarian law'.[60] Furthermore, the ECtHR has, in several cases, applied the ECHR to the conduct of hostilities, for instance during Russian airstrikes in Chechnya in 2011.[61] See section 2 for more details on the application of IHRL in times of armed conflict.

3.7 The Danish Ministry of Foreign Affairs, *The Copenhagen Guidelines and Principles on the Handling of Detainees in International Military Operations*, October 2012

The Copenhagen Principles[62] were initiated by the Danish Ministry of Foreign Affairs in 2007 and concluded on 19 October 2012 when sixteen states 'welcomed' the Copenhagen Process Principles and Guidelines.[63] The ICRC was invited to participate as an observer. The Copenhagen Guidelines apply to international military operations in the context of non-international armed conflict, and peace operations.[64]

The purpose of the Copenhagen Guidelines is not to create new legal obligations or authorizations under international law, but to develop principles to guide the implementation of the existing obligations with respect to detention in international military operations.[65]

Nonetheless, in 2013, shortly after the adoption of the Copenhagen Guidelines, the UK Ministry of Defence claimed, in a case before the UK High Court of Justice, that the Guidelines could be seen as evidence of CIHL. The case concerned the UK

[59] Program on Humanitarian Policy and Conflict Research, 'Commentary on the HPCR Manual on International Law Applicable to Air and Missile Warfare' (Published paper, Mar. 2010): 6.

[60] ECtHR (GC), *Hassan v. The United Kingdom*, App. no. 29750/09, 16 Sept. 2014, para. 103.

[61] See ECtHR, *Kerimova v. Russia*, 3 May 2011.

[62] The Copenhagen Principles and Guidelines can be found here: <http://um.dk/en/~/media/UM/English-site/Documents/Politics-and-diplomacy/Copenhangen%20Process%20Principles%20and%20Guidelines.pdf>. Consult the chapter by Bruce 'Ossie' Oswald in this volume for a more thorough and comprehensive description and discussion of the Guidelines.

[63] Eighteen states participated in the meeting on 19 Oct. 2012, namely: Argentina, Australia, Canada, China, Denmark (Host), France, Finland, Germany, Malaysia, the Netherlands, Norway, the Russian Federation, South Africa, Sweden, Turkey, Uganda, United Kingdom, United States of America. Two States—Sweden and Russia—were unwilling to welcome the Copenhagen Guidelines without noting the lack of reference to international human rights norms in the Copenhagen Guidelines. See the text.

[64] 'The Chairman's Commentary to the Copenhagen Process: Principles and Guidelines' in the Copenhagen Principles and Guidelines, para. 1.2.

[65] Principle II in the Copenhagen Principles and Guidelines.

military's detention of an Afghan detainee in Afghanistan in 2010. However, this was rejected by the Court:

> The MOD's contention that a legal power to detain exists as a matter of customary IHL is primarily based on a set of principles and guidelines developed in the Copenhagen Process on the Handling of Detainees in International Military Operations ... The MOD [cannot] rely on the Copenhagen Process Principles as evidence of customary international law. I note in any event that the Copenhagen Process Principles again do not themselves purport to provide a legal basis for detention. Principle 4 merely requires that detention must be justified on the basis of 'applicable international law.'[66]

There are no references to human rights standards in the Copenhagen Guidelines, either in the introductory remarks or in the sixteen principles contained in the Guidelines.

The delegation of Sweden stated during the final meeting in October 2012 in Copenhagen that the Swedish interpretation of the reference to international law in principle 16[67] is that this also includes human rights law, and that Sweden would have preferred if this had been stated explicitly in principle 16.[68] Likewise, the Russian Federation indicated at the final meeting in Copenhagen that the 'Copenhagen Process could contribute more to the safeguarding of the humane treatment of detainees by placing greater emphasis on their inherent rights which derive from the international human rights law and the international humanitarian law'.[69]

3.8 The NATO Cooperative Cyber Defence Centre of Excellence, *Tallinn Manual on the International Law Applicable to Cyber Warfare*, 2013

In 2009, the NATO Cooperative Cyber Defence Centre of Excellence[70] invited an independent international group of experts to produce a manual on the law governing cyber warfare.[71] The editorial committee for the Manual consisted of six persons.[72] ICRC was invited as an observer. The Manual is applicable to international and non-international armed conflicts.

[66] UK, High Court of Justice, [2014] EWHC 1369 (QB), 2 May 2014, paras 262, 266, and 267.

[67] Principle 16 reads: 'Nothing in *The Copenhagen Process Principles and Guidelines* affects the applicability of international law to international military operations conducted by the States or international organizations; or the obligations of their personnel to respect such law; or the applicability of international or national law to non-State actors.'

[68] Minutes of the '3rd Copenhagen Conference on the Handling of Detainees in International Military Operations', 18–19 Oct. 2012, <http://um.dk/en/~/media/UM/English-site/Documents/Politics-and-diplomacy/Official%20minutes_CP%20ny.pdf>.

[69] Minutes of the '3rd Copenhagen Conference on the Handling of Detainees in International Military Operations', 18–19 Oct. 2012, <http://um.dk/en/~/media/UM/English-site/Documents/Politics-and-diplomacy/Official%20minutes_CP%20ny.pdf>.

[70] The Centre is an international military organization based in Tallinn, Estonia, and accredited in 2008 by NATO as a 'Centre for Excellence'. See: <http://www.ccdcoe.org>.

[71] *Tallinn Manual on the International Law Applicable to Cyber Warfare* (2013).

[72] Namely Michael Schmitt (General Editor and Director of the project), William H. Boothby, Bruno Demeyere, Wolff Heintschel von Heinegg, James Bret Michael, and Thomas Wingfield.

It is highlighted in the introduction to the Manual that:

> there are no provisions that directly deal with cyber "warfare". Similarly, because State cyber practice and publicly available expressions of *opinio juris* are sparse, it is sometimes difficult to definitively conclude that any cyber-specific customary international law norm exists. This being so, any claim that every assertion in the Manual represents an incontrovertible restatement of international law would be an exaggeration ... the Rules set forth in the Tallinn Manual reflect consensus among Experts as to the applicable *lex lata*, that is, the law currently governing cyber conflict. It does not set forth *lex ferenda* best practice, or preferred policy.[73]

There are no references to IHRL and substantive IHRL is not reflected in the Manual, for example in relation to the rules on detained persons or children. It is highlighted in the introduction of the Manual that it is 'without prejudice to other applicable fields of international law, such as international human rights'.[74]

3.9 GCPEA, *The Lucens Guidelines for Protecting Schools and Universities from Military Use during Armed Conflict*, December 2014

The Global Coalition to Protect Education from Attack (GCPEA)[75] was established in 2010 by organizations from the fields of education in emergencies and conflict-affected fragile states.[76]

The Lucens Guidelines were drafted by a former British military officer and a drafting committee including state representatives and other experts after consultations with experts from governments, militaries, UN agencies, and international and human rights organizations. In November 2012, GCPEA convened a group of experts in Lucens, Switzerland, in order to consult them on the document. The experts included representatives from twelve states, as well as the human rights and humanitarian law community. The Guidelines were finalized via a state-led process headed by Norway and Argentina in December 2014.

Under the leadership of Norway and Argentina, states participated in consultations on the Safe Schools Declaration in May 2015.[77] By signing the Declaration, states can endorse the Guidelines and commit themselves to 'use the Guidelines, and bring them into domestic policy and operational frameworks as far as possible and appropriate'. Furthermore, by signing the Declaration, states agree to 'meet

[73] *Tallinn Manual on the International Law Applicable to Cyber Warfare* (2013): 19.

[74] *Tallinn Manual on the International Law Applicable to Cyber Warfare* (2013): 18.

[75] Global Coalition to Protect Education from Attack, *Draft Lucens Guidelines for Protecting Schools and Universities from Military Use during Armed Conflict*, Oct. 2014, <http://www.protectingeducation.org/draft-lucens-guidelines-protecting-schools-and-universities-military-use-during-armed-conflict>.

[76] GCPEA is governed by a steering committee consisting of: CARA (Council for At-Risk Academics), Human Rights Watch (HRW), Institute of International Education/IIE Scholar Rescue Fund, Protect Education in Insecurity and Conflict (PEIC), Save the Children, UNICEF, UNESCO, and UNHCR.

[77] Global Coalition to Protect Education from Attack, 'Safe Schools Declaration', May 2015, <http://www.protectingeducation.org/sites/default/files/documents/safe_schools_declaration-final.pdf>.

on a regular basis, inviting relevant international organizations and civil society, so as to review the implementation of this declaration and the use of the guidelines'.

It is laid down in the introduction to the Guidelines that they respect international law as it stands and do not propose to change it. They are not legally binding in themselves and do not affect existing obligations under international law. The Guidelines are intended to generate a shift in behaviour that will lead to better protections for schools and universities in times of armed conflict.

The legal framework applicable to the targeting of schools and universities during armed conflicts is found primarily in IHL. It is, however, highlighted in the Guidelines that while IHL 'contains all the rules governing targeting, it is less focused on the use of schools in support of the military effort, which is also affected by international human rights law. It is, therefore, important to acknowledge at the outset that the law of armed conflict is complemented by international human rights law.'

3.10 Conclusion

A number of new soft law instruments have been adopted in the last two decades regulating areas of armed conflict that states have been unwilling or unable to regulate in treaty law. These instruments cover a wide range of important issues, including: sea warfare; air and missile warfare; cyber warfare; interpretation of the notion of direct participation in hostilities; non-international armed conflicts; private military companies; detention in international military operations (in non-international armed conflicts); and protecting schools and universities from military use and attack during armed conflict.

These areas are—most often—covered by the general rules in existing IHL hard law, for example in the Geneva and Hague Conventions, but more specific and detailed tailor-made rules have been identified in the above-mentioned soft law instruments.

This development gives rise to a number of observations, discussed in section 4.

4. Observations and Discussion

4.1 From hard law to soft law

During the last twenty years and particularly over the last decade, there has been a shift in how armed conflict is regulated: from hard law to soft law.

As mentioned, armed conflict has traditionally been regulated by hard law, that is, treaties and customary international law. Starting with the adoption of the very first Geneva Convention in 1864 on protection of wounded in armies in the field, a large number of conventions have been adopted restricting means and methods of warfare (the Hague Conventions) and protecting persons who are not, or are no longer, taking part in hostilities (the Geneva Conventions).

In addition to treaty law, CIHL has played an important role in regulating armed conflict in particular in the eighteenth and nineteenth centuries before states agreed on the first Geneva and Hague Conventions in the late nineteenth century. In recent years, there has again been much focus on CIHL and how it can assist in regulating armed conflict, particularly non-international armed conflict. The first ICRC endeavour to identify CIHL was the San Remo Manual on International Law applicable to Armed Conflicts at Sea from 1994. This led to the ICRC initiating its own large-scale CIHL Study in 1996.

Soft law has traditionally played an insignificant role in regulating armed conflict. It is only during the last two decades that a large number of soft law instruments have emerged as described in section 3. This is decades behind developments in the human rights field, where a large number of soft law documents have been adopted, for example by various UN bodies including the UN General Assembly and the Human Rights Council, and by treaty bodies since the 1970s.[78]

The move towards government of this field via soft law instruments may cause concern. It is of utmost importance in times of armed conflict to have clear, precise, and binding instructions for the soldiers involved in the fighting. Guidelines or optional principles are not very helpful in the chaos of war.

4.2 From the involvement of the ICRC and all states—to the involvement of a few selected experts and a few states

Another observation is that the role of ICRC in developing new soft law instruments applicable in armed conflict has diminished and now seems to be rather limited. This development seems to be at odds with the agreement among states that one of the important roles of the ICRC is 'to work for the understanding and dissemination of knowledge of international humanitarian law applicable in armed conflicts and *to prepare any development thereof*' (emphasis added). This is laid down in the Statutes of the International Red Cross and Red Crescent Movement, adopted by, among others, all states parties to the Geneva Conventions on the Twenty-Fifth International Conference of the Red Cross, in October 1986.[79]

Also in practice, the ICRC has historically played a crucial role in developing new rules for armed conflict. In fact, it has been claimed that the ICRC has been the 'main driving force behind the development of international humanitarian law for 140 years'.[80]

[78] See e.g.: in relation to the administration of justice see, inter alia: Standard Minimum Rules on the Treatment of Prisoners, 1977; Code of Conduct for Law Enforcement Officials, 1979; and the Basic Principles on the Use of Force and Firearms by Law Enforcement Officials, 1990. A list of human rights soft law instruments can be found at: <http://www.ohchr.org/EN/ProfessionalInterest/Pages/UniversalHumanRightsInstruments.aspx>.

[79] International Conference of the International Red Cross and Red Crescent Movement, *Handbook of the International Red Cross and Red Crescent Movement* (14th edn, 2008), <https://www.icrc.org/eng/assets/files/publications/icrc-002-0962.pdf>. The International Conference is the supreme deliberative body of the International Red Cross and Red Crescent Movement. It brings together all the components of the Movement and all the states parties to the Geneva Conventions. It normally meets once every four years.

[80] F. Bugnion, 'The Role of the Red Cross in the Development of International Humanitarian Law: The International Committee of the Red Cross and the Development of International Humanitarian Law', *Chicago Journal of International Law* vol. 5 (Summer 2004): 1.

The role of the ICRC in preparing new IHL treaty law has typically been threefold, namely (i) to take the initiative and seek the support of states for a new IHL treaty; (ii) to prepare the draft treaty that is used for deliberations at an International Conference comprising all states parties (i.e. all states, since the Geneva Conventions have been ratified by all states); and (iii) to participate in the deliberations at the International Conference in which all states are participating.[81]

The existing IHL hard and soft law standards drafted and adopted with the assistance of the ICRC and the Red Cross Movement have been adopted pursuant to a transparent, inclusive, and open consultative process involving all states.[82] In terms of the more recent soft law instruments, it is evident that the role of the ICRC has been limited to that of a passive observer on the same footing as other international organizations such as the UN, NATO, EU, and the Council of Europe. The new soft law instruments have been developed by: a small group of selected international experts (often the same experts); a small group of selected states (see section 3); or a combination of selected experts and selected states (e.g. the HPCR *Manual on International Law Applicable to Air and Missile Warfare*, which was drafted by a small group of experts and then presented to a small group of selected states for their views and comments). It is not clear how the experts and states involved have been selected.

Whether the reason for this is that the ICRC has deliberately been excluded from the drafting process, or rather that the ICRC itself has decided to play a less active role in the drafting of soft law instruments, is not clear. In any event, it is clear that there has been a remarkable change in who is developing new IHL rules: from the involvement of ICRC and all states, to the involvement of a small, selected group of experts and a few selected states.

Furthermore, it is clear that the new soft law IHL instruments developed by a few experts and/or a few states in what appears to be a more closed and exclusionary process will not have the same broad legitimacy as the IHL rules that have been developed by the ICRC and adopted at an international conference including all states. The ICRC has, as described, an international mandate from all states to develop new rules applicable in armed conflict and, furthermore, IHL treaty law has traditionally been discussed and adopted by all states at international conferences often organized by the ICRC.

4.3 Blurred description of legal authority—hard or soft law?

The nine new soft law instruments described in section 3 are referred to as manuals, guidance, papers, documents, and studies. Their names therefore indicate that they

[81] Bugnion (2004): 3.

[82] For an example of a transparent, inclusive, and open drafting process, see the existing ICRC initiatives on strengthening compliance with IHL and the protection of persons deprived of their liberty. More information about these initiatives can be found at: <https://www.icrc.org/eng/what-we-do/other-activities/development-ihl/index.jsp>.

are of a non-binding character. However, there are major differences in how they describe their legal authority.

Three instruments clearly identify themselves—in their name and introductory section—as soft law instruments of a non-binding character, namely: the Montreux Document, which seeks to 'provide guidance on a number of difficult and unclear practical and legal points' (see section 3.4); the Copenhagen Guidelines and Principles, which seek to 'develop principles to guide the implementation of existing obligations' (see section 3.7); and *The Lucens Guidelines for Protecting Schools and Universities from Military Use during Armed Conflict* (see section 3.9).

On the other side of the spectrum, three instruments—those that the ICRC has been actively involved in preparing, the San Remo Manual on Armed Conflicts at Sea (see section 3.1), the study on *Customary International Humanitarian Law* (see section 3.2), and the *Interpretative Guidance on the Notion of Direct Participation in Hostilities* (see section 3.5)—claim to be straightforward expressions of customary international law or an authoritative 'interpretation of IHL within existing legal parameters' (see the Interpretive Guidance) and thus binding on all states as hard law. In this sense, it can be disputed whether they are 'real' soft law instruments. However, they have been included in this overview because a number of states have been unwilling to accept the identified rules as customary international law or as an interpretation of hard law standards. It is likely that these states would qualify the instruments as soft law instruments.

Finally, the last three instruments—the San Remo Manual on Non-International Armed Conflict (see section 3.3), the Manual on Air and Missile Warfare (see section 3.6), and the Tallinn Manual on Cyber Warfare (see section 3.8)—are all described as non-binding soft law instruments, but at the same time it is claimed in the introductory paragraphs of the instruments that the identified rules in the manuals reflect (at least partially) *lex lata*, for example customary international law.

Hence, many of the guidelines and manuals seem to reflect a blurred mix of hard and soft law standards. Some instruments are clearly labelled as soft law instruments, but at the same time seek to gain authority from including hard law obligations; that is, customary international law.

Furthermore, even though a manual or guideline is clearly described as a non-binding soft law document containing guiding principles, there is evidently a risk that the document will be used—or possibly misused—as evidence of customary IHL, as the UK Ministry of Defence tried to do with the Copenhagen Principles (see section 3.7).

4.4 From soft law to hard law? States 'acceding' to a soft law instrument by means of a unilateral declaration

States must undertake a certain procedure to become legally bound by a treaty, that is by acceding or ratifying the treaty, meaning that a state becomes a participating state to the treaty.[83] The same is not expected or required in terms of soft law instruments. Soft law instruments comprise non-binding rules and states may, of their own free will and discretion, decide whether they want to follow the guidance and best practice often contained in these instruments.

Given this background, it is remarkable that states can 'accede' to two of the abovementioned soft law instruments. The Montreux Document on Private Military Companies (see section 3.4) establishes a mechanism where states can 'join' the instrument and become a 'participating State of the Montreux Document'—as it is described in the instrument and on the homepage about the instrument.[84] States can become a 'party to' or 'join' the document by communicating their support for the document to the Federal Department of Foreign Affairs of Switzerland (FDFA). The FDFA maintains a webpage about the Montreux Document and updates the webpage upon receipt of supporting statements from states.[85]

A similar mechanism is established in the *Lucens Guidelines for Protecting Schools and Universities during Armed Conflict* (see section 3.9). By signing a so-called Safe Schools Declaration, states can endorse the Guidelines and commit to use the Guidelines and to meet on a regular basis to review the implementation of the guidelines (see section 3.9). Such unilateral statements on the support for and effective implementation of a soft law instrument—and possible international supervision in the form of regular meetings of states 'parties'—are not known in relation to IHRL soft law instruments. In the UN General Assembly and the UN Human Rights Council, states can vote in favour of or against a soft law IHRL document, for example a UN resolution. However, this does not entail a commitment to support or, indeed, implement the soft law instrument at the domestic level.

Hence, this appears to be a novel way to seek the implementation of non-binding soft law instruments. We may question the international law implications of a state signing such a unilateral declaration and expressing its commitment to support and implement a non-binding soft law instrument. Can such a unilateral declaration potentially transform soft law standards into hard law obligations? The answer will depend on the wording of the concrete declaration, and it is outside the scope of this chapter to discuss this in further detail. However, it should be recalled that the ICJ, in the *Nuclear Test* case in 1974, found that France was bound under international law by public statements from its President and Foreign and Defence Ministers to cease nuclear testing in the South Pacific. Based on this ruling, the International Law Commission (ILC) has laid down a basic guiding principle: 'Declarations publicly made and manifesting the will to be bound may have the effect of creating legal obligations.'[86]

[83] See Art. 1(b) of the Vienna Convention on the Law of Treaties.

[84] Swiss Federal Department of Foreign Affairs, 'Participating States of the Montreux Document', <https://www.eda.admin.ch/eda/en/fdfa/foreign-policy/international-law/international-humanitarian-law/private-military-security-companies/participating-states.html>.

[85] Swiss Federal Department of Foreign Affairs, 'Participating States of the Montreux Document', <https://www.eda.admin.ch/eda/en/fdfa/foreign-policy/international-law/international-humanitarian-law/private-military-security-companies/participating-states.html>.

[86] ILC, Guiding Principles Applicable to Unilateral Declarations of States Capable of Creating Legal Obligations, with commentaries thereto (2006), UN Doc. A/61/10, Guiding Principle 1.

4.5 Are customary international humanitarian law and human rights law reflected in recent soft law instruments regulating armed conflict?

As described in section 4.3, all seven soft law instruments clearly incorporate, draw on, or refer to CIHL. This is not surprising, since CIHL is clearly a relevant legal source in international as well as non-international armed conflict.

Similarly, it is evident, as discussed in section 2, that IHRL is a relevant source of law in armed conflicts. Hence, it is remarkable that only three of the nine described soft law instruments reflect or incorporate international human rights norms, namely: the ICRC study on *Customary International Humanitarian Law* (section 3.2); the Montreux Document (section 3.4), and the Lucens Guidelines (section 3.9).

The rest of the described soft law instruments deliberately exclude IHRL. In some soft law instruments, IHRL is perceived as irrelevant to the subject matter dealt with in the instrument; in others, IHRL is perceived as relevant but considered to lie outside the scope of the instrument.

A large proportion of the new soft law instruments thus reflect an outdated legal position that prevailed more than twenty years ago, namely that IHL and IHRL are two distinct and separate systems of norms, with IHL only applicable in armed conflict and IHRL only applicable in times of peace. As a consequence of this situation, states bear the risk of being criticized by human rights bodies if they follow soft law instruments excluding IHRL, while European states even run the risk of a case being held against them by the ECtHR and being ordered to provide redress and compensation.

For example, if a state is carrying out preventive detention of a detainee in a non-international armed conflict for security reasons, as provided for in the Copenhagen Guidelines on the Handling of Detainees—or if a state launches a missile in a populated area in an armed conflict, in line with guidance on collateral damage assessments provided in the HPCR *Manual on International Law Applicable to Air and Missile Warfare*—there is a potential risk that these state actions would conflict with the more restrictive standards on the right to life and the right to liberty in IHRL hard law.

5. Concluding Observations

It has been argued in this chapter that, at the normative level, there has been a remarkable change in how armed conflict has been regulated within the last fifteen years. This has included a change from hard law to soft law standards—from standards being prepared by the ICRC and discussed, drafted, and adopted by states in an open and transparent process, to soft law standards being prepared and adopted by a small group of selected experts/organizations and a few selected states in an often more closed and non-transparent process. These soft law instruments identify international rules and claim to be universally relevant, rather than relevant only to the states involved in drafting and adopting the instrument. This development may be cause for concern, as there is a risk of fragmentation and polarization of IHL soft law standards.

There are also major differences between the development, role, and function of soft law in the fields of IHRL and IHR.

With regard to the *development of soft law standards*, IHL soft law is, as mentioned, often drafted and adopted by means of a rather closed and non-transparent process by a small number of experts and states. This is not the case with IHRL soft law. This difference may be explained by the fact that, with regard to IHRL, there are well-established formal structures, institutions, and procedures for creating soft law, in particular the UN Human Rights Council and the various UN treaty bodies. This is not the case for IHL. As highlighted by the ICRC, 'the Geneva conventions, are an exception among international treaties in that they do not provide States with a regular opportunity to meet in order to take stock of and exchange opinions on ways of enhancing observance of this body of laws'.[87] Given this background, the ICRC is currently carrying out a consultation process with states with a view to establish a forum for regular meetings between states.[88] The 'Meeting of States' should serve as a dedicated forum for states to discuss issues of common concern and matters related to the implementation of and compliance with IHL, with the goal of strengthening respect for this body of law.[89]

The lack of a formal state forum and structures for discussing and elaborating soft law instruments may explain why experts, international organizations, and various groups of states have begun drawing up new soft law standards on their own initiative. A 'Meeting of States' could potentially function as a forum for drafting and adopting IHL soft law standards and, in this way, counter the risk of fragmentation and polarization of IHL soft law.

The lack of a formal state forum and structures for adopting soft law instruments within the field of IHL may also explain the process of states 'acceding'/'joining'/'endorsing' IHL soft law instruments described in section 4.4. A similar process is not known in relation to IHRL soft law instruments.

There are also important differences with regard to the *role and function* of soft law in the area of IHL and IHRL. It is often argued that in a rapidly changing and developing world order, soft law is a 'vital intermediate stage towards a more rigorously binding system, permitting experiment and rapid modification'.[90] In areas where a norm gap exists, soft law can function as a temporary and intermediate norm-filler until hard law norms have been adopted or emerge (in terms of

[87] ICRC, Background Document for the Fourth Meeting of States on Strengthening Compliance with International Humanitarian Law (23 and 24 Apr. 2005): 6.

[88] The question was discussed at the 32nd International Conference of the Red Cross and Red Crescent in Dec. 2015 and it was recommended that the ICRC continues the consultation process and seeks to 'find agreement on features and functions of a potential forum of States and to find ways to enhance the implementation of IHL'. See: para. 2 in the adopted resolution on 'Strengthening Compliance with International Humanitarian Law', 8–10 Dec. 2015.

[89] ICRC, 'Strengthening Compliance with International Humanitarian Law' (8–10 Dec. 2015).

[90] H. Thirlway, *The Sources of International Law* (Oxford: Oxford University Press, 2014): 164.

customary international law). Within the human rights field, soft law has often played a norm-filling or a norm-creating role as discussed in the Introduction to this book. Its purpose has essentially been to address human rights norm gaps.

There is, arguably, no norm gap in contemporary armed conflict. Rather there is—in addition to IHL—an abundance of various international hard law norms, including, most prominently, IHRL, CIHL, and binding chapter VII resolutions from the UN Security Council. Norms that are not elaborated directly to regulate situations of armed conflict or specific types of armed conflict (e.g. non-international armed conflicts or transnational non-international armed conflicts) sometimes directly conflict with standards in IHL. Hence, in the area of armed conflict, it might provocatively be argued that soft law plays the role of a *norm-excluder* rather than a norm-filler or norm-creator. It is remarkable that many of the new soft law instruments dealt with in this chapter deliberately exclude IHRL, even though there is a strong consensus among judicial bodies, states, and international organizations that human rights is a relevant legal source in times of armed conflict.

This new trend may be cause for some concern. Rules applicable in times of armed conflict, including soft law standards, should preferably be based on broad international consensus and should take into consideration and reflect all international norms applicable in armed conflict, including international human rights law.

8

Addressing and Resolving Internal Displacement

Reflections on a Soft Law 'Success Story'

Megan Bradley and Angela Sherwood

1. Introduction

By 2015, there were more people displaced by conflict and human rights violations than at any point since the end of the Second World War.[1] Some 19.5 million of the global displaced population are refugees who have sought asylum outside their country of origin, and are protected by formal agreements such as the 1951 Convention relating to the status of refugees, or the 1969 Organization for African Unity Convention governing the specific aspects of refugee problems in Africa. However, almost twice as many people—over 38 million worldwide—have been uprooted within their own countries by violence and human rights abuses, while millions are internally displaced every year by natural disasters.[2]

Because IDPs (internally displaced persons) remain within their own countries, protecting and assisting them is, first and foremost, the responsibility of the national government—even when these governments are directly complicit in generating displacement crises in the first place. Efforts to ensure a more systematic response to internal displacement crises gained steam in the late 1980s, and advanced significantly with the nomination of a Representative of the UN Secretary-General (RSG) on IDPs, who marshalled an international team of legal experts to lead the development of the 1998 Guiding Principles on Internal Displacement ('Guiding Principles').[3] Based on international human rights and humanitarian law and analogous refugee law, the Guiding Principles have been widely endorsed by states, international organizations, and non-governmental organizations as a key standard

[1] Megan Bradley's work on this chapter was supported with a grant from the Social Sciences and Humanities Research Council of Canada.

[2] 'Worldwide displacement hits all time high as war and persecution increase', UNHCR News Stories, 18 June 2015, <http://www.unhcr.org/558193896.html>.

[3] UN High Commissioner for Refugees (UNHCR), 'Guiding Principles on Internal Displacement', 22 July 1998, ADM 1.1, PRL 12.1, PR00/98/109.

clarifying the rights of IDPs, and the primary responsibility of states to protect them. Indeed, the Guiding Principles are regarded in many quarters as one of the most successful examples of the use of 'soft law' standards to influence responses to a human rights issue on local, national, and international levels, providing a model that has been emulated by advocates working on a range of other concerns.[4] Further reflecting the Guiding Principles' success, in 2009 African Union (AU) member states adopted the AU Convention for the protection and assistance of IDPs in Africa (Kampala Convention).[5] Based significantly on the Guiding Principles, the Convention entered into force in December 2012.[6]

At the same time as the approach to internal displacement laid out in the Guiding Principles has become broadly recognized and accepted, even to the point of codification in hard laws such as the Kampala Convention, the number of people uprooted within their own countries has continued to climb, owing to massive new displacement crises as well as to the increasingly protracted nature of displacement situations. That is, IDPs have been unable to access solutions to their predicament.[7] This situation is at odds with the Guiding Principles and the Kampala Convention, which indicate that upholding the rights of IDPs entails not only protection and assistance at the height of crises, but also support for the sustainable resolution of displacement. In the parlance of the forced migration regime, IDPs have a right to a 'durable solution' to their displacement. This challenge is addressed in detail in an important but under-examined tool, the 2010 Inter-Agency Standing Committee (IASC) Framework on Durable Solutions for Internally Displaced Persons.[8] Like the Guiding Principles, the IASC Framework was developed under the leadership of the RSG on IDPs. Building on the Guiding Principles, the rights-based IASC Framework identifies three potential 'durable solutions' to internal displacement: return and reintegration of IDPs in their

[4] R. Cohen, 'Lessons learned from the Development of the Guiding Principles on Internal Displacement' (Working Paper, Georgetown University Institute for the Study of International Migration Working Paper, 2013).

[5] African Union, 'African Union Convention for the Protection and Assistance of Internally Displaced Persons in Africa (Kampala Convention)', 22 Oct. 2009, <http://www.unhcr.org/4ae9bede9.html>.

[6] A. M. Abebe, 'The African Union Convention on Internally Displaced Persons: Its Codification Background, Scope, and Enforcement Challenges', *Refugee Survey Quarterly* vol. 29 (2010): 28–57. The Kampala Convention was the world's first regional convention on internal displacement, but was preceded by a binding sub-regional standard, the Great Lakes Protocol. The Great Lakes Protocol is outside the scope of this chapter; for further discussion of this standard see: C. Beyani, 'Recent Developments: The Elaboration of a Legal Framework for the Protection of Internally Displaced Persons in Africa', *Journal of African Law* vol. 50 (2006): 187–97.

[7] As of 2011 the majority of the world's IDPs were living in protected displacement situations that had lasted at least five years. See: IDMC and Brookings-LSE Project on Internal Displacement, 'IDPs in Protracted Displacement: Is Local Integration a Solution?' (Report from the Second Expert Seminar on Protracted Internal Displacement, 19–20 Jan. 2011) <http://www.internal-displacement.org/publications/2011/idps-in-protracted-displacement-is-local-integration-a-solution>.

[8] IASC, 'IASC Framework on Durable Solutions for Internally Displaced Persons' (Brookings-Bern Project on Internal Displacement, Washington DC, 2010). The IASC is the main international mechanism for coordination between humanitarian actors within and outside the UN system. It also involves major development agencies. See <http://www.humanitarianinfo.org/iasc/>.

communities of origin; local integration in the communities where they sought shelter; or relocation and sustainable integration elsewhere within their country.[9] According to the Framework, 'durable solutions' have been achieved when IDPs 'no longer have specific assistance and protection needs that are linked to their displacement and such persons can enjoy their human rights without discrimination on account of their displacement'.[10]

Previous scholarship has extensively analysed the origins and evolution of the Guiding Principles, and their remarkable influence as a soft law tool.[11] Building on this foundation, this chapter explores how the Guiding Principles and subsequent standards including the IASC Framework have contributed to the construction of the critical concept of 'durable solutions', and shaped discourse and practice on this issue. It advances the literature by using a systematic analysis of national laws and policies on IDPs, and two fieldwork-informed case studies on efforts to resolve internal displacement as a lens through which to examine some of the particular contributions and constraints of soft law in addressing a complex human rights, humanitarian, and development issue. This focus is warranted because the resolution of displacement remains under-examined, notwithstanding the emergence of this issue as a defining concern for practitioners and for IDPs themselves. Our case studies bring into focus some of the strengths and limitations of efforts to ensure the implementation of soft law standards (as well as related hard law standards such as the Kampala Convention) through 'domestication' in national laws and policies.

We argue that the development of a soft law standard was essential to establishing the IDP issue on national and international agendas, and to making progress in understanding and better protecting the rights of IDPs, including as they pertain to the resolution of displacement. That is, to borrow the terms discussed by Gammeltoft-Hansen, Lagoutte, and Cerone in their Introduction to this volume, in this case soft law had both a 'norm-filling' and 'norm-creating' function. The strategy advanced by the architects of the IDP soft law framework of emphasizing the primary responsibility of states for those displaced within their borders, including by encouraging the integration of soft law standards into national laws and policies on IDPs, has had considerable traction, as evidenced by the adoption of scores of national laws and policies on the rights of IDPs and hard law standards such as the Kampala Convention, as well as by the engagement of donors,

[9] IASC Framework: A-1. [10] IASC Framework: 5.

[11] On the significance of the Guiding Principles as a soft law standard, see e.g.: Cohen (2013); P. Orchard, 'Protection of Internally Displaced Persons: Soft Law as a Norm-Generating Mechanism', *Review of International Studies* vol. 36 (2010): 281–303; W. Kälin, 'How Hard is Soft Law? The Guiding Principles on Internal Displacement and the Need for a Normative Framework' (Ralph Bunch Institute Round Table, City University of New York, 19 Dec. 2001); P. Orchard, 'Implementing a Global Internally Displaced Persons Protection Regime', in *Implementation and World Politics: How International Norms Change Practice*, ed. A. Betts and P. Orchard (Oxford: Oxford University Press, 2014); W. Kälin, 'The Guiding Principles on Internal Displacement as International Minimum Standard and Protection Tool', *Refugee Survey Quarterly* vol. 24 (2005): 27–36; T. Weiss and D. Korn, *Internal Displacement: Conceptualization and Its Consequences* (Abingdon: Routledge, 2006).

international organizations, and NGOs in responding to IDP situations. These developments both reflect and have influenced the emergence of a 'durable solutions discourse' that shapes how the resolution of displacement and the roles of different actors in this process are understood. However, norms on durable solutions remain contested and minimally interpreted, and struggle to exert influence in complex post-conflict and post-disaster contexts where even domestic laws are often not systematically and equitably implemented. Some government actors and humanitarian practitioners working in highly impoverished countries have suggested that rights-based tools such as the IASC Framework set an impossibly high bar for the standards that need to be achieved in order for a displacement situation to be understood to have ended.[12] Such sceptical perspectives are particularly evident in Haiti, where massive numbers of people were displaced by the January 2010 earthquake. In contrast, in other countries such as Sri Lanka, governments' rhetorical embrace of soft law principles on durable solutions has served as a foil to deflect criticism for the abuse of IDPs in practice.[13]

The chapter begins by providing a snapshot of the strategies underpinning the successful development and diffusion of the Guiding Principles.[14] It then considers the influence of soft law standards on durable solutions discourse and practice, highlighting the development of the IASC Framework and the approach to durable solutions articulated in the Kampala Convention as a hard law instrument significantly shaped by previous soft law standards. It deepens discussion of these issues through an analysis of how soft law-informed national laws and policies on internal displacement address the question of durable solutions, and through examination of the relationship between soft law and the pursuit of durable solutions in Haiti and Sri Lanka. In this chapter, as Chinkin urges, we understand soft law in its broad sense, ranging from formal agreements with only 'soft obligations ("legal soft law"), to non-binding or voluntary resolutions and codes of conduct formulated and accepted by international and regional organizations ("non-legal soft law"), to statements prepared by individuals in a non-governmental capacity, but which purport to lay down international principles'.[15]

[12] A. Sherwood, M. Bradley, L. Rossi, R. Gitau, and B. Mellicker, *Supporting Durable Solutions to Urban, Post-Disaster Displacement: Challenges and Opportunities in Haiti* (Washington, DC: Brookings/IOM, 2014).

[13] These cases were selected because they display important contrasts in terms of, inter alia, the causes of displacement, and the use of soft law standards by government officials and international actors. The Haiti case study draws on extensive fieldwork undertaken by the second author in Port-au-Prince from Oct. 2013 to Aug. 2014. The Sri Lanka case study is informed by fieldwork undertaken by the first author in 2013.

[14] Following the Guiding Principles, we view IDPs as those who 'have been forced or obliged to flee or to leave their homes or places of habitual residence, in particular as a result of or in order to avoid the effects of armed conflict, situations of generalized violence, violations of human rights or natural or human-made disasters, and who have not crossed an internationally recognized State border'.

[15] C. Chinkin, 'The Challenge of Soft Law: Development and Change in International Law', *International and Comparative Law Quarterly* vol. 38 (1989): 851. This definition may be interpreted as somewhat incongruent with the conception of soft law forwarded in the Introduction to this volume.

2. The Guiding Principles on Internal Displacement: A Soft Law Success Story

The development of the Guiding Principles was crucial to putting the IDP issue on the map, and to navigating states' concerns that addressing the rights and well-being of IDPs was a pretext for external meddling in internal affairs. Informed by the concept of 'sovereignty as responsibility' articulated by Francis Deng, the first RSG on IDPs, the Guiding Principles were developed at the request of the UN Commission on Human Rights, and were based largely on commitments that states had already made under binding international human rights and humanitarian law.[16] Rather than creating new legal commitments for states—an undertaking beyond the purview of an independent group of legal experts—the architects of the Principles engaged in 'norm-filling' by drawing out the implications of states' prior legal commitments for the IDP issue, endeavouring to clarify the rights of IDPs and the obligations of different actors, particularly states, at all stages of displacement.[17] This approach meant that it was unnecessary to present the Principles for formal state approval. Instead, RSG Deng simply delivered the Guiding Principles to the UN Commission on Human Rights in 1998, which 'took note' of the tool. Following this quiet introduction into the international arena, the Guiding Principles' proponents launched a steady, strategic campaign to raise awareness of and support for the Principles at the local, national, and international levels.

The success of this approach is in large part attributable to the eminent appropriateness of soft law for addressing a thorny issue such as internal displacement that is primed to rankle 'sovereignty-sensitive' states, and that did not, at least initially, seem possible to tackle through the development of new hard law instruments.[18] Success was also attributable to the strong focus of the Principles' proponents on translating and disseminating the tool, and gradually shoring up support through recognition of the standard in scores of resolutions passed by UN bodies and regional organizations. This culminated in the recognition by 193 heads of state at the 2005 UN World Summit of the Guiding Principles as an 'important international framework for the protection of IDPs'.[19] The Principles were

[16] On 'sovereignty as responsibility' see e.g.: R. Cohen and F. M. Deng, *Masses in Flight: The Global Crisis of Internal Displacement* (Washington, DC: Brookings Institution Press, 1998); F. Deng, *Sovereignty, Responsibility and Accountability* (Washington, DC: Brookings Institution Press, 1995).

[17] Some scholars have argued that the Guiding Principles did significantly more than simply restate existing law, but rather had a more explicitly 'norm-creating' function. See e.g.: Orchard (2010).

[18] As Gammeltoft-Hansen, Lagoutte, and Cerone note in the introduction of this volume, in 'some areas today, soft law constitutes a primary reference point, and yet there seem to be no immediate prospects for codification or crystallization of soft law into hard law'. This has certainly been the case in regards to the Guiding Principles. While welcoming the emergence of binding regional agreements such as the Kampala Convention, some leading IDP advocates continue to maintain that attempting to negotiate a UN treaty on internal displacement would not be advisable. See e.g.: W. Kälin, 'The Future of the Guiding Principles on Internal Displacement', *Forced Migration Review*, Special Issue (2008a): 38–9.

[19] UN General Assembly, 'World Summit Outcome: Resolution/Adopted by the General Assembly', 24 Oct. 2005, A/RES/60/1, para. 132.

integrated into training programmes and, perhaps most significantly, there was a strong focus amongst advocates on promoting their incorporation into domestic laws and policies on IDPs. The Kampala Convention shares this strong focus on the incorporation of IDP protection into domestic legal standards, explicitly requiring states parties to develop national laws on IDPs as the means of implementing the agreement.[20]

As Orchard observes, a 'central property of soft law as a norm-generating mechanism is its ability to contribute to the internalization of new norms within states by becoming entrenched in domestic legislation'.[21] Ideally, internalization results in norms having a 'taken-for-granted' quality that makes 'conformance with the norm almost automatic'.[22] Internalization of the Guiding Principles has been supported through national and international advocacy efforts, the development of tools for law and policy-makers, and the deployment of international advisers who spearheaded—sometimes with only modest domestic involvement—drafting processes.[23] As a result of such efforts, between 1998 and 2014, at least twenty-six countries adopted national laws or policies on IDPs.[24] This strong focus on domestic law and policy-making is in keeping with the positioning of internal displacement as first and foremost a matter of state responsibility in human rights discourse, and reflects the prominent role of lawyers with professional dispositions to focus on law and policy as a means to address internal displacement. Indeed, the development of a domestic legal framework for responding to IDPs is recognized as a key benchmark for assessing the extent to which states are shouldering their responsibilities towards their internally displaced populations.[25] However, as the following sections suggest, the efficacy of this approach in terms of concretely supporting the *resolution* of internal displacement has been limited by a range of factors, including the quality of the domestic laws and policies themselves; contested interpretations

[20] The comparatively rapid negotiation and entry into force of the Kampala Convention is a testament to the efficacy of the soft law-based approach adopted by the 'norm entrepreneurs' behind the Guiding Principles, but is largely outside the scope of this chapter. For further details, see e.g.: Abebe (2010) and M. Asplet and M. Bradley, 'Strengthened Protection for Internally Displaced Persons in Africa: The Kampala Convention Comes into Force', *American Society of International Law (ASIL) Insights* vol. 16 (2012), <https://www.asil.org/insights/volume/16/issue/36/strengthened-protection-internally-displaced-persons-africa-kampala>.

[21] Orchard (2010): 286.

[22] T. Risse and K. Sikkink, 'The Socialization of International Human Rights Norms into Domestic Practices: Introduction', in *The Power of Human Rights*, ed. T. Risse, S. C. Roppe, and K. Sikkink (Cambridge: Cambridge University Press, 1999): 15; Orchard (2010): 286.

[23] These tools include: Brookings-Bern Project on Internal Displacement, 'Protecting Internally Displaced Persons: A Manual for Law and Policymakers' (Washington, DC: Brookings-Bern Project on Internal Displacement, 2008) and Brookings-LSE Project on Internal Displacement, Internal Displacement Monitoring Centre and Norwegian Refugee Council, 'National Instruments on Internal Displacement: A Guide to their Development' (Geneva: IDMC, 2013).

[24] For a compendium of these standards, see the IDP Laws and Policies Index, <http://www.brookings.edu/about/projects/idp/resources/idp-policies-index>. This index includes more than fifty documents from over twenty-six countries. Notably, in addition to national standards, several laws and policies have been adopted at the sub-national level, and courts, particularly in Colombia, have developed a substantial body of jurisprudence on the rights of IDPs.

[25] Brookings-Bern Project on Internal Displacement, 'Addressing Internal Displacement: A Framework for National Responsibility' (Washington, DC: Brookings Institution, 2005).

of durable solutions concepts; and, more generally, the deeply political and economic nature of the pursuit of durable solutions.

3. The Role of Soft Law in Discourse and Standard-Setting on Durable Solutions

The Guiding Principles are comparatively brief in their discussion of durable solutions to displacement—indeed, they do not use the term 'durable solutions', but rather couch the provisions on the resolution of displacement in section V on 'Principles Relating to Return, Resettlement and Reintegration'. Principle 28, the main provision on the resolution of displacement, indicates that:

> Competent authorities have the primary duty and responsibility to establish conditions, as well as provide the means, which allow internally displaced persons to return voluntarily, in safety and with dignity, to their homes or places of habitual residence, or to resettle voluntarily in another part of the country. Such authorities shall endeavour to facilitate the reintegration of returned or resettled internally displaced persons.

Principle 28 goes on to stress the need to ensure the 'full participation' of IDPs in the process, while Principle 29 addresses non-discrimination against former IDPs; their right to equal access to public services and participation in public affairs; and the obligation of 'competent authorities' to facilitate the restitution of IDPs' lost property or, where this is not possible, 'appropriate compensation or another form of just reparation'. Principle 30 addresses the need for international actors to have access to IDPs to support return, resettlement, and reintegration.

Building on this foundation, over the course of the past ten years a range of related soft law standards and other tools have been developed that address the resolution of displacement. These standards import the term 'durable solutions' from the international refugee regime, where a trinity of durable solutions are promoted, including voluntary return to refugees' country of origin; local integration in the country of asylum; or resettlement to a third country. There are some important distinctions between the concepts and discourse surrounding 'durable solutions' for refugees and IDPs. First, vis-à-vis refugees, the term 'durable solutions' pertains significantly to refugees' lack of effective *citizenship*. While the pursuit of durable solutions for refugees certainly involves broad concerns around stability, peacebuilding, and development, the primary problem is, arguably, the 'regularization' of refugees' status, either through repatriation, or the acquisition of citizenship in the country of asylum or a resettlement state. In contrast, as IDPs are typically citizens (or 'habitual residents') of the country in which they are displaced, the 'regularization' of their citizenship status is not the predominant concern. Whereas voluntary repatriation is the only 'solution' to which refugees have a legal right, as citizens or habitual residents of the state in which they are displaced, soft law standards (and related binding standards such as the Kampala Convention) stress that IDPs have the right to freely choose a solution to their displacement.[26] These standards and

[26] See e.g.: Art. 11(2) of the Kampala Convention.

tools position the resolution of displacement as a human rights protection concern, and generally recognize that achieving durable solutions requires not only the support of humanitarian actors, but also development and, in post-conflict contexts, peacebuilding actors.[27] This approach is certainly consistent with the 'rights-based' perspective that has defined international discussions on the IDP issue, but does not necessarily readily resonate with the conceptual frameworks and working cultures of the development actors and operational agencies involved in supporting durable solutions to displacement in the field. It may also clash with local priorities and interpretations of different human rights.

3.1 From soft to hard law: durable solutions in the Kampala Convention

Like the Guiding Principles, the Kampala Convention is fairly brief in its discussion of durable solutions. Unlike the Principles, however, the Convention explicitly employs the term 'durable solutions', a testament to the increased traction of the concept in the eleven years between the release of the two standards. Indeed, the first objective of the Convention is to 'Promote and strengthen regional and national measures to prevent or mitigate, prohibit and eliminate root causes of internal displacement as well as provide for durable solutions' (Article 2.a). In a demonstration of how soft law can prompt the development of more robust binding commitments, as noted by Gammeltoft-Hansen, Lagoutte, and Cerone in the Introduction to this collection, the Convention builds on the Guiding Principles with fortified provisions on choice between durable solutions, and the active participation of IDPs in the process. While the Guiding Principles simply state that 'Special efforts should be made to ensure the full participation of internally displaced persons in the planning and management of their return or resettlement and reintegration',[28] the Convention insists that 'States Parties *shall* enable internally displaced persons to make a free and informed choice on whether to return, integrate locally or relocate by consulting them on these and other options and ensuring their participation in finding sustainable solutions.'[29] The Convention also importantly advances the normative framework by explicitly recognizing local integration as a legitimate durable solution to displacement.[30]

The Convention additionally strengthens protections relating to redress for IDPs—an issue that may directly shape the pursuit of durable solutions. Whereas the Principles address only the loss of 'property and possessions', the Convention

[27] See the 2013 report of the UN Special Rapporteur on the human rights of IDPs to the General Assembly; Brookings-LSE Project on Internal Displacement, 'Durable Solutions to Internal Displacement: Exploring the Roles of Development, Humanitarian and Peacebuilding Actors' (Washington, DC, 2013).

[28] Guiding Principles, 28.2.

[29] Kampala Convention, Art. 11.2, emphasis added.

[30] The Guiding Principles address 'return, resettlement and reintegration'. Principle 28 is intended to incorporate local integration, but this term is not used in the text of the Principles, leaving space for states to resist this sometimes politically unpopular approach to resolving displacement. See: W. Kälin, *The Guiding Principles on Internal Displacement: Annotations* (American Society of International Law and Brookings Institution, Washington, DC, 2nd edn, 2008): 125–31.

tacitly recognizes that displacement may be associated with a much wider range of losses affecting not only IDPs but also other stakeholders such as host community members. The Convention thus indicates that 'States Parties shall provide persons *affected by displacement* with effective remedies', and shall 'establish an effective legal framework to provide just and fair compensation and other forms of reparations, where appropriate, to internally displaced persons for damage incurred as a result of displacement, in accordance with international standards'.[31]

Despite these important advances, the Convention (unsurprisingly, given the political sensitivity of the issue) leaves open a range of key questions concerning, for example, the particular conditions that authorities are obliged to establish in order to enable solutions. These issues are addressed in greater detail in a subsequent tool, the IASC Framework on Durable Solutions for Internally Displaced Persons.

3.2 The IASC Framework on Durable Solutions for Internally Displaced Persons

A rights-based tool, the IASC Framework was developed under the leadership of Walter Kälin, the legal expert who led the drafting of the Guiding Principles and subsequently became the second RSG on IDPs.[32] The release of the IASC Framework was the culmination of a long process of consultation and debate with organizations involved in supporting durable solutions. As with the Guiding Principles, the IASC Framework was presented to the UN Human Rights Council, and subsequently translated and disseminated. While the Guiding Principles focus primarily on the responsibilities of states, the main audience for the IASC Framework is the range of international actors involved in supporting durable solutions.[33] The Framework sets out rights-based principles, processes, and criteria that should inform efforts to support durable solutions for IDPs uprooted by conflicts, natural disasters, or other causes. The Framework characterizes the resolution of displacement as a long-term process of progressive realization of interlinked rights and social goods, and articulates four key criteria that shape the extent to which IDPs have obtained a durable solution. According to the Framework, IDPs who have secured a durable solution will be able to equitably enjoy:

- Long-term safety, security and freedom of movement;
- An adequate standard of living, including at a minimum access to adequate food, water, housing, health care and basic education;

[31] Kampala Convention, Art. 12.1, Art. 12.2, emphasis added; Asplet and Bradley (2012).

[32] Other important standards that are largely outside the scope of this chapter include the 2005 UN Principles on Housing and Property Restitution for Refugees and Displaced Persons (Pinheiro Principles). For analyses of this standard, see e.g.: A. Smit, 'Private Rights and Public Interests: Property Restitution, Transitional Justice and Post-conflict Restitution', in *Forced Migration, Reconciliation and Justice*, ed. M. Bradley (Montreal: McGill-Queen's University Press, 2015); A. Smit, *The Property Rights of Refugees and Internally Displaced Persons: Beyond Restitution* (London: Routledge, 2012); M. J. Ballard, 'Post-Conflict Property Restitution: Flawed Legal and Theoretical Foundations', *Berkeley Journal of International Law* vol. 28 (2010): 1–36.

[33] IASC, Framework: 3.

- Access to employment and livelihoods; and
- Access to effective mechanisms that restore their housing, land and property or provide them with compensation.[34]

Depending on the circumstances, achieving durable solutions to displacement may also necessitate IDPs' equitable enjoyment of:

- Access to and replacement of personal and other documentation;
- Voluntary reunification with family members separated during displacement;
- Participation in public affairs at all levels on an equal basis with the resident population; and
- Effective remedies for displacement-related violations, including access to justice, reparations and information about the causes of violations.[35]

Despite efforts to popularize the IASC Framework, many humanitarian and development practitioners remain unaware of this standard. Some of those who are familiar with the standard but work in post-disaster contexts point out that it is predominantly geared to concerns that arise in post-conflict contexts, overlooking the particular challenges faced after disasters. Others admit that rather than helping them determine what concrete actions they can and should take, reading the Framework leaves them feeling overwhelmed at the complexity of the issue, and the high bar that, according to the Framework, needs to be reached in order to declare that durable solutions have been achieved. This suggests that the ambitious nature of 'norm-filling' soft law standards can sometimes inadvertently overwhelm rather than empower practitioners, particularly when the principles articulated in soft law standards are not linked to practical implementation advice, and stretch beyond the commitments and interpretations that resonate with states.

3.3 Soft law and the evolution of discourse on durable solutions

Soft law has had a significant role in shaping discourse on durable solutions. This role has been characterized by tension between the political goals and aspirations of actors such as states and international organizations; the focus of normative standards on these actors' roles and responsibilities in terms of human rights; and the complex empirical realities surrounding displacement situations.

For example, when the development of the IASC Framework began, the discussion focused on the notion of 'ending' displacement, with the 2007 pilot version of the Framework bearing the title 'When Displacement Ends: A Framework for Durable Solutions'. However, some scholars and practitioners suggested that as the experience of forced migration shapes a displaced person's entire life, and is thus never really 'over', it would be preferable to shift the discourse away from a focus on 'ending' displacement. This perspective is at odds with the preferences

[34] IASC, Framework: A-1. [35] IASC, Framework: A-1.

of governments and operational agencies looking to close files and declare particular interventions a success. Yet by the time the Framework was finalized in 2010, references to the notion of 'ending' displacement, or displacement situations being 'over', had been assiduously removed from the text, replaced by the more amorphous concept of the 'resolution' of displacement through the attainment of 'durable solutions'. While this is for some an important if nuanced substantive difference, others regard this shift as mere semantics, a reflection of the Framework's 'academic' approach.

Further in this vein, soft law standards on IDPs, and related agreements such as the Kampala Convention, tend to focus on the roles and responsibilities of governments and international organizations. This has perpetuated the notion that these actors 'provide' solutions to displacement, obscuring the reality that it is typically IDPs themselves who take the lead in carving out solutions to their own displacement. For example, while the Guiding Principles tread carefully around this issue, emphasizing authorities' duty to establish the conditions needed to 'allow' IDPs to return, resettle, and reintegrate, the IASC Framework more forthrightly states that the 'primary responsibility to provide durable solutions for IDPs ... needs to be assumed by the national authorities'.[36] Similarly, the preamble to the Kampala Convention highlights African states' 'common vision of providing durable solutions to situations of internally displaced persons'.[37] As experiences in Haiti demonstrate, the 'solutions' IDPs advance for themselves may sit uncomfortably within the parameters of rights-based international durable solutions discourse, not to mention the preferences of national authorities and elites, and must be better understood and accounted for in national and international strategies to support the resolution of displacement.

4. Interpreting and Applying IDP Soft Law in Support of Solutions

Section 3 detailed how IDP advocates achieved the remarkable commitment of states to new soft law standards on internal displacement, and how these standards have shaped the development of a durable solutions discourse. In this section, we examine efforts to increase compliance with soft law standards through their integration into domestic frameworks, whether in the form of laws or policies, focusing in particular on the significance of these efforts for the resolution of displacement.[38] We also examine two case studies in which IDP soft law played very different roles.

Since the 1990s, nearly half of the states facing major internal displacement crises have developed new laws or policies on IDPs. This trend may be taken to reflect considerable levels of state acceptance of the view at the heart of soft law standards

[36] IASC Framework: 11. [37] Kampala Convention, Art. 2.a.

[38] J. Wyndham, 'A Developing Trend: Laws and Policies on Internal Displacement', *Human Rights Brief* vol. 14 (2006): 7–70.

such as the Guiding Principles that national authorities have primary and particular responsibilities towards those displaced within their borders. It also suggests that states perceive there to be considerable costs, reputational and otherwise, to non-compliance with IDP soft law.[39] However, our examination of national laws and policies on IDPs suggests that many of these standards diverge considerably from soft law norms, particularly in relation to the resolution of displacement. That said, particularly in domestic instruments focusing on conflict-related displacement situations, the incorporation of concepts such as durable solutions is becoming increasingly common, and the instruments developed appear to be increasingly consistent with the language and principles of the Guiding Principles and the IASC Framework.

While the development of these instruments is, overall, a critical step towards improved protection and assistance for IDPs, this analysis underscores that it cannot be taken for granted that national laws and policies necessarily translate into increased support for durable solutions as they are understood in soft law standards.[40] Diversity in local interpretation of norms reflects 'the thickness [or thinness] of shared understandings that support the rule'.[41] Even when the Guiding Principles and related tools inform the development of domestic instruments and the practice of international actors, social contexts influence interpretations of IDPs' rights and entitlements. In analysing domestic instruments and the two case studies presented in this chapter, we are concerned not only with whether soft law principles have made their way into domestic legislation, but also with how the interpretation and application of norms on IDPs reflect particular understandings of displacement and socio-economic and political environments.

In addition to substantial variation between domestic texts, we note the significant roles of international, non-state institutions in promoting the development of these instruments, and transplanting soft law concepts, meanings, and interpretations—with varying results—into different contexts.[42] International, non-state actors can also destabilize domestic interpretation and application of soft law norms on IDPs, as they may approach the question of internal displacement with different vocabularies and normative traditions. For example, while humanitarian actors may be familiar with IDP soft law, and seek to promote durable solutions in line with standards such as the IASC Framework, actors focused on issues such as urban development and shelter may approach the resolution of displacement from the standpoint of the 'right to housing', or the 'right to the city'. These different approaches may produce conceptual and interpretative tensions, as related

[39] Orchard (2014).

[40] This analysis is informed by interdisciplinary human rights scholarship. See e.g.: *The Practice of Human Rights: Tracking Law between the Global and the Local*, ed. M. Goodale and S. Engle Merry (Cambridge: Cambridge University Press, 2007).

[41] J. Ellis, 'Shades of Grey: Soft Law and the Validity of Public International Law', *Leiden Journal of International Law* vol. 45 (2012): 317.

[42] S. Engle Merry, 'International Law and Sociolegal Scholarship: Toward a Spatial Global Legal Pluralism', in *Special Issue Law and Society Reconsidered*, ed. A. Sarat (*Studies in Law, Politics and Society* vol. 41, 2007): 149–68.

but distinct human rights agendas with different priorities and methodologies.[43] The cases explored in this section also illustrate how, when soft law norms seem particularly abstract or difficult to apply in particular displacement contexts, or when actors have vested interests in advancing particular interpretations of key concepts, international and domestic institutions will create and seek to justify new interpretations of these norms. The reflexivity between law and practice is a rich terrain to explore questions that go beyond the legal character and processes of developing IDP soft law, to engage in critical analysis of the factors that affect the understanding, quality, and influence of soft law tools and related national instruments over time. In this way, the IDP issue opens up valuable insights on the role of soft law and its ability to regulate intense and rapidly changing environments shaped by conflict and disaster.

4.1 Addressing internal displacement and durable solutions through national laws and policies

While the domestication of IDP soft law through the development of national laws and policies has broadly been a major success of the IDP movement, a closer look at these instruments reveals dissonance in relation to the international normative framework, and, in some instances, barriers to durable solutions. Building on Orchard's discussion of IDP soft law implementation, we consider how domestic instruments reflect and shape normative understandings of displacement and durable solutions forwarded in soft law, and thus coordinate the behaviour of actors through a particular 'discursive opportunity structure'.[44] In other words, how and to what extent do understandings of IDPs and durable solutions pass from the international soft law context to the domestic context?

The benefits of national laws and policies on IDPs have been discussed widely in the literature. National instruments are often seen as reflective of growing state recognition of and commitment to a vulnerable population.[45] Schrepfer captures the international community's high expectations of these instruments, arguing that developing national laws and policies on IDPs 'strengthens capacities, as it clarifies basic notions, concepts and normative ideas framing and strategizing a response to internal displacement, and may even lead to a more efficient use and allocation [of resources]'.[46] Other key benefits cited include the possibility that these instruments

[43] I. Venzke, *How Interpretation Makes International Law: On Semantic Change and Normative Twists* (Oxford: Oxford University Press, 2012): 35.

[44] L. Graham, 'Advancing the Human Right to Housing in Post-Katrina New Orleans: Discursive Opportunity Structures in Housing and Community Development', *Housing Policy Debate* vol. 22 (2012): 5–27.

[45] Wyndham (2006); N. Schrepfer, 'Addressing Internal Displacement through National Laws and Policies: A Plea for a Promising Means of Protection', *International Journal of Refugee Law* vol. 24 (2012): 667–91.

[46] Schrepfer (2012): 676.

can provide clarity over legal conflicts; facilitate coordination; allocate roles and responsibilities; and systematize responses.[47]

While scholars have praised the IDP 'norm cascade' since the 1990s, it is important to note that many national laws and policies have been developed in reference to specific displacement crises and have narrow applicability. Many national instruments discuss in their preambles the details of the conflict-based displacement that led to the need for a law or policy; comparatively few explicitly include other displacement scenarios such as natural disasters.[48] These documents may not necessarily inform future displacement situations, although it may be hoped that they establish a productive political or legal context for states to act on their responsibilities toward IDPs.

Orchard identifies some of the consistencies between domestic laws and the IDP soft law framework.[49] In his analysis of thirty-nine laws and policies, Orchard indicates that twenty-nine address the provision of international assistance; twenty-four recognize that IDPs are protected by international law; twenty-one cite or highlight domestic laws that protect IDP rights. While seventeen mention the Guiding Principles explicitly, only seven embrace the conception of an IDP established in the Guiding Principles.[50] Building on Orchard's work, our qualitative analysis of a similar but somewhat larger sample of fifty-five national laws and policies examines the 'frames' that structure efforts to mobilize action and marshal resources in response to a particular issue such as internal displacement.[51] Variations in the framing of the IDP concept itself, the hardships and violations associated with displacement, and what constitutes a durable solution all shed light on the motivations behind these instruments, their efficacy, and the traction of IDP soft law in diverse domestic contexts.

It is instructive to look at how the representation of 'the IDP' within these texts relates to the international normative framework. The way in which the concept of an IDP is framed has fundamental importance if assistance and protection is

[47] Wyndham (2006); Schrepfer (2012).

[48] Only five states—Kenya, Angola, Uganda, Afghanistan, and the Philippines—provide some descriptive detail on displacement resulting from natural disasters. Liberia, Sudan, Nepal, Azerbaijan, Iraq, and Turkey have policies that include 'natural disasters' in the definition or description of an IDP, but these documents largely discuss displacement resulting from conflict scenarios. E.g., Iraq's National Policy on Displacement (2008) lists a series of consequences from displacement that are clearly conflict related; its goals likewise reflect the resolution of conflict-related displacements. The remaining laws and policies analysed do not explicitly include displacement owing to natural disasters in their definitions or scenarios. In fact, Art. 2 of Russia's 1995 Federal Law on Forced Migrants actually states that 'A person shall *not* be recognized as a Forced Migrant if he/she has left the place of his residence because of the economic reasons or because of a famine or of an epidemic, or because of the emergency situations of the natural or of the technogenic character' (emphasis added).

[49] Orchard (2014). [50] Orchard (2014): 8.

[51] R. D. Benford and D. A. Snow, 'Framing Processes and Social Movements: An Overview and Assessment', *Annual Review of Sociology* vol. 26 (2000): 611–39. Our sampling frame includes all the laws and policies listed in the Brookings-LSE Index of Laws and Policies on Internal Displacement as of Apr. 2015. In cases where a particular country has four or more such documents, the most current and comprehensive law or policy was selected for analysis (this concern applied to only five countries, Iraq, Bosnia and Herzegovina, Colombia, Turkey, and Uganda).

to last over the entire displacement cycle. It is therefore troubling that few states have embraced the flexible and encompassing definition laid out in the Guiding Principles, and incorporated in subsequent documents such as the Kampala Convention and the IASC Framework. For example, Nepal's national framework states that only those who lived in 'legal areas' before the displacement crisis may be considered IDPs.[52] Laws and policies from various former Soviet states detail an application process for IDP 'status'; only some establish or detail an appeals process to contest denial of status.[53] Some policies, furthermore, convey that IDPs are only those in camps. For instance, Liberia's legal framework from 2002 declares 'its commitment to respect the rights of all Liberians *in IDP camps* to return to their places of origin or habitual residence with the full protection of the law'.[54] Some national laws and policies link negative connotations to the IDP concept. For instance, some indicate that IDPs require a top-down 're-socialization' or 'rehabilitation' process (such as Sri Lanka and Nepal) while others paint IDPs as welfare dependants, emphasizing the need to wean them off aid (rather than, say, treating them as victims of traumatic and destructive circumstances, or agents who have a role to play in their own recovery).[55] These representations illuminate how states view their IDP populations and may seek to use national laws and policies as a tool to limit rather than to bolster their entitlements.

Diverging from international soft law standards, hardly any national instruments recognize that IDPs actually have a *right* to a durable solution, but rather express a commitment to create the conditions for the resolution of displacement, establish funds for the settlement of IDPs, or specify certain settlement options that can be made available to IDPs. In most instances there are gaps in the representation of durable solutions, with only one or two settlement options mentioned—usually return and resettlement. Even when durable solutions are not explicitly referenced, many of the criteria outlined in the IASC Framework receive some mention in the description of the resolution of displacement. These include issues such as access to safety and security, an adequate standard of living, livelihoods support, property restitution, family reunification, documentation, and participation in public affairs. 'Access to effective remedies and justice' was the least likely of the eight IASC Framework criteria to be included in domestic laws and policies. Unlike

[52] Government of Nepal, National Policy on Internally Displaced Persons, 2007.

[53] Under the Guiding Principles, being an IDP is not to be understood as a legal 'status'.

[54] Government of Liberia, Declaration on the Rights and Protection of Liberian IDPs, 2002, emphasis added.

[55] This imagery of the IDP is sprinkled throughout e.g. Sri Lanka's 2002 National Framework for Relief Rehabilitation and Reconciliation (RRR Framework), which at one point bluntly states: 'The tendency for residents of camps and welfare centers to become passive recipients of handouts from relief agencies should be counteracted by every means' (p. 24). Art. 20 of section IV (Sanction) of Peru's *Law Concerning the Internally Displaced* (Law No. 28223) states that 'any person who, taking advantage of the circumstances may have declared untrue facts and conditions, and because of them may have obtained rights and benefits not due to him/her, automatically loses these rights and benefits, as well as being penalized in accordance with the applicable legislation'. Strikingly, there are no such statements for the application of sanctions or penalties for anyone who obstructs the provision of assistance to IDPs, or is complicit in arbitrary displacement.

in standards such as the IASC Framework, in the majority of national laws and policies on internal displacement, supporting durable solutions is presented as an expressly humanitarian undertaking. While the vast majority of the policies state that IDPs have either a right to or can benefit from *humanitarian* assistance, it is rare that *development* actors are mentioned, although soft law tools including the Guiding Principles and the IASC Framework recognize that they have critical roles to play. Important exceptions to this are found in some Latin American laws and policies as well as in some of the newer policies created in Iraq and Afghanistan, which mention the resolution of displacement and its relationship to the protection of social, economic, and cultural rights.[56]

In the majority of instruments, there is a heavy emphasis on return as the preferred and expected option, with various policies mentioning the need to encourage IDPs to return, or to 'build confidence in them that home is safe'.[57] In most of the national laws and policies we reviewed, IDPs are presented as people who have an original place of permanency and belonging, and should be assisted for national and economic stability reasons to return to these places. This focus on return is particularly evident in instruments developed in the 1990s and in the early years of the twenty-first century; more recent instruments are more likely than earlier documents to contain the term 'durable solutions' and to reference the three settlement options—a testament to soft law's contribution to popularizing a 'durable solutions discourse'. Various instruments, especially those from the mid-1990s to mid-2000s, seem to conflate return and resettlement; using resettlement as a synonym for return further entrenches the notion, contrary to soft law standards, of return as the only supported option. Even when policies recognize IDPs' right to freedom of movement, many instruments only provide details on support and entitlements for returnees.

Indeed, only a few instruments explicitly identify local integration as an option for IDPs, reflecting the historical neglect of local integration in international discourse.[58] In national instruments, states sometimes explicitly or tacitly restrict free movement and settlement options. For example, Angola's Council of Ministers' Decree indicates that efforts to resolve the country's displacement crisis shall 'take into account the local administrations' priorities regarding territorial regulations in the identification of resettlement or return areas'.[59] Sudan's 2009 National Policy on IDPs states that IDPs 'can live wherever they want to live freely inside the Sudan *without violating the rights and obligations of other citizens*'.[60] Such provisions reflect

[56] Strong statements on social, cultural, and economic rights are made in Guatemala's Agreement on Resettlement of the Population Groups Uprooted by the Armed Groups (1994) as well as in the numerous laws and policies developed in Colombia, which also reference the state's obligation to facilitate social justice.

[57] Text taken from Uganda's 2008 Camp Closure Guidelines. Similar phrasing and concepts are echoed in national instruments from Sri Lanka, Sierra Leone, and Turkey.

[58] E. Ferris, 'Resolving Internal Displacement: Prospects for Local Integration' (Washington, DC, Brookings-LSE Project on Internal Displacement, 2011).

[59] Government of Angola, Angola's Council of Ministers' Decree 79/02 on Norms on the Resettlement of Displaced Populations, 2002.

[60] Government of the Republic of Sudan, National Policy for Internally Displaced Persons, 2009, emphasis added.

the diverse and complex ways in which IDPs' rights, particularly as they relate to the resolution of displacement, intersect with the rights and responsibilities of other actors and populations, sometimes resulting in competing claims and conflicts. IDP soft law and related tools do not, for the most part, provide concrete guidance on how to navigate and resolve these dilemmas. Reflecting this gap, few laws or policies seem to envision, or provide guidance for dealing with, legal conflicts that emerge between IDPs' right to pursue the durable solution of their choice, on the one hand, and state or private rights to land upon which IDPs may have taken refuge, and where they may wish to remain. Some instruments, such as Kenya's 2012 Prevention, Protection, and Assistance to Internally Displaced Persons and Affected Communities Act, do suggest that the government has the responsibility to find land for IDPs as necessary, although others link the clearance of temporary IDP settlements (camps) with the perceived need to return private and public land back to 'productive use'.[61]

IDP soft law stresses the need for the *process* of pursuing durable solutions to adhere to rights-based principles, including as they relate to questions of voluntariness or choice, and the active participation of IDPs in decision-making. Reflecting this soft law concern, most national laws and policies use the word 'voluntary' in relation to settlement options. However, the majority of these documents do not put IDPs at the heart of the process, failing to connect the principle of voluntary movement with choice regarding IDPs' place of permanent residence. Some instruments also embrace relatively restrictive conceptions of what voluntariness entails. For example, the 2008 Uganda Camp Closure guidelines indicate that once 50 per cent of the camp population has left, camp phase-out can legitimately commence, suggesting that residual populations have less robust process-related rights protections. In most national instruments, IDP participation is usually discussed at the level of 'consultation' and rarely as 'decision-making'. The paternalism that pervades these documents provides little discursive room for IDPs to express their voice, choice, and agency. Interestingly, some national policies that address development-induced displacement, as well as conflict or natural disaster-induced displacement, seem to include a more active role for IDP participation and access to public hearings or fora.[62]

Overall, analysis of the body of national laws and policies on IDPs that have emerged over the past twenty-five years demonstrates that while soft law has had a significant and evolving influence on domestic frameworks, in many instances

[61] See e.g. several of Uganda's 2008 Camp Closure Guidelines, or Guatemala's Agreement on Resettlement of the Population Groups Uprooted by the Armed Groups (1994). Section 1.3 (Housing) of the Republic of Georgia's State Strategy for Internally Displaced Persons—Prosecuted (2007) states, 'almost the half [*sic*] (45%) of IDPs are accommodated in collective centers. These buildings have lost their primary function, which in many cases has resulted in their depreciation … the economic development of the country is hindered as in many cases the half-ruined buildings and their uncared for neighborhoods represent disadvantageous factors for urban development of cities, the revival and management of resorts and industrial infrastructure, and the attraction of new investors.'

[62] See e.g.: Government of the Republic of Kenya, Prevention, Protection and Assistance to Internally Displaced Persons and Affected Communities Act, 2012.

domestic interpretations of obligations towards IDPs vary considerably from international standards. Variance from international standards is somewhat more evident when it comes to addressing the question of durable solutions; this is perhaps unsurprising, given the political and economic sensitivities associated with efforts to resolve displacement crises.[63] To be sure, there are some national laws and policies that hew closely to international norms. For example, Afghanistan's national policy reflects soft law standards in many important ways. It conveys a broad conceptualization of durable solutions as a humanitarian and development issue, and makes clear and explicit statements about security of tenure and access to land as important elements of durable solutions. The policy also, in a particularly progressive fashion, states the need for IDPs to 'benefit from Master Urban Plans to regularize many of the informal settlements' and 'from improved land titling, so that they get security of tenure and can make improvements to their shelters without fear of eviction'.[64] Policies such as the one adopted in Afghanistan underscore the importance of incorporating a wide range of different actors into the policy-making process in order to productively navigate the interpretative challenges that accompany efforts to translate international soft law norms on IDPs into national standards. In general, however, the creation of domestic standards may be a double-edged sword: while they may systematize and strengthen domestic commitment to international norms, restrictive or narrow interpretations of the state's obligations towards IDPs may also make it more difficult for the displaced to lay claim to the full range of rights identified in international IDP soft law. And yet, as the following case studies demonstrate, the development of national instruments on IDPs and the quality of these standards are only two aspects of the myriad ways in which soft law shapes the resolution of displacement. As experiences in Sri Lanka demonstrate, the drafting of national laws and policies that closely track soft law norms may serve as a foil for abuses against IDPs. Meanwhile, experiences in Haiti—where soft law norms have not been incorporated into domestic instruments—illustrate both the limitations of soft law and universal norms as well as the ways in which they nonetheless influence practice.

4.2 Sri Lanka: strategic state manipulation of soft law

Gammeltoft-Hansen, Lagoutte, and Cerone question whether it can be 'presumed that soft law necessarily fulfils a progressive role' in interpreting and enacting international human rights law. The Copenhagen Process, for example, was framed by a restrictionist agenda from the outset. Experiences in Sri Lanka further underscore that it cannot be presumed that the effects of soft law are necessarily positive, by

[63] Assessing whether the variance between international and domestic standards is more pronounced in soft law-informed cases than in hard law-informed cases is beyond the scope of this chapter. However, the more rigorous monitoring structures accompanying some hard law frameworks could potentially encourage the development of domestic laws and policies that are more systematically attuned to international principles.

[64] Government of Afghanistan, National Policy on Internal Displacement, 2013.

demonstrating how even soft law frameworks that have been hailed as progressive and are intended to assist states in effectively interpreting and upholding their responsibilities can be twisted by state authorities to limit rather than advance their citizens' rights.

Sri Lanka has a long and complex history of internal displacement caused by natural disasters and, in particular, the conflict between the government and the Liberation Tigers of Tamil Eelam (LTTE). More than 800,000 Sri Lankans were internally displaced over the course of the conflict, which ended in 2009 with the annihilation of the LTTE in a final government offensive. By late 2013, 760,000 of those who had been displaced in the conflict were registered as having returned to their areas of origin in northern and eastern Sri Lanka.[65] However, many IDPs have not actually been able to reclaim their lost homes and lands, and do not enjoy the protections the IASC Framework identifies as critical components of the sustainable resolution of displacement. Nonetheless, by 2014 the Sri Lankan government recognized only 22,000 people as IDPs.[66]

The government of Sri Lanka (particularly under the presidency of Mahinda Rajapaksa, 2005–15) has employed its own 'take' on durable solutions discourse, using the term 'resettlement' to refer both to the return of IDPs to their homes, and to their relocation in other areas. Actors such as the UN mandate-holders on internal displacement have challenged this discursive move, pointing to the conceptualizations of return, local integration, and resettlement mapped out in the Guiding Principles and IASC Framework, and encouraging the Sri Lankan government to adopt these concepts. However, the Sri Lankan government has resisted this recommendation, and has capitalized on the arguable 'blurriness' of soft law standards on some key issues, including what in particular constitutes 'return'. On the face of it, Guiding Principle 28 gives a clear indication that return entails IDPs voluntarily going back 'to their homes or places of habitual residence' in 'safety and with dignity'. Yet what does this mean when homes or 'places of habitual residence' have been destroyed? Is there a right to return to the razed land? What happens in cases in which the displaced were renters, or resided under informal or customary, communal arrangements? In the absence of clear and widely accepted answers to such questions, the government's elision of return and resettlement has papered over the persistent concerns of those who have returned to their areas of origin but have not been able to repossess their property, and has facilitated the government's assertion that it has upheld its citizens' rights through the rapid resolution of the displacement situation.

[65] Special Rapporteur on the Human Rights of Internally Displaced Persons, 'Report of the Special Rapporteur on the Human Rights of Internally Displaced Persons, Chaloka Beyani: Mission to Sri Lanka', Submitted to 26th Session of the UN Human Rights Council, Geneva, A/HRC/26/33/Add.4, 2014.

[66] Special Rapporteur on the Human Rights of Internally Displaced Persons, 'Report of the Special Rapporteur on the Human Rights of Internally Displaced Persons, Chaloka Beyani: Mission to Sri Lanka', Submitted to 26th Session of the UN Human Rights Council, Geneva, A/HRC/26/33/Add.4, 2014.

At present, Sri Lanka does not have a national law or policy on IDPs, although over the course of 2013 the Ministry of Resettlement published and updated a draft resettlement policy; there is no clear timeline for the finalization of this policy. Similarly, at earlier stages the government has engaged in inconclusive policy-making processes ostensibly intended to domesticate soft law principles on IDPs. For example, in 2008, the Human Rights Commission of Sri Lanka drafted a comprehensive IDP protection bill, while the Ministry of Disaster Management and Human Rights convened a national consultation on IDPs, which resulted in the development of a draft durable solutions strategy based on the document that eventually became the IASC Framework. Both drafts were hailed as laudably comprehensive and in line with IDP soft law, and yet neither instrument was ever finalized, much less implemented. Indeed, by 2009, the government was engaged in a final offensive against the LTTE characterized by mass displacement and extreme human rights violations.

The development of IDP policies may in some instances 'reflect the government having decided to make a strategic rhetorical commitment to the norms embodied within the Guiding Principles with no plan to follow through on implementation'.[67] Orchard identifies two possible reasons for states adopting policies they have no intention to implement.[68] First, states may be motivated by reputational concerns; second, they may be persuaded by international organizations and NGOs to engage in the law or policy development process, but without sustained pressure from these organizations, implementation falls by the wayside. The government of Sri Lanka's behaviour reflects both of these dynamics, but also points to a third, related possibility: states may strategically engage in the development of national policies, based on soft law standards, as a way of deflecting criticism and negative repercussions from donors and other powerbrokers. This goes beyond abstract concerns about reputation to cold calculation of how states under international pressure create the political space necessary to pursue their perceived interests—in this case, the annihilation of the LLTE and the assertion of Sinhalese dominance over the predominantly Tamil north. The reflections of national and international staff working on IDP issues in Sri Lanka bolster this conclusion. Looking back on the 2008 process, for example, some UN staff suggest the international community was 'being led by the nose' by the government, which engaged with the UN and international law simply to legitimize itself.[69] As the leader of a prominent national NGO expressed it, the government 'played the game beautifully'; the durable solutions strategy was a 'masterpiece' such that upon reading it, 'You get convinced, wow, Sri Lanka is a model of resettlement.'[70] However, as the subsequent war demonstrated, the government did not intend to respect these domestic documents, or the international principles on which they were based. Rather, the process was undertaken with a view to 'pacifying the international community'.[71] IDP advocates in Sri Lanka

[67] Orchard (2014): 117. [68] Orchard (2014): 118.
[69] Interview, Colombo, 15 Jan. 2013; Interview, Colombo, 16 Jan. 2013.
[70] Interview, Colombo, 17 Jan. 2013. [71] Interview, Colombo, 22 Jan. 2013.

stress that in spite of this experience, international norms on IDPs remain highly relevant, and it is important not to give up hope on the possibility of successfully incorporating them into domestic law. However, this troubled history emphasizes that in the hands of a manipulative government, soft law can play a very different, and much more nefarious, role than its proponents intend.[72]

4.3 The role of soft law in Haiti's displacement crisis

Experiences in Haiti reveal a very different set of dynamics around the role of IDP soft law, but similarly point to both the relevance and limitations of soft law standards. On 12 January 2010, a 7.0 magnitude earthquake in Haiti's capital, Port-au-Prince, killed hundreds of thousands, destroyed 300,000 homes, and displaced over 1.5 million people.[73] Soft law played a limited but complex role in national and international responses to the displacement crisis. While soft law tools on internal displacement, particularly the IASC Framework, reflect a predominant focus on conflict-generated displacement, and are arguably best attuned to challenges faced in rural environments, the urban, post-disaster context in Haiti raised questions about the salience of the IDP and durable solutions concepts. Key standards including the IASC Framework were not necessarily well known amongst national and international actors, and some of those familiar with the relevant soft law tools were openly sceptical about their relevance in Haiti. In contrast to Sri Lanka and the countries reviewed in section 4.2 on national laws and policies, the Haitian government did not develop an explicit national law or policy on IDPs, nor did it integrate the question of internal displacement into key documents such as the draft national housing policy. It is nonetheless important to consider the role of IDP soft law in this case, as some national and international actors did appeal to and 'cherry-pick' from soft law principles in an attempt to legitimize their policies and interventions. At the same time, these standards served as the foundation for external critiques of the failure to support durable solutions for uprooted Haitians. Experiences in Haiti bring into focus the limits of soft law as a tool to promote durable solutions for IDPs, and the considerable work that remains to be done to build understanding and acceptance of soft law standards, particularly as they relate to durable solutions.

[72] In its engagement with the international community, the government of Sri Lanka has oscillated between being completely dismissive and 'car[ing] exceptionally'. Some suggest that the previous government's decision to engage with the IDP soft law standards promoted by the international community is attributable to the connections between IDP crises, war crimes, and the spectre of accountability for egregious human rights violations. (Interview, Colombo, 16 Jan. 2013; Interview, Colombo, 22 Jan. 2013.)

[73] 105,000 houses were destroyed and 208,164 were badly damaged. See: Amnesty International, *Nowhere to Go: Forced Evictions in Haiti's Displacement Camps* (London: Amnesty, 2013).

4.3.1 Context and factors limiting the traction of soft law standards in Haiti

From the outset, efforts to gain traction in Haiti for soft law standards on IDPs faced an uphill battle. The early response to the disaster was characterized by an idealistic discourse of 'building back better', but as the scale and complexity of the challenges became clear, and media scrutiny increased, national and international actors refocused on the seemingly more immediate and manageable task of addressing the hundreds of thousands of Haitians in some 1,500 often squalid camps. Thousands of IDPs did not take shelter in camps, but instead stayed with friends and family. However, the concept of internal displacement become synonymous with residency in camps, and the resolution of the displacement crisis with camp closures, rather than with the more complex challenge of supporting durable solutions as per the IASC Framework. Camp closures were achieved primarily through the application of a 'rental subsidy cash grant' mechanism, whereby IDPs residing in camps that the government wished to close were given a minimum $500 grant to subsidize the cost of obtaining a year of rental accommodation. For some IDPs, this helped them to establish themselves in decent accommodation, but for many if not most this approach did not translate into a durable solution: in the face of unaffordable rents and lack of access to livelihoods, many were unable to stay in their rented accommodation, and instead moved to informal settlements springing up on the outskirts of Port-au-Prince.[74]

Observers such as the UN Special Rapporteurs on the right to housing and the human rights of IDPs have raised concerns about this approach to camp closure, pointing out that it runs the risk of facilitating evictions, and falls short of standards such as the IASC Framework. However, such rights-based critiques have held little sway in a society characterized by the highest levels of poverty and income inequality in the western hemisphere.[75] Haiti's crisis conditions, patterns of vulnerability and exploitation, and marked divisions between the elite and the subordinate classes are an extension of practices of slavery and abusive colonial and post-colonial governance.[76] In this light, it is unsurprising that recovery has varied dramatically between social classes, with property holders faring far better than those without property,[77] and that in such a context, soft law standards—and even domestic laws—are implemented or neglected depending largely on elites' interests.

The adoption of soft law standards on durable solutions was a particularly hard sell in Haiti given the complexity of housing, land, and property issues. Soft law standards on durable solutions stress the need to uphold IDPs' housing, land, and property rights, calling for 'effective and accessible' mechanisms to restore lost homes. However, interpreting and upholding these norms proved challenging if

[74] K. Leader, *Rapport de stage professionnel: étude préliminaire sur la zone de Canaan et Jérusalem* (Port-au-Prince, Haiti: Ministère de la Planification et de la Coopération Externe, 2014).

[75] A. Dupuy, 'Disaster Capitalism to the Rescue: The International Community and Haiti after the Earthquake', *NACLA Report on the Americas* vol. 43 (2010): 14–19.

[76] For an in-depth account of historical patterns of injustice see: P. Farmer, 'Blood, Sweat, and Baseballs: Haiti in the West Atlantic System', *Dialectical Anthropology* vol. 13 (1988): 83–99.

[77] Sherwood et al. (2014): 30.

not implausible in the context of a land system governed not so much by law as by informal arrangements shaped by deeply inequitable power relations. The actors involved in land governance in Haiti extend far beyond the formal institutions that are the typical duty-bearers under soft law frameworks, with powerful elites, land mafias, criminal gangs, and highly autonomous NGOs all influencing, to different degrees, the extent to which IDPs could access land on which to pursue a durable solution. Only 5 per cent of Haitian land is recorded in the national cadastral office,[78] and there is currently no complete source of information on ownership and legally enforceable property rights. All this has further limited the practical application of soft law standards on durable solutions, and prompted some to question whether tools such as the IASC Framework are relevant in Haiti.

In the absence of a robust and regulated housing, land, and property rights system in Haiti, squatting and informal land use arrangements have become widespread practices that help the poor access affordable places to live, but also contribute to urban mismanagement and chaos. Haiti's legal framework has not dealt adequately with urban informality: domestic law is outdated, conservative, inefficient, and certainly not a basis of legal empowerment for landless and renter populations.[79] For example, the Haitian Constitution stipulates a right to housing, but has not specified the content of this right nor developed it in line with international standards.[80] In such a context, even if a national law or policy on IDPs were to be developed based on soft law standards, it would be at odds with and inevitably struggle to counterbalance this broader body of 'anti-poor' domestic laws, starkly reflecting the limitations of the 'internalization' approach that has been the focus of efforts to encourage the implementation of soft laws on IDPs.

Experiences in Haiti also show how emerging and established soft and hard law frameworks can compete with each other, sometimes detrimentally. Competing legal and ideological goals linked to notions of property rights and urban development have created some fundamental inconsistences and normative tensions regarding support for IDPs. Actors have walked a political tightrope in their efforts to promote the right of IDPs to access the land and housing they need, while ensuring that they do not impede the rights of non-IDPs who hold land and require security in it. It has also been unclear how to mesh normative frameworks on IDPs with emerging concepts such as the 'right to the city', and how to better draw out socio-economic rights that are less prominent within IDP frameworks and discourse. In short, Haiti is an environment full of rights-based dilemmas and thus problematizes the capacity of soft law frameworks to settle conflicts between different social interests and values, and to facilitate judgments on the hard social and political questions that arise in times of crisis.

[78] G. Calhan, 'Forced Evictions, Mass Displacement, and the Uncertain Promise of Land and Property Restitution in Haiti', *Hastings Race & Poverty LJ* vol. 11 (2014): 170.

[79] Interview with Haitian Lawyer, Port-au-Prince, July 2014.

[80] Amnesty International, *'15 Minutes to Leave': Denial of the Right to Adequate Housing in Post-Quake Haiti* (2015).

4.3.2 Conceptualizing internal displacement in Haiti: local views and normative legitimization

Finnemore and Sikkink suggest that normative strength and socialization depend on the construction of appropriate and persuasive cognitive frames that resonate with familiar understanding of issues, reflect shared standards and logics, and clarify what the norm is and what constitutes a violation.[81] In Haiti, soft law translated into an early focus on IDPs by a broad spectrum of international actors, who convinced several government institutions to recognize and commit to assisting IDPs. However, the narrow conception in Haiti of IDPs as those living in camps diverted attention from IDPs living with host families, as well as from the concerns that continued to face Haitians after leaving camps. This dynamic illustrates how restrictive local interpretations of soft law principles can attenuate soft law frameworks' core protection goals.

To understand the limited traction of core IDP soft law concepts in Haiti, it is instructive to examine the arguments and dynamics that affected the emergence of this narrow interpretation. Given the massive number affected by the disaster, and the fact that the majority slept away from their homes for at least the first two months after the earthquake, stakeholders found themselves asking: 'To be classified as an IDP, how far away from your home do you have to be, and for how long?' This question was motivated by the understanding amongst international actors that they had a particular obligation to this special category of concern, but also by the sense that it was operationally necessary to differentiate between 'real' IDPs and others who lost their homes but were not to be targeted for help. Lack of confidence in the IDP definition as too broad, unclear, and logistically unmanageable led to a system-wide decision to confer the IDP label only on those in government-recognized camps. In this way, actors could isolate a manageable 'caseload' of victims to whom aid workers could 'provide' solutions, and thus meet their institutional goals.

Scepticism about the IDP concept was not only a definitional issue or related to reputational concerns. The normative framework on IDPs is underpinned by the view that because IDPs typically encounter particular and often extreme vulnerabilities compared to the non-displaced population, targeted protection and assistance efforts are warranted. Some actors questioned the legitimacy of IDPs as a category of concern, doubting that IDPs faced particular vulnerabilities or extreme need compared to the rest of the impoverished population. The Haitian government in particular questioned the wisdom of funnelling assistance to what they saw as a somewhat arbitrary and internationally constructed category of individuals, especially when many sectors of society in Port-au-Prince suffered from similar crisis conditions. This is not to mention the dire lack of livelihoods and high levels of food insecurity that existed outside the city. These comparisons soon

[81] M. Finnemore and K. Sikkink, 'International Norm Dynamics and Political Change', *International Organization* vol. 52 (1998): 887–917.

led to IDPs in camps being branded as abusers of international welfare systems, generating doubt about the wisdom of investing efforts in supporting 'durable solutions' for this population.[82] As a member of civil society lamented: the 'skepticism of "who is in camps and why" was a harmful discourse that questioned the integrity of IDPs in camps and made it easy to dismiss IDPs as people in need, justifying short-sighted, camp-closure programmes' rather than more sustained support for durable solutions as soft law standards require.[83] Debate continues on the legitimacy of IDP soft law concepts in determining who should be assisted and to what extent, despite a growing body of evidence confirming that even years after the earthquake, many IDPs continue to face significant and enduring vulnerabilities as a result of their displacement.[84]

4.3.3 Questioning and engaging soft law frameworks

In Port-au-Prince, where nearly 70 per cent of residents lived in slum conditions even before the earthquake, the traction of soft law frameworks such as the IASC Framework has been limited by their ambitious nature.[85] The systematic protection of human rights is a core objective of the durable solutions process as outlined in the IASC Framework, which implies that progress must be made towards satisfying a wide range of human rights in order to determine that displacement has been resolved. This undertaking did not fit the short-term timeframe pushed by the Haitian government, donors, and even the media to 'end' the displacement crisis.[86] Aid institutions felt ill equipped to support this expansive conception of durable solutions for a population whose rights have never been wholly recognized in the first place, generating a high degree of scepticism that human rights standards, and the soft law concept of 'durable solutions' in particular, could provide an operational roadmap towards resolving displacement.

Despite the major displacement situation in Haiti, few national and international actors have detailed familiarity with the normative framework on durable solutions. Amongst those introduced to the IASC Framework, the tool was often perceived as an idealistic or 'academic' set of human rights standards with little practical import. While some strongly supported soft law norms on durable solutions, many saw the IASC Framework in particular as too cumbersome, demanding, resource-intensive, and, in the most antagonistic perspectives, inequitably preferring IDPs over the non-displaced urban poor (even though the Framework clearly indicates that support for durable solutions should benefit both IDPs and the non-displaced

[82] It was not uncommon to see 'for rent' or 'for sale' signs on tents in IDP camps, for example.

[83] Interview with Haitian civil society member, Port-au-Prince, May 2014.

[84] Sherwood et al. (2014).

[85] A. Moloney, 'Unclear Land Rights Hinder Haiti's Reconstruction', ReliefWeb, <http://reliefweb.int/report/haiti/unclear-land-rights-hinder-haitis-reconstruction>.

[86] S. Levine, S. Bailey, and B. Boyer, *Avoiding Reality: Land, Institutions and Humanitarian Action in Post-earthquake Haiti: Humanitarian Policy Group Working Paper* (London: Overseas Development Institute, 2012).

population). Consequently, the IASC Framework was only selectively used to rhetorically demonstrate support for IDPs, but was never fully institutionalized as a foundation for policy-making or practice.

The lack of detailed knowledge of the IASC Framework and clear guidance on how it may be applied resulted in a situation in which key concepts and principles could be bent or reinterpreted, sometimes with unfortunate consequences for IDP protection. For example, while the IASC Framework stresses the importance of IDP choice regarding durable solutions, and opposes the notion of a hierarchy of solutions, national and international actors singled out return as the most expedient, and thus 'preferred', solution. Various, murky meanings were ascribed to 'return': private property owners were the first to receive concerted support to leave camps and return to their properties. The cash grants eventually provided to renters did not generally enable them to 'return' to their former places of residence. Yet, trying to fit the model of durable solutions, international organizations portrayed the grants as enabling IDPs to 'return' to their communities, or to the status of being renters—a contortion of terminology arguably intended to position the provision of rental subsidies as a solution rather than a quick fix to advance camp closures. In an environment in which there were comparatively low levels of knowledge of and respect for soft law standards, this discursive move was not challenged as early as it might have been.

While soft law frameworks did not significantly inform the development of major camp closure interventions, they came to underpin important critiques of these efforts. Many Haitian civil society members lambasted rental subsidy programmes as a violation of state obligations to progressively satisfy the right to housing.[87] At the same time, some officials working with international organizations recognized their responsibility to support not only camp closures but durable solutions, and expressed doubt that the provision of rental assistance satisfied the definitions and criteria pertaining to durable solutions. Some international actors endeavoured to promote IDP choice regarding durable solutions by advancing alternative options such as local integration through the incorporation of former camps into surrounding communities; even so, these efforts usually failed because of local land politics and high material incentives to 'return' all IDPs to where they belonged. Still, IDP soft law sometimes provided a foundation for international organizations' scrutiny of the extent to which responsibilities to protect IDPs are being respected. For example, the Inter-American Commission on Human Rights drew on the Guiding Principles in granting precautionary measures to Haitian IDPs facing threat of evictions, and successfully directed the Haitian government to adopt a moratorium on evictions from camps.[88]

Five years after the earthquake, many IDPs and other disaster-affected people are independently pursuing settlement in informal communities on the outskirts

[87] Interviews with Haitian civil society groups, Port-au-Prince, Mar.–May 2014.

[88] N. Phillips, K. Bergin, J. Goldsmith, and L. Carr, 'Enforcing Remedies from the Inter-American Commission on Human Rights: Forced Evictions and Post-Earthquake Haiti', *Human Rights Brief* vol. 19 (2011): 13–18.

of the city as their 'solution' of choice. The durability of this process remains to be seen and is often delegitimized by institutional actors as a violation of rule of law and sustainable development principles. Unlike the visions of settlement (or relocation) laid out in soft law frameworks, most of the resettlement that takes place in Haiti is unplanned and informal. At the time of writing, residents of these areas still faced the challenge of political recognition and acceptance. Haitian IDPs who have ended up in informal settlements are generally no longer recognized as IDPs by any formal actors, and are instead frequently derided as land grabbers trying to scam free housing on government land. All this suggests that while the development and dissemination of the Guiding Principles and related tools such as the IASC Framework represents a remarkable soft law success story, norms on durable solutions face a variety of interpretations and can be extremely difficult to apply to complex social and political landscapes.

5. Conclusion

As part of the norm-creation process, IDP soft law has successfully raised the profile of an issue of growing international concern; sparked the development of national laws and policies that concretize soft law norms; placed scrutiny on state duties and responsibilities; and initiated a community of practice to monitor and help deliver on a set of standards around how and to what extent people can rebuild their lives after displacement. IDP advocates' use of soft law tools has supplied human rights activists and the field of international law with lessons in strategy and tactics on establishing new issues on the international agenda, and navigating concerns around intrusion on state sovereignty.

As Gammeltoft-Hansen, Lagoutte, and Cerone point out, soft law can potentially lead to 'the ultimate and authoritative determinations of open-ended legal questions'. As a soft law standard, the Guiding Principles on Internal Displacement and related tools such as the IASC Framework have certainly shaped the discourse surrounding 'durable solutions' for IDPs, and have influenced interpretation of the issue as a long-term challenge requiring cooperation between national authorities and international humanitarian and development actors. These documents have also, if only to a modest extent, informed the integration of durable solutions into national laws and policies on IDPs. In addition, they have to varying degrees shaped the practices of actors working to support durable solutions to displacement. However, given the complex political and economic interests at stake in efforts to resolve displacement crises, states have continued to embrace and push conceptions of durable solutions that do not necessarily mesh with these standards, which, as soft law tools, lack strong mechanisms to contest such interpretations. Further, soft law tools on internal displacement still generally do not provide 'ultimate and authoritative' responses to some of the thorniest questions surrounding the pursuit of durable solutions, such as: to what extent are states and international actors required to invest resources to make each of the three durable solutions realistic options for IDPs? In practice, the right to choose a durable solution is often pared down to the 'right' to accept the particular solution that is most politically acceptable, materially feasible, and enforceable within domestic legal systems. Given often profound resource constraints, and the need to equitably consider and support the rights and well-being of non-displaced communities, is it acceptable to channel support to a particular solution, such as return? How are solutions such as 'return' to be defined, especially when original homes have been destroyed, or when populations were highly marginalized and mobile prior to their displacement? What are the rights of secondary occupants who move onto displaced persons' former lands, and how do these relate to IDPs' right to return?[89]

In other words, while the use of soft law to tackle internal displacement is, overall, a success story, it is an inevitably limited one. IDP soft law tools do not yet comprehensively fill the interpretation gap arising from the hard law instruments from which they are derived. Given the complexity of particular displacement situations, perhaps comprehensive legal responses to the deeply political questions they raise are not possible. In this way, IDP soft law mirrors the weaknesses and limitations of international law—particularly international human rights and humanitarian law—more generally. International law is not a 'silver bullet' to the resolution of displacement crises, but a foundation to inform political and socio-economic interventions in support of IDPs.

[89] The Pinheiro Principles address some of these questions, advocating a precise interpretation of the right of return as the almost unfettered right of displaced persons to reclaim their lost homes or lands. However, the Pinheiro Principles have been extensively critiqued as misinterpreting or offering an insufficiently nuanced interpretation of obligations on this issue. See e.g.: Ballard (2010).

PART II

EMERGING HUMAN RIGHTS REGIMES

9

The Role of Soft Law in the Progressive Development of Indigenous Peoples' Rights

Felipe Gómez Isa

1. Introduction

Indigenous peoples have been systematically excluded from the process of evolution of International Human Rights Law.[1] The International Labour Organization (ILO) adopted in 1957 and 1989 the two major conventional instruments for the recognition and protection of indigenous peoples' rights (ILO Convention No. 107 and ILO Convention No. 169, respectively). Despite the current relevance of ILO Convention No. 169, it faces significant problems in terms of scope (only twenty-two states have ratified it so far), content, and effective mechanisms for implementation.

In the 1970s and 1980s the United Nations (UN) started to pay increasing attention to the situation of indigenous peoples worldwide, introducing a number of initiatives to adequately deal with their claims and opening institutional spaces for their meaningful participation. Against the background of the emerging mobilization of indigenous peoples at both domestic and international level, certain relevant soft law documents were adopted, and UN human rights treaty bodies and UN specialized agencies gradually focused on the marginalized situation of indigenous peoples. The most remarkable achievement within this movement has been the adoption, on 13 September 2007, of the United Nations Declaration on the Rights of Indigenous Peoples[2] (UNDRIP) by an overwhelming majority at the UN General Assembly. Since the 1980s, the adoption of such a document was one of the main demands of indigenous organizations and representatives. Being fully aware of its non-binding nature, they were convinced that the UN

[1] F. Gómez Isa, 'The Right to Development: Translating Indigenous Voice(s) into Development Theory and Practice', in *Improving Delivery in Development: The Role of Voice, Social Contract, and Accountability, The World Bank Legal Review* vol. 6, ed. J. Wouters, A. Ninio, T. Doherty, and H. Cissé (Washington, DC: The World Bank, 2015): 91.

[2] UN Doc. GA Resolution 61/295, 13 Sept. 2007.

Declaration could play a relevant role in the dynamic and challenging interplay between hard and soft law, thus contributing significantly to the recognition and implementation of indigenous rights at both domestic and international level. In this sense, the Declaration's context and content, as well as the institutional architecture for its implementation and the circumstances under which it was adopted, help clarify its legal scope and likelihood of influencing both state behaviour and the actions of international organizations as regards indigenous peoples, in particular the UN.

This chapter is aimed at exploring the potential, as well as the limitations and contradictions,[3] of soft law instruments (*primary* soft law) and soft law decisions and general comments (*secondary* soft law) in terms of fostering the process of progressively developing indigenous peoples' rights. In fact, in spite of its very recent adoption, the Declaration has already had far-reaching legal implications. For example, in November 2007, Bolivia not only adopted a law that incorporated the UNDRIP into its domestic legal system, but also included some of its provisions in the new Constitution approved in 2009. Along the same lines, certain domestic courts, the Inter-American Court of Human Rights, the African Commission on Human and Peoples' Rights, and the UN human rights treaty bodies have used the UNDRIP as the legal basis for some ground-breaking decisions affirming indigenous rights.

The second part of the chapter analyses the contradictory nature of international law as far as indigenous peoples are concerned. While traditional international law played a significant role in the process of subjugation and domination of indigenous peoples, contemporary international law has been used by indigenous peoples as a privileged avenue for articulating their claims and calling for reparation of the historical injustices perpetrated against them. The third section analyses the emergence of soft law as a conceptual category, its main contours, and its influence on both international law in general and international human rights law in particular. This essay's core lies in section 4, where I delineate how soft law has been of utmost importance for the evolution of indigenous peoples' rights in the last decades. The UNDRIP has marked the culmination of the progressive process of recognition of indigenous rights. Irrespective of its uncertain legal nature, it has become an indispensable point of reference when interpreting the rights of indigenous peoples at both domestic and international level, thus performing a *norm-filling* function. At the same time, some provisions of the UNDRIP have already become customary law, or are in the process of emerging as new customary rules of international law. By virtue of this evolutionary legal process, soft law can also play what the editors of this volume refer to as a *norm-creating* role.[4]

[3] On the 'ambiguous and multifaceted' role of soft law in the development of contemporary International Human Rights Law see the Introduction to this volume.

[4] The editors distinguish between the *norm-filling* and the *norm-creating* function of soft law.

2. Indigenous Peoples and International Law

Traditional international law played a major role in the dramatic history of the conquest of indigenous peoples, the usurpation of their sovereignty, and the dispossession of their lands, territories, and resources.[5] The emerging international legal order in Europe became a powerful instrument in the hands of conquerors to dominate and subjugate indigenous peoples in the Americas.[6] Since its inception, given the role played by the main European powers in its creation and the subordinate position of indigenous peoples and other non-Western countries and societies,[7] international law could be characterized as a hegemonic discourse and source of domination.[8] This situation continued unaltered until very recently, when contemporary international law progressively changed its approach to indigenous peoples. But it is quite remarkable that even in the first half of the twentieth century the West still believed itself to be entrusted with a 'civilizing mission' to save non-European peoples from ignorance and backwardness.[9] In line with this approach, the first international treaty adopted by the International Labour Organization (ILO) in 1957 to deal specifically with indigenous issues largely retained an assimilationist paradigm.[10] As stated in Article 2 of the Indigenous and Tribal Populations Convention (Convention No. 107, 1957), 'Governments shall have the primary responsibility for developing co-ordinated and systematic action for the protection of the populations concerned and their *progressive integration* into the life of their respective countries' (emphasis added).[11]

Post-Second World War international law recognized two core principles that have been of utmost importance to the struggle of indigenous peoples for recognition as distinct peoples in need of specific protection. The first principle relates to the purpose of the then-nascent United Nations of 'promoting and encouraging

[5] P. Keal, *European Conquest and the Rights of Indigenous Peoples: The Moral Backwardness of International Society* (New York: Cambridge University Press, 2003).

[6] J. Anaya, *Indigenous Peoples in International Law* (Oxford: Oxford University Press, 2004, 2nd edn). See also: A. Anghie, *Imperialism, Sovereignty and the Making of International Law* (Cambridge: Cambridge University Press, 2004).

[7] E. Pulitano, 'Indigenous Rights and International Law: An Introduction', in *Indigenous Rights in the Age of the UN Declaration*, ed. E. Pulitano (Cambridge: Cambridge University Press, 2012): 4.

[8] B. Rajagopal, *International Law from Below: Development, Social Movements and Third World Resistance* (Cambridge: Cambridge University Press, 2003).

[9] This is the essence of some provisions found in the Covenant of the League of Nations (1919), the constitutive treaty of the first international organization. According to Art. 22, a provision that has to be read in a colonial context, 'to those colonies and territories which as a consequence of the late war have ceased to be under the sovereignty of the States which formerly governed them and which are inhabited by *peoples not yet able to stand by themselves* under the strenuous conditions of the modern world, there should be applied the principle that the well-being and development of such peoples form a *sacred trust of civilization ...*' (emphasis added).

[10] P. Thornberry, *Indigenous Peoples and Human Rights* (Manchester: Manchester University Press, 2002): 329–33; J. M. Salgado, *Convenio 169 de la OIT sobre Pueblos Indígenas* (Neuquén: Universidad Nacional del Comahue, 2006): 29–30.

[11] Besides, ILO Convention No. 107 refers to indigenous 'populations' rather than peoples. The recognition as true peoples and nations is one of the main claims of the global indigenous movement.

respect for human rights and for fundamental freedoms for all without distinction as to race, sex, language, or religion'.[12] The second principle affirms the right of peoples to self-determination,[13] a principle that paved the way for the second process of decolonization after the 1960s.[14] These two principles served as the theoretical frame by means of which indigenous peoples articulated their main claims in the 1970s and 1980s.[15] International law, particularly international human rights law, became a very powerful discursive resource for indigenous peoples to advance their demands both domestically and at international fora. In Rhiannon Morgan's view, 'the global indigenous movement is just one example of a movement that has grasped the transformative, dynamic potential lodged in the discourse of human rights, drawing on its manipulability and malleability to foster the reform of human rights'.[16] At the same time, and as part of the process of empowering indigenous peoples, the United Nations has since the 1970s been increasingly receptive to claims by indigenous peoples,[17] opening institutional spaces and avenues for their

[12] Art. 1.3 of the United Nations Charter (1945).

[13] Art. 1.2 of the United Nations Charter establishes as one of the purposes of the UN 'to develop friendly relations among nations based on respect for the principle of equal rights and *self-determination of peoples*' (emphasis added).

[14] As stated by the Declaration on the Granting of Independence to Colonial Countries and Peoples, GA Res. 1514 (XV), 14 Dec. 1960, 'All peoples have the right to self-determination; by virtue of that right they freely determine their political status and freely pursue their economic, social and cultural development.' The conventional proclamation of the right of peoples to self-determination is to be found in common Art. 1 of the two human rights covenants adopted in 1966. The problem with this decolonization process is that, as Siegfried Wiessner explains, 'the choice as to the political future of colonized peoples was not given to the individual peoples conquered, but to the inhabitants of territories colonized by European conquerors, within the borders drawn by the colonizers'. The colonial powers used the Roman legal category of *uti possidetis* to maintain the borders that were delineated by them at the Berlin Conference of 1884. S. Wiessner, 'Indigenous Self-Determination, Culture, and Land: A Reassessment in Light of the 2007 UN Declaration on the Rights of Indigenous Peoples', in Pulitano (2012): 7, 36. As a consequence of this interpretation of the right to self-determination limited to the colonial context, indigenous peoples were not considered as potential beneficiaries of such a right. One of the most difficult issues during the process of negotiation of the UNDRIP was precisely the incorporation of the right of indigenous peoples to self-determination. Art. 3 of the UNDRIP does ultimately recognizes this controversial right, a right that has to be interpreted in light of Arts 4 and 46.1 of the Declaration. As James Anaya has stressed, 'reflecting the state of contemporary international law in relation to this principle as well as the demands of indigenous peoples themselves, the affirmation of self-determination in the Declaration is deemed compatible with the principle of territorial integrality and political unity of States', Report of the Special Rapporteur on the Situation of Human Rights and Fundamental Freedoms of Indigenous People, S. James Anaya, UN Doc. A/HRC/9/9, 11 Aug. 2008, para. 37.

[15] On the so-called *indigenous emergence* during the 1970s and 1980s: A. Brysk, *From Tribal Village to Global Village: Indian Rights and International Relations in Latin America* (Stanford, Calif.: Stanford University Press, 2000). See also: S. Martí i Puig, 'Emergencia indígena y política en América Latina tras la Década de los Pueblos Indígenas', in *La plasmación política de la diversidad: autonomía y participación política en América Latina*, ed. F. Gómez Isa and S. Ardanaz (Bilbao: Universidad de Deusto, 2011): 165–78.

[16] R. Morgan, *Transforming Law and Institution: Indigenous Peoples, the United Nations and Human Rights* (Farnham: Ashgate, 2011): 43.

[17] A very lucid analysis of the increasing involvement of the UN in indigenous issues by one of the key players within the Organization can be found in: A. Willemsen-Diaz, 'How Indigenous Peoples' Rights Reached the UN', in *Making the Declaration Work: The United Nations Declaration on the Rights of Indigenous Peoples*, ed. C. Charters and R. Stavenhagen (Copenhagen: IWGIA, 2009): 16–31.

participation and the advancement of their demands.[18] Indigenous peoples used the United Nations as a mobilizing structure to increase visibility of their marginalized position and to pursue some strategic goals in terms of recognition and protection.[19] In a sense, the period saw a very promising process of *decolonization* of both international law and the United Nations.[20] This process has allowed indigenous peoples to transform from mere victims to actors, and from objects of protection to subjects of rights,[21] thus opening the door to their acquisition of some forms of international legal personality.[22] The culmination of this legal and institutional development was the creation of the UN Permanent Forum on Indigenous Issues in 2000, a unique body in which states and indigenous representatives participate on an equal footing,[23] and the adoption of the UNDRIP in 2007. As the Committee on the Rights of Indigenous Peoples of the International Law Association (ILA) has affirmed, all these developments demonstrate that 'indigenous persons and peoples are back not only as fully entitled holders of individual human rights, but as collective actors with distinct rights and status under international law'.[24]

[18] A number of bodies were created to deal specifically with indigenous issues (Working Group on Indigenous Peoples; Working Group on a Draft Declaration on indigenous peoples' rights; Permanent Forum on Indigenous Issues; Special Rapporteur on the Rights of Indigenous Peoples; and Expert Mechanism on the Rights of Indigenous Peoples). The General Assembly of the UN also proclaimed two consecutive UN Decades on Indigenous Peoples (1994–2003, and 2005–14). The UN Permanent Forum on Indigenous Issues has recently called for a Third International Decade of the World's Indigenous Peoples. In its view, 'over the course of the two Decades, we have seen some progress ... However, we need to ensure and reinvigorate momentum to genuinely implement the UN Declaration ... A Third Decade can provide a framework and consolidate clear milestones for the achievement of the UN Declaration ...' 'A Third International Decade of the World's Indigenous Peoples', United Nations Permanent Forum on Indigenous Issues (Dalee Sambo Dorough, Chairperson, 7 Nov. 2014), <http://www.un.org/esa/socdev/unpfii/documents/Communication-UNPFII%20Chair-3decade.pdf>.

[19] I. Bellier and M. Préaud, 'Emerging Issues in Indigenous Rights: Transformative Effects of the Recognition of Indigenous Peoples', *The International Journal of Human Rights* vol. 16 (2012): 474–88.

[20] Post-1945 international law and institutions have been used by the West (itself an imagined community) to construct and impose a new set of rational truths based on particular values, norms, and socio-political organizations that have been defined as universal. Post-colonial studies have demonstrated that international law and institutions, among many other structures of power, were used by the West to maintain its hierarchies and modes of domination. Indigenous peoples' struggles have aimed to decolonize both the theory and practice of the 'ideological-institutional complex' known as international law. On this challenging processes see the illuminating essay by Sundhya Pahuja, *Decolonizing International Law: Development, Economic Growth and the Politics of Universality* (Cambridge: Cambridge University Press, 2011).

[21] F. Gómez Isa, 'Pueblos indígenas: de objeto de protección a sujetos de derechos', in *Vulnerabilidad y protección de los derechos humanos*, ed. M. C. Barranco and C. Churruca (Valencia: Tirant lo Blanch, 2014): 167–85.

[22] D. S. Dorough, 'The Significance of the Declaration on the Rights of Indigenous Peoples and Its Future Implementation', in Charters and Stavenhagen (2009): 265. See also: A. Meijknecht, *Towards International Personality: The Position of Minorities and Indigenous Peoples in International Law* (Oxford: Intersentia, 2001).

[23] A description of the process that led to the creation of the PFII and its main functions in L. García-Alix, *The Permanent Forum on Indigenous Issues* (Copenhagen: IWGIA, 2003).

[24] International Law Association, *Rights of Indigenous Peoples*, Report of the Hague Conference (2010): 2.

3. Soft Law in the Evolution of International Law

Under traditional international law, the sources for the emergence of law were primarily treaties and customary law. Accordingly, the creation of international rules was a predominantly state-led process. Contemporary international law-making has become a much more complex, dynamic, and, sometimes, contradictory process, with a number of norms, ranging from hard law conventions to soft law instruments, and with a multiplicity of actors participating. Nevertheless, as the long delay in the process that led to the adoption of the UNDRIP clearly shows, 'the political will of states remains crucial to the law-making activities of non-state actors'.[25]

In this new scenario, soft law plays an increasingly relevant role, especially in the field of international human rights law. Soft law basically plays three main roles in the progressive development of international law.[26] First, soft law instruments can perform an *interpretative function*, providing useful guidelines to fill gaps and lacunae in existing normative standards. Secondly, soft law can have a *crystallizing effect* on norms that are in a process of emergence as customary international law, that is, a soft law instrument such as a declaration adopted by a significant majority of states at the UN General Assembly can be the final stage of the formation of a given norm. The third function is a *prospective function*, since soft law instruments proclaim new rules aimed at generating international consensus so that these new norms can be accepted as legally binding, as either customary law or conventional law. In fact, many human rights treaties were preceded by declarations adopted by the UN General Assembly,[27] and in this sense have a performative character.[28]

The presence of soft law in the current international legal panorama is essentially due to the growing relevance of international organizations in world politics (in particular the UN), the emergence of so-called third-world countries following the process of decolonization, and the progressive participation of a myriad of actors (both state and non-state actors)[29] in the norm-creation processes. This has led to

[25] A. Boyle and C. Chinkin, *The Making of International Law* (Oxford: Oxford University Press, 2007): 49.

[26] While the editors of this volume refer to two main functions of soft law (*norm-filling* and *norm-creating* function), I think that the second of these functions can be further divided into the *crystallizing* and the *prospective* functions.

[27] C. Joyner, 'UN General Assembly Resolutions and International Law: Rethinking the Contemporary Dynamics of Norm-Creation', *California Western International Law Journal* vol. 11 (1981): 470.

[28] A very illuminating analysis of the concept of performativity, from a legal anthropological angle, as applied to the multifaceted processes around the UNDRIP can be found in I. Bellier, 'La *Performativité* de la Déclaration des droits de peoples autochtones', *Cultures-Kairós: revue d'anthropologie des pratiques corporelles et des arts vivants* no. 4 (2014), <http://revues.mshparisnord.org/cultureskairos/index.php?id=960>.

[29] For a reflection on the role that non-state actors play in contemporary international law see: *Participants in the International Legal System: Multiple Perspectives on Non-state Actors in International Law*, ed. J. d'Aspremont (Abingdon: Routledge, 2011). See also: *Non-state Actor Dynamics in International Law: From Law-Takers to Law-Makers*, ed. M. Noortmann and C. Ryngaert (Farnham: Ashgate, 2010).

a necessary flexibilization of the methods for forming international law, which had been rooted in legal positivism and Article 38.1 of the Statute of the International Court of Justice (1945).[30] Soft law is now a well-established legal category, and contemporary international law has to accommodate it within the varied processes for creating and implementing international norms. An in-depth analysis of current practice shows that the legal value of human rights norms is not the key element in promoting compliance with these norms, and in a number of cases formally non-binding rules have played an even more effective role in encouraging human rights compliance.[31]

While the role played by soft law in contemporary international human rights law is undeniably relevant, there are also strong reasons to advocate a cautious approach.[32] First of all, an anarchic and chaotic proliferation of soft law instruments can undermine the consistency and integrity of international law itself. In this sense, Prosper Weil has affirmed that international law 'est malade de ses normes', given that 'the multiplication of *soft* instruments is a symptom of the weakness of the international legal system'.[33] In Weil's opinion, there exists a clear 'normativity threshold' that serves to distinguish between law and non-law. If that is not the case, and the threshold is not clearly established, international law may become a 'relative' legal system.[34] Other scholars counter that this threshold cannot be strictly delineated, since there is a grey area between law and non-law within which the resolutions of international organizations play a pre-eminent role, and that the legality–legitimacy dialectic will always be present.[35] Accordingly, a certain degree of relative normativity is 'inevitable',[36] being inherent to every legal system, and soft law can become a vital tool for the interpretation of existing international norms and the formulation of new customary rules and general principles.

The quality of international norms is also a serious concern associated with the increasing role played by soft law. In the context of the emergence of the so-called third-generation human rights in the 1980s, Philip Alston warned against the excessive speed and ease with which new rights were being created through soft law instruments,[37] giving rise to a disturbing 'inflation of rights'.[38] The process of

[30] A. D'Amato, 'International Soft Law, Hard Law, and Coherence', *Northwestern Public Law Research Paper*, no. 08-01 (2008): 1–31.

[31] D. Shelton, 'Commentary and Conclusions', in *Commitment and Compliance: The Role of Non-binding Norms in the International Legal System*, ed. D. Shelton (Oxford: Oxford University Press, 2000): 449.

[32] See the Introduction to this volume.

[33] P. Weil, 'Vers une normativité relative en Droit International', *Revue générale de droit international public* vol. 86 (1982): 6–9.

[34] Weil (1982): 9.

[35] A. Pellet, 'Le Bon Droit et l'ivraie: plaidoyer pour l'ivraie (remarques sur quelques problèmes de méthode en droit international du développement)', in *Le Droit des peuples à disposer d'eux mèmes: méthodes d'analyse du Droit International. Mélanges offerts à Charles Chaumont* (Paris: Pedone, 1984): 488.

[36] U. Fastenrath, 'Relative Normativity in International Law', *European Journal of International Law* vol. 4 (1993): 306.

[37] P. Alston, 'Conjuring up New Human Rights: A Proposal for Quality Control', *American Journal of International Law* vol. 78 (1984): 607.

[38] S. M. Helmons, 'Considérations finales', in *Droits de l'homme et droit au développement*, ed. S. M. Helmons (Bruxelles: Bruylant, 1989): 88.

legalizing new human rights must be governed by proper reflection, methodological rigour, precision regarding their content, and the participation of the relevant stakeholders.[39] Therefore, the quality of the norm-creation process is a precondition for ensuring its future effectiveness and implementation by avoiding a 'legal jungle' of inconsistent norms and divergent interpretations.[40] Ultimately, Alston was proposing a process of 'quality control',[41] to eliminate, to the extent possible, mere rhetoric and proclamations of wishful thinking.[42]

Another distinctive feature of soft law is the conflation of law and politics.[43] Although international law itself is a highly political process,[44] some scholars argue that soft law instruments are sometimes extremely contaminated by political considerations. This situation can lead to the perception of soft law norms as political tools rather than legal instruments, thus affecting their very legal nature. During the 1960s and 1970s, the newly independent countries that emerged from the process of decolonization conceived international law, in particular the UN General Assembly resolutions, as a powerful tool for transforming asymmetric power relations between states. René-Jean Dupuy has referred to these soft law norms as a 'droit de finalité',[45] a set of norms aimed at establishing a new political and economic order at the international level.[46] This has been eloquently expressed by Professor Carrillo Salcedo:

> although their legal value is doubtful, many UN General Assembly resolutions are instruments aimed at promoting changes in the international legal system. Especially if they are adopted by a majority of states, they question existing international law, and send a clear message as to the aspirations of the majority of the international community.[47]

As we will see, this is one of the most relevant characteristics of the UNDRIP, since it encapsulates the profound aspirations of the world's indigenous peoples, thus gaining significant political and moral force. This, in fact, is the source of the considerable legitimacy of this soft law document, 'rather than its claimed international legal character'.[48] And, as Claire Charters has very rightly stated, 'the greater

[39] M. Flory, 'Introduction générale', in *Droits de l'homme et droit au développement*, ed. M. Flory, A. Mahiou, and J. R. Henry (Paris: CNRS, 1984): 13.

[40] Weil (1982): 6–7.

[41] Alston (1984): 618.

[42] R. Ida, 'Formation des normes internationals dans un monde en mutation: critique de la notion de Soft Law', in *Le Droit international au service de la paix, de la justice et du développement: Mélanges Michel Virally* (Paris: Pedone, 1991): 334.

[43] J. Donelly, 'In Search of the Unicorn: The Jurisprudence and Politics of the Right to Development', *California Western International Law Journal* vol. 15 (1985): 477.

[44] Makau Mutua has referred to a 'symbiotic' relation between international law, human rights, and politics, M. Mutua, 'Politics and Human Rights: An Essential Symbiosis', in *The Role of Law in International Politics*, ed. M. Byers (Oxford: Oxford University Press, 2000): 149–75.

[45] R. J. Dupuy, 'Droit déclaratoire et droit programmatoire: de la coutume sauvage a la *soft law*', in *L'Élaboration du droit international public* (Paris: Pedone, 1975): 133.

[46] The most relevant instrument was the Declaration on the Establishment of a New International Economic Order, UN Doc. UNGA Resolution 3201 (S-VI), 1 May 1974.

[47] J. A. Carrillo Salcedo, *Curso de derecho internacional público* (Madrid: Tecnos, 1991): 132.

[48] S. Allen, 'The UN Declaration on the Rights of Indigenous Peoples and the Limits of the International Legal Project', in *Reflections on the UN Declaration on the Rights of Indigenous Peoples*, ed. S. Allen and A. Xanthaki (Oxford: Hart Publishing, 2011): 225.

the perception of the Declaration on the Rights of Indigenous Peoples' legitimacy, the greater the likelihood that states will give effect to its provisions',[49] irrespective of its legal status.

So far, we have analysed the emergence of soft law as a well-established category in contemporary international law, its potential to generate new rules of law, and certain related difficulties. Section 4 will comprise a reflection on the role played by soft law in the progressive recognition of indigenous peoples' human rights.

4. Soft Law and Indigenous Peoples' Rights

We must acknowledge from the outset that soft law, in particular the UNDRIP, has had an enormous impact in the remarkable development of indigenous peoples' rights over the last two decades. A priority of the global indigenous movement had always been the elaboration of a declaration,[50] given the relatively negative experience of the two existing ILO conventions on indigenous peoples. The adoption of ILO Convention 169 in 1989, replacing ILO Convention No. 107 (1957),[51] was a relevant step forward for the recognition of indigenous rights,[52] but states have been very reluctant to ratify it.[53] The choice of a soft law document such as the UNDRIP therefore 'guaranteed the adoption of an instrument of universal scope that all indigenous peoples may use to foster their rights',[54] circumventing the obstacle posed by the poor number of ILO conventions ratifications.

[49] C. Charters, 'The Legitimacy of the UN Declaration on the Rights of Indigenous Peoples', in Charters and Stavenhagen (2009): 280.

[50] As one of the key players in the process of adoption of the UNDRIP has underlined, 'there was more or less general agreement on all sides that the UN Working Group on Indigenous Populations should in the first instance produce a declaration, eventually to be adopted by the UN General Assembly. The possibility of a convention was also mentioned, but there seemed to be general agreement that this kind of instrument would emerge further down the road, possibly inspired by the declaration', E. I. Daes, 'The UN Declaration on the Rights of Indigenous Peoples: Background and Appraisal', in Allen and Xanthaki (2011): 22.

[51] Twenty-seven states ratified this convention. Since the adoption of ILO Convention 169, Convention 107 is no longer open for ratification. However, it is still in force in eighteen countries that have not yet ratified Convention 169.

[52] A comprehensive analysis of this convention can be found in, L. Rodríguez-Piñero, *Indigenous Peoples, Post-colonialism and International Law: The ILO Regime (1919–1989)* (Oxford: Oxford University Press, 2005).

[53] As of Dec. 2015, twenty-two states have ratified ILO Convention No. 169 (Argentina, Plurinational State of Bolivia, Brazil, Central African Republic, Chile, Colombia, Costa Rica, Denmark, Dominica, Ecuador, Fiji, Guatemala, Honduras, Mexico, Nepal, Netherlands, Nicaragua, Norway, Paraguay, Peru, Spain, and Bolivarian Republic of Venezuela), <http://www.ilo.org/dyn/normlex/en/f?p=1000:11300:0::NO:11300:P11300_INSTRUMENT_ID:312314>.

[54] M. Barelli, 'The Role of Soft Law in the International Legal System: The Case of the United Nations Declaration on the Rights of Indigenous Peoples', *International and Comparative Law Quarterly* vol. 58 (2009): 965.

4.1 Participation of indigenous peoples

Another significant advantage of using the avenue of a soft law document instead of an international treaty is that 'it normally allows for the more active participation of non-state actors'.[55] It should be noted that this was the case with indigenous peoples, since they participated very actively in all stages of the process leading to the adoption of the UNDRIP.[56] Since the creation of the UN Working Group on Indigenous Populations (WGIP) in 1982 by what was then the Sub-Commission on Prevention of Discrimination and Protection of Minorities (the Sub-Commission),[57] and the decision in 1985 to adopt a draft Declaration on the rights of indigenous peoples, followed by the creation of the Working Group on the Draft Declaration (WGDD) in 1995, the meaningful participation of the global indigenous movement has become one of the key features of the lengthy process of negotiation and adoption of the UNDRIP.[58]

At the time of the creation of the WGIP, a body composed of five independent experts, only NGOs with consultative status before the UN Economic and Social Council (ECOSOC) could participate as observers in the meetings of the working groups created by the Sub-Commission. This was an obstacle for indigenous organizations wanting to participate in the WGIP, since almost no indigenous organization had consultative status before the ECOSOC at that time. The first chairperson of the WGIP, Asbjorn Eide, took a decision that was to have significant consequences for the process of institutionalizing indigenous participation at the UN bodies dealing with indigenous issues. He opened up the working group to indigenous representatives, thus effecting a dramatic change in the tradition of participation of NGOs in working groups. Although this decision met with some objections, he received strong support from Theo Van Boven, Director of the UN Human Rights Center. As Eide has lucidly explained,

> to fulfil the mandate of reviewing developments concerning indigenous populations and to work towards developing the corresponding standards, there was a need to have the best possible experts present, and the best experts were the indigenous representatives themselves.[59]

The same dilemma was faced by the WGDD when it was created in 1995 by the then UN Commission on Human Rights (CHR)[60] aimed at adopting a draft Declaration on the rights of indigenous peoples. Indigenous peoples' representatives were concerned about the strict rules on NGO participation established by the CHR, and lobbied extensively to gain similar spaces for participation to those

[55] Barelli (2009): 965.

[56] A. Xanthaki, *Indigenous Rights and United Nations Standards: Self-Determination, Culture and Land* (Cambridge: Cambridge University Press, 2007): 102.

[57] ECOSOC Resolution 1982/34, 7 May 1982.

[58] I. Bellier, 'Les Peuples autochtones aux Nations Unies: un nouvel acteur dans la fabrique des normes internationales', *Critique Internationale* vol. 54/1 (2012).

[59] A. Eide, 'The Indigenous Peoples, the Working Group on Indigenous Populations and the Adoption of the UN Declaration on the Rights of Indigenous Peoples', in Charters and Stavenhagen (2009): 34.

[60] UN Commission on Human Rights, Resolution 1995/32, 3 Mar. 1995.

existing within the WGIP. While not meeting the degree of openness that characterized the WGIP, indigenous organizations also had the chance to participate significantly throughout the negotiation process. In Rhiannon Morgan's view, 'during the drafting of the UNDRIP, indigenous representatives succeeded in pressing for unprecedented levels of inclusiveness and participation, allowing not only for the extensive input of indigenous perspectives as to the content of their rights but also some degree of control over decision-making processes'.[61] The truth is that indigenous peoples' representatives and organizations benefited immensely from this democratic culture of openness, and since then have occupied an increasing number of spaces within UN bodies dealing with indigenous issues. The increasing participation of civil society movements and other transnational actors in the 'state-centric system of international law has itself been part of the democratisation trend' of contemporary international law-making.[62]

4.2 Legal implications of the UNDRIP

The adoption of the UNDRIP on 2007 by the UN General Assembly was the culmination of a challenging process initiated more than twenty years ago in which indigenous peoples themselves were the main driving force.[63] The adoption also reflects the deep aspirations of the world's indigenous peoples and their confidence in international law and human rights law as powerful tools to modify entrenched patterns of domination and exclusion that have affected indigenous peoples since colonial times.[64] To a great extent, the UNDRIP is an attempt to repair historical wrongs suffered by indigenous peoples.[65] As established by the UNDRIP in its preamble, 'indigenous peoples have suffered from *historic injustices* as a result of, inter alia, their colonization and dispossession of their lands, territories and resources, thus preventing them from exercising, in particular, their right to development in accordance with their own needs and interests'.[66]

[61] Morgan (2011): 41. This process did not count with the support of the USA. In its view, 'this process was unfortunate and extraordinary in any multilateral negotiating exercise and sets a poor precedent with respect to UN practice', United States, 'Observations of the United States with respect to the Declaration on the Rights of Indigenous Peoples: Explanation of Vote by Robert Hagen, U.S. Advisor, on the Declaration on the Rights of Indigenous Peoples, to the UN General Assembly', 13 Sept. 2007.

[62] Boyle and Chinkin (2007): 43.

[63] I. Bellier, 'Retour sur la négotiation de la Déclaration des Droits des Peuples Autochtones: reconnaître le principe d'égalité pour avancer des interprétations pragmatiques', in *Le Statut des peoples autochtones: à la croisée des saviors*, ed. S. P. Dassonville (Paris: Karthala, 2012): 73–96.

[64] H. P. Glenn, 'The Three Ironies of the UN Declaration on the Rights of Indigenous Peoples', in Allen and Xanthaki (2011): 174.

[65] F. Gómez Isa, 'Repairing Historical Injustices: Indigenous Peoples in Post-Conflict Scenarios', in *Rethinking Transitions: Equality and Social Justice in Societies Emerging from Conflict*, ed. G. O. Aguilar and F. Gómez Isa (Cambridge-Antwerp: Intersentia, 2011): 265–300.

[66] Para. 5 of the Preamble (emphasis added). In James Anaya's view, this preambular paragraph of the Declaration 'stresses the essentially remedial purpose of the instrument. Far from affirming special rights per se, the Declaration aims at repairing the ongoing consequences of the historical denial of the right to self-determination and other basic human rights affirmed in international instruments of general applicability', Report of the Special Rapporteur on the Situation of Human Rights and

Concerning the legal status of the rights recognized in the UNDRIP, we must first distinguish between the legal value of the Declaration itself and the normative character of the substantive rights included in the UNDRIP.

4.2.1 The UNDRIP and existing international law

To a great extent, many of the provisions embodied in the UNDRIP do not create new rights, but may be considered a reaffirmation of existing customary international law.[67] As James Anaya, former Special Rapporteur on the situation of human rights and fundamental freedoms of indigenous people, has argued, the Declaration 'reflects the existing international consensus regarding the individual and collective rights of indigenous peoples in a way that is coherent with, and expands upon, international developments, including the interpretations of other human rights instruments by international bodies and mechanisms'.[68] A similar view is expressed by Luis Rodríguez-Piñero, who claims that 'most of the substantive rights enshrined in the Declaration, notably in key areas such as indigenous peoples' self-determination, autonomy, participation, land and resource rights, cultural rights, and social and economic rights, relate to already existing human rights obligations derived from general treaties, as well as to specific legally-binding instruments on indigenous rights, such as ILO Convention 169'.[69] The same conclusion can be found in a recent resolution adopted by the International Law Association (ILA). According to this authoritative opinion,[70] 'the 2007 UNDRIP as a whole cannot yet be considered as a statement of existing customary international law. However it includes several key provisions which correspond to existing state obligations under customary international law.'[71] Among the UNDRIP norms that may be regarded as evidence of customary international law, the ILA included the following: the right of indigenous peoples to self-determination, autonomy, and self-government; the right to participate in national decision-making with respect to decisions that may affect them; the right to free, prior, and informed consent (FPIC) on projects significantly impacting their rights and ways of life; the right to cultural identity; the right to lands, territories, and resources, including restitution of ancestral lands

Fundamental Freedoms of Indigenous People, S. James Anaya, UN Doc. A/HRC/9/9, 11 Aug. 2008, para. 36.

[67] J. Anaya and S. Wiessner, 'The UN Declaration on the Rights of Indigenous Peoples: Towards Re-empowerment', *Jurist* (3 Oct. 2007), <http://jurist.org/forum/2007/10/un-declaration-on-rights-of-indigenous.php>.

[68] Report of the Special Rapporteur on the Situation of Human Rights and Fundamental Freedoms of Indigenous People, S. James Anaya, UN Doc. A/HRC/9/9, 11 Aug. 2008, para. 43.

[69] L. Rodríguez-Piñero, 'Where Appropriate: Monitoring/Implementing of Indigenous Peoples' Rights under the Declaration', in Charters and Stavenhagen (2009): 336.

[70] It has to be taken into account that, according to Art. 38.1.d of the Statute of the International Court of Justice (1945), 'the teachings of the most highly qualified publicists of the various nations can be considered as *subsidiary* means for the determination of rules of law' (emphasis added).

[71] Resolution No. 5/2012, 75th Conference of the ILA, Sofia, 26–30 Aug., para. 2.

of which they have been deprived in the past; the right to establish their own educational institutions and media; and the right to reparation and redress for wrongs indigenous peoples have suffered.[72]

This position was explicitly rejected by those states that voted against the UNDRIP (the United States, Canada, Australia, and New Zealand).[73] The clearest opposition came from the United States (USA), denying

> any possibility that this document is or can become customary international law ... As this declaration does not describe current state practice or actions that states feel obliged to take as a matter of legal obligation, it cannot be cited as evidence of the evolution of customary international law.[74]

While recognizing the relevance of the position of these states, it should be noted that they 'represent only a minority of states specially affected by the Declaration'.[75] As a consequence of this, the position of these states would be unable to prevent the emergence of international customary law.[76] However, it is likely that they could have been considered persistent objectors, given that they opposed the text of the UNDRIP from the earliest drafting stages. Fortunately for the indigenous peoples' cause, these four states have changed their official positions vis-à-vis the UNDRIP and endorsed it, having repeatedly reiterated that the Declaration is neither legally binding nor a statement of current international law, and will not influence their domestic legal orders.

Some of the provisions of the UNDRIP can even be considered as evidence of already existing rights under general international law, thus having an *erga omnes* effect. Among those norms that have turned into *ius cogens* norms, we may refer to 'the right of peoples and individuals to be free from any kind of discrimination, in particular that based on their indigenous origin or identity',[77] the right not to be subjected to any act of genocide,[78] the right to practise their own cultural traditions and customs,[79] or 'the right to participate in decision-making in matters which would affect their rights'.[80]

[72] Resolution No. 5/2012, 75th Conference of the ILA, Sofia, 26–30 Aug., para 2.

[73] For further details on the statements made by these countries, see Léticia Villeneuve's contribution in this volume.

[74] United States, 'Observations of the United States with respect to the Declaration on the Rights of Indigenous Peoples: Explanation of Vote by Robert Hagen, U.S. Advisor, on the Declaration on the Rights of Indigenous Peoples, to the UN General Assembly', 13 Sept. 2007.

[75] Barelli (2009): 967.

[76] M. Meza-Lopehandía, 'El derecho internacional de los derechos humanos y los pueblos indígenas', in *Los pueblos indígenas y el derecho*, José Aylwin (coord.) (Santiago de Chile: LOM Ediciones, 2013): 466.

[77] Art. 2, UNDRIP. [78] Art. 7.

[79] Art. 11. On the role of indigenous customary law for the development of indigenous peoples and for the establishment of an intercultural justice and equity, see the illuminating essay by B. Tobin, *Indigenous Peoples, Customary Law and Human Rights: Why Living Law Matters* (New York: Routledge, 2014).

[80] Art. 18.

4.2.2 The legal value of the UNDRIP

As we already know, resolutions of the UN General Assembly are not binding per se, since they are considered 'recommendations' by Article 13.1 of the UN Charter.[81] However, under certain circumstances, some scholars argue that the General Assembly can have a 'quasi-legislative competence',[82] and can participate in the process of progressive development of international law. When the resolution is adopted as a 'Declaration', the likelihood of having legal effects is much higher,[83] as was the case with the Universal Declaration of Human Rights (1948). Some Declarations of the UN General Assembly, especially those aimed at proclaiming legal principles and adopted by a significant majority, can be considered an expression of the *opinio iuris* of states,[84] one of the required elements for the formation of new rules of customary law if followed by consistent state practice. Thus, in 1962, the Office of Legal Affairs of the UN Secretariat adopted a highly relevant opinion regarding the legal nature of Declarations adopted by the UN General Assembly. According to this Memorandum, a Declaration 'is a formal and solemn instrument, suitable for rare occasions when principles of great and lasting importance are being enunciated'.[85] Therefore, with the adoption of the UNDRIP as a 'Declaration', the international community is recognizing that the rights and principles enshrined in the UNDRIP are of special significance, generating expectations of maximum compliance. Provided that these expectations are followed by state practice, 'a

[81] Art. 13.1 of the UN Charter: 'The General Assembly shall initiate studies and make *recommendations* for the purpose of: a) promoting international co-operation in the political field and encouraging the progressive development of international law and its codification; b) promoting international co-operation in the economic, social, cultural, educational, and health fields, and assisting in the realization of human rights and fundamental freedoms for all without distinction as to race, sex, language, or religion' (emphasis added).

[82] R. Falk, 'On the quasi-legislative competence of the General Assembly', *American Journal of International Law* vol. 60 (1960): 782. Along the same lines see: O. Y. Asamoah, *The Legal Significance of the Declarations of the General Assembly of the United Nations* (The Hague: Martinus Nijhoff Publishers, 1966): 2.

[83] But 'there is no magic in the label', as the ILA has underlined, International Law Association, 'Statement of Principles Applicable to the Formation of Customary International Law' (Final Report of the Committee, London Conference, 2000): 63.

[84] According to the International Court of Justice (ICJ), the '*opinio iuris* may, though with all due caution, be deduced from, *inter alia*, the attitude of the Parties and the attitude of States towards certain General Assembly resolutions, and particularly resolution 2625 (XXV) entitled Declaration on Principles of International Law concerning Friendly Relations and Co-operation among States in accordance with the Charter of the United Nations'. The effect of consent to the text of such resolutions cannot be understood as merely that of a 'reiteration or elucidation' of the treaty commitment undertaken in the Charter. On the contrary, it may be understood as an acceptance of the validity of the rule or set of rules declared by the resolution by themselves, ICJ Reports, 'Military and Paramilitary Activities in and against Nicaragua (Nicaragua v. United States of America), Merits, Judgment' (1986): 100, para. 188. This position has been reiterated by the ICJ in an advisory opinion issued in 1996. In its view, 'General Assembly resolutions, even if they are not binding, may ... provide evidence important for establishing the existence of a rule or the emergence of an *opinio iuris*', ICJ Reports, 'Legality of the Threat or Use of Nuclear Weapons, Advisory Opinion' (1996): 226, para. 70. A criticism of this line of reasoning by the ICJ can be found in M. Mendelson, 'The Nicaragua Case and Customary Law', *Coexistence* vol. 26 (1989): 85.

[85] Memorandum of the Office of Legal Affairs, UN Secretariat, UN Doc. E/CN.4/L.610, 2 Apr. 1962.

Declaration can be considered as an instrument enunciating obligatory rules for states as customary law'.[86]

When trying to ascertain the legal value of the UNDRIP, three elements are of utmost importance: the circumstances of the instrument's adoption, the precision and normative nature of its content, and the existence of implementation mechanisms.

The adoption of the UNDRIP in 2007 is the result of more than twenty years of intense and controversial negotiations in which indigenous peoples and their close allies achieved very significant levels of participation. Undoubtedly, the way in which this process was conducted, together with its highly positive outcomes, will come to influence international norm-creation exercises in other areas of international law in general, and international human rights law in particular. H. Patrick Glenn situates the Declaration within a broader international law movement. In his view, the Declaration 'would represent not simply a use or application of international law, in novel circumstances, but a major shift in the nature and direction of international law itself'.[87]

The inclusiveness of the process and the support from a number of bodies and instances within the UN, and from states themselves, provides the Declaration with a high degree of legitimacy that is certain to increase compliance. The UN has been highly supportive from the outset, and we have already mentioned how relevant bodies such as the WGIP and the WGDD have adapted their procedural rules to the specificities and needs of indigenous representatives and organizations. The World Conference on Human Rights (1993) issued a strong call for the promotion and protection of the rights of indigenous peoples. According to the Vienna Declaration and Programme of Action, 'States should, in accordance with international law, take concerted positive steps to ensure respect for all human rights and fundamental freedoms of indigenous people, on the basis of equality and non-discrimination, and recognize the value and diversity of their distinct identities, cultures and social organization.'[88] At the same time, the World Conference urged the WGIP 'to complete the drafting of a declaration on the rights of indigenous people'[89] and recommended 'that the General Assembly proclaim an international decade of the world's indigenous people'.[90] This recommendation was welcomed by the General Assembly, which proclaimed the International Decade for the World's

[86] Memorandum of the Office of Legal Affairs, UN Secretariat, UN Doc. E/CN.4/L.610, 2 Apr. 1962.

[87] Glenn (2011): 174. A very similar position has been expressed by Will Kymlicka, for whom the Declaration can be seen 'as a victory for international law itself', W. Kymlicka, 'Beyond the Indigenous/Minority Dichotomy?', in Allen and Xanthaki (2011): 183.

[88] Vienna Declaration and Programme of Action, World Conference on Human Rights, UN Doc. A/CONF.157/23, 12 July 1993, para. 20.

[89] Vienna Declaration and Programme of Action, World Conference on Human Rights, UN Doc. A/CONF.157/23, 12 July 1993, para. II, 28.

[90] Vienna Declaration and Programme of Action, World Conference on Human Rights, UN Doc. A/CONF.157/23, 12 July 1993, para. II, 32.

Indigenous People (1995–2004).[91] In spite of certain shortcomings,[92] especially the failure to adopt the Declaration on the rights of indigenous peoples, a number of relevant institutional developments must be highlighted, in particular the creation of the Permanent Forum on Indigenous Issues (PFII, 2000) and the Special Rapporteur on the rights of indigenous peoples, two remarkable achievements on the part of the global indigenous movement. A Second International Decade of the World's Indigenous People (2005–14)[93] was announced by the General Assembly, with one of the basic goals of this new Decade being the adoption of the Declaration. The 2005 World Summit also focused specifically on the issue of the rights of indigenous peoples. As stated in the World Summit Outcome, 'we reaffirm our commitment to continue making progress in the advancement of the human rights of the world's indigenous peoples at the local, national, regional and international levels, including through consultation and collaboration with them, and to present for adoption a final draft United Nations declaration on the rights of indigenous peoples *as soon as possible*'.[94] All these initiatives, and many others not mentioned in this chapter, unequivocally signal a 'systemic interest in indigenous concerns within the UN system'.[95]

The final vote on the UNDRIP at the UN General Assembly is also an indication of the international consensus regarding the document. As one scholar has highlighted in this respect,

> the adoption of resolutions such as the UNDRIP should not be taken to have an intrinsic impact on customary international law, but rather to function as an inspiration for future practice and as an occasion for individual states to make collateral statements that clarify their attitude with regard to the customary law of indigenous rights.[96]

The International Law Association (ILA) has also stressed the importance of looking beyond the votes on a specific resolution. According to the ILA, 'the circumstances of adoption need to be examined closely. It is necessary to examine, not just who voted for the resolution as a whole, but also the explanations or comments accompanying each vote and the paragraph by paragraph votes of States.'[97] As we know, 144 states voted in favour of the Declaration, eleven abstained,[98] and four voted against. In an interesting development since 2007, the four states that voted against have now all endorsed the Declaration. Along the same lines, two of the abstaining states, Colombia and Samoa, have also made up their mind to

[91] Resolution 48/163, 18 Feb. 1994.

[92] A very critical analysis of the outcomes of the First Indigenous Decade can be found in, J. Corntassel, 'Partnership in Action? Indigenous Political Mobilization and Co-optation During the First UN Indigenous Decade (1995–2004)', *Human Rights Quarterly* vol. 29 (2007): 137–66.

[93] Resolution 59/174, 24 Feb. 2005.

[94] Resolution 60/1, 16 Sept. 2005 (emphasis added).

[95] Morgan (2011): 28.

[96] E. Voyiakis, 'Voting in the General Assembly as Evidence of Customary International Law?', in Allen and Xanthaki (2011): 222.

[97] International Law Association, *Rights of Indigenous Peoples*, Report of the Hague Conference (2010): 58.

[98] Azerbaijan, Bangladesh, Bhutan, Burundi, Colombia, Georgia, Kenya, Nigeria, Russian Federation, Samoa, and Ukraine.

subsequently endorse the Declaration. This overwhelming support for the UNDRIP shows a clear commitment on the part of the international community to support protection of the rights enshrined in the Declaration and promote compliance, and can be considered as clear evidence of *opinio iuris* which, if accompanied by consistent state practice, may give rise to new rules of customary international law.

The second element to be taken into account deals with the precision and normative content of the rights incorporated in the UNDRIP. First of all, it should be observed that the Declaration is the longest human rights instrument ever adopted in the UN. It was negotiated over a period of more than twenty years, allowing for substantive consultations and proposals as well as the development of highly precise provisions, in terms of both content and scope. Besides, as we have already mentioned, many of the provisions are evidence of pre-existing customary international law and conventional law, especially ILO Convention 169.[99] As proclaimed in the Declaration itself, 'the rights recognized herein constitute the minimum standards for the survival, dignity and well-being of the indigenous peoples of the world'.[100]

The final determining factor for calibrating the legal value of the UNDRIP is the existence of mechanisms for its implementation. The UNDRIP does not create specific follow-up mechanisms, but it relies on existing bodies at both international and state level. The only body explicitly mentioned is the Permanent Forum on Indigenous Issues (PFII), which is thus placed 'at the forefront in ensuring the effective implementation of the Declaration'.[101] According to Article 42 of the Declaration,

> The United Nations, its bodies, including the Permanent Forum on Indigenous Issues, and specialized agencies, including at the country level, and States shall promote respect for and full application of the provisions of this Declaration and follow up the effectiveness of this Declaration.

In Luis Rodríguez-Piñero's view, the main goal of this provision is 'mainstreaming and operationalizing'[102] the promotion of the rights enshrined in the Declaration within the activities of UN bodies, specialized agencies, regional organizations, and states. Therefore, measures for implementing the UNDRIP will need to be taken at three parallel and interrelated levels: international, regional, and national.

At the *international level*, it is clear that a large number of UN bodies and specialized agencies are increasingly using the UNDRIP as a point of reference when interpreting international legal standards and their mandates. First of all, the mechanisms created specifically to address indigenous issues refer explicitly to the UNDRIP as an interpretative guide. The PFII, which aims to mainstream

[99] This position is also advanced by the newly nominated UN Special Rapporteur on the rights of indigenous peoples, V. Tauli-Corpuz, Report of the Special Rapporteur of the Human Rights Council on the Rights of Indigenous Peoples, UN Doc. A/69/267, 6 Aug. 2014, para. 13.

[100] Art. 43.

[101] Barelli (2009): 978.

[102] L. Rodríguez-Piñero, 'La "implementación" de la Declaración: las implicaciones del Artículo 42', in *La declaración sobre los derechos de los pueblos indígenas: hacia un mundo intercultural y sostenible*, ed. N. Álvarez, D. Oliva, and N. Zúñiga (Madrid: Los Libros de la Catarata, 2009): 74–5.

indigenous issues throughout the whole UN system,[103] plays a pivotal role and is thus in a key position for implementing the UNDRIP. In its 2008 session, the PFII welcomed the adoption of the Declaration and stated that it would constitute 'its legal framework'.[104] Similarly, the Special Rapporteur on the situation of human rights and fundamental freedoms of indigenous people (SR) was also entrusted with the mandate of promoting the UNDRIP,[105] and has worked very hard to make this possible. As stated by James Anaya, former SR, the UNDRIP

> represents an authoritative common understanding, at the global level, of the minimum content of the rights of indigenous peoples, upon a foundation of various sources of international human rights law … The principles and rights affirmed in the Declaration constitute or add to the normative frameworks for the activities of United Nations human rights institutions, mechanisms and specialized agencies as they relate to indigenous peoples.[106]

Finally, the recently created Expert Mechanism on the Rights of Indigenous Peoples[107] (EMRIP) is another body that can significantly contribute to implementation of the UNDRIP. Given its technical and advisory function as a body composed of five independent experts, the EMRIP is in a 'privileged position to contribute to promoting authoritative interpretations of the standards of the Declaration'.[108]

UN specialized agencies are also paying an increasing attention to indigenous peoples in their daily work. The United Nations Educational, Scientific, and Cultural Organization (UNESCO) has promoted a strong link between cultural diversity, human dignity, environmental protection, and indigenous peoples.

[103] In 2002, the Inter-Agency Support Group on Indigenous Issues (IASG) was created to support the PFII in the goal of promoting dialogue and cooperation between UN bodies and agencies dealing with indigenous issues. The IASG is composed of thirty-one bodies, departments, funds and agencies of the UN. See J. Burger, 'Making the Declaration Work for Human Rights in the UN System', in Charters and Stavenhagen (2009): 309–10. The IASG adopted a very interesting statement just after the adoption of the UNDRIP in 2007. In its opinion, 'this landmark action of the United Nations bears political, legal, symbolic and moral significance, as well as constituting a crucial opportunity for the UN system and other inter-governmental organizations to critically reflect upon their engagement with indigenous peoples' issues and, according to Article 42 of the Declaration, to promote respect and full application of its provisions and follow-up effectiveness', <http://www.un.org/esa/socdev/unpfii/en/iasg.html>.

[104] UN Permanent Forum on Indigenous Issues, 'Report of the Seventh Session', UN Doc. E/C.19/2008/23. Some members of the PFII have claimed that, given the special legitimacy and radical novelty of the UNDRIP, it should have some legally binding effects. This view has been expressed, among others, by Bartolomé Clavero, for whom 'although the Declaration is not a treaty between states, it constitutes a convention or covenant between states and peoples, between the member states of the United Nations and indigenous peoples', *Nota sobre el Alcance del Mandato contenido en el Artículo 42 de la Declaración sobre los Derechos de los Pueblos Indígenas y el mejor modo de satisfacerlo por parte del foro permanente para las cuestiones indígenas*, Submitted by Bartolomé Clavero, UN Doc. E/C.19/2008/CRP.6, 26 Mar. 2008, 9. A legally sound criticism of this position can be found in Rodríguez-Piñero (2009): 74.

[105] Human Rights Council, Resolution 6/12, 28 Sept. 2007.

[106] Report of the Special Rapporteur on the Situation of Human Rights and Fundamental Freedoms of Indigenous People, S. James Anaya, UN Doc. A/HRC/9/9, 11 Aug. 2008, paras 85 and 88.

[107] Human Rights Council, Resolution 6/36, 14 Dec. 2007.

[108] Rodríguez-Piñero (2009): 334–5.

Accordingly, one of the guiding principles of the UNESCO Convention on the Protection and Promotion of the Diversity of Cultural Expressions (2005) is precisely the equal dignity and respect of all cultures. As proclaimed in Article 3 of the Convention, 'the protection and promotion of the diversity of cultural expressions presuppose the recognition of equal dignity of and respect for all cultures, including the cultures of persons belonging to minorities and indigenous peoples'. As a clear signal of UNESCO's commitment to the UNDRIP, the Organization participated in the Task Team of the Inter-Agency Support Group on Indigenous Issues (IASG) that adopted the United Nations Development Group (UNDG) *Guidelines on Indigenous Peoples' Issues*[109] in February 2008, issued to help orient UN country teams in their efforts to mainstream and integrate the principles of the Declaration in development programmes at the country level.

The World Health Organization (WHO) has also been very active in the promotion of indigenous peoples' right to health. In the Geneva Declaration on the Health and Survival of Indigenous Peoples (1999), the WHO expressed its deep concern that 'the health of Indigenous Peoples in every region of the world is acknowledged to be in a poor state due to the negation of our way of life and world vision, the destruction of our habitat, the decrease of bio-diversity, the imposition of substandard living and working conditions, the dispossession of traditional lands and the relocation and transfer of populations'. Since then, the WHO Assembly has adopted a number of resolutions to promote the right of indigenous peoples to the highest attainable standard of health.[110]

Last but not least, the World Bank has also adopted some relevant policy guidelines on indigenous peoples and has paid increasing attention to the normative developments related to indigenous peoples' rights.[111] In its Revised Operational Policy and Bank Procedure on Indigenous Peoples, the World Bank recognizes that indigenous peoples 'play a vital role in sustainable development and that their rights are increasingly being addressed under both domestic and international law'.[112]

[109] United Nations Development Group, *Guidelines on Indigenous Peoples' Issues*, UN Doc. HR/P/PT/16, 1 Feb. 2008, in <http://www.ohchr.org/Documents/Publications/UNDG_training_16EN.pdf>.

[110] For instance, resolution 54.16 (May 2001) requested the WHO to develop a global strategy on indigenous health. See also resolutions 47.27, 48.28, 49.26, 50.31, 51.24, and 53.10 on the WHO's contribution to achieving the objectives of the International Decade of the World's Indigenous Peoples. On the involvement of the WHO in indigenous issues, see WHO Activities on the Health of Indigenous and Tribal Peoples, UN Doc. E/CN.19/2002/2/Add.8, 9 Apr. 2002.

[111] World Bank Legal Department, Legal Note on Indigenous Peoples (8 Apr. 2005).

[112] World Bank, OP/BP 4.10, Indigenous Peoples, July 2005 (revised Apr. 2013), in <http://go.worldbank.org/TE769PDWN0>. The revision that was adopted in 2013 can be viewed as a missed opportunity to have mentioned the UNDRIP as a standard to be considered by the Bank when implementing development projects affecting indigenous peoples. See in this sense J. Burger, 'The UN Declaration on the Rights of Indigenous Peoples: From Advocacy to Implementation', in Allen and Xanthaki (2011): 57. The Inter-American Development Bank has also adopted an Operational Policy on Indigenous Peoples. Unlike the World Bank, the Inter-American Development Bank explicitly mentions 'the emergence of an international legal framework on the rights of indigenous peoples, including the adoption in 1989 of ILO Convention 169 …, as well as the drafting of important new

The UN human rights treaty bodies have gradually begun incorporating indigenous peoples' rights into their interpretations of human rights conventions.[113] More recently, they have referred explicitly to the UNDRIP as a point of reference when interpreting legal standards for international human rights. Along these lines, the recent World Conference on Indigenous Peoples invited the human rights treaty bodies 'to consider the Declaration in accordance with their respective mandates', and encouraged states 'to include ... information on the situation of the rights of indigenous peoples, including measures taken to pursue the objectives of the Declaration, in reports to those bodies'.[114]

The pioneers of attempting to mainstream indigenous peoples' rights into their work were the Human Rights Committee (HRC) and the Committee on the Elimination of All Forms of Racial Discrimination (CERD). The HRC has progressively interpreted the cultural rights enshrined in Article 27 of the International Covenant on Civil and Political Rights (ICCPR), linking them to the way in which indigenous peoples enjoy their lands and natural resources. Accordingly, the HRC has observed that 'culture manifests itself in many forms, including a particular way of life associated with the use of land resources, *especially in the case of indigenous peoples*. That right may include such traditional activities as fishing or hunting and the right to live in reserves protected by law'.[115] In a very similar way, the CERD has also established strong links between racial discrimination and the dispossession of indigenous peoples' land and cultural rights. The CERD has affirmed that it is 'conscious of the fact that in many regions of the world indigenous peoples have been, and are still being, discriminated against and deprived of their human rights and fundamental freedoms and in particular that they have lost their land and resources to colonists, commercial companies and State enterprises. Consequently, the preservation of their culture and their historical identity has been and still is jeopardized.'[116] Accordingly, 'the Committee especially calls upon States parties to recognize and protect the rights of indigenous peoples to own, develop, control

instruments such as the *United Nations Declaration on the Rights of Indigenous Peoples* and the OAS Draft American Declaration on the Rights of Indigenous Peoples. These instruments in turn have played an instrumental role in the adoption by many countries in the region of constitutional and legal provisions recognizing the pluriethnic and multicultural nature of their societies and the specific rights of indigenous peoples' (emphasis added), Inter-American Development Bank, Operational Policy on Indigenous Peoples, GN-2296, 11 Mar. 2004, Annex I, para 1.4, <http://publications.iadb.org/bitstream/handle/11319/1876/Profile%20of%20the%20Operational%20Policy%20on%20Indigenous%20Peoples.pdf?sequence=1>.

[113] Thornberry (2002): 116. See the very useful Compilation of the indigenous-related jurisprudence of the relevant UN human rights treaty bodies by Fergus Mackay (comp.), *Indigenous Peoples and United Nations Human Rights Bodies* (Moreton-in-Marsh: Forest Peoples Programme, 2013), <http://www.forestpeoples.org/topics/un-human-rights-system/publication/2013/indigenous-peoples-and-united-nations-human-rights-bo>.

[114] Outcome Document of the High-Level Plenary Meeting of the General Assembly Known as the World Conference on Indigenous Peoples, UN Doc. A/RES/69/2, 22 Sept. 2014, para. 29.

[115] Human Rights Committee, General Comment No. 23: Article 27 (Rights of Minorities), 8 Apr. 1994, UN Doc. CCPR/C/21/Rev.1/Add.5, para. 7 (emphasis added).

[116] CERD, General Recommendation 23, Rights of Indigenous Peoples (1997), UN Doc. A/52/18, para. 3.

and use their communal lands, territories and resources and, where they have been deprived of their lands and territories traditionally owned or otherwise inhabited or used without their free and informed consent, to take steps to return those lands and territories'.[117]

The Convention on the Rights of the Child (CRC) was one of the first core human rights treaties that explicitly recognized the rights of indigenous children,[118] and the Committee on the Rights of the Child has been increasingly active in trying to promote the UNDRIP. As the Committee affirmed in a recent General Comment expressly devoted to the rights of indigenous children, the UNDRIP 'provides important guidance on the rights of indigenous peoples'.[119] Other treaty bodies such as the Committee on the Elimination of All Forms of Discrimination Against Women (CEDAW Committee) and the Committee on Economic, Social, and Cultural Rights (Com. ESCRs) are also paying increasing attention to the specific concerns of indigenous peoples and are developing relevant decisions and observations using the UNDRIP as the legal point of reference. The CEDAW Committee has focused on the particularly marginalized position of indigenous women in relation to the enjoyment of a number of human rights.[120] When the Committee issued its Concluding Observations on Nepal, it declared that it was 'deeply concerned about the multiple forms of discrimination against disadvantaged groups of women such as Dalit and indigenous women'.[121] Similarly, the Com. ESCRs has explicitly referred to the specific needs and the especially vulnerable situation of indigenous peoples in terms of a number of rights. For instance, in the context of the right to food, the Committee emphasized that 'a particular vulnerability is that of many indigenous population groups whose access to their ancestral lands may be threatened'.[122] The same rationale has been applied by the

[117] CERD, General Recommendation 23, Rights of Indigenous Peoples (1997), UN Doc. A/52/18, para. 5.

[118] According to Art. 30 of the CRC (1989), 'in those States in which ethnic, religious or linguistic minorities or persons of indigenous origin exist, a child belonging to such a minority or who is indigenous shall not be denied the right, in community with other members of his or her group, to enjoy his or her own culture, to profess and practise his or her own religion, or to use his or her own language'.

[119] UN Committee on the Rights of the Child (CRC), General Comment No. 11 (2009): Indigenous Children and their Rights under the Convention [on the Rights of the Child], UN Doc. CRC/C/GC/ 11, 12 Feb. 2009.

[120] This is the case with access to health by indigenous women. As stated by the Committee, 'there are societal factors that are determinative of the health status of women and men and can vary among women themselves. For that reason, special attention should be given to the health needs and rights of women belonging to vulnerable and disadvantaged groups, such as … indigenous women …', CEDAW Committee, General Recommendation No. 24 (1999): Women and Health (Art. 12), UN Doc. A/54/38/Rev. 1, 5 Feb. 1999, para. 6.

[121] CEDAW Committee, Concluding Observations, Nepal, UN Doc. CEDAW/C/NPL/CO/4–5, 29 July 2011, para. 39. However, there are a number of concluding observations on states with indigenous peoples that did not make any reference to indigenous women (Bangladesh, Costa Rica, Kenya, South Africa, and Algeria), in Mackay (2013): 130.

[122] Committee on ESCRs, General Comment No. 12: The Right to Adequate Food (Art. 11), UN Doc. E/C.12/1999/5, 12 May 1999, para. 13.

Committee regarding the indigenous peoples' rights to education,[123] health,[124] and water.[125]

This promising evolution experienced by human rights treaty bodies has made it clear that 'whenever issues relating to human rights violations against indigenous peoples by states are raised they will utilize the UNDRIP as *the* interpretative standard by which to judge state compliance under the conventions'.[126]

At the *regional level*, both the Inter-American Court of Human Rights[127] and the African Commission on Human and Peoples' Rights[128] are using the UNDRIP

[123] The Committee highlighted that States must 'fulfil (facilitate) the acceptability of education by taking positive measures to ensure that education is culturally appropriate for minorities and indigenous peoples', Committee on ESCRs, General Comment No. 13: The Right to Education (Art. 13), UN Doc. E/C.12/1999/10, 8 Dec. 1999, para. 50.

[124] 'The Committee considers that indigenous peoples have the right to specific measures to improve their access to health services and care. These health services should be culturally appropriate, taking into account traditional preventive care, healing practices and medicines. States should provide resources for indigenous peoples to design, deliver and control such services so that they may enjoy the highest attainable standard of physical and mental health. The vital medicinal plants, animals and minerals necessary to the full enjoyment of health of indigenous peoples should also be protected. The Committee notes that, in indigenous communities, the health of the individual is often linked to the health of the society as a whole and has a collective dimension. In this respect, the Committee considers that development-related activities that lead to the displacement of indigenous peoples against their will from their traditional territories and environment, denying them their sources of nutrition and breaking their symbiotic relationship with their lands, has a deleterious effect on their health', Committee on ESCRs, General Comment No. 14: The Right to the Highest Attainable Standard of Health (Art. 12), UN Doc. E/C.12/2000, 11 Aug. 2000, para. 27.

[125] 'States parties should ensure that there is adequate access to water for subsistence farming and for securing the livelihoods of indigenous peoples', Committee on ESCRs, General Comment No. 15: The Right to Water (Arts. 11–12), UN Doc. E/C.12/2002/11, 20 Jan. 2003, para. 7.

[126] M. B. Trask, 'Afterword: Implementing the Declaration', in Pulitano (2012): 335. The recently created *universal periodic review* (UPR) by the UN Human Rights Council can also be considered as a window of opportunity for mainstreaming indigenous peoples' rights and the UNDRIP within the UN human rights bodies. Accordingly, the World Conference of Indigenous Peoples encouraged 'Member States to include, as appropriate, information on the situation of the rights of indigenous peoples, including measures taken to pursue the objectives of the Declaration … during the universal periodic review', Outcome Document of the High-Level Plenary Meeting of the General Assembly Known as the World Conference on Indigenous Peoples, UN Doc. A/RES/69/2, 22 Sept. 2014, para. 29. On the limited impact of the UPR on indigenous rights so far, see: D. O. Martínez, *Los pueblos indígenas a la conquista de sus derechos* (Madrid: Boletín Oficial del Estado, 2012): 878–9. An interesting analysis of how the rights of indigenous peoples were dealt with during the first cycle of the UPR can be found in N. Higgins, 'Advancing the Rights of Minorities and Indigenous Peoples: Getting UN Attention Via the Universal Periodic Review', *Netherlands Quarterly of Human Rights* vol. 32/4 (2014): 379–407.

[127] A general overview of the impact of the Inter-American system for human rights on the UNDRIP can be found in: M. S. Campbell, 'Contribución del sistema interamericano en la definición e interpretación de la Declaración de la ONU sobre los Derechos de los Pueblos Indígenas', in *Los derechos indígenas tras la Declaración: el desafío de la implementación*, ed. F. Gómez Isa and M. Berraondo (Bilbao: Universidad de Deusto, 2013): 113–36.

[128] On the conflicting emergence of indigenous peoples' rights in the African context, see: F. Viljoen, *International Human Rights Law in Africa* (Oxford: Oxford University Press, 2012); F. Mukwiza Ndahinda, *Indigenousness in Africa: A Contested Legal Framework for Empowerment of Marginalised Communities* (The Hague: Asser Press, 2011); Jeremie Gilbert, 'Indigenous Peoples' Human Rights in Africa: The Pragmatic Revolution of the African Commission on Human and Peoples' Rights', *International and Comparative Law Quarterly* vol. 60 (2011): 245–70. On the position of African States vis-à-vis the process of adoption of the UNDRIP and the UNDRIP itself, see: A. K. Barume, 'Responding to the Concerns of the African States', in Charters and Stavenhagen (2009): 170–83.

as one of the legal bases for their findings and decisions.[129] The UNDRIP, and the positive vote by Suriname at the UN General Assembly, were used by the Inter-American Court of Human Rights in its judgment on *Saramaka People v. Suriname*,[130] a case in which the Court affirmed the indigenous peoples' rights over land, territories, and natural resources. The Court affirmed that states have the obligation 'to obtain the consent of indigenous and tribal peoples to carry out large-scale development or investment projects that have a significant impact on the right of use and enjoyment of their ancestral territories'.[131] This is a far-reaching decision, since the Court implicitly recognized that these standards are operative principles of international law irrespective of the normative scope of the Declaration and despite the fact that the state involved in this specific case is not a party to ILO Convention 169. More recently, the Inter-American Court has also explicitly referred to the UNDRIP in the *Case of Kichwa Indigenous People of Sarayaku v. Ecuador*.[132] The decision of this regional human rights Court to resort to the UNDRIP must be seen as a very positive step towards its implementation in the Americas. In Loreto Ferrer's view, the decisions by the Inter-American Court 'constitute authorized interpretations of the rights enshrined in the American Convention ... and other legal instruments. Therefore, they have *erga omnes* effects.'[133] Accordingly, the provisions of the UNDRIP must be used by states at least 'as parameters to interpret their human rights obligations'.[134]

The African Commission on Human and Peoples' Rights (ACHPR) has also been open to incorporating the UNDRIP in the legal framework it is bound to apply. Just some two months after the approval of the UNDRIP, the ACHPR welcomed its adoption and stated that 'the Declaration will become a very valuable tool and a point of reference for its efforts to ensure the promotion and protection of indigenous peoples' rights on the African continent'.[135] In a memorable decision

[129] The European Union (EU) has also used the authority of the UNDRIP to grant an exception to its general ban on the import of seal products to Inuit traders who hunt seals in accordance with their traditional customs for the purpose of subsistence. According to Art. 3.1 of Regulation No. 1007/2009 of the European Parliament and of the Council on trade in seal products, 'the placing on the market of seal products shall be allowed only where the seal products result from hunts traditionally conducted by Inuit and other indigenous communities and contribute to their subsistence'. The Preamble of this Regulation makes an explicit reference to the UNDRIP: 'The fundamental economic and social interests of Inuit communities engaged in the hunting of seals as a means to ensure their subsistence should not be adversely affected. The hunt is an integral part of the culture and identity of the members of the Inuit society, and as such *is recognized by the United Nations Declaration on the Rights of Indigenous Peoples*', *Official Journal of the European Union*, L 286/36, 31 Oct. 2009 (emphasis added).

[130] Inter-American Court of Human Rights, *Saramaka People v. Suriname (Preliminary Objections, Merits, Reparations, and Costs)*, Judgment of 28 Nov. 2007, Series C No. 172, paras 131 and 138.

[131] Inter-American Court of Human Rights, *Saramaka People v. Suriname (Preliminary Objections, Merits, Reparations, and Costs)*, Judgment of 28 Nov. 2007, Series C No. 172, para. 129.

[132] Inter-American Court of Human Rights, *Case of Kichwa Indigenous People of Sarayaku v. Ecuador (Merits and Reparations)*, Judgment of 27 June 2012, Series C No. 245, paras 160 and 166.

[133] L. Ferrer, 'The Application of the United Nations Declaration on the Rights of Indigenous Peoples in Latin America', in *Indigenous Peoples' Human Rights in Domestic Courts*, ed. L. Ferrer and P. Borraz (Madrid: Almaciga, 2013): 294.

[134] Ferrer in Ferrer and Borraz (2013).

[135] ACHPR, Resolution 121 (XXXXII) on the UN Declaration on the Rights of Indigenous Peoples, 28 Nov. 2007.

in May 2009,[136] the African Commission stated that the forcible eviction of the Endorois people from their traditional lands near Lake Bogoria by the government of Kenya without prior consultation and with no provision for compensation was a violation of a number of rights under the African Charter on Human and Peoples' Rights (ACHPR) and under the UNDRIP.[137] The African Commission has also urged that existing treaty obligations be interpreted in light of the provisions of the UNDRIP. The UNESCO World Heritage Convention (1972) does not require the free, prior, and informed consent of indigenous peoples to inscribe indigenous sites on the World Heritage List. Against this background, the World Heritage Committee inscribed Lake Bogoria National Reserve on the World Heritage List without the free, prior, and informed consent of the Endorois, and despite the fact that the Endorois Welfare Council had urged the Committee to defer the nomination because of the lack of meaningful consultation. The ACHPR first considered that the decision constituted 'a violation of the Endorois' right to development under Article 22 of the African Charter'.[138] At the same time, the Commission urged the World Heritage Committee and UNESCO to review their procedures 'in order to ensure that the implementation of the World Heritage Convention is consistent with the UN Declaration on the Rights of Indigenous Peoples'.[139]

At the *national level*, indigenous peoples' rights have also been gradually recognized both legislatively and judicially,[140] opening avenues for their effective implementation.[141] First of all, many states, especially in Latin America, have

[136] *Centre for Minority Rights Development (Kenya) and Minority Rights Group International on behalf of Endorois Welfare Council v. Kenya*, Communication 276/2003, para. 232. The African Commission relied to a great extent on the indigenous jurisprudence of the Inter-American Court of Human Rights, in a clear example of cross-fertilization between regional human rights systems.

[137] P. Borraz, 'The Endorois Case: Indigenous Peoples' Rights in the African Regional Human Rights System', in Ferrer and Borraz (2013): 211–16.

[138] ACHPR, Resolution 197 on the Protection of Indigenous Peoples' Rights in the Context of the World Heritage Convention and the Designation of Lake Bogoria as a World Heritage Site, 5 Nov. 2011, para. 1.

[139] ACHPR, Resolution 197 on the Protection of Indigenous Peoples' Rights in the Context of the World Heritage Convention and the Designation of Lake Bogoria as a World Heritage Site, 5 Nov. 2011, para. 2.

[140] Countries that have affirmed the right of indigenous peoples to their cultural identity, their cultural rights, land rights, right to autonomy and participatory rights include Argentina, Australia, Bangladesh, Botswana, Brazil, Cambodia, Canada, Chile, Colombia, Costa Rica, India, Laos, Malaysia, Mexico, New Zealand, Nicaragua, Norway, Paraguay, Peru, South Africa, and Taiwan, among many others, International Law Association, 'Rights of Indigenous Peoples', Interim Report (The Hague Conference, 2010): 49–50.

[141] In the aftermath of the adoption of the UNDRIP, the Japanese Diet adopted a resolution recognizing the Ainu as an indigenous people, *Resolution on Recognition of Ainu as Indigenous People*, No. 169th Diet Session, 6 June 2008, <http://www.kantei.go.jp/jp/singi/ainu/konkyo.pdf>. Nepal and the Philippines have used the UNDRIP as a normative reference in their processes of constitutional reform, in Report of the Special Rapporteur on the Situation of Human Rights and Fundamental Freedoms of Indigenous People, S. James Anaya, UN Doc. A/HRC/9/9, 11 Aug. 2008, para. 53. A less successful experience refers to Bangladesh, where the government refused to incorporate some provisions of the UNDRIP in the Constitution. On the other hand, the debate on the UNDRIP had positive effects on the position of indigenous peoples in public discourse. See an interesting account of this process in E. Gerharz, 'Recognizing Indigenous People, The Bangladeshi Way: The United Nations Declaration, Transnational Activism and the Constitutional Amendment Affair of 2011', *Indigenous Policy Journal* vol. 24/4 (2014).

undergone constitutional changes for the incorporation of indigenous peoples' rights, thus heralding the emergence of so-called multicultural constitutionalism.[142] The most significant development was in Bolivia,[143] where a law[144] was adopted to explicitly incorporate the UNDRIP in the country's domestic legal system. At the judicial level, the Colombian Constitutional Court,[145] the Constitutional Court of Peru,[146] and the Supreme Court of Belize have all used the UNDRIP in certain decisions. It is worth noting that the Supreme Court of Belize issued 'the first court judgment ever to apply the UNDRIP ... barely a month after its adoption'.[147] The Supreme Court referred specifically to Belize's vote in favour of the UNDRIP as a clear commitment to future compliance in the *Case of the Maya Villages of Belize*. As stated by the Supreme Court, 'General Assembly resolutions are not ordinarily binding on member states. But where these resolutions or Declarations contain principles of general international law, states are not expected to disregard them.'[148] And the Court continued emphasizing that 'it is of some signal importance ... that Belize voted in favour of the

[142] See e.g.: D. L. Van Cott, *The Friendly Liquidation of the Past: The Politics of Diversity in Latin America* (Pittsburgh: University of Pittsburgh Press, 2000); *Multiculturalism in Latin America: Indigenous Rights, Diversity and Democracy*, ed. R. Sieder (London: Palgrave, 2002); D. Bonilla Maldonado, *La constitución multicultural* (Bogotá: Siglo del Hombre Editores, 2006); B. Clavero, 'Derechos indígenas y constituciones latinoamericanas', in *Pueblos indígenas y derechos humanos*, ed. M. Berraondo (coord.) (Bilbao: Universidad de Deusto, 2006): 313–38; *Pueblos indígenas: constituciones y reformas políticas en América Latina*, ed. R. Yrigoyen Fajardo (Lima: Instituto Internacional de Derecho y Sociedad, 2010).

[143] The new constitutions of Bolivia (2009) and Ecuador (2008) are leading examples of a new wave of constitutionalism known as *plurinational constitutionalism*. See: A. Schilling-Vacaflor and R. Kuppe, 'Plurinational Constitutionalism: A New Era of Indigenous-State Relations?', in *New Constitutionalism in Latin America: Promises and Practices*, ed. D. Nolte and A. Schilling-Vacaflor (Farnham: Ashgate, 2012): 347–70; C. Mamani Condori, 'Bolivia: pueblos indígenas y estado plurinacional', in Isa and Ardanaz (2011): 179–98.

[144] *Ley 3760 de los derechos de los pueblos indígenas*, 7 Nov. 2007. Along the same lines, the Parliament of Nicaragua adopted a formal statement to welcome the adoption of the UNDRIP, and to promote the 'harmonization of the domestic legal system' with the provisions of the UNDRIP, *Declaración A.N. No. 001-2008*, 11 Mar. 2008, para. 4.

[145] F. Gómez Isa, 'Cultural Diversity, Legal Pluralism, and Human Rights from an Indigenous Perspective: The Approach by the Colombian Constitutional Court and the Inter-American Court of Human Rights', *Human Rights Quarterly* vol. 36 (2014): 736 and following. A recent decision by the Colombian Constitutional Court on prior consultation to indigenous peoples used ILO Convention 169, the jurisprudence of the Inter-American Court of Human Rights, and the UNDRIP as the legal foundations, Corte Constitucional de Colombia, Sentencia T-129, 3 Mar. 2011, 72. An in-depth analysis of this decision can be found in: C. Zapata, 'Judgement T-129 of 2011 of the Colombian Constitutional Court', in Ferrer and Borraz (2013): 333–8.

[146] The Constitutional Court of Peru has also referred to ILO Convention 169, the jurisprudence of the Inter-American Court of Human Rights and the UNDRIP to reaffirm the rights of indigenous peoples to their lands and territories in the *Tres Islas indigenous community Case*, Sentencia del Tribunal Constitucional, Exp. No. 01126-2011-HC/TC, 11 Sept. 2012, para. 23.

[147] Maia S. Campbell and S. James Anaya, 'The Case of the Maya Villages of Belize: Reversing the Trend of Government Neglect to Secure Indigenous Land Rights', *Human Rights Law Review* vol. 8/2 (2008): 377.

[148] *Manuel Coy, Maya Village of Conejo, Manuel Caal, Perfecto Makin, Melina Makin Claimants v. Attorney General of Belize, Minister of Natural Resources, and Environmental Defendants*, Supreme Court of Belize, 18 Oct. 2007, para. 131.

Declaration'.[149] Finally, the Court was of the view that Article 26 of the UNDRIP reflects 'the growing consensus and the general principles of international law on indigenous peoples and their lands and resources'.[150]

While we must welcome these progressive jurisprudential developments at domestic level, we also cannot ignore that 'what initially seemed a positive trend towards the materialization of ... the Declaration at the domestic level, turned out to be isolated events'.[151] Loreto Ferrer goes on to express further caution: 'since the adoption of the Declaration, most Latin American states have been reluctant to accept its applicability in the domestic sphere, being relegated to just an aspirational document ... Many judges and magistrates in the region do not know the Declaration or see it as an aspirational document.'[152]

In sum, as this chapter has shown, there is a significant emerging practice at the international, regional, and domestic levels that provides solid ground for the conclusion that the UNDRIP has become a point of reference when interpreting and applying indigenous rights, and that at least some of the key provisions of the UNDRIP have already become customary international law, or are in the process of emerging as new rules of customary law.

5. Conclusions

Indigenous peoples have used contemporary international law and international institutions as close allies in their struggle for recognition and the elimination of historically rooted patterns of subjugation, dispossession, and cultural assimilation. As part of this evolution, indigenous peoples have become subjects of rights under international law rather than objects of protection. Soft law norms have played a major role in this process, contributing significantly to the transformation of the dynamics of international law, and paving the way for its flexibilization, deformalization, and, ultimately, democratization. The UNDRIP, adopted in 2007 by the UN General Assembly 'as a standard of achievement to be pursued in a spirit of partnership and mutual respect',[153] must be seen as the culmination of a long and difficult journey in which indigenous peoples themselves and their representatives

[149] *Manuel Coy, Maya Village of Conejo, Manuel Caal, Perfecto Makin, Melina Makin Claimants v. Attorney General of Belize, Minister of Natural Resources, and Environmental Defendants*, Supreme Court of Belize, 18 Oct. 2007, para. 131.

[150] *Manuel Coy, Maya Village of Conejo, Manuel Caal, Perfecto Makin, Melina Makin Claimants v. Attorney General of Belize, Minister of Natural Resources, and Environmental Defendants*, Supreme Court of Belize, 18 Oct. 2007, para. 131.

[151] Ferrer (2013): 292. Similar concerns have also been expressed by Stephen Allen. In his view, 'instead of adducing evidence of uniform or consistent behaviour regarding adherence to certain indigenous rights on the part of such states, many indigenous advocates marshal the best *particular* practice of the most 'enlightened' states on indigenous/human rights issues. This data is then presented as evidence of the *general* practice of affected states ... They ignore any practices to the contrary', S. Allen, 'The UN Declaration on the Rights of Indigenous Peoples and the Limits of the International Legal Project', in Allen and Xanthaki (2011): 233–4.

[152] Ferrer (2013): 292.

[153] UNDRIP, Preamble, para. 24.

have been the driving force and key participants. Many of the provisions enshrined in the Declaration simply reaffirm existing customary rules of international law, while others point to future developments in what it may be considered a norm-creating function. Irrespective of the uncertain legal nature of the UNDRIP per se, it has become an unavoidable point of reference when dealing with indigenous peoples' rights. The recent experience of UN bodies, specialized agencies, human rights treaty bodies, regional human rights courts, and commissions, as well as some domestic courts, clearly demonstrates the strong persuasive authority and interpretative function of the UNDRIP. The challenge ahead is to systematically mainstream the provisions of the Declaration into the routines of those bodies, thus enabling its effective implementation at both the international and the domestic level.[154]

[154] For an alternative view, outlining the possible risks associated with the mainstreaming and progressive 'hardening' of human rights soft law, see Léticia Villeneuve's contribution to this volume.

10

Could the Progressive 'Hardening' of Human Rights Soft Law Impair its Further Expansion?

Insights from the UN Declaration on the Rights of Indigenous Peoples

Léticia Villeneuve

1. Introduction

The adoption of the United Nations Declaration on the Rights of Indigenous Peoples (UNDRIP) in September 2007[1] was celebrated as a historic achievement in the quest towards full recognition and protection of indigenous peoples' rights at the international level. The document was welcomed by the UN and a vast majority of its member states who voted in favour. It was also saluted by indigenous peoples and their representatives, as the UNDRIP's drafting process had opened its doors to indigenous participation and contribution. Even if the UNDRIP was adopted in a soft law form, it was welcomed overall as a sign of progress for the indigenous rights movements and the UN human rights regime more generally.[2]

Beyond this positive narrative, however, the UNDRIP's adoption process presented some anomalies that are worth investigating: when the document was presented to the UN General Assembly (UNGA) four states opposed its adoption, a stance that had barely ever been witnessed in the history of UN Declarations on human rights.[3] This cast some shadow on a declaration meant to be a true 'standard

[1] UNGA Res. 61/295 (13 Sept. 2007).

[2] In Chapter 9 of this volume, Felipe Gómez Isa discusses the case of the UNDRIP, presenting its positive impact in the development of an international indigenous rights regime. Indeed, as stated in that chapter, the UNDRIP has a great transformative potential for indigenous peoples. This chapter, however, highlights the potential risks associated with the 'hardening' of soft law principles from the angle of state practice and the impact such developments can have on the further development of human rights regimes in a soft form.

[3] The only other occurrence being the United States' opposition to the Declaration on the Right to Development. UNGA Res. 41/128 (4 Dec. 1986).

of achievement',[4] and raised important questions about state practice and the law's further development in the field of human rights.

Indeed, soft law[5] is increasingly recognized as a distinct and useful category in international law-making. It is often presented as an optimal institutional arrangement in contexts where a harder, binding form is not possible or desirable, or to pave the way to the development of binding norms.[6] Still, its non-binding status does not deprive soft law of all significant effects in the international community. In some cases, as this chapter aims to show, soft law can also gain greater weight and potentially create legal obligations, going beyond its initially non-binding status and beyond what its parties consented to at the drafting and adoption stage of particular instruments.[7] This progressive development (and eventual 'hardening') of soft law can be welcomed positively as it fuels the expansion of normative orders in areas not covered by conventional, binding instruments. The impact of such evolution, however, can raise important issues for the further development of soft law, when new instruments are drafted and presented to states and other actors for adoption.

While the development of soft law has received some attention from scholars from the angle of implementation and compliance,[8] issues faced at the commitment stage have remained under-theorized, both in international legal and political scholarship.[9] Indeed, common wisdom posits that its non-binding nature alone makes decisions on commitment easy and largely inconsequential for its parties, no matter if the soft law instrument is envisioned to create new standards to be followed or simply to be used as a tool of cheap talk. As it is believed that a party can maintain control of the requirements of implementation over time (an element that

[4] UNGA Res. 61/295 (n. 1), Preamble.

[5] For the purposes of this chapter, soft law is defined as referring to written international instruments, which are non-binding at the time of adoption, but create particular expectations of future behaviour and are likely to have legal effects. While this does not exclude instruments drafted and adopted by/for non-state actors, this chapter will primarily focus on soft law instruments devised and adopted by states, since states remain the central actors and traditional reference point in international law-making.

[6] K. W. Abbott and D. Snidal, 'Hard and Soft Law in International Governance', *International Organization* vol. 54 (2000): 421.

[7] A similar process is described in Megan Bradley and Angela Sherwood's chapter in this volume, in relation to the regime governing the protection of internally displaced persons. In that case, a soft law instrument (the Guiding Principles on Internal Displacement) gained enough traction to act as a standard-setter in the field and permeated international and domestic instruments (albeit with more or less success in practice). The main difference with the case at hand is that the Guiding Principles emanated from an independent international body, not from an initial act of adoption by state actors.

[8] See e.g.: E. Brown Weiss, *International Compliance with Nonbinding Accords* (Washington, DC: American Society of International Law, 1997); D. Shelton, *Commitment and Compliance: The Role of Non-Binding Norms in the International Legal System* (Oxford: Oxford University Press, 2003).

[9] E.g. Shelton's *Commitment and Compliance* volume is mostly about the latter. Studies on commitment are usually rather focusing on binding treaties (e.g.: O. A. Hathaway, 'Why Do Countries Commit to Human Rights Treaties?', *Journal of Conflict Resolution* vol. 51 (2007): 588), or on the trade-offs between hard and soft law (e.g.: Abbott and Snidal (2000)).Commitment to soft law on its own has yet to be fully explored.

contributes to the attractiveness of soft law forms), decisions to join should remain an easy matter.

This chapter, however, argues that commitment to a soft law instrument may involve a more complex decision-making process than conventional wisdom suggests, at least for the states parties involved. A growing body of precedents now points to the potential 'harder' effects of soft law, and this does not go unnoticed in state practice. As a result, it is likely that precedents and interpretations granting greater political and legal weight to instruments adopted in a soft form will fuel uncertainty and apprehension. As new soft law instruments are presented to states for adoption, an initially non-binding status can no longer act as a guarantee that legal effects are not to arise at an ulterior stage.

This appears quite clearly when investigating the opposition to the adoption of the UN Declaration on the Rights of Indigenous Peoples (UNDRIP), an unusual occurrence in the recent history of human rights soft law. While all but one of such declarations (adopted through UNGA resolutions) have historically been adopted without opposition[10] (if not without a vote), the UNDRIP was initially opposed by Australia, Canada, New Zealand, and the United States.[11] Looking through these four countries' positions and motives for opposing the adoption of the UNDRIP, an instance not easily reconciled with common assumptions regarding commitment to soft law,[12] this chapter posits that the potential, and potentially 'harder', effects of soft law are increasingly taken into account in state practice. It argues that this can form the basis of opposition to a soft law instrument, if the possibility of harder obligations arising from it in the future would prove costly to a participating state. It will also argue that existing precedents in human rights soft law coupled with advocates' continued attempts to boost the legal value of such instruments increase the likelihood that further developments will face resistance.

This chapter will first survey the functions and potential effects of human rights soft law as demonstrated by existing precedents, especially in the United Nations framework. It will then move to a thorough analysis of the opposition to the adoption of the UNDRIP and uncover the political and legal underpinnings of the process. It will show that the four opposing states' declarations directly map onto

[10] The only exception: the United States of America voted against the UN Declaration on the Right to Development in 1986. UNGA Res. 41/128 (4 Dec. 1986).

[11] UNGA Res. 61/295 (13 Sept. 2007).

[12] From a rationalist standpoint, commitment to international instruments is to be expected when benefits are to outweigh the potential costs. Soft law is often presented as a low-cost, low-stakes alternative to hard law, which can still yield benefits (Abbott and Snidal (2000)). In the field of human rights specifically, normative pressures mean that commitment can be accompanied by reputational benefits (which some states are keen to reap even if they do not intend to comply—see: O. Hathaway, 'The Cost of Commitment', *Stanford Law Review* vol. 55 (2003); E. M. Hafner-Burton and K. Tsutsui, 'Justice Lost! The Failure of International Human Rights Law to Matter Where Needed Most', *Journal of Peace Research* vol. 44 (2007): 407), while opposition is likely to carry reputational costs. As such, commitment to a soft law instrument on human rights is the expected standard of behaviour (especially when UN declarations are concerned) while opposition is puzzling, unless states perceive potentially greater costs outweighing the reputational impact. Such costs have yet to be explored in existing accounts of commitment to soft law.

the potential developments foreseen for a soft law instrument, as each voiced clear objections to all potential avenues through which the UNDRIP could follow the lead of the previous 'hardening' of provisions contained in soft law instruments in the United Nations system. It will finally explore what this case could mean for the further development of human rights instruments, highlighting the emergence of competing narratives on the effects of soft law and the issues it raises for its further expansion.

2. Functions and Effects of Soft Law: Precedents within the UN System

It is now increasingly recognized that soft law can play an important role in the progress of normative development in the international community, in spite of an initially non-binding status. The functions soft law serves, and the effects it carries, can be largely political,[13] but there is also room in the international legal order for soft law instruments to 'harden' in various ways, and eventually create legal obligations not necessarily foreseen at the time of their adoption. Soft law can thus be seen as a precursor of harder legal instruments (soft law as norm-creating), or as a complement to existing instruments (soft law as norm-filling).[14] Through both these routes, provisions contained in a soft law instrument can evolve into binding standards and carry effects equivalent, to a certain extent, to those of hard law. This section will briefly address the most common and widely recognized of these eventualities, along with an exploration of precedents involving UNGA declarations, especially in the field of human rights.[15]

2.1 Soft law as norm-creating

There are multiple examples of soft law instruments, in their norm-creating role, paving the way for harder instruments in the international legal order. This has occurred with many UNGA declarations over the past fifty years. On matters of human rights, out of twenty-two UNGA declarations,[16] seven led to the adoption

[13] I.e. it can influence behaviour or act as a signalling device, outside the legal sphere and without relying on the shadow of legal obligation.

[14] For a further discussion of soft law's norm-creating and norm-filling roles, see the Introduction to this volume.

[15] The chapter focuses on UN General Assembly declarations considering their particular nature (they undeniably fall under our definition of soft law; still, they are adopted in the general plenary body of an international organization with close to universal membership, which confers a particular aura of legitimacy upon them and makes them the best candidates to illustrate the potential 'hardening' of soft law). They are also the type of instruments bearing the greatest insights into the specific case at hand, the UNDRIP.

[16] Ninety-one 'declarations' have been adopted by the UNGA since 1945, with twenty-two classified as related to human rights. United Nations, 'Declarations and Conventions Contained in General Assembly Resolutions—Human Rights', <http://www.un.org/documents/instruments/docs_subj_en.asp?subj=32>.

of a binding treaty, including the first and most famous of all, the Universal Declaration on Human Rights (UDHR).[17] Indeed, a majority of the provisions set out for the first time in the UDHR have subsequently been detailed and formalized through the adoption of the International Covenant on Civil and Political Rights[18] and the International Covenant on Economic, Social, and Cultural Rights,[19] slightly less than twenty years after the adoption of the non-binding instrument.[20] Similarly, the 1959 Declaration on the Rights of the Child[21] was followed by the 1989 Convention on the Rights of the Child.[22] The same pattern was repeated with instruments dedicated to the elimination of racial discrimination,[23] the elimination of discrimination against women,[24] the rights of persons with disabilities,[25] the protection against torture,[26] and the protection against enforced disappearance.[27] Hence, examples of UNGA declarations leading to harder forms within the UN treaty structure, beyond their initial soft status, are not scarce.

In all cases, there is significant overlap between the content of the instrument adopted in a soft, declaratory form and the final provisions of the hard instrument adopted as a multilateral treaty within the UN structure. Provisions contained in a soft law instrument can play a determinant role in the elaboration of further, binding instruments under international law. At times, the exact wording put forward in the soft instrument is transposed in the subsequent binding convention, albeit with greater details. This highlights the potentially crucial importance of negotiations on the final text of soft law provisions, as they could subsequently be replicated in harder forms.

[17] UNGA Res. 217 A (III) (10 Dec. 1948).

[18] International Covenant on Civil and Political Rights (adopted 16 Dec. 1966, entered into force 23 Mar. 1976) 999 UNTS 171 (ICCPR).

[19] International Covenant on Economic, Social, and Cultural Rights (adopted 16 Dec. 1966, entered into force 3 Jan. 1976) 993 UNTS 3 (ICESCR).

[20] The obligations included in the two Covenants are usually presenting greater detail than their UDHR counterparts. Still, almost all articles of the UDHR are reflected in one or the other (if not in both) covenants (with the exception of the right to property—Art. 17 of the UDHR), and almost all provisions of the Covenants are reflected in the UDHR (apart from Art. 27 of the ICCPR on minority rights).

[21] UNGA Res. 14/1386 (20 Nov. 1959).

[22] Convention on the Rights of the Child (adopted 20 Nov. 1989, entered into force 2 Sept. 1990) 1577 UNTS 3.

[23] UNGA Res. 18/1904 (20 Nov. 1963) and International Convention on the Elimination of All Forms of Racial Discrimination (adopted 7 Mar. 1966, entered into force 4 Jan. 1969) 660 UNTS 195.

[24] UNGA Res. 12/2263 (7 Nov. 1967) and Convention on the Elimination of All Forms of Discrimination against Women (adopted 18 Dec. 1979, entered into force 3 Sept. 1981) 1249 UNTS 13.

[25] UNGA Res. 30/3447 (9 Dec. 1975) and Convention on the Rights of Persons with Disabilities (adopted 13 Dec. 2006, entered into force 3 May 2008) 2515 UNTS 3.

[26] UNGA Res. 30/3452 (9 Dec. 1975) and Convention against Torture and Other Cruel, Inhuman, or Degrading Treatment or Punishment (adopted 10 Dec. 1984, entered into force 26 June 1987) 1465 UNTS 85.

[27] UNGA Res. 47/133 (18 Dec. 1992) and International Convention for the Protection of All Persons from Enforced Disappearance (adopted 20 Dec. 2006, entered into force 23 Dec. 2010) 2715 UNTS Doc. A/61/448.

Soft law can also fulfil a norm-creating role in cases where it is not necessarily meant to pave the way for the adoption of hard law.[28] This has been the course followed by other UNGA declarations, including in the field of human rights. The fact that the non-binding instrument is not followed by a harder covenant drafted on similar bases does not deprive the instrument of all possible political and legal effects. In fact, in the absence of binding standards, a soft law instrument can act as a reference point,[29] both domestically and internationally.[30]

2.2 Soft law as norm-filling

Soft law can also play a norm-filling role, and stand as a complement to existing instruments (soft and hard). It can be devised and used, both in domestic and international institutions, as an interpretative device for harder instruments or to fill a gap left open by existing instruments.

It is not rare to see soft law assume this norm-filling function in the judicial realm. Courts may refer to UNGA declarations, for instance, either in situations where there are no other standards to apply, or when the binding standards are not applicable in a given case. For instance, in the case brought by Nicaragua to the International Court of Justice (ICJ) against the United States in the 1980s,[31] the Court could not use the UN Charter as the basis of obligations arising for the United States.[32] However, the Court decided that it could apply similar provisions, as expressed in the UN General Assembly Resolution 2625.[33] In that particular case, the Court referred to the soft law instrument as evidence of *opinio juris* in the recognition of customary international law (CIL), a point which will be addressed further in section 2.3.

[28] In fact, hard legalization is not (and does not have to be) the end goal, as highlighted by the authors in the Introduction to this volume.

[29] It is the case, e.g., with the Declaration on human rights defenders (Declaration on the Right and Responsibility of Individuals, Groups and Organs of Society to Promote and Protect Universally Recognized Human Rights and Fundamental Freedoms, UNGA Res. 53/144 (9 Dec. 1998)). Adopted in 1998, it was never followed by a binding instrument, but still acts as an accepted standard on the issue and is periodically called upon in international proceedings on the matter (e.g. in the Universal Periodic Review spearheaded by the United Nation's Human Rights Council).

[30] The substance and wording of provisions contained in international soft law instruments can easily be replicated in other instruments and jurisdictions (international or domestic), and can thus make their way into harder legalized forms beyond the UN system. International soft law provisions can act as a reference point in these other jurisdictions as well (in spite of their non-binding status), even if they are not necessarily formally incorporated as law in these other regimes. Felipe Gómez Isa's chapter in this volume offers a thorough account of such occurrences in the case of the UNDRIP (at domestic, regional, and international levels).

[31] *Military and Paramilitary Activities in and against Nicaragua (Nicaragua v. United States of America)* (Merits) [1986] ICJ Rep. 14 (Nicaragua).

[32] Since the US declaration of acceptation of the jurisdiction of the Court excluded such possibility.

[33] Declaration on Principles of International Law Concerning Friendly Relations and Co-operation among States in Accordance with the Charter of the United Nations, UNGA Res. 25/2625 (24 Oct. 1970).

2.3 Soft law and its legal effects

A corollary to their norm-creating and norm-filling roles is that soft law instruments can potentially be recognized as having greater legal value and give rise to legal obligations. This can happen either through soft law instruments bearing direct legal effects (in very specific contexts), or seeing some of the provisions contained in soft law instruments 'harden', generally through the emergence and recognition of a rule of CIL.

As per the first scenario, there is a possibility for soft law to carry direct legal effects.[34] This is usually contingent, however, on the particular institutional context of an instrument's adoption. Soft law instruments adopted within international organizations, for example, will have direct legal effects within the organization itself. It will be part of the organization's legal framework and will be considered binding as far as its internal affairs are concerned, even if it is not directly binding for its member states.[35]

Soft law instruments, or, more specifically, particular provisions within one, can also potentially integrate the realm of hard law and give rise to legal obligations. This can happen if they are recognized as part of the body of CIL, itself a direct source of internationally binding obligations.[36] In fact, a soft law instrument can be linked through various ways to the development of a customary practice and its recognition as law. It can do so through fostering consistent state practice (by providing a focal point and establishing common norms in a given issue-area), or providing evidence of *opinio juris* (the belief that a norm conveys a legal obligation),[37] the two constitutive elements for the recognition of CIL.[38] Soft law can also influence the formation and recognition of CIL by encouraging states to define and formalize the content of existing customary practices.

[34] Without the need for it to be first recognized by a court or transposed in a binding instrument.

[35] T. Gruchalla-Wesierski, 'A Framework for Understanding Soft Law', *McGill Law Journal* vol. 30 (1984): 52.

[36] As recognized in Art. 38 of the ICJ Statute: 'international custom, as evidence of general practice accepted as law'. United Nations, Statute of the International Court of Justice (24 Oct. 1945), <http://www.icj-cij.org/documents/index.php?p1=4&p2=2&p3=0>.

[37] H. Hannum, 'The Status of the Universal Declaration of Human Rights in National and International Law', *Ga. J. Int'l & Comp. L.* vol. 25 (1995): 321–2.

[38] In fact, some analysts go even further in their treatment of soft law's links with CIL, suggesting that the attitude of a state towards the adoption of a soft law instrument (at the voting stage) could not only show evidence of *opinio juris* (voting in favour as evidence of that state's belief that the instrument reflects the status of customary norms), but also evidence of that state's practice in accordance with the emerging norm (voting in favour as evidence of 'state practice'). See e.g.: discussion in E. Voyiakis, 'Voting in the General Assembly as Evidence of Customary International Law?' in *Reflections on the UN Declaration on the Rights of Indigenous Peoples*, ed. S. Allen and A. Xanthaki (Oxford: Hart, 2011). This paper takes the more widely accepted view that voting behaviour can form potential evidence of *opinio juris*, rather than of state practice per se. Still, notwithstanding the debate on the role of voting behaviour in the formation of CIL, there is still a strong case to be made that voting towards the adoption of a soft law instrument can at least constitute a unilateral act giving rise to expectations that the state will behave accordingly. When a state participates in the adoption of a soft law instrument, the instrument will legitimize conforming conduct by establishing the presumption that acts conforming to the provisions of the instrument are done in good faith. Gruchalla-Wesierski (1984): 62.

In this respect, the UDHR, the first UNGA declaration (which also acted as a precursor to binding covenants in the international legal order), constitutes a precedent of a great magnitude. Indeed, even though it has been clearly adopted as a non-binding, aspirational document, some of its provisions have since been increasingly recognized as reflecting the state of CIL[39] and considered binding *erga omnes*.[40] Furthermore, since the UDHR is at the heart of the UN human rights system, its provisions mention, in a relatively general way, rights that were subsequently detailed in other soft and hard instruments. The argument being made that the UDHR is part of the body of CIL is then sometimes used as a basis to claim that other documents detail rights which should equally be recognized as CIL.[41]

The links between UNGA resolutions and the formation and recognition of CIL have been at times enhanced by International Court of Justice decisions. Indeed, there are precedents in the Court's history where it directly considered soft law instruments in its evaluation of the presence of CIL. In the landmark Nicaragua case, for instance, the ICJ suggested that consensus on an UNGA resolution on a matter can contribute to proving *opinio juris* and establishing the presence of a norm of CIL.[42] Again, the Court established that the consent of member states to a resolution of a declaratory nature can constitute a mark of acceptance of the validity of the substantive rules it contains. In the case of Resolution 2625, it remarked that 'the adoption by States of this text affords an indication of their *opinio juris* as to customary international law on the question'.[43] Such views are not uncontestably accepted in the international legal community,[44] but they certainly constitute

[39] The UN Treaty Collection website notes: 'Some instruments entitled "declarations" were not originally intended to have binding force, but their provisions may have reflected customary international law or may have gained binding character as customary law at a later stage. Such was the case with the 1948 Universal Declaration of Human Rights.' See also: V. Lowe, *International Law* (Oxford: Oxford University Press, 2007): 93; Hannum (1995): 321–6. The latter reviews multiple positions, from both academic research and diplomatic history, in support for provisions of the UDHR constituting CIL. Accounts are not unanimous, as not every actor is ready to ascribe customary law value to the whole of the document, but there is overwhelming support to the effect that the UDHR, in large parts, provides strong evidence of CIL. Some would argue, in that regard, that there is a stronger case to be made for civil and political rights than for its provisions on economic, social, or cultural rights.

[40] I.e. even on states that did not necessarily consent to its adoption initially (apart from situations where a state would place itself in the position of 'persistent objector'). See e.g.: O. Elias, 'Persistent Objector', in *Max Planck Encyclopedia of Public International Law* (Oxford: Oxford University Press, 2009).

[41] As Felipe Gómez Isa notes in the case of the UNDRIP, it is important to distinguish between the legal value of an instrument itself, and that of the substantive rights it contains. For an exploration of the links between provisions of the UNDRIP and existing CIL see his chapter in this volume.

[42] *Military and Paramilitary Activities in and against Nicaragua (Nicaragua v. United States of America)* (Merits) [1986] ICJ Rep. 14 (Nicaragua): 188.

[43] *Military and Paramilitary Activities in and against Nicaragua (Nicaragua v. United States of America)* (Merits) [1986] ICJ Rep. 14 (Nicaragua): 191.

[44] Voyiakis reports on criticism of the decision on the grounds that the '*Nicaragua* methodology fails to note that States can support or oppose a given GA Resolution on different grounds and on the basis of very different views as to whether that Resolution reflects or ought to reflect customary international law'. Voyiakis (2011): 220.

precedents that fuel uncertainty regarding the legal status of soft instruments, even when initially adopted in a non-legally binding form.

Finally, beyond the realm of usual CIL, provisions contained in a soft law instrument can be given stronger legal value and give rise to legal obligations if they were deemed to reflect in substance general principles of law[45] or *jus cogens*,[46] as recognized within the sources of international law by the Statute of the International Court of Justice.

As seen, soft law can carry or lead to the recognition of binding obligations for its parties in various ways. This highlights the potential fluidity between soft and hard law, and the possibility that the distinctiveness of the former gradually becomes less salient as it gains similar attributes to the latter. In this respect, both categories could appear redundant, and the distinction, useless. There is, however, a major difference warranting the distinctiveness of those categories, and it is rooted in the degree of certainty regarding the legal effects of the instrument: while hard law is (by definition) creating legal obligations, the possibility for soft law to lead to the same outcome is acknowledged, but by no means automatic. The key difference is thus the uncertainty regarding soft law's potential legal effects, a point to which we now turn.

2.4 Uncertainty surrounding the legal effects of soft law

Section 2.3 was a brief overview of soft law's functions and potential effects. As such, the cases mentioned are solely a few examples of precedents within the UN human rights system, where provisions contained in soft law instruments have evolved to acquire greater legal value beyond their adoption as part of non-binding resolutions or declarations. But such evolution is by no means linear or systematic. This highlights a core issue with soft law instruments from the standpoint of state practice: the uncertainty regarding the potential value of its provisions, as to whether or not it might eventually give rise to legal obligations.

Indeed, it is important to recall that there is no agreement, either in theory or in practice, on the actual effects of soft law instruments. This is partly due to the variety of instruments categorized as 'soft',[47] and partly because soft law's effects can be changing as distinct instruments evolve in practice. This process is not formalized in any specific way; rather, it happens organically.[48] Many factors can come into

[45] 'General principles of law recognized by civilized nations' in the wording of the ICJ Statute.

[46] I.e. 'peremptory norm of general international law'. Vienna Convention on the Law of Treaties (adopted on 23 May 1969, entered into force 27 Jan. 1980) 1155 UNTS 331.

[47] As Gruchalla-Wesierski, Chinkin, and many contributors to this volume have pointed out, the term soft law can be used to refer to many different concepts, e.g. legal soft law, non-legal soft law; Gruchalla-Wesierski (1984); C. M. Chinkin, 'The Challenge of Soft Law: Development and Change in International Law', *International and Comparative Law Quarterly* vol. 38 (1989): 850. Even when focusing on soft law instruments, the concept will refer to a variety of instruments adopted through different instances, to fulfil different functions (norm-creating or norm-filling), and used by different actors for various purposes.

[48] The creation of a soft law instrument is often not regulated by formal procedural requirements. This is considered by Posner and Gersen as a constitutive dimension of its soft character. E. Posner and

play in determining what course an instrument will follow, and that can partially be independent of the will or consent of states parties who adopted the instrument in the first place (i.e. it could be the result of a concerted effort from states who were initially parties to the soft instrument and consent to work towards a binding framework on the same issue,[49] but it could also happen through the evolution of organizational practices within the UN,[50] the action of non-state actors and lobby groups,[51] or through court proceedings,[52] without necessarily involving an additional expression of consent from initial states parties).

Still, the potential harder effects of soft law have been confirmed over time by precedents such as the cases mentioned here. Such precedents and interpretations are likely to fuel uncertainty and apprehension, as states parties who are not totally comfortable with the content of new soft law instruments presented for adoption can no longer rely on the 'soft' status of the instrument to deny it all potential legal effects.[53] There is no way to know with absolute certainty, at the adoption stage, which form a soft law instrument is likely to take in the future, and what kind of legal obligations could arise from it. But it is no longer possible to simply assume that the provisions adopted as part of a soft, non-binding instrument will remain as such. This chapter argues that this does not go unnoticed and is increasingly acknowledged in state practice, in ways that are likely to affect the way states approach commitment to new soft law instruments in the future. This becomes clear when examining the adoption process of one recent UNGA declaration, the UNDRIP, and the unusual state behaviour it triggered.

J. Gersen, 'Soft Law: Lessons from Congressional Practice', *Stanford Law Review* vol. 61 (2008): 573. E.g. there is no formal basis in the UN Charter (or in the UNGA Rules of Procedure) providing for special resolutions to be adopted as 'declarations'. UN, Rules of Procedure of the General Assembly, A/520/Rev.17, <http://www.un.org/en/ga/search/view_doc.asp?symbol=A/520/rev.17&Lang=E>.

[49] Considering that soft law can be a tool building 'compromise over time'. Abbott and Snidal (2000): 446.

[50] See e.g.: J. E. Alvarez, *International Organizations as Law-Makers* (Oxford: Oxford University Press, 2005); A. E. Boyle and C. M. Chinkin, *The Making of International Law* (Oxford: Oxford University Press, 2007).

[51] M. E Keck and K. Sikkink, *Activists beyond Borders: Advocacy Networks in International Politics* (New York: Cornell University Press, 1998); *Non-state Actors and Human Rights*, ed. P. Alston (Oxford: Oxford University Press, 2005); *Non-state Actor Dynamics in International Law: From Law-Takers to Law-Makers*, ed. M. Noortmann and C. Ryngaert (Aldershot: Ashgate, 2010); D. Hollis, 'Why State Consent Still Matters: Non-State Actors, Treaties, and the Changing Sources of International Law', *Berkeley Journal of International Law* vol. 23 (2005): 1.

[52] See e.g.: C. J. Tams and J. Sloan, *The Development of International Law by the International Court of Justice* (Oxford: Oxford University Press, 2014); K. J. Alter, *The New Terrain of International Law: Courts, Politics, Rights* (Princeton: Princeton University Press, 2014).

[53] Voyaiakis raises a similar point in respect to the intrinsic role of voting behaviour in the formation of CIL. Voyiakis (2011): 220–1. This chapter considers that it is equally valuable for other paths through which soft law could 'harden'.

3. Opposition to the UNDRIP: Resistance to the Potential Hardening of Soft Law?

The UNDRIP was adopted as part of UNGA Resolution 61/295, on 13 September 2007. The adoption of this instrument, detailing human rights provisions in the particular context of indigenous peoples, was, however, far from an easy process. It was the result of nearly twenty-five years of debates and negotiations among member states of the UN, between member states and indigenous peoples, and between indigenous peoples themselves.[54]

The voting record on the Declaration at the UNGA was the following: 144 votes in favour, eleven abstentions, and four oppositions. The four opposition votes were cast by Australia, Canada, New Zealand, and the United States.[55] Such behaviour was a puzzling occurrence within the history of the UNGA, especially on matters pertaining to human rights. Only once before had a member state cast a vote in opposition to the adoption of a declaration which fell under the human rights category.[56] Moreover, a majority of such declarations (fourteen out of twenty-two in UN history) had been adopted by acclamation, signifying consensus among the members of the Assembly.[57]

The four states that opposed the adoption of the Declaration made statements in explanation of their vote, at the UNGA, right before draft resolution A/61/L.67 was submitted for the member states' approval. All of them started by stressing their commitment to indigenous rights and their long-standing involvement in the work of the various committees leading to the draft Declaration. However, all four claimed that it was not possible for them to vote in favour. In fact, eschewing the option of avoiding commitment through abstention (or absence on voting), they further claimed that they had to formally oppose the adoption of the UNDRIP. They did so for very similar reasons, calling upon comparable arguments. This section exposes, in essence, the official explanation of these states' objections to the UNDRIP.[58] Their remarks can be grouped in two categories, as they relate to the UNDRIP's content or to its soft form and possible effects.

[54] A. Eide, 'The Indigenous Peoples, the Working Group on Indigenous Populations and the Adoption of the UN Declaration on the Rights of Indigenous Peoples', in *Making the Declaration Work: The United Nations Declaration on the Rights of Indigenous Peoples*, ed. C. Charters and R. Stavenhagen (Copenhagen: IWGIA, 2009): 34. The extent to which this could be due to the specificities of the case and/or of the subject matter will be explored in this chapter. For further details on this process, see the chapter by Felipe Gómez Isa in this volume.

[55] UNGA Res. 61/295 (n. 1).

[56] The United States of America, on the UNGA Declaration on the Right to Development. For UN declarations on human rights, see: United Nations, 'Declarations and Conventions Contained in General Assembly Resolutions—Human Rights', <http://www.un.org/documents/instruments/docs_subj_en.asp?subj=32>.

[57] United Nations, 'Declarations and Conventions Contained in General Assembly Resolutions—Human Rights', <http://www.un.org/documents/instruments/docs_subj_en.asp?subj=32>.

[58] Data includes statements made at the UNGA in explanation of the vote, official documents published by the relevant governmental bodies in explanation of the states' position, as well as statements by the relevant departments or heads of state and official governmental press releases.

3.1 Statements related to the UNDRIP's content

First, all four countries had strong substantive objections to some of the Declaration's provisions. The main preoccupations of the quartet were with articles revolving around land rights, resources, and redress,[59] particularly the requirements of recognition of indigenous land rights in spite of other legal rights to land (including claims settled with indigenous populations) in their domestic legal framework. Regarding the use of resources, they critiqued the Declaration's requirement of 'free, prior and informed consent' of the peoples concerned for a state to make use of indigenous land or resources contained therein. Canada, New Zealand, and the United States claimed that it would effectively give indigenous peoples a veto power over a democratic government's decision, or 'imply different classes of citizenship, where indigenous people have a right of veto that other groups or individuals do not have'.[60]

Another central aspect of the opposition to the Declaration relates to the right to self-determination. Australia expressed its 'dissatisfaction' with the references to such a right in the document, as it conceived of self-determination solely in external terms and thus claimed that it was inadequate for the UNDRIP.[61] The United States was particularly concerned with the fact that, instead of articulating a new concept of self-determination as self-government within the state, the Working Group took what the US representative dubbed a 'wholly inappropriate approach of reproducing the text of ICCPR and ICESCR article 1 in article 3 of the Declaration, with no intention that both articles mean the same thing or define the same legal obligations'.[62] Such ambiguities were exacerbated by the lack of a definition of 'indigenous peoples' in the Declaration, a conscious and long-argued choice of the Working Group, but explicitly dissatisfactory to Australia and the United States.

An additional overarching concern was the incompatibility of the text of the Declaration with these states' domestic frameworks. All four states mentioned it as an integral part of their justification for refusing to support the Declaration. New Zealand, for instance, claimed that the main argument precluding its adoption of the Declaration was that it 'include[d] provisions that are ... fundamentally incompatible with [its] democratic processes, [its] legislation and [its] constitutional arrangements'. The other states coupled the argument about the incompatibility with their domestic frameworks with broader comments on the 'failure' of the Declaration to ensure its meaningfulness, potential for implementation, and wide support of the international community,[63] or to become a 'strong' text 'which could have provided practical guidance to all States'.[64]

59 I.e. Arts 19, 26, 28, and 32.

60 UN Doc. A/61/PV.107, 14 (New Zealand).

61 UN Doc. A/61/PV.107, 12 (Australia).

62 United States, 'Observations of the United States with Respect to the Declaration on the Rights of Indigenous Peoples'.

63 UN Doc. A/61/PV.107, 12 (Australia).

64 UN Doc. A/61/PV.107, 13 (Canada).

These four states stressed those substantive objections as the core of their incapacity to implement the provisions of the Declaration as it stood.[65] Some articles were deemed 'overly broad and unclear and ... susceptible of a wide variety of interpretations' by Canada,[66] while the United States lamented that the text was 'confusing and risk[ed] endless conflicting interpretations and debate about its application'.[67] Moreover, they complained that 'the aspirational principles and collective rights described in the declaration [were] typically written in extremely general and absolute terms'.[68] This last point is particularly puzzling since broad guidelines and principles, in more or less precise formulations, are the hallmark of most declaratory, aspirational documents.

For all of the opposing states, however, the opposition to some provisions of the Declaration was expressed along with a commitment in principle to the promotion and protection of indigenous peoples' rights. This challenges expectations of state commitment to soft law instruments, especially in the field of human rights. Indeed, if all four states agreed in principle to the idea of a declaration on indigenous peoples' rights, commitment should not have raised any major issue. If states firmly considered that they were to remain in control and, thus, be able to evaluate the potential obligations arising from the instrument in its soft form and the extent of the required implementation efforts,[69] substantive concerns would have been effectively alleviated.

3.2 Statements related to the UNDRIP's soft form

When looking at the nature of the instrument, it is important to recall that, like other UNGA resolutions, the UNDRIP was widely recognized by the UN member states (across voting positions) as a non-legally binding, aspirational document. Among its opponents, Australia, Canada, and the United States unequivocally agreed on that point. Australia stated that 'it [was] the clear intention of all states that it be an aspirational declaration with political and moral force, but not legal force',[70] a point echoed in identical form by the United States in its supplementary observations[71] and shared equally by Canada.[72]

New Zealand adopted a more nuanced stance, as it did not clearly deny all legal value for the instrument. Instead, it insisted on the importance to be conferred on the document, in contrast to other actors stressing its aspirational nature. It contended that 'it [could] not accept that a state [could] responsibly take such a

65 New Zealand, e.g., claimed that 'this text is ... clearly unable to be implemented by many states, including those that will be voting in favour of its adoption'. UN Doc. A/61/PV.107, 14.

66 UN Doc. A/61/PV.107, 13.

67 UN Doc. A/61/PV.107, 15.

68 UN Doc. A/61/PV.107, 15.

69 Characteristics which are commonly presented as advantages of soft law forms.

70 UN Doc. A/61/PV.107, 12.

71 The exact wording of the Australian statement is part of the United States' supplementary observations. United States, 'Observations of the United States with Respect to the Declaration on the Rights of Indigenous Peoples'.

72 UN Doc. A/61/PV.107, 13.

stance [focusing on a merely aspirational nature] towards a document that purports to declare the contents of the rights of indigenous people'.[73] The fact that it took the Declaration 'very seriously', coupled with disagreements regarding its content, served as central justification for its opposition. This alludes to a greater value granted to the instrument, compared to what its counterparts were ready to admit. In fact, the three others went further and insisted that the 'declaration does not provide a proper basis for legal actions, complaints, or other claims in any international, domestic, or other proceedings'.[74]

Still, New Zealand joined the three other opponents of the Declaration in declaring that the text of the Declaration was not to be considered 'reflective of international law'.[75] All four states went into further details, by making it clear that they did not consider that the UNDRIP entertained any link with CIL. As Australia put it: 'this declaration does not describe current state practice or actions states consider themselves obliged to take as a matter of law, it cannot be cited as evidence of the evolution of customary international law'.[76] Once again, it echoed word for word a comment made by the United States in its supplementary observations.[77] It is easy to identify, in this statement, claims denying the presence of both state practice and *opinio juris*, the two constitutive elements of CIL. The United States further rejected 'any possibility that this document is or can become customary international law'.[78] New Zealand made a similar statement, claiming that the Declaration 'does not state propositions which are reflected in State practice or which are or will be recognised as general principles of law'.[79]

3.3 Opposition as a clear intent not to be bound

The four states devoted a substantial part of their interventions to arguments related to the content of the Declaration. Most of their comments referred to a level of precision too low to act as a clear guide for the state, thus rendering domestic implementation imprecise and impossible when coupled with the particulars of their domestic situation and legal framework. However, considering that the instrument is deemed to be in a soft, aspirational form, such oppositions to the particular wording (or claims about lack of precision therein) should not, in theory, be an impediment to state commitment. Indeed, if states can remain in control of the interpretation to be given to soft law provisions and the extent to which they intend to implement them and comply with them, substantive provisions should not prevent a state from agreeing to the instrument in principle. In this case, opposing

[73] UN Doc. A/61/PV.107, 14 (New Zealand).

[74] As stated by Australia (UN Doc. A/61/PV.107, 12).

[75] UN Doc. A/61/PV.107, 12.

[76] UN Doc. A/61/PV.107, 12 (Australia).

[77] United States, 'Observations of the United States with Respect to the Declaration on the Rights of Indigenous Peoples'.

[78] United States, 'Observations of the United States with Respect to the Declaration on the Rights of Indigenous Peoples'.

[79] UN Doc. A/61/PV.107, 15.

states' motives for disagreeing with the content of the Declaration rather appeared to take their source in the increased or potentially 'harder' obligatory value that these states envision for the instrument, following its adoption.

Arguments on the form and effects of the instrument made a great part of the four opposing states' interventions in explanation of their vote. However, such points were not called upon as justifications for their behaviour; the remarks on the form and effects of the instrument were not framed as arguments per se, as they were not formulated and expressed by any of them as constituting a reason not to commit to the Declaration. Why, then, would states feel the need to dedicate a substantial part of their interventions to such a matter? This chapter argues that they did so in an attempt to block possible interpretations that could arise, on the basis of the adoption of the Declaration at the UNGA, to grant an increased value to the UNDRIP in international law. When coupling the potential effects of soft law surveyed above with the remarks made at the UN on that occasion, it clearly appears that the four opposing states' interventions raised all potential functions and effects of soft law, only for the purpose of denying the very possibility of them all.

First, thinking of the potential of soft law as a precursor of more intensely legalized forms, Australia made it clear that the UNDRIP could not 'provide a basis for the elaboration of other international instruments, whether binding or non-binding'.[80] As such, it was also denying its potential to constitute a new standard filling a gap in existing rights instruments and act as a reference point for further developments and claims. Likewise, conceiving of the possibility that soft law acts as a complement to existing instruments, Australia, Canada, and the United States insisted that the UNDRIP could not form a basis for actions, complaints, or other claims, thus denying it any complementary value in legal proceedings.

On another level, states' declarations showed a strong insistence on denying all links or possibility that the UNDRIP would eventually be linked to CIL, which definitely rings a 'persistent objector' bell. Indeed, the theory of the persistent objector posits that a new norm of CIL 'will not be binding on persistent objectors who have demonstrated their unwillingness to be bound by it before the rule becomes established'.[81] There is no ambiguity in the four actors' statements: they clearly opposed the fact that the Declaration could form CIL, as well as the idea that it could evidence any constitutive aspect of CIL (state practice and *opinio juris*). To this end, they even highlighted the fact that they had opposed the current text of the Declaration since the early stages of its drafting. What such insistence reveals is a clear concern on these states' part that the provisions of the UNDRIP could be recognized as CIL and, should recognition happen, the intention for their state not to be bound by the new customary provisions.

Finally, even when focusing on the political impacts of the Declaration, the four opposing states objected to the possibility that the UNDRIP could become the new

[80] UN Doc. A/61/PV.107, 12. This is something that Australia will not be able to control or limit in any way. Hence, such a worry shows their concern with limiting *all* possible effects of soft law for the UNDRIP.

[81] Elias (2009).

reference point in terms of indigenous peoples' rights. They attempted to stress the disagreement (or at least, the lack of consensus) around the instrument to undermine its legitimacy, claiming that it '[could] not enjoy universal support to become a true standard of achievement'.[82] By insisting on the lack of consensus as a fundamental shortcoming of the document, the opposing states tried to limit its possible political impact just as much as its (potential) legal value.

In sum, the four opposing states expressed that the basis of their objection was related to the content of the Declaration. Still, they dedicated a substantial part of their statements in explanation of their position, to address clearly each of the potential functions and effects a soft law instrument and its provisions could gain over time, only to deny the possibility of them all in the case at hand. This cannot be mere coincidence. It shows both a belief in the potential effects of provisions contained in a soft law instrument, and a clear intent not to be bound should such unintended effects materialize after the adoption of the Declaration.

3.4 Further insights from belated adoption of the UNDRIP

Within a few years of the vote consecrating the adoption of the UNDRIP,[83] all opponents reversed their position and endorsed the instrument.[84] Such behaviour is also quite unusual. Indeed, contrary to treaty instruments (which are usually open to ratification at any time a state so wishes) the endorsement of a UNGA declaration is usually to be made on the voting day. Beyond that, no procedure exists for a state to formally modify its position towards a given UNGA resolution (and declarations contained therein). The only way for a state to express its desire to modify its position is through a unilateral declaration of its intent to do so. Such

82 United States, 'Observations of the United States with Respect to the Declaration on the Rights of Indigenous Peoples', 15.

83 Australia approved it on 3 Apr. 2009. Australia, 'Statement of Support to the United Nations Declaration on the Rights of Indigenous Peoples, The Hon Jenny Macklin MP', 3 Apr. 2009, <http://www.un.org/esa/socdev/unpfii/documents/Australia_official_statement_endorsement_UNDRIP.pdf>. Canada did so on 12 Nov. 2010: Aboriginal Affairs and Northern Development Canada, 'Canada's Statement of Support on the United Nations Declaration on the Rights of Indigenous Peoples', 12 Nov. 2010, <http://www.aadnc-aandc.gc.ca/eng/1309374239861/1309374546142>. New Zealand on 20 Apr. 2010. NZ Ministry of Foreign Affairs and Trade, 'Statement by Hon Dr Pita Sharples, Minister of Maori Affairs, Ninth Session of the United Nations Permanent Forum on Indigenous Issues', 19 Apr. 2010, <https://www.beehive.govt.nz/release/supporting-un-declaration-restores-nz039s-mana>. The United States approved it on 16 Dec. 2010. The White House, 'Remarks by the President at the White House Tribal Nations Conference', 16 Dec. 2010, <http://www.whitehouse.gov/the-press-office/2010/12/16/remarks-president-white-house-tribal-nations-conference>.

84 It is important to note that two of the states who initially abstained during the vote on the UNDRIP, Colombia and Samoa, also reversed their position. This might confirm the tendency towards universal endorsement of the Declaration and its provisions (see Felipe Gómez Isa's chapter in this volume). In the case of Colombia, it could contribute further evidence to the emergence of a regional custom. But it could also be a response to pressures to rally, from and for domestic or international actors and constituencies. The behaviour of these two actors is outside the scope of this chapter, which focuses on the four opposing states (considering that formal opposition is a truly unusual—and somewhat more consequential—stance regarding the adoption of UNGA human rights declarations). Still, the interplay with the position of abstaining states, especially in terms of belated acceptance of the Declaration, would warrant further research.

a move, however, is not formally recorded at the UN and does not alter the voting record.[85]

Rather than undermining this chapter's claims, the statements made by those four states as they were changing their positions confirm that the fear of 'harder' effects for soft law was at the heart of their decision not to join it in the first place. Indeed, all opposing states eventually supported the Declaration, without any changes having been made to its content, form, or drafting process. What appears to have changed, above all, is their evaluation of the form of the instrument and its potential effects.[86] After what the United States presented as a 'thorough review' process,[87] all states re-evaluated their position and concluded that it was possible to make qualified statements of acceptance, interpreting the provisions of the Declaration within the boundaries of their own domestic constitutional, legal, and political frameworks.[88] They still restated that the adoption of the Declaration does not carry direct legal effects in their domestic legal order and does not change their existing constitutional and legal frameworks, even if the level of openness to such an eventuality differed among the four states.[89] In sum, they considered it was possible to interpret the Declaration and its potential effects in a manner consistent with their domestic orders and objectives, something that was not possible when the Declaration was first presented for adoption.

Obviously, many factors can lead to such a change of position.[90] What we can notice, though, is that the instrument is valued and that the potential for it to

[85] Therefore, there is no data readily available on the frequency of such changes in a state's position. Considering the nature of the procedure and of the instruments concerned, we can reasonably presume that it is not a frequent occurrence.

[86] Or the acceptability of such a scenario, in the case e.g. of a new government taking a different stance on the issue.

[87] US Department of State, 'UN Declaration on the Rights of Indigenous Peoples Review' (16 Dec. 2010): 1.

[88] E.g. Canada declared that it was now 'confident [that it] can interpret the principles expressed in the Declaration in a manner that is consistent with [its] Constitution and legal framework'. Aboriginal Affairs and Northern Development Canada, 'Canada's Statement of Support on the United Nations Declaration on the Rights of Indigenous Peoples', 12 Nov. 2010, <http://www.aadnc-aandc.gc.ca/eng/1309374239861/1309374546142>. New Zealand noted that its statement of support for the Declaration 'reaffirms the legal and constitutional frameworks that underpin New Zealand's legal system, noting that those existing frameworks define the bounds of New Zealand's engagement with the declaration'. New Zealand, 'National Government to Support UN Rights Declaration (Statement by PM John Key)', 20 Apr. 2010, <http://www.beehive.govt.nz/release/national-govt-support-un-rights-declaration>. Australia qualified their statement of support with mention of their interpretation of problematic provisions (e.g.: 'Article 46 makes it clear that the Declaration cannot be used to impair Australia's territorial integrity or political unity.... While there is continuing international debate about the meaning of "free, prior and informed consent", we will consider any future interpretations in accordance with Article 46.' Australia, 'Statement of Support to the United Nations Declaration on the Rights of Indigenous Peoples, The Hon Jenny Macklin MP', 3 Apr. 2009), <http://www.un.org/esa/socdev/unpfii/documents/Australia_official_statement_endorsement_UNDRIP.pdf>.

[89] Australia, New Zealand, and the United States have touched upon the possibility of modifying their domestic legal frameworks in various (albeit limited) ways following the standards set forth in the Declaration.

[90] One could think of, e.g., pressures from domestic constituencies or domestic or international lobby groups, changes of governments (which happened in all opposing states except Canada between

become binding (or for claims to arise on its basis) is acknowledged by states. This explains the insistence to mention that it will not directly be changing domestic legal orders, or evidence the development of any obligation under international law. Even in the reversal of their position, we still find in those four states' positions a firm intent not to be bound by the provisions of the document, or at least, a firm intent not to be bound unless the state can autonomously work out the content of the duties imposed on it by the Declaration and integrate them in its domestic framework to its liking, not through an obligation arising *erga omnes* from the Declaration's provisions.

4. What This Case Could Mean for the Further Developments of Human Rights Soft Law

Opposition to a soft law instrument in the realm of human rights is relatively rare and can seem like a counter-intuitive position, especially from democratic states which are generally publicly positioning themselves as human rights advocates.[91] The case of the UNDRIP is close to the only time this has ever been witnessed in the history of UN General Assembly declarations on such matters. As this chapter has shown, states' opposition to this particular instrument was not rooted primarily in a disagreement with the core principles of the Declaration,[92] but rather in a desire to limit the potential effects of the instrument and to preclude the possibility that some of its provisions could become binding in the absence of a further explicit expression of state consent.[93] Only apprehensions regarding the latter possibility can explain their reluctance to commit to the UNDRIP.

The adoption of the Declaration is a relatively recent occurrence, though. As such, it is important to reflect on what this case (and the associated responses it elicited from states) could mean for the further development of soft law in the realm of human rights. Could such behaviour be replicated as new instruments are presented to states for adoption? Is the case symptomatic of a nascent trend or just an outlier in an otherwise relatively uniform body of state practice?

the UN vote and the belated statement of acceptance), or a re-evaluation of the effects of the instrument a few years after its adoption (mitigating initial fears about obligations to arise from commitment to the document).

[91] This links to the important reflection raised by this volume, exploring the roles of soft law as both a potential tool for progress and a locus of interpretative struggles. It therefore has the potential to expand or limit normative developments in the field of human rights. See the Introduction to this volume.

[92] And this is further evidenced by their belated rallying, without any changes to the Declaration itself, its form or drafting process.

[93] In this respect, the limited control of UN member states over the drafting process of the Declaration probably exacerbated fears as to the levels of state control over its further developments. See section 4.2 for further remarks on the drafting process.

4.1 Specificities of the UNDRIP case: substance and process

The case of the UNDRIP is peculiar in a few respects. First, its substance relates to salient domestic issues in former colonial states where there are unresolved disputes with indigenous populations, concerning land rights for instance. As such, there would be a point in saying that the issue is more sensitive and harder to address for states in that situation like the four opposing ones: the full implementation of the provisions of the Declaration could prove extremely costly materially (e.g. in relation to land rights and natural resources exploitation) as well as affect the essence of those states' sovereignty (since it would require a re-evaluation of their exclusive jurisdiction over parts of their territory). Thus, the fact that some of the substantive rights included in the Declaration are rights to be claimed against the state itself (as opposed to others that would, for instance, impose negative duties on states not to infringe on citizens' rights) sets the Declaration apart from other instruments of a similar type.

The UNDRIP is also quite unique in terms of the process leading to its adoption.[94] Indeed, a broad range of participants were involved in its development since very early stages (states, subsidiary bodies of the UN, NGOs, etc.). But more importantly, it included, almost from the start, a strong representation of the beneficiaries of the rights set forth in the instrument, representatives of various indigenous peoples.[95] States were thus not able, in that case, to negotiate and amend the text in the usual framework of state-centric fora, a point mentioned initially by the opposing states as a regrettable aspect of the whole process.[96] While this can be seen as a unique feature of this case, it also reflects broader dynamics in the evolution of the international legal order, where new actors (international organizations, non-state actors, private entities) are increasingly participating in the development of soft law standards, curtailing states' exclusive jurisdiction on it and limiting their ability to control the evolution of an instrument once they actually commit to it. Some states' responses to that challenge in the UNDRIP case are thus rather likely to be replicated in the future.

Finally, non-state actors' involvement in that case was not only important at the drafting stage: organized domestic groups, as well as transnational ones, also mobilized to push for the full implementation of the Declaration as soon as it was adopted. Such groups may have a greater political weight in states where there are important indigenous communities, and where they can actually enter the political arena to advance their claims, either through domestic (democratic) institutions, or through multilateral bodies of which their state is a party. While this would necessitate further research, the case of the UNDRIP points towards the possibility

[94] For a more detailed account of the process and of indigenous peoples' participation at various stages, see Felipe Gómez Isa's chapter in this volume.

[95] Victoria Tauli-Corpuz, 'How the UN Declaration on the Rights of Indigenous Peoples Got Adopted', <http://www.tebtebba.org/index.php/all-resources/category/20-un-declaration-on-the-rights-of-indigenous-peoples>.

[96] The United States initially went as far as saying that 'the process was unfortunate and extraordinary in any multilateral negotiating exercise and [set] a poor precedent with respect to United Nations practice', UN Doc. A/61/PV.107, 15.

that these factors could now make it harder for democratic states to join soft law instruments as a tool of cheap talk.[97] Where institutions exist to oversee the implementation of an instrument and where organized groups are politically mobilized, domestically or transnationally, to request full compliance with soft standards, states might have to think twice about joining without any kind of qualifying statement. The fear of signing a blank cheque through the adoption of a theoretically non-binding instrument, from which obligations of an undefined nature could potentially arise, may be enough to warrant opposition on sensitive (and potentially costly) topics, in spite of the usual normative pull of human rights instruments.

4.2 Competing narratives on the value of soft law

In this light, what emerges from the exploration of the initial opposition to the UNDRIP, and the developments of the instrument since its adoption, are two competing narratives on the value and effects of soft law. While activists constantly attempt to boost the legal value of soft law instruments to achieve further progress in the development of human rights regimes, such push is likely to fuel resistance from traditional actors who will be increasingly reluctant to commit to new soft law instruments if they are not fully ready to endorse the obligations that could arise from them.

On the one hand, soft law instruments are increasingly used by advocates to further normative developments on human rights issues. Pushes are made for the full implementation of soft instruments by states parties (and other actors, where applicable). In an attempt to secure the implementation and development of human rights regimes, soft instruments can be presented and used in similar ways to hard law; distinction is not always made between those two types of instruments when formulating rights claims, and the non-binding nature of soft law is rarely mentioned. Instead, attempts are often made to boost its legal value, by presenting it as reflective of international law (through CIL, general principles of international law, or its links with existing binding norms).

We can definitely witness this in the paths taken by proponents of the UNDRIP over the last few years. Not only have there been strong lobbying efforts within opposing countries and internationally to foster wider adoption of the Declaration, but we have also seen a global push in favour of its full implementation.[98] The language used often presents the UNDRIP as the state of international law on the matter, by reference to other binding instruments or to its own provisions as forming CIL.[99]

On the other hand, such attempts to maximize the value of soft law and pressure for its full implementation can logically have an adverse effect on states. Indeed,

[97] This is in line with an argument made by Hathaway regarding binding human rights treaties. See: O. Hathaway, 'The Cost of Commitment', *Stanford Law Review* vol. 55 (2003).

[98] See e.g.: the proceedings of the 2014 World Conference on Indigenous Peoples and its outcome document. 'Outcome Document of the High-Level Plenary Meeting of the General Assembly known as the World Conference on Indigenous Peoples.' UNGA Res. 69/1 (22 Sept. 2014).

[99] Especially on matters such as the right to self-determination, or the requirements of free, prior, and informed consent.

attempts to boost the legal value of existing instruments, beyond their non-binding status upon adoption, can make states increasingly reluctant to sign on to new instruments of the same kind. Once again, this is based on existing precedents and fears that consent to the non-binding instrument could lead to further developments in international law without a renewed expression of direct consent. States who deal with sensitive issues domestically are likely to continue to insist on the non-binding status of existing soft law instruments in those issue-areas. They are also likely to play down the significance of their complying behaviour with the standards evoked in soft law instruments when they happen to coincide.[100] This is a clear example of an attempt to limit the possibility for a soft law instrument to be recognized as the applicable standard in a given rights regime, even when state practice is conforming to it. The more powerful and successful attempts to boost the value of existing soft law instruments are, the more we can expect reluctance from states to join new instruments, in ways similar to the opposition it triggered to the UNDRIP.

In this context, reluctant states can also be prompted to deal with soft law in ways similar to how they would approach commitment to binding instruments, contributing to the blurring of the distinction between hard and soft law. This has also been witnessed in the UNDRIP case: opposing states waited for a certain period of time before joining the instrument,[101] delivered qualifying statements with their adoption in ways that resemble treaty reservations, or consistently opposed particular provisions they would not want to be bound by (to trigger a status of persistent objector).

The positive news for advocates of normative development through human rights soft law-making in that ongoing confrontation is that it consecrates soft law as a force to be reckoned with in the development of international law. However, this comes at a cost: if the line between hard and soft law is increasingly blurred, the advantages that come with soft law in international law-making (flexibility, adaptability, etc.) might be at risk. In sum, the more soft law advocates stretch the limits of state consent after the adoption of a soft law instrument and attempt to push for the recognition of binding obligations arising from it, the likelier the chances that it will cause a backlash in state practice, and nourish a reluctance to commit to further instruments. Soft law could thus fall prey to its own success.

5. Conclusion

Using insights from the UNDRIP and the opposition it initially fostered, this chapter has aimed to explore issues of state commitment to human rights soft law. It has shown that the possibility for soft law instruments to give rise to 'harder',

[100] E.g., Canada noted in its opposing statement that it would continue to take effective action for the promotion of indigenous peoples rights, based on other obligations, but stressed that 'such effective action ... would not be undertaken on the basis of the provisions of this Declaration'. UN Doc. A/61/PV.107, 13.

[101] This is common in the case of treaties open for ratification, but unusual for a soft law instrument with a one-off voting procedure.

potentially binding effects over time is acknowledged in state practice. It has argued that such recognition is likely to change the ways in which states approach questions of commitment to new instruments, and even form the basis of opposition to a non-binding human rights instrument (if any obligation arising beyond the bounds of initial consent could prove costly to a potential party).

In doing so, it has uncovered competing narratives on the value and effects of soft law in practice. This exercise was mostly of an exploratory nature, as no definitive trend has emerged yet (and whether one will eventually is likely to be highly dependent on issue-areas). Still, this chapter has made the point that while the way in which soft law's advocates use existing instruments can lead to successful normative developments, it can also feed back into state practice and change state actors' responses to both existing and new soft law instruments. Indeed, advocates' attempts to obtain the most out of a non-binding instrument in terms of human rights protection could well lead to increased opposition from states to join new instruments of that kind, if they felt their control over the obligations such instruments could create without explicit consent was in jeopardy. It remains to be seen whether different equilibria between competing views of soft law will emerge in practice. These could likely be dynamic, renegotiated over time and across substantive fields. And this could be something worth preserving, if soft law is to maintain its distinct strengths in an international legal order that is fast evolving.

11

The UN Guiding Principles on Business and Human Rights

A Confusing 'Smart Mix' of Soft and Hard International Human Rights Law

Stéphanie Lagoutte

1. Introduction

The UN Guiding Principles on Business and Human Rights (UNGPs) restate and compile relevant human rights obligations and create soft law standards addressing both states and business enterprises.[1] In this respect, the UNGPs interact with both international hard and soft human rights law, as well as with voluntary corporate social responsibility (CSR) standards, which business enterprises may choose to follow. The novelty brought by the interaction between CSR and human rights is twofold. In the field of CSR, the UNGPs are welcomed as a game-changer, as they create 'a new CSR paradigm driven by systematic precision based on legal concept'.[2] In the field of human rights, the UNGPs introduce a focus on non-state actors as duty-bearers in a set of human rights standards endorsed by a central UN human rights body, the Human Rights Council (HRC). The UNGPs directly address non-state actors, that is, business enterprises, and outline their 'responsibility to respect'[3] human rights in their activities.[4] This responsibility is to be implemented through specific procedures such as due diligence and reporting.

[1] UNGPs Guiding Principles on Business and Human Rights: Implementing the United Nations 'Protect, Respect and Remedy' Framework, Annex to the Report of the Special Representative of the Secretary-General on the issue of human rights and transnational corporations and other business enterprises, J. Ruggie (Human Rights Council, Seventeenth session, Agenda item 3, Promotion and protection of all human rights, civil, political, economic, social, and cultural rights, including the right to development, Advance Edited Version Distr.: General, 21 Mar. 2011, Original: English, A/HRC/17/31).

[2] Y. Aftab, 'The Intersection of Law and Corporate Social Responsibility: Human Rights Strategy and Litigation Readiness for Extractive Companies', *Rocky Mi. Min. L. Inst.* vol. 19 (2014): 60.

[3] Guiding Principle (GP) 11 and 12.

[4] GP 11 and 12.

While at first sight the field of application of human rights law seems to expand through the UNGPs, at least in terms of expectations by some actors, it remains in fact unchanged in terms of actual legal protection. Hence, a discrepancy may occur between, on the one hand, civil society views (and discourse) on the emergence of new obligations for states and private actors and, on the other hand, the very clear opinion emanating from states that only international treaties and customs create international obligations.[5] In the case of the UNGPs on human rights and business, associating CSR discourse and actual legal obligation in the same instrument makes it difficult to distinguish the mandatory elements from the voluntary ones within the field of human rights and business. The introduction of new actors (i.e. business enterprises) as possible subjects, or at least addressees, of UN-endorsed standards only reinforces this confusion.

This chapter deals with the functions of soft law in international human rights law by examining the UNGPs. I argue that the UNGPs are a challenging, and sometimes confusing, international instrument for public international law and international human rights law in terms of form and content. Non-binding soft law provisions may have to some extent political consequences for states, but their implications as far as non-state actors, such as business enterprises, are concerned are very difficult to identify.

The main purpose of this chapter is therefore to seek clarification as to the nature and the contents of the UNGPs and analyse the effects of the emergence of such soft law instruments in international human rights law. Chapter 12 of this volume by Christoph Good also takes the UNGPs as its starting point, considering their consequences in terms of the role of new actors, law-making, and norm-shaping for private actors.

Following a short overview of the UNGPs on business and human rights and some preliminary reflections on the role of soft law in international human rights law, this chapter asks whether the UNGPs represent a new category of soft law. I finally argue that dressing voluntary standards that apply to both states and business companies in the ornament of international law language blurs the extent and contents of the legal obligations of the state.

2. The UNGPs on Business and Human Rights: State Duties and Business Responsibilities

Global and multi-level governance approaches to the human rights and business field have yielded major achievements over the past decade. Broad multilateral soft law standards have been adopted, such as the OECD Guidelines for Multinational Enterprises[6] or the ILO Declaration on Fundamental Principles and Rights at

[5] C. Chinkin, 'Normative Development in the International Legal System', in *Commitment and Compliance: The Role of Non-binding Norms in the International Legal System*, ed. D. Shelton (Oxford: Oxford University Press, 2000): 21–42 at 42.

[6] The OECD Guidelines for Multinational Enterprises are annexed to the OECD Declaration on International Investment and Multinational Enterprises first adopted in 1976. The Guidelines are

Work.[7] Multi-stakeholder initiatives, such as the UN Global Compact in 2000, have been launched and supported by private companies, states, civil society organizations, labour organizations, and also several UN agencies. At the same time, sectorial guidelines and codes of conduct have been adopted[8] and many multi-stakeholder initiatives have been launched on issues pertaining to the human rights and business field.[9]

The UNGPs take stock of existing human rights obligations, regulations and policies, multi-governance initiatives, good practices and challenges, and CSR developments within the field of human rights and business. They provide for a well-structured presentation of relevant issues in the form of guiding principles. Based on the 'Protect, Respect, and Remedy' Framework for business and human rights presented by Special Representative of the Secretary General (SRSG) Professor John Ruggie to the UN HRC,[10] the UNGPs define and unpack the distinction that exists between the state *duty to protect human rights* and the corporate *responsibility to respect human rights.*[11] They provide for a set of principles that states and businesses must apply, should apply, or ought to consider applying (depending on the case) to prevent, mitigate, or redress human rights-related abuses by business enterprises. In March 2011, the UNGPs were endorsed by the HRC. Subsequently a Working Group on the issue of human rights and transnational corporations and other business enterprises was established by an HRC resolution in June 2011.[12]

The UNGPs are presented, and to some extent accepted, as a common reference point that provides a basis for new initiatives in the field of human rights and business. The author of the UNGPs, John Ruggie, has repeatedly emphasized that the UNGPs are only 'the end of the beginning' and a 'common foundation from which thinking and action of all stakeholders would generate cumulative progress over

far-reaching recommendations addressed by governments to multinational enterprises operating in or from adhering countries. They have been revised several times since 1976.

[7] The Declaration adopted by the ILO in 1998 declares that all ILO members, even if they have not ratified the Conventions in question, have an obligation to respect, to promote and to realize, in good faith and in accordance with the Constitution, the principles concerning the fundamental rights which are the subject of those Conventions (e.g. freedom of association, right to collective bargaining, elimination of forced or compulsory labour, abolition of child labour, elimination of discrimination).

[8] See e.g.: Voluntary Principles for Security and Human Rights (2000), which concern extractive sector companies, Code of Conduct for Private Security Service Providers (2010), the OECD Due Diligence Guidelines for Responsible Supply Chains of Minerals from Conflict-Affected and High Risk Areas (2011); The FAO Voluntary Guidelines on the Responsible Governance of Tenure of Land, Fisheries, and Forests in the Context of National Food Security (2012), etc.

[9] Such as the Extractive Industries Transparency Initiative—EITI (2003) or the Kimberley Process on conflict diamonds (2002).

[10] Report of the Special Representative of the Secretary-General on the issue of human rights and transnational corporations and other business enterprises, *Protect, Respect and Remedy: A Framework for Business and Human Rights*, 7 Apr. 2008 (A/HRC/8/5).

[11] Respectively GP 1 (state duty to protect human rights) and GP 11 and 12 (business responsibility to respect human rights).

[12] Resolution endorsing the UNGPs and establishing the Working Group on the issue of human rights and transnational corporations and other business enterprises, HRC, 17th session, 33rd meeting, 16 June 2011 (A/HRC/17/4).

time'.[13] There is a general expectation that an uptake of the UNGPs in the work of the UN, in a global governance framework as well as at the domestic and local level, will take place in the years to come. This has already been the case since June 2011.[14] The UN Working Group on the issue of human rights and transnational corporations and other business enterprises (UNWG) plays a central role in the uptake of the UNGPs.[15]

In terms of contents, the state's duty to protect, defined by Pillar 1 of the UNGPs, focuses on the positive obligation of the state to safeguard individuals' human rights against abuses committed by non-state actors. The human rights obligation of states with regard to business activities is to ensure that business enterprises do not indirectly infringe upon human rights. Where a state is unable or unwilling to protect individuals against human rights-related abuses, another state (the home state in the case of transnational business activities) or the business enterprise itself may have a responsibility to take action. Pillar 3 of the UNGPs, which addresses the roles of state and non-state actors in securing access to remedy, reiterates in Guiding Principle 5 the international human rights duty of states 'to take appropriate steps to ensure, through judicial, administrative, legislative or other appropriate means, that when such abuses occur within their territory and/or jurisdiction those affected have access to effective remedy'.

Pillar 2 prescribes the business enterprises' responsibility to respect human rights and defines its central element: a due diligence obligation for business enterprises to address the human rights impacts of their activities at home and through their subsidiaries and other business relationships abroad. According to the UNGPs, business enterprises are expected to prevent and mitigate human rights impacts directly linked to their operations, products, and services as well as to provide remedies to potential victims. The main tools envisaged by Pillars 2 and 3 are human rights impact assessments, the integration of human rights policies into operations, human rights monitoring and auditing, as well as transparent reporting to relevant stakeholders and providing remedies to victims.

The nature of the state duties listed in the UNGPs is twofold: first, a reminder of international human rights obligations undertaken by states through previous international and regional treaties and conventions and, second, recommendations to take action in specific ways and regarding selected issues. Taking action means for example that states should be proactive in ensuring companies operating

[13] Report of the Special Representative of the Secretary-General on the issue of human rights and transnational corporations and other business enterprises, J. Ruggie, 21 Mar. 2011, A/HRC/17/31, para. 13. See also: R. Mares, 'Business and Human Rights after Ruggie: Foundations, the Art of Simplification and the Imperative of Cumulative Progress', in *The UN Guiding Principles on Business and Human Rights: Foundations and Implementation*, ed. R. Mares (The Hague: Brill, 2012): 85–105 at 86.

[14] European Commission's 'Renewed EU Strategy 2011–14 for Corporate Social Responsibility', COM(2011), 681 final, 25 Oct. 2011: The Commission regards the UNGPs as providing authoritative guidance; OECD Guidelines for Multinational Enterprises, Recommendations for Responsible Business Conduct in a Global Context, 25 May 2011.

[15] HRC Resolution 17/4 of 16 June 2011 (A/HRC/17/4). In June 2014, the HRC, at its twenty-sixth session, decided to extend the Working Group's mandate for a period of three years (A/HRC/26/22).

in conflict-affected areas do not become involved in human rights abuses,[16] or a reminder that states may regulate extraterritorial activities of companies domiciled or listed in their jurisdiction.[17] Accordingly, the state duty to protect consists of a 'smart mix'[18] of legally binding obligations and soft law commitments. The nature of the corporate responsibility to respect human rights has been detailed and discussed in many commentaries to the UNGPs.[19] It is in any case certain that the UNGPs do not create direct human rights obligations for companies under international law. An attempt to create such human rights obligations imposed directly on business enterprises has failed in the past,[20] as such an endeavour raises enormous conceptual, legal, and practical challenges.[21]

Since the endorsement of the UNGPs by the HRC, the discussion surrounding the creation of a legally binding UN treaty on human rights and business that would impose obligations on states, and possibly also business enterprises, has been kept alive by non-governmental organizations and a group of states within the UN system.[22] On 26 June 2014, the HRC voted in favour of a resolution that represents a step towards a legally binding instrument on business and human rights. The HRC resolution establishes an open-ended intergovernmental working group to elaborate an international legally binding instrument on transnational corporations and other business enterprises with respect to human rights.[23]

16 GP 7. 17 GP 2. 18 Commentary under GP 3.

19 J. Knox, 'The Ruggie Rules: Applying Human Rights Law to Corporations', in Mares (2012): 51–83; See also Part III The Nature and the Extent of Corporate Obligations (several contributions) in *Human Rights Obligations of Business: Beyond the Corporate Responsibility to Respect?*, ed. S. Deva and D. Bilchitz (Cambridge: Cambridge University Press, 2013), 191–268.

20 Norms on the Responsibilities of Transnational Corporations and Other Business Enterprises with Regard to Human Rights, 2003, UN Doc. E/CN.4/Sub.2/2003/12/Rev.2.

21 Summed up in a 2005 Report of the UN High Commissioner on Human Rights on the responsibilities of transnational corporations and related business enterprises with regards to human rights, UN Doc. E/CN.4/ 2005/91. See also: J. Ruggie, 'Business and Human Rights: The Evolving International Agenda', *American Journal of International Law* (2007): 822.

22 Republic of Ecuador Government statement to the UN HRC: Statement on Behalf of a Group of Countries at the 24th Session of the Human Rights, General Debate—Item 3 'Transnational Corporations and Human Rights', Geneva, Sept. 2013. See also; NGO Joint Statement: Call for an international legally binding instrument on human rights, transnational corporations and other business enterprises, authored by Treaty Alliance (CETIM, Dismantle Corporate Power Campaign, ESCR-Net, FIAN, FIDH, Franciscans Intl., Friends of the Earth Intl., Transnational Institute) and signed by more than 500 organizations, 28 Apr. 2014. Both documents are available on the website of the Business and Human Rights Resource Centre (<http://www.business-humanrights.org>). See also: Issue Brief by J. Ruggie: *A UN Business and Human Rights Treaty?* Harvard Kennedy School, 28 Jan. 2014.

23 HRC Resolution L.22, A/HRC/26/L.22/Rev.1. The final vote was 20 in favour, 14 against, and 13 abstentions.

3. Preliminary Reflections on Soft Law in International Human Rights

Soft law instruments such as the UNGPs challenge the boundaries of international human rights law and thereby international human rights protection. While the increased use of soft law in human rights law expands the outreach of a human rights discourse, it is arguable that this also contributes to reducing the specificities of international human rights law and brings it back within the realm of ordinary public international law.

A question central to this volume is whether soft law poses specific challenges to human rights law, distinct from those otherwise posed by soft law in international law due to the specific features of international human rights law.[24] A comprehensive discussion of the legal nature and specificities of international human rights law would exceed the limited objectives of this chapter.[25] It is not my intention here to reopen the debate regarding the fragmentation of international law and the specific nature of human rights law.[26] International human rights law is part of public international law; it is created by states, which commit themselves to a number of obligations.

Two main features are, however, traditionally seen as specific to international human rights. First, when adopting human rights instruments, states commit themselves to protecting the rights of third parties to the treaty, that is individuals. Human rights law therefore defines its addressees in 'direct contradiction to the Statist orientation of traditional international law'.[27] The human rights obligations that states take upon themselves have been defined as *erga omnes* or 'objective' obligations. The International Court of Justice and the European Court of Human Rights have in several decisions emphasized the idea that human rights treaties protect the common interest of all contracting states, independently of each state's own interest.[28] As a consequence of this jurisprudential construction, the international and regional regime of treaty reservations and denunciations has caved in to interpretation by international and regional human rights mechanisms, which do not allow reservations or have decided to set them aside in many instances.[29]

[24] See the Introduction to this volume.

[25] Ongoing debates on the legal nature and specificities of international human rights law, see e.g.: M. Addo, *The Legal Nature of International Human Rights* (Leiden/Boston: Martinus Nijhoff Publishers, 2010).

[26] Addo (2010) and M. Kamminga, 'Impact on State Succession in Respect of Treaties', in *The Impact of Human Rights Law on General International Law*, ed. M. Kamminga and M. Scheinin (Oxford: Oxford University Press, 2009).

[27] Addo (2010).

[28] ICJ Advisory Opinion concerning *Reservations to the Genocide Convention*, 1951, ICJ Rep. at 15 and ICJ Judgment *Barcelona Traction*, 1970 ICJ Rep. at 32; ECtHR Judgment *Ireland v. UK*, 18 Jan. 1978, A.25, at 239. See also: P. Weil, 'Towards Relative Normativity in International Law', *American Journal of International Law* vol. 77 (1983): 413–42, at 431–3.

[29] On reciprocity, reservations, and denunciations in international human rights law, see e.g.: F. Sudre, *Droit européen et international des droits de l'homme*, 11th edn (Paris: PUF, 2012): 61; *Reservations*

The second specific feature of international human rights law is its high degree of legalization supported by the establishment of independent supranational supervision, 'from fully empowered judicial bodies to weak oversight agencies'.[30] State action is monitored across the globe and individuals bring petitions, applications, or claims against states before the UN treaty bodies or the three regional human rights courts (and the two Commissions). In order for the international human rights supervisory and monitoring organs to function properly, there needs to be close dialogue between these supranational mechanisms, domestic courts, and especially domestic administration, creating synergies and resistances in the implementation of human rights obligations. This dialogue may be superficial, difficult, and much resistance may appear at the domestic level. However, this ongoing interaction promotes the framing and shaping of international human rights law. This is not to say that soft law standards have no part to play in this interaction; nevertheless, they do not afford individuals the same *legal* protection.

This preliminary reflection is mostly an expression of concern. In public international law, when adopting soft law instruments, states only reduce the quality—or the strength—of their commitment to each other. In international human rights law, they are simply reducing the legal quality of the protection they otherwise could afford individuals. In the case of the UNGPs, I will now show that simply crystallizing the state of affairs in the field of human rights and business does not add anything to the international legal protection of individuals. However, the UNGPs send out a signal to a variety of actors and propose some tools that may be picked up by both states and business enterprises.

4. New Soft Law

The UNGPs present the characteristics of what Dinah Shelton labels 'secondary soft law instruments',[31] that is, non-binding standards produced by intergovernmental bodies and institutions. The UNGPs are an international soft law standard developed by an expert appointed by the UN Secretary General and endorsed by a UN body, the HRC. The UNGPs are the first instrument in a new category of soft law that has been developed under the auspices of the HRC over the past few years. It resembles, however, several other soft law instruments.

to Human Rights Treaties and the Vienna Convention Regime: Conflict, Harmony or Reconciliation, ed. I. Ziemele (Leiden: Martinus Nijhoff Publishers, 2004).

[30] Addo (2010): 469.

[31] Shelton (2000): 449. Primary soft law is described as normative texts not adopted in treaty form, such as Declarations. They declare new norms or elaborate, reaffirm, or further elaborate previously accepted binding & non-binding norms.

4.1 Other UNGPs and similar instruments (guidelines, principles, etc.)

UNGPs, as a generic category, are a relatively new category of international soft law instruments elaborated under the auspices of the HRC. Since John Ruggie started to work on the UNGPs on Business and Human Rights, the HRC has mandated other UN Special Procedures to elaborate guiding principles. In addition to the UNGPs on business and human rights, two sets of guiding principles have been adopted in 2012: the Guiding Principles on Foreign Debt and Human Rights[32] and the Guiding Principles on Extreme Poverty and Human Rights.[33] A third set of Guiding Principles on Security of Tenure for the Urban Poor has been presented to the HRC[34] but not yet endorsed. In addition, the Guiding Principles on Internal Displacement were elaborated under the auspices of the former Human Rights Commission in 1998.[35] The Commission expressed its appreciation of the Guiding Principles in a late 2004 resolution.[36] Earlier in the history of the UN, similar sets of principles were developed by experts and 'endorsed' by UN human rights bodies. One of the main examples is the Standard Minimum Rules for the Treatment of Prisoners, which were adopted by the First United Nations Congress on the Prevention of Crime and the Treatment of Offenders, held in Geneva on 30 August 1955, and later approved by the Economic and Social Council.[37]

The UN General Assembly has also adopted guiding principles and other types of guidelines such as the 1991 Guiding Principles on Humanitarian Emergency Assistance[38] or the 1985 United Nations Standard Minimum Rules for the Administration of Juvenile Justice (the 'Beijing Rules').[39] Guiding principles and other types of guidelines are developed within the expert bodies of the Council of Europe and adopted by the Committee of Ministers, which is the executive organ of the Council of Europe.[40] In the African human rights system, the African Commission on human and peoples' rights has taken the lead on adopting

[32] GPs endorsed by an HRC Resolution 20/10 (July 2012). The GPs are set forth in the report of the Independent Expert on extreme poverty and human rights (A/HRC/20/23, 10 Apr. 2011).

[33] HRC Resolution 21/11 (Sept. 2012) which 'adopted' the GPs set forth in the report of the Special Rapporteur on extreme poverty and human rights (A/HRC/21/11, Sept. 2012). The resolution was adopted without a vote.

[34] Report of the Special Rapporteur on adequate housing (A/HRC/25/54).

[35] E/CN.4/1998/53/Add.2. [36] E/CN.4/RES/2004/55.

[37] Resolutions 663 C (XXIV) of 31 July 1957 and 2076 (LXII) of 13 May 1977.

[38] Adopted by UN General Assembly Resolution 46/182 (A/RES/46/182).

[39] A/RES/40/33. See also inter alia: the 1998 Body of Principles for the Protection of All Persons under Any Form of Detention or Imprisonment (A/RES/43/173) or the 1990 United Nations Rules for the Protection of Juveniles Deprived of their Liberty (A/RES/45/113).

[40] Guiding Principles for the Fight Against Corruption (Resolution (97) 24 on the 20 GPS for the fight against corruption, adopted by the Committee of Ministers on 6 Nov. 1997); Guidelines on child-friendly health care adopted by the Committee of Ministers on 21 Sept. 2011 or Guidelines of the Committee of Ministers of the Council of Europe on child-friendly justice adopted on 17 Nov. 2010.

Guidelines relevant to specific human rights issues.[41] This is also the case in the Inter-American human rights system.[42]

Guiding principles in this relatively new category, endorsed by the HRC, compile existing human rights principles. They 'reflect and are consistent with international human rights law and international humanitarian law'[43] and, as mentioned in the UNGPs on business and human rights, do not create any new international law obligations.[44] These Guiding Principles restate the relevant rights in a given context (e.g. the internally displaced, business enterprise activities, or the urban poor), thereby seeking to clarify unclear areas and addressing gaps that might have been identified, for instance the focus of the UNGPs on business and human rights within the state business nexus (public enterprises, procurement, privatization, and support for exports and investment).

In all cases, the HRC has closely followed the elaboration of preliminary reports and draft versions of the guiding principles by the special UN bodies and procedures in charge. Contrary to instruments adopted by central political bodies of international organizations (i.e. the UN General Assembly or the Committee of Ministers of the Council of Europe), the UN Guiding Principles are not formally negotiated among states. Their endorsement, through the adoption of a resolution by the HRC, may however be accompanied by a vote of the forty-seven states members of the HRC. The resolution endorsing the UNGPs and establishing the UNWG was adopted without a vote.[45] Prominent scholars have described this adoption as unanimous endorsement of the UNGPs by the HRC.[46] Adoption without a vote in fact signals an emphasis on consensus more than unanimity. It can indeed be seen as a sign of goodwill of the states members of the HRC, especially when compared to the much narrower state adhesion to such soft law instruments when adopted by a simple majority vote at the HRC.[47]

[41] E.g. Principles and Guidelines on Fair Trial and Legal Assistance in Africa, adopted by the African Commission on human and peoples' rights at its 33rd session in Niamey, Niger, 29 May 2003 or the Robben Island Guidelines, i.e. Guidelines and measures for the prohibition and prevention of torture, cruel, inhuman and degrading treatment and punishment in Africa adopted by the African Commission on human and peoples' rights at its 32nd session in Banjul, the Gambia, 23 Oct. 2002.

[42] See e.g.: Principles and Best Practices on the Protection of Persons Deprived of Liberty in the Americas, Inter-American Commission on Human Rights, Resolution 1/08 of 13 Mar. 2008.

[43] Guiding Principles on Internal Displacement, para. 9.

[44] Nothing in these Guiding Principles should be read as creating new international law obligations, or as limiting or undermining any legal obligations a state may have undertaken or be subject to under international law with regard to human rights (UNGPs, General Principles, p. 1).

[45] HRC, 17th session, 33rd meeting, 16 June 2011 (A/HRC/17/4). It may be noted that the Guiding Principles on Extreme Poverty and Human Rights (report of the SR to the HRC A/HRC/21/ 11 Sept. 2012) have also been adopted without a vote by Resolution 21/11 (27 Sept. 2012).

[46] M. Addo, 'The Reality of the United Nations Guiding Principles on Business and Human Rights', *Human Rights Law Review* vol. 14 (2014): 133–47 at 141. Addo says that the uniqueness of the UNGPs lies in the unanimity of their endorsement.

[47] 2012 Guiding Principles on foreign debt and human rights: the resolution endorsing the GPs was adopted by a recorded vote of 31 to 11 (Western states), with 5 abstentions. As is often the case with HRC resolutions, the distribution of the votes gives a fairly clear idea of the political disputes at stake between the states members of the HRC.

Guiding principles and guidelines adopted by the UN General Assembly or the Committee of Ministers of the Council of Europe are negotiated and debated among the member states of the organization. Hence UN guiding principles such as the UNGPs only represent an initial crystallization of the states' goodwill. As Karin Buhmann notes, 'acceptance by the Human Rights Council does not make for formal international law by itself, but it paves the way for further efforts that may eventually reach the UN General Assembly for formal adoption',[48] in the form of hard or soft law instruments. As UNGPs have a rather uncertain position in the formal taxonomy of soft law due to their lack of prior adoption by a political body (executive or parliamentary organ), their adoption process tries to compensate for the lack of state involvement in their elaboration. In order to ensure the adoption of the UNGPs by the HRC and potential future compliance by all states and other duty-bearers defined in the UNGPs, Ruggie opted for a broad consultation approach.

4.2 Relevant features of the elaboration of the UNGPs

The work of John Ruggie on the Framework and the UNGPs has been closely scrutinized by all actors and abundantly commented on by scholars.[49] The UNGPs are a typical case of expert-driven soft law. They build on extensive work by Professor John Ruggie and his team during his mandate as Special Representative of the Secretary General on the issue of human rights and transnational corporations and other business enterprises (2005–11). A lot of Ruggie's work is based on surveys that seek to identify whether the practice of human rights and business fits with more theoretical and scholarly views on the application of international human rights law to business. This relates, for example, to the responsibility of business enterprises to respect human rights, or to the extraterritorial application of human rights to the activities of business enterprises operating outside the home state.[50] The results of this research and analysis have been submitted to several rounds of consultation at the international, regional, and national levels with all stakeholders: relevant state organs, national human rights institutions, multinational and national private corporations, civil society, and human rights experts and scholars.

As far as international law-making is concerned, it is common for civil society, national human rights institutions, and experts to be consulted by UN institutions as well as other international and regional organizations. Private actors, such as

[48] K. Buhmann, 'The Development of the 'UN Framework': A Pragmatic Process Towards a Pragmatic Output', in Mares (2012): 85–105 at 86.

[49] See inter alia two previously cited anthologies: Mares (2012) and Deva and Bilchitz (2013).

[50] See e.g.: *Survey of Scope and Patterns of Alleged Corporate-Related Human Rights Abuse*, Addendum to the Report of the Special Representative of the Secretary General on the issue of human rights and transnational corporations and other business enterprises, 23 May 2008 (A/HRC/8/5/Add.2) or *Corporate Responsibility under International Law and Issues in Extraterritorial Regulation: Summary of Legal Workshops*, Addendum 2 to the Report of the Special Representative of the Secretary General on the issue of human rights and transnational corporations and other business enterprises, 9 Feb. 2007 (A/HRC/4/35/Add.2).

business enterprises, on the other hand, are not usually involved in such processes for elaborating human rights standards. In the case of the UNGPs on business and human rights, carrying out broad consultation was part of the mandate originally given to the SRSG by the Human Rights Commission in 2005[51] and became the core element of his methodology.[52] Ruggie needed to get the support of traditional actors in international human rights law-making (states, NHRI, international NGO networks, human rights experts, etc.) to achieve endorsement at the level of the HRC. He also needed to involve some of the future addressees of the UNGPs via consultation with private corporations, employer organizations, chambers of commerce, trade unions, and practitioners working with private corporations.

The combination of targeted surveys and broad multi-stakeholder consultations had the benefit of disseminating information on the guiding principles prior to their endorsement by the HRC. This helped to build some form of consensus among all stakeholders (state, business enterprises, and civil society) regarding the existence and contents of the UNGPs, and guide the SRSG in identifying and making strategic choices for the drafting of the final document. This process does not negate the fact that half the principles contained in the UNGPs establish standards for addressees who did not participate in their formal adoption.

4.3 The new addressees

It is a feature of international human rights law that states are not at the centre of reciprocal engagements with other states but commit not to violate and to actively protect the human rights of *individuals*. Non-state actors are a known figure in human rights, both as the recipient of the protection and as a possible 'indirect human rights abuser' (e.g. a husband beating his wife, a company engaging in discrimination, a private militia killing people), whose negative actions states have an obligation to regulate, sanction, and redress.

The UNGPs on business and human rights directly address, for the first time, a category of non-state actors (business enterprises), in their own right, and elaborate a series of responsibilities with which they should comply.[53] In this respect, business enterprises become the addressees of a set of norms endorsed by the United Nations. A UN Special Procedure (the Working Group) is in charge of ensuring the dissemination and implementation of these principles,[54] by addressing business enterprises in its recommendations on implementation[55] after conducting country visits.[56]

[51] Resolution 2005/69 of the UN Commission on Human Rights.

[52] Buhmann (2012): 101–4.

[53] Humanitarian law addresses also non-state actors (rebel forces in the Common Art. 3 to Geneva Conventions), but define no obligations for them other than the one they define for any party to a conflict.

[54] A/HRC/RES/17/4, 6(a).

[55] A/HRC/RES/17/4, 6(b).

[56] A/HRC/RES/17/4, 6(d).

This chapter is not the place to dwell on the nature of the corporate *responsibility* to respect human rights and on the possible existence of a corporate *obligation* to respect human rights.[57] It goes without saying that business enterprises are paramount stakeholders and actors in the business and human rights field, but this does not give them a formal role in the creation of soft law. Likewise, the role played by these new addressees during the consultations on the UNGPs does not give them any new formal status under international human rights law. States remain the driving force in creating international law, while other stakeholders (civil society, experts, business organizations, etc.) are consulted to give expert/technical advice and feedback in the form of criticisms and/or support.

Further, business enterprises do suffer from a representation problem on the global stage. In fact, the new addressees of the UNGPs (i.e. transnational, multinational companies, or other business enterprises) constitute an endless category. The International Organization of Employers, the International Chamber of Commerce, as well as the multinationals that were active in the debates, meetings, and consultations on the UNGPs and continue to provide expertise and push agendas with the UNWG through the Annual Forum,[58] cannot be considered to be representative of *all* the potential business addressees of the UNGPs.

The above difficulty in no way detracts from what is fundamentally new in the UNGPs: that they address new actors and recommend that they take action. Consequently, the UNWG is directly addressing business enterprises in its work, as can be seen in the UNWG country visit reports. In the three country visit reports available so far, recommendations have been directly addressed to business enterprises. Under the title 'Recommendations to Business', the report on Mongolia addresses seven recommendations directly to business enterprises.[59] The report on the visit to Ghana has a section devoted to recommendations to business and international development partners. Two main types of private actor are directly addressed by the UNWG: business enterprises and industry, and private sector associations.[60] The report on the visit to the USA differs slightly, as there is no set of recommendations directly addressed to business enterprises as specific entities. The seventeen recommendations are mostly addressed to US public authorities (government, counties, municipalities, etc.). A few specific business sectors are, however, mentioned directly: companies in the agricultural sector, coal companies, and the financial sector, as well as business associations and networks.[61]

[57] There is an abundant literature on the topic. A 2013 anthology, Deva and Bilchitz (2013), takes an in-depth look at the UNGPs, considering that the pragmatic approach followed by Ruggie led to a text that does not take the human rights obligations of private corporations seriously. They examine further how companies can be made accountable for human rights violations.

[58] An Annual Forum has been organized by the UNWG and held in Geneva each year since 2012.

[59] Report on the visit to Mongolia, Addendum to the Report of the Working Group on the issue of human rights and transnational corporations and other business enterprises, 2 Apr. 2013, A/HRC/23/32/Add.1, para. 95 (a–g).

[60] Report on the visit to Ghana, Addendum to the Report of the Working Group on the issue of human rights and transnational corporations and other business enterprises, 6 May 2014, A/HRC/26/25/Add.5, paras 82 and 83.

[61] Report on the visit to the USA, Addendum to the Report of the Working Group on the issue of human rights and transnational corporations and other business enterprises, 6 May 2014, A/HRC/26/25/Add.4, para. 102, respectively (h), (l), (o), and (p).

5. An Instrument that Blurs the Contents of International Human Rights Law?

Ruggie's work is successful in connecting the language of public international law with the practical discourse of CSR.[62] Dressing CSR in international law language may indeed give the illusion of moving CSR beyond voluntary standard, while in fact CSR stays within the realm of voluntary commitments by business enterprises. The UNGPs on business and human rights do not provide any clarification as to what the authoritative dimension of human rights in business might be. The UNGPs simply restate a social responsibility of business via the process of due diligence.[63] As unambiguously explained by Ruggie,

> the term 'responsibility' to respect, rather than 'duty', is meant to indicate that respecting rights is not an obligation that current international human rights law generally imposes directly on companies, although elements may be reflected in domestic laws. At the international level, the corporate responsibility to respect is a standard of expected conduct acknowledged in virtually every voluntary and soft-law instrument related to corporate responsibility, and now affirmed by the Council itself.[64]

In addressing corporate responsibility to respect human rights through the vehicle of a UN instrument, Ruggie needed to render an accurate picture of international human rights law. In consequence the integration of the business human rights responsibility discourse into a UN soft law instrument has inevitably led to the abandonment of any pretence that business enterprises should have actual human rights obligations. The language used by Ruggie inevitably reflects this reality. In parallel with the dichotomy of state duty and business responsibility, the UNGPs consequently implement a distinction between human rights *violations* committed by states, through actions or lack of action, and the human rights *abuses* committed by business enterprises. Here the UNGPs refer to actions or lack of action by business enterprises that may amount to a breach of law and engage their civil responsibility and/or in the most serious cases will amount to criminal offences. More precisely, we may talk about *human rights-related* abuses by business enterprises or human rights *impacts*, as referred to in several places of the UNGPs. The use of *impacts* is criticized heavily by Deva, who states that 'it is by and large uncontroversial that companies can *violate* human rights'[65] and that the word 'impact' devalues the importance attached to human rights and the consequences of their violation on a victim. Deva seems to argue that Ruggie chose to depart from a conception

[62] C. Parker and J. Howe, 'Ruggie's Diplomatic Project and its Missing Regulatory Infrastructure', in Mares (2012): 273–301 at 273.

[63] Parker and Howe in Mares (2012): 278.

[64] Business and human rights: further steps toward the operationalization, Report of the SRSG on the issue of human rights and transnational corporations and other business enterprises, J. Ruggie, 2010, A/HRC/14/27/2010, para. 55.

[65] D. Surya, 'Treating Human Rights Lightly: A Critique of the Consensus Rhetoric and the Language Employed by the Guiding Principles', in Deva and Bilchitz (2013): 96–7.

of rights that would create legal obligations for both states and non-state actors. Nonetheless, using the language of international law and applying international human rights law thinking to business enterprises, Ruggie had no real choice other than to make the difference between the two categories of commitments (and infringements of these commitments) very explicit.

Although the language of the UNGPs is coherent, there are two main areas where the UNGPs and their subsequent interpretation do create—or maintain—a degree of confusion as to the actual contents and extent of international human rights law.

5.1 The state duty to protect: connecting hard law and soft law?

As far as the UNGPs are concerned, a state human rights duty is both something the state *must* do and something the state *should* do. There is no distinct boundary between hard and soft law commitment. The first area of confusion concerns the actual lack of connection between Pillars 1 and 2 of the UNGPs.

As mentioned above, GP 1 restates the state obligation to protect against human rights abuses within their territory and/or jurisdiction by business enterprises through taking appropriate steps to prevent, investigate, punish, and redress such abuses via effective policies, legislation, regulations, and adjudication. Linking GP 1 to Pillar 2, one may deduce that states have an obligation to regulate the activities of business enterprises and thereby require that business enterprises assess, mitigate, report, and, if necessary, redress the human rights impacts that their activities may produce. In other words, voluntary CSR commitments would become compulsory requirements that states must adopt. These types of legal requirement are not unknown, as some states do require some form of non-financial reporting for certain types of company.[66] According to the UNGPs, this is an avenue open to any state.

The commentary under GP 3 refers directly to due diligence and reporting and recommends states to 'encourage, and where appropriate require, business enterprises to communicate how they address their human rights impacts'.[67] More precisely, the UNGPs recommend that the state consider implementation of their pre-existing regulatory requirements on these matters, as well as the possible introduction of such requirements or the development of means to encourage companies to adopt due diligence and reporting processes on a voluntary basis.

The connection between GP 1 and Pillar 2 is not complete: passing laws requiring mandatory due diligence and reporting is a recommended option that international

[66] See e.g.: the German Corporate Governance Code or the Danish legislation on CSR. According to a 2008 provision of the Danish Act on financial reporting, a large company or a financial institution must either give information on its CSR policy, its implementation, the results that have been achieved and the expectations for the future or expressly state that the company will not be engaging in CSR. In 2012 an amendment was adopted by the Danish Parliament to specifically include human rights (and climate policies) in this legal requirement (comply or explain) for reporting on CSR, available in Danish at: <http://www.ft.dk/samling/20111/lovforslag/l125/html_som_vedtaget.htm>. Mandatory impact assessment is also known from comparable fields such as environment or health.

[67] GP 3, d.

human rights law does not, however, impose on states. The drafters of a legally binding instrument on human rights and business, if they choose not to impose direct obligation on business enterprises, could design such a state obligation to regulate the human rights impacts of business enterprise activities.[68]

5.2 Which extraterritoriality?

When dealing with extraterritoriality in the context of human rights and business, the main issue at stake is the exercise of extraterritorial jurisdiction by a 'home' state over the overseas activities of a transnational company with some link to that state (domicile, registration, or listing in the territory or within the jurisdiction of the state). Navigating between a few legal obligations and many soft law recommendations, the UNGPs reflect the confusion that already exists as to which type of extraterritoriality is at stake: on the one hand, a possible extraterritorial human rights obligation of the state to ensure by law that business enterprises domiciled on their territory do not commit human rights-related abuses abroad and, on the other hand, the mere possibility of applying extraterritorial jurisdiction in criminal prosecution or civil litigation to business enterprise operations outside the state.

Extraterritoriality is mentioned indirectly in the text of GP 2 which is worded in a highly cautious and non-committal manner: 'States should set out clearly the expectation that all business enterprises domiciled in their territory and/or jurisdiction respect human rights throughout their operations.' Focusing primarily on an extraterritorial application of the human rights obligation of the state, the 'minimal'[69] wording of GP 2 is explained by the fact that, at present, states are not required under international human rights law to regulate the extraterritorial activities of businesses domiciled in their territory and/or jurisdiction. In international human rights law, the extraterritorial application of the human rights obligation of states requires a certain degree of control by the state on the situation occurring outside the territorial jurisdiction. The relevant and extensive case law of the European Court of Human Rights thus deals primarily with military operations or other forms of military presence abroad.[70]

In the field of human rights and business, there is fierce debate regarding the actual existence—and possible future development—of an extraterritorial human rights obligation of the state.[71] Some human rights treaty bodies already ask that home states take steps to prevent abuses abroad by business enterprises domiciled within their territorial jurisdiction. For example, the Committee on Economic,

[68] See section 6.

[69] D. Augenstein and D. Kinley, 'When Human Rights Responsibilities Become Duties: The Extraterritorial Obligations of States that Bind Corporations?', in Deva and Bilchitz (2013): 275.

[70] Overview of this case law in the Factsheet on extraterritorial jurisdiction available on the website of the ECtHR.

[71] Augenstein and Kinley in Deva and Bilchitz (2013): 271–94; O. De Schutter, *Extraterritorial Jurisdiction as a Tool for Improving the Human Rights Accountability of Transnational Corporations*, Dec. 2006 (background paper to the seminar organized in collaboration with the Office of the UN High Commissioner for Human Rights in Brussels on 3–4 Nov. 2006).

Social, and Cultural Rights has stated in its General Comment on the right to water that 'steps should be taken by states parties to prevent their own citizens and companies from violating the right to water of individuals and communities in other countries'.[72] Transnational activities that have critical human rights impacts such as child trafficking have compelled the Committee on the Rights of the Child to urge states to take action in order to prosecute and punish those engaging in trafficking. Article 3(1) of the Optional Protocol on Sale of Children, Child Prostitution, and Child Pornography requires that such offences be criminalized, whether they are committed 'domestically or transnationally or on an individual or organized basis'.[73]

Independently of the existence of any international human rights obligations, states have chosen to adopt direct extraterritorial legislation[74] or to extend their civil and or criminal jurisdiction to acts that have taken place outside their own territory.[75] In the USA, the Alien Tort Statute of 1789 has opened up the possibility of victims obtaining redress for *human rights violations* by companies operating outside their territory of domicile. This was a rather exceptional development and has been significantly toned down following the 2013 *Kiobel* judgment of the US Supreme Court.[76] However, numerous cases against multinational companies have been pursued in many countries on the basis of tort (negligence arising from a breach of a company's duty of care). Even though there has not yet been a final legal determination on the point of establishing an extraterritorial duty of care for parent companies that could serve as the basis of an 'extraterritorial' tort claim,[77] cases are not dismissed from the outset on the basis of lack of territorial jurisdiction.[78]

[72] Para. 33 of General Comment 15 on the right to water (E/C.12/2002/11). See also CESCR General Comment 14 on the right to the highest attainable standard of health (E/C.12/2000/4), at para. 39 for similar comments to General Comment 15, para. 33 in relation to influencing third party actions abroad.

[73] Optional Protocol on sale of children, child prostitution, and child pornography (General Assembly Resolution A/RES/54/263 of 25 May 2000), see also Arts 3.2, 4.2, and 4.3. See also inter alia CRC concluding observations, Lebanon, UN Doc. CRC/C/LBN/CO/3, 8 June 2006, at para. 82(e). See also the international framework for combating terrorism, which relies heavily on states establishing extraterritorial jurisdiction or the 2000 International Convention for the Suppression of the Financing of Terrorism. For references to several other standards: De Schutter (2006).

[74] See e.g.: the United States legislation re the fight against corruption or consumer protection: US Foreign Corrupt Practice Act of 1977 and US Dodd–Franck Act of 2010, section 1502 on conflict free minerals. See also: UK Bribery Act of 2010.

[75] J. Zerk, *Corporate Liability for Gross Human Rights Abuses: Towards a Fairer and More Effective System of Domestic Law Remedies*, a study prepared for the Office of the UN High Commissioner for Human Rights (2014): 31–9.

[76] *Esther Kiobel v. Royal Dutch Petroleum Co.*, 133 S. Ct 1659 (2013). Until the *Kiobel* judgment in 2013, the US Alien Tort Statute of 1789 had been interpreted by US federal courts 'as implying that they have jurisdiction over enterprises either incorporated in the United States or having a continuous business relationship with the United States, where foreigners, victims of violations of international law wherever such violations have taken place, seek damages from enterprises which have committed those violations or are complicit in such violations as they may have been committed by State agents' (De Schutter (2006): 6).

[77] R. Meeran, 'Access to Remedy: The United Kingdom Experience of MNC Tort Litigation for Human Rights Violation', in Deva and Bilchitz (2013): 378–402. See also e.g. the list of tort cases litigated in the UK at 388.

[78] E.g. the Quebec Superior Court of Justice in the *Anvil* judgment of 27 Apr. 2011: the Court dismissed a motion to strike the claim brought by Anvil based on lack of jurisdiction. In so doing,

The above and recent developments in the field of extraterritoriality show that there are many possibilities for increasing access to effective remedy for victims of human rights-related abuses committed in host countries, even though there is no legal obligation for states to do so.

6. Towards a Legally Binding Instrument

Efforts to elaborate an international legally binding human rights and business instrument have been renewed with the establishment in 2014 of an open-ended intergovernmental working group 'whose mandate is to elaborate an international legally binding instrument to regulate, in international human rights law, the activities of Transnational Corporations and Other Business Enterprises'.[79]

So far, the actual contents of such an instrument has been the subject of much debate.[80] Ruggie himself has suggested that it is necessary to start looking into gross human rights abuses.[81] One avenue could be an extension of international criminal jurisdiction to include legal persons as perpetrators of (or complicit in) international crimes through the introduction of a new treaty or the extension of ICC jurisdiction. Another option could be to look into linking non-binding and binding elements found in the UNGPs and to work towards the creation of an obligation for the state to regulate the activities of business enterprises, for example through compulsory due diligence and reporting procedures for some or all business enterprises. Finally, a few proposals have been made towards strengthening the legal obligations of states and business enterprises, such as a creating international human rights remedies that would target business enterprises,[82] or imposing an obligation on states to create a duty of care for parent companies via a new international legally binding instrument on human rights and business.[83]

the Court left the door open for extraterritorial human rights claims against Canadian corporations in Quebec courts. The Quebec Court of Appeal ultimately overturned that decision and dismissed the case but not on the grounds of lack of jurisdiction. See also the judgment against Royal Dutch Shell and its subsidiary SPDC, District Court of The Hague, 30 Jan. 2013. Even in the USA, Circuits Court judgments have looked into whether claims had a sufficient link to the US territory in order to determine whether or not the presumption against extraterritorial application of the ATS could be displaced. When the alleged violations concerned conduct that occurred entirely abroad (the claim does not affect or concern the US territory), the presumption against extraterritorial application cannot be lifted, *Al Shimari et al. v. CACI Premier Tech., Inc.*, 2014 WL 2922840 (4th Cir. 30 June 30 2014); *Cardona et al. v. Chiquita Brands International*, No. 12-14898 (11th Cir. 24 July 2014), J. Martin dissenting.

[79] Establishment by the HRC in June 2014 of an open-ended intergovernmental working group to elaborate an international legally binding instrument on transnational corporations and other business enterprises with respect to human rights, HRC Resolution L.22, A/HRC/26/L.22/Rev.1.

[80] An account of the difficulties that surrounded the adoption of the resolution can be found at <http://business-humanrights.org/en/binding-treaty/un-human-rights-council-sessions>.

[81] Issue Brief by J. Ruggie, *A UN Business and Human Rights Treaty?* Harvard Kennedy School, 28 Jan. 2014.

[82] M. Nowak, 'The Need for a World Court of Human Rights', *Human Rights Law Review* vol. 7 (2007): 251–9.

[83] As advocated by Amnesty International, *Injustice Incorporated: Corporate Abuses and the Human Right to Remedy* (Amnesty International, 2014), 202.

In any case, the elaboration and negotiation of such a legally binding instrument, albeit with only a very narrow scope, will not be an easy road to travel.

7. Conclusion

The UNGPs are an important development in the global governance of business.[84] They are not merely a governance instrument or simple manual; they may only constitute international secondary soft law, but the formality of their endorsement brings them within the realm of international law. As an international soft law instrument, the UNGPs represent a major innovation, as they address business enterprises which are actors but not (yet) fully-fledged subjects of international law, define a form of commitment for them, and recommend precise action to fulfil this responsibility.

From the outset, the UNGPs are *standard-filling* as they unpack and explain the human rights obligations of states in the field of human rights and business. In doing so, they also touch on unexplored areas of international human rights law and seem to aim, in the long term, at *creating* new standards. The UNGPs are a first step towards expanding state obligations to protect (establishing obligatory due diligence and HR reporting, or mandatory standards for situations where the state plays a predominant role in the conducting of business activities, etc.) and formulating an actual human rights obligation for business enterprises, so far in the form of a responsibility to respect. This last point requires an extensive conceptual rethink of international law and a massive amount of political will within the international community. Its realization in practice would also require major adjustments to domestic and international legislation on criminal, administrative, and civil jurisdiction and procedures.

It is too early to predict the effects of such an instrument. As the UNGPs mostly take stock of pre-existing developments within the field of human rights and business, the effects of the UNGPs as such are difficult to trace. In this respect, the establishment, work, and, in June 2014, the mandate renewal of the UNWG on human rights may make a difference. In addition to being a focal point for human rights and business within the human rights system, the UNWG is in a unique position to mainstream issues with potentially considerable effects, push topical agendas, and feed into other processes and initiatives at the international, regional, and domestic level. Through country visits, the working group has the opportunity to remind states of their human rights obligations as well as to recommend a large range of actions that should be undertaken by both state and non-state actors. By promoting national action plans and providing guidance to states to develop such plans, the working group is building on existing practice as well as enhancing

[84] S. Aaronson and I. Higham, '"Re-Righting Business": John Ruggie and the Struggle to Develop International Human Rights Standards for Transnational Firms', *Human Rights Quarterly* vol. 35 (2013): 333–64.

the tool that it deems paramount to the dissemination and implementation of the UNGPs. More recently, the UNWG is pushing the human rights and business agenda in the UN, for instance by promoting the mainstreaming of issues relevant to human rights and business in the work of UN treaty bodies and in the Universal Periodic Review.

Needless to say, the role played by non-legally binding standards in the field of human rights and business has been colossal and paramount to the developments leading to the endorsement of the UNGPs by the HRC. There is indeed nothing problematic about non-binding instruments as such. As Shelton explains, these standards 'offer a flexible and efficient way to order responses to common problems. They are not law and they do not need to be in order to influence conduct in the desired manner.'[85] A soft law instrument such as the UNGPs does not reduce or undermine the pre-existing legally binding obligation for states to protect human rights. It might even pave the way towards creating, in an admittedly distant future, new international obligations for both states and business enterprises. However, there is a danger that such state obligations may become diluted by the declaration of new duties and responsibilities, which amount, when unpacked, to a long list of possible actions to be taken by various actors.[86] Therefore, all actors must focus on the principal matter in hand: the protection of human rights. This means that business enterprises must, as a minimum, respect the laws of the countries in which they are operating and states must regulate, monitor, and redress the human rights-related abuses that businesses may commit within their jurisdiction.

Soft law blurs some of the lines drawn by international human rights law; in some cases, it works towards reducing state commitment; in our case it seeks to expand the field of human rights at the risk of creating misperceptions among all stakeholders and false expectations among right-holders. When actual human rights violations occur, the disputes are, so far, ultimately settled by state organs (courts of justice). In such situations, as Prosper Weil puts it, there is no hesitation as to which standards apply: 'on one side of the line, there is born a legal obligation that can be relied on before a court or an arbitrator ...; on the other side, there is nothing of the kind.'[87] This remains true today: no matter how blurred the frontiers between hard law and soft law have become, states continue clearly to perceive the difference.

[85] D. Shelton, 'International Law and "Relative Normativity"', in *International Law*, ed. M. D. Evans (Oxford: Oxford University Press, 2010): 169.

[86] S. Lagoutte, 'New Challenges Facing States within the Field of Human Rights and Business', *Nordic Journal of Human Rights* vol. 33 (2015): 158–80.

[87] Weil (1983): 417.

12

Mission Creeps

The (Unintended) Re-enforcement of the Actor's Discussion in International Law through the Expansion of Soft Law Instruments in the business and Human Rights Nexus

Christoph Good

1. Introduction

The phenomenon of a rising number of mechanisms with soft law content in international law in general[1] and in the human rights arena in particular[2] over the last few decades can be interpreted as a shift in the regulative paradigm of international law.[3] Especially in the field of human rights—to some extent containing a category of absolute rights[4]—this development raises various questions, primarily regarding the effectiveness of these non-binding forms of regulation, their impact on the existing human rights protection framework, and their interaction with pre-existing binding treaty norms.[5] Not surprisingly, most legal scholars therefore predominantly focus on the dichotomy of soft versus hard law and the direct consequences for the actual level of protection of international human rights.

Following Stéphanie Lagoutte's chapter, which focuses primarily on understanding the exact nature of the UN Guiding Principles on business and human rights and disentangling their contents, this chapter seeks to address the cross-cutting issue of

[1] A. Boyle, 'Soft Law in International Law-Making', in *International Law*, ed. M. D. Evans (Oxford: Oxford University Press, 2014, 4th edn): 118–36, 118f.

[2] Regarding the number of soft law instruments see for example the OHCHR overview of universal human rights instruments on: <http://www.ohchr.org/EN/ProfessionalInterest/Pages/UniversalHumanRightsInstruments.aspx>.

[3] T. Meyer, 'Collective Decision-Making in International Governance', AJIL Unbound blog [Agora: The End of Treaties], 28 Apr. 2014, <http://www.asil.org/blogs/collective-decision-making-international-governance-agora-end-treaties>.

[4] O. de Schutter, *International Human Rights Law* (Cambridge: Cambridge University Press, 2014, 2nd edn): 295ff. and N. Mavronicola, 'What is an "Absolute Right"? Deciphering Absoluteness in the Context of Article 3 of the European Convention on Human Rights', *Human Rights Law Review* vol. 12 (2012): 723–58.

[5] D. Shelton, 'Human Rights', in *Commitment and Compliance: The Role of Non-binding Norms in the International Legal System*, ed. D. Shelton (Oxford: Oxford University Press, 2003): 345–464.

the business and human rights nexus as a paragon for recent soft law developments in international human rights law.[6] To demonstrate the apparently unintended side effects of newly developed human rights soft law instruments, the chapter describes the emergence of specific but functionally varying soft law-related mechanisms in the field of business and human rights and analyses their regulative consequences (section 2). Based on these general remarks, special attention is given to the peculiar effects of new developments on the issue of recognition of actors/subjects in international (human rights) law and the correlated changes in norm-shaping for private actors. Furthermore, we will examine whether these new soft law-driven intra-human rights developments have effects on fundamental paradigms of public international law (section 3).

2. The Business and Human Rights Nexus

2.1 A narrative of legislative failure?

The business and human rights nexus has occupied a prominent position in the international law agenda since the 1970s.[7] The predominant narrative sees the nexus as the unwavering (but for a long time unsuccessful) attempt by the international community to regulate the negative impacts of economic globalization, itself conceptually very welcome, and to influence the behaviour of transnational corporations (TNCs), which at least in the 1970s were a new phenomenon. While there was broad agreement from the beginning that international law was the most promising regulative toolset for tackling the negative externalities of economic globalization, the opinions of the states parties were highly divided in terms of which concrete regulative measures to take.[8] As a record from the time, Seymour J. Rubin's *AJIL* article on the discussions on and organizational structure of the UN Commission on Transnational Corporations established in 1974 depicts the struggles quite clearly.[9] In very simplified terms, one might say that within the UN bodies the greater part of state representatives of the global

[6] See e.g.: the UN Guiding Principles on Business and Human Rights (UN Doc. A/HRC/17/31) adopted in 2011, the new human rights chapter within the OECD Guidelines for Multinational Enterprises revised in 2011 (<http://dx.doi.org/10.1787/9789264115415-en>) or the Voluntary Principles on Security and Human Rights (<http://www.voluntaryprinciples.org/>) established in 2000.

[7] See e.g.: D. G. Arnold, 'Transnational Corporations and the Duty to Respect Basic Human Rights', *Business Ethics Quarterly* vol. 20 (2010): 371–99, 372ff. and J. G. Ruggie, 'Business and Human Rights: The Evolving International Agenda', *American Journal of International Law* (*AJIL*) vol. 101 (2007): 819–40, 819f.

[8] See e.g.: D. Weissbrod and M. Kruger, 'Human Rights Responsibilities of Businesses as Non-state Actors', in *Non-state Actors and Human Rights*, ed. P. Alston (Oxford: Oxford University Press, 2005): 315–50, 318ff.

[9] S. J. Rubin, 'Reflections Concerning the United Nations Commission of Transnational Corporations', *AJIL* vol. 70 (1976): 73–91.

south lobbied for a binding convention, whereas their counterparts in the global north favoured a more flexible regulative approach. Within the responsible UN Commission, the role of the states as exclusive regulative players was unquestioned. Nevertheless, the parallel—but formally entirely separate—argumentative proxy war between NGOs and business representatives on the topic further complicated the state-driven discussions.[10] Caught up in the concurrent interplay of these discourses, promising first regulative drafts such as the Draft United Nations Code of Conduct (1988)[11] and some years later the Norms on Responsibilities (2003)[12] were doomed to failure.[13]

At the same time, other efforts in this direction were being made outside the scope of international law: partly motivated by a desire to avoid the discussion on international legally binding and non-binding regulations, business-driven voluntary policy initiatives took up the issue and integrated the business and human rights nexus partly into the emerging corporate social responsibility debate.[14] The most prominent example to date is unquestionably the creation of the Global Compact[15] in 2000.[16] Many more initiatives followed and were adopted by corporations, as demonstrated by the impressive numbers in the EU's revised CSR strategy published in 2011.[17] The relative success of these private non-law approaches had—at least to some extent—repercussions on the international law discourse.[18]

[10] See e.g.: P. Alston, 'Non-state Actors and Human Rights', in *International Human Rights—The Successor to International Human Rights in Context: Law Politics and Morals—Text and Materials*, ed. P. Alston and R. Goodman (Oxford: Oxford University Press, 2013): 1461–1515 at 1477; J. Martens, 'Corporate Influence on the Business and Human Rights Agenda of the United Nations' (Misereor, Brot für die Welt and Global Policy Forum Working Paper, Aachen, Berlin, Bonn, New York, 2014): 6–10; as well as the joint comments of the International Chamber of Commerce and the International Organization of Employers on the draft norms on the responsibilities of transnational corporations and other business enterprises with regard to human rights (UN Doc. E/CN.4/2/2003/NGO/44).

[11] Draft United Nations Code of Conduct on Transnational Corporations (UN Doc. E/1988/39/ Add.1).

[12] Norms on the Responsibilities of Transnational Corporations and Other Business Enterprises with Regard to Human Rights (UN Doc. E/CN.4/Sub.2/2003/12/Rev.2).

[13] For further details see: Arnold (2010): 374–6 as well as Weissbrodt and Kruger (2005): 318–21.

[14] For a detailed analysis see: F. Wettstein, 'CSR and the Debate on Business and Human Rights: Bridging the Great Divide', *Business Ethics Quarterly* vol. 22 (2012): 739–70 at 745–7.

[15] 'United Nations Global Compact' <https://www.unglobalcompact.org/AboutTheGC/index.html>.

[16] A. Rasche, 'A "Necessary Supplement": What the United Nations Global Compact is (and is not)', in *Corporate Social and Human Rights Responsibilities: Global Legal and Management Perspectives*, ed. K. Buhmann, L. Roseberry, and M. Morsing (Basingstoke: Palgrave Macmillan, 2011): 52–76 at 56–8.

[17] European Commission, *A Renewed EU Strategy 2011–14 for Corporate Social Responsibility* (Brussels, 2011), COM (2011): 681.

[18] This can be seen in the fact that the mandate of the newly appointed special representative to the SG on the issue of human rights and transnational corporations and other business enterprises contained e.g. the obligation 'to compile a compendium of best practices of ... transnational corporations and other business enterprises'. See Commission on Human Rights Res. 2005/69 (UN Doc. E/CN.4/ RES/2005/69) para. 1(e).

2.2 The legislative breakthrough on an international level: the UNGPs and their recent regulative dissemination

In 2005, the newly appointed special representative on the issue of human rights and transnational corporations, John Ruggie, revitalized the blocked state-driven discussions on the international legal regulation of the business and human rights nexus—whether binding or non-binding. Over a period of three years, Ruggie and his team analysed the complex reasons for the failure of the previous regulative projects as well as the advantages and disadvantages of extra-legal policy initiatives. In addition, the stakeholder representatives in the process were repeatedly consulted.[19] The first major result of this extensive undertaking was the 'Protect, Respect, and Remedy' Framework,[20] which was unanimously 'welcomed' by the HRC in 2008. A second result was the operationalization of the framework in the form of the UN Guiding Principles (UNGPs),[21] realized between 2008 and 2011, which the HRC then adopted by consensus in July 2011.[22] A key factor in the broad acceptance of the framework and the UNGPs within the community of states, with whom the final decision rested, was the inherent promise that both framework and principles were based exclusively on pre-existing state obligations.[23] They were 'sold' as a compilation and clarification of existing state obligations under international law and not as the creation of new international obligations or the weakening of pre-existing norms.[24] Whether this characterization is entirely correct will not be our concern in this chapter.[25] Instead, we shall focus exclusively on the methodological aspects of the UNGPs and their follow-up processes.

[19] See for a self-description: J. G. Ruggie, 'Global Governance and "New Governance Theory": Lessons from Business and Human Rights', *Global Governance* vol. 20 (2014): 5–17 at 6–8. For a critical assessment of these development see also the chapter by Stéphanie Lagoutte in this volume.

[20] UN Doc. A/HRC/8/5.

[21] UN Doc. A/HRC/17/31. An interesting aspect of the UNGPs from a legislative perspective is the fact, that the legal text itself already contains *ex ante* its authoritative interpretation.

[22] HRC Res. 17/4 (UN Doc. A/HRC/RES/17/4) para. 1.

[23] The 'fear' of new binding obligations can be seen in the heated discussions at the HRC in summer 2014 related to the finally nevertheless adopted Ecuador proposal regarding the development of a binding instrument on business and human rights (see e.g.: L. C. Backer, 'And a Treaty to Bind them All: On Prospects and Obstacles to Moving from the GPs to a Multilateral Treaty Framework, a Preliminary Assessment', Law at the End of the Day Blog, 3 July 2014, <http://lcbackerblog.blogspot.dk/2014/07/and-treaty-to-bind-them-allon-prospects.html>).

[24] 'Nothing in these Guiding Principles should be read as creating new international law obligations, or as limiting or undermining any legal obligations a State may have undertaken or be subject to under international law with regard to human rights.' See General Principles (UN Doc. A/HRC/17/31).

[25] For a critical analysis see e.g.: S. Deva, 'Treating Human Rights Lightly: A Critique of the Consensus Rhetoric and the Language Employed by the Guiding Principles', in *Human Rights Obligations of Business: Beyond the Corporate Responsibility to Respect?*, ed. S. Deva and D. Bilchitz (Cambridge: Cambridge University Press, 2013): 78–104 and C. López, 'The "Ruggie Process": From Legal Obligations to Corporate Social Responsibility', in Deva and Bilchitz (2013): 58–77. For a critical assessment regarding the *legal* consequences see also the chapter by Stéphanie Lagoutte in this volume.

When compared to the enormous amount of time taken initially to find any regulative framework at all to deal with the business and human rights nexus, the speed of its regulative dissemination is remarkable. Very quickly, a huge number of uptakes and follow-up projects to the 'Protect, Respect, and Remedy' Framework and the UNGPs were developed and endorsed at both the national and international level. Landmark uptakes include the decision of the EU to call on all its member states to adopt a national action plan for the implementation of the UNGPs in their national legislation and policy developments.[26] Furthermore, the EU not only directed states in their dissemination activities, but also developed sectorial implementation guides for corporations.[27] Similar developments have recently been seen at the UN level and within the OECD framework.[28]

2.3 Soft law approaches in the UNGPs: monolithic or network functions?

Due to their explicitly non-binding nature, the UNGPs can easily be situated within the broad and expanding realm of soft law in the human rights field.[29]

[26] European Commission (2011), para 4.8.2. Similar issues are currently discussed in the broader framework of the Council of Europe. In 2011, the Committee of Ministers requested the Steering Committee for Human Rights (CDDH) to elaborate a study on the feasibility and the added value of new standard-setting work of the Council of Europe on corporate social responsibility in the field on human rights. At the beginning of 2013, the Committee of Ministers requested the CDDH to elaborate, by the end of 2015, a political declaration supporting the UNGPs as well as a non-binding instrument, which may include a guide of good practice, addressing gaps in the implementation of the Guiding Principles at the European level. To perform these tasks, a Drafting Group on Human Rights and Business (CDDH-CORP) has been set up. In their third meeting the CDDH-CORP articulated inter alia the recommendation, that all Council of Europe members participate in the developments of national action plans regarding the implementation of the UNGPs; see CDDH-CORP (2014) R3, Appendix III, para. 4 (with further clarification in the 'Appendix to the Recommendations', para. I b). For further information see <http://www.coe.int/t/dghl/standardsetting/hrpolicy/other_committees/hr_and_business/default_EN.asp>.

[27] Until now specific guidance for the sectors; 'oil and gas' (European Commission, *Oil and Gas Sector Guide on Implementing the UN Guiding Principles on Business and Human Rights* (Brussels, 2013), <https://ec.europa.eu/anti-trafficking/sites/antitrafficking/files/oil_and_gas.pdf>); 'information and communication technologies' (European Commission, *ICT Sector Guide on Implementing the UN Guiding Principles on Business and Human Rights* (Brussels, 2013), <https://ec.europa.eu/anti-trafficking/sites/antitrafficking/files/information_and_communication_technology_0.pdf>), and 'employment and recruitment agencies' (European Commission, *Employment and Recruitment Agencies Sector Guide on Implementing the UN Guiding Principles on Business and Human Rights* (Brussels, 2013), <https://ec.europa.eu/anti-trafficking/sites/antitrafficking/files/employment_and_recruitment_agencies.pdf>) were created. Furthermore, a more general report focused on the implementation of the UNGPs in small and medium size enterprises (European Commission, *My Business and Human Rights: A Guide to Human Rights for Small and Medium Enterprises* (Brussels, 2013), <http://ec.europa.eu/DocsRoom/documents/10375/attachments/1/translations/en/renditions/native>).

[28] See e.g.: M. K. Addo, 'The Reality of the United Nations Guiding Principles on Business and Human Rights', *Human Rights Law Review* vol. 14 (2014): 133–47 at 142–5. Regarding the UN, a landmark decision was the mainstreaming of the UNGPs within all UN institutions in 2012 (UN Doc. A/HRC/21/21). One of the most recent uptakes can be seen in the Principles for Responsible Investment in Agriculture and Food Systems, an international soft law agreement, approved by the Committee on World Food Security in Oct. 2014 (<http://www.fao.org/3/a-au866e.pdf>).

[29] Regarding the question whether the UNGPs are soft law at all see e.g.: J. Nolan, 'The Corporate Responsibility to Respect Human Rights: Soft Law or not Law?', in Deva and Bilchitz (2013): 138–61.

Furthermore, the rush of uptakes of the UNGPs easily accomplishes the criterion of 'traction' introduced earlier in this volume.[30] However, not much is gained by this broad categorization with regard to the mechanism's legal effects. This leads to the central question of this volume, namely: what consequences for international human rights law follow from the use of soft law norms and their implementation in legal instruments in this specific area? To properly answer this question, some introductory statements must be made. First and foremost, however redundant this may initially seem, it is essential to clarify the nature of the specific human rights content established by the UNGPs. Answering this question is a necessary step if we are to evaluate what concrete function soft law norms and their instrumentalization have in this specific context and what consequences they exert on the material dimension of human rights law in relation to business activities.

2.3.1 The human rights content of the UNGPs

In contrast to their clear title, 'Guiding Principles on Business and Human Rights', literally suggesting a compilation of pre-existing principles, the human rights content of the UNGPs can be interpreted quite differently: directly after their endorsement by the HRC, the OHCHR celebrated the UNGPs in their news section as an 'unprecedented step ... to provide for the first time a global standard for preventing and addressing the risk of adverse impacts on human rights linked to business activity'.[31] This interpretation of the UNGPs as a new standard creates the impression that their introduction entailed the creation of designated new human rights content—in other words, that the UNGPs were intended as a substantive 'topping' added to the existing human rights framework with special emphasis on the business and human rights nexus. The central point is mainly the alleged new obligation of corporations to respect human rights in all their activities.[32]

The Special Representative, John Ruggie, described the function of the UNGPs quite differently in his introductory commentary to the draft of the principles in 2011: they were constructed as a 'common global platform for action on which cumulative progress can be built'[33] and do not create any new obligations but elaborate 'the implications of existing standards and practices for States and businesses; integrating them within a single, logically coherent and comprehensive template'.[34] In contrast to the former, content-oriented interpretation, the latter view suggests a procedural understanding of the UNGPs. They are not considered a 'topping', but rather assume the role of an 'incubator'. Depending on the interpretation of the

[30] See Introduction to this volume.

[31] 'New Guiding Principles on Business and Human Rights Endorsed by the UN Human Rights Council', OHCHR, <http://www.ohchr.org/en/NewsEvents/Pages/DisplayNews.aspx?NewsID=11164>.

[32] Within the UNGPs, the corporate's obligation to respect human rights is articulated in Principles 11 to 24. For a critical analysis of the nature of the corporate obligation to respect human rights see the chapter by Stéphanie Lagoutte in this volume.

[33] UN Doc. A/HRC/17/31, para. 13.

[34] UN Doc. A/HRC/17/31, para. 14.

UNGPs chosen, different expectations with regard to the function of the soft law instrument are raised, and different promises articulated.

2.3.1.1 Direct promise of soft law in the case of the UNGPs: 'hardening' the obligation to respect and 'changing the rules of the game'

Under the interpretation of the UNGPs as a 'topping', the recourse to soft law is used as a functional preparatory step within a designated multilateral treaty-making process with intended side effects on customary international law.[35] According to this classical international law understanding, soft law could best be described as 'auxiliary regulative means', in the sense of a preparatory step to the exclusively inter-governmental process of 'hardening' norms. Consequently, this soft law dimension always entails a progressive element, clearly defined by a goal that must be reached. At the same time, a limitation of regulative means is inherent to this type of soft law approach, since in most cases only one type of regulation is suitable. In concrete terms, a specific set of norms on the obligation of corporations to respect human rights in the form of an international binding treaty or covenant would seem to be the instrument of choice. The soft law stage of the norm is itself only transitional in nature, and once the 'hard' norm is established, the soft law instrument becomes superfluous. Furthermore, this type of soft law regulation encourages and follows a classical top-down approach for implementation.

Bearing the long history of the creation of the UNGPs in mind, it is obvious that the inclusion of new material content in the UNGPs aims precisely at realizing this typical soft law function. This at least seems to be the expectation that especially supportive civil society organizations and states parties of the global south repeatedly express in relation to the UNGPs and their role with regard to the corporate obligation to respect human rights.[36] Whether such an expectation can ultimately be fully satisfied is hard to tell.[37] In fact, an early test case in the international law arena—the discussions regarding Ecuador's proposal for the development of a binding instrument on the human rights accountability of corporations in the HRC in June 2014[38]—overcame the initial hurdle of passing the HRC, but at the same time revealed the fragility of the consensus reached on the matter itself. This is further evidenced by the statements from the representatives of the USA, Italy (on behalf

[35] In general to the preparatory character of soft law see: Boyle (2014): 123–5 and D. Thürer, 'Soft Law', in *Max Planck Encyclopaedia of Public International Law*, ed. R. Wolfrum (Oxford: Oxford University Press, 2009): para. 32.

[36] With regard to the involvement of civil society organizations see e.g. the support of the Ecuador resolution to develop a binding instrument for human rights accountability of corporations by the 'Treaty Alliance'—a network of more than 500 civil society organizations from all over the globe, <http://www.treatymovement.com/>.

[37] For the interplay of national and international corporate human rights obligations see e.g.: J. L. Černič, 'Corporations and Human Rights: Towards Binding International Legal Obligations?', in *Business and Human Rights*, ed. M. K. Sinha (Los Angeles et al.: Sage Publications, 2013): 1–51, 26f. For an outline of possible 'ways ahead' see also the chapter by Stéphanie Lagoutte in this volume.

[38] See: HRC, Elaboration of an International Legally Binding Instrument on Transnational Corporations and Other Business Enterprises with Respect to Human Rights (UN Doc. A/HRC/26/L.22/Rev.1), 24 June 2014.

of the EU), and Ireland during the discussions at the related HRC session and their almost hysterical evocation of the risks to which the achievements of the UNGPs would be exposed if this step towards hardening them were taken.[39] The biggest real risk posed by this approach seems to be the return of political deadlock in the UN's legislative procedure, as witnessed during the debates on the Draft United Nations Code of Conduct (1988) and the Norms on Responsibilities (2003).[40]

2.3.1.2 Indirect promise of soft law in the case of the UNGPs: 'making the existing system fully operable'

On the other hand, the view of the UNGPs as an 'incubator' suggests a different interpretation of the function of soft law. In this case, soft law operates more as a 'coordinating device'.[41] Its instrumental function is not so much progressive change, but aims predominantly at managing and optimizing the existing regulative system. With regard to the UNGPs this function is expressed by the persistent invocation of the creation of a 'level playing field' for all competitors as a central goal. In direct contrast to the promises of the 'hardening' process, the regulative framework is much broader and designed to work for an indefinite period of time by assuming a clear governance role. The endorsement of the UNGPs is 'just the end of the beginning'.[42] In specific terms, such soft law governance mechanisms seem to blur the line between preparatory works and classical intergovernmental drafting processes of international law. A further characteristic of this type of procedural soft law approach is the regular transfer of expertise to an institution that acts as a focal point. In the case of the UNGPs, this function is delegated to the newly established UN Working Group on the issue of human rights and transnational corporations and other business enterprises.[43] Additionally, both the regulative framework itself and the created focal point institution have an inherent 'canonizing' function, in the sense that they authoritatively compile and interpret the existing obligations as well as the instruments by which compliance with the obligations can be achieved.[44] Nevertheless, the framework is flexible with regard to the resources applied to fulfil the purpose. As the Special Representative stated during the elaboration of the 'Protect, Respect, and Remedy' Framework, 'no silver bullet can resolve the business and human rights challenge'.[45] The creation of a

[39] See: HRC, 37th Meeting/26th Regular Session (Video), 26 June 2014, <http://webtv.un.org/search/ahrc26l.22rev.1-vote-item3-37th-meeting-26th-regular-session-human-rights-council/3643474570001?term=A/HRC/26/L.22>.

[40] See e.g.: N. Jägers, 'Will Transnational Private Regulation Close the Governance Gap?', in Deva and Bilchitz (2013): 295–328 at 295.

[41] See: A. T. Guzman and T. L. Meyer, 'International Soft Law', *Journal of Legal Analysis* vol. 2 (2010): 171–225 at 188–92.

[42] UN Doc. A/HRC/17/31, para. 13.

[43] For its tasks and working methods see Addo (2014): 136–41.

[44] A recent practical example of its canonizing function can be seen in the development of a model National Action Plan that defines the benchmark for the member states; see <http://www.ohchr.org/EN/Issues/Business/Pages/NationalActionPlans.aspx>.

[45] HRC, 'Business and Human Rights: Mapping International Standards of Responsibility and Accountability for Corporate Acts: Report of the Special Representative of the Secretary-General on

corresponding 'hard' law regulation is an option, but not the ultimate or exclusive goal. The scope is wider and gives credit to all possible types of regulation and compliance mechanisms far beyond the scope of national and international law.[46] It includes other regulative systems, especially 'a civil governance system involving stakeholders affected by business enterprises ... [and] corporate governance'.[47] This broadening of the regulative means, demonstrated by the hybridity of the respective governance mechanisms, challenges existing legal techniques to describe its function. The most promising approaches for tackling these new legal and paralegal regulations from a theoretical perspective seem to be the emerging legal pluralism and transnational law discourses.[48]

Meanwhile, the flurry of uptakes at the international and national level perpetuates not only the canonized content of the UNGPs but also their procedural nature. A cursory glance at the published national action plans on the issue of business and human rights[49] reveals that 'hard law' regulations are the exception rather than the rule. The only exception is the evolving emergence of reporting obligations on non-financial matters.[50] At the same time, this tendency towards more transparency can be interpreted as a push for the emergence of extra-legal accountability mechanisms in the area of civil governance, such as consumer pressure, boycotts, or the freezing of investments.[51] Consequently, the monopolizing tendency of the UNGPs on the entire regulative area of the business and human rights nexus blurs the pre-existing fixed functions of soft law mechanisms and challenges the classical international law notion of soft law as a regulative auxiliary.

2.3.2 *A uniting element: the challenge of integrating corporations and other stakeholders in the realm of human rights*

This brief analysis of the soft law dimensions of the UNGPs supports the assumption that the new regulative approach they comprise challenges the classic notion of the dominant international law framework in general and its soft law understanding in particular.[52] Even though both interpretations of the function of soft law

the Issue of Human Rights and Transnational Corporations and Other Business Enterprises' (UN Doc. A/HRC/4/035), 9 Feb. 2007, para. 88.

[46] Jägers in Deva and Bilchitz (2013): 301. [47] Ruggie (2014): 9.

[48] For an instructive overview of the ongoing discussion see e.g.: P. Zumbansen, 'Law and Legal Pluralism: Hybridity in Transnational Governance', in *Regulatory Hybridization in the Transnational Sphere*, ed. P. Jurčys, P. F. Kjaer, and R. Yatsunami (Leiden/Boston: Martinus Nijhoff Publishers, 2013): 49–70 at 60–2 and J. Klabbers, 'Of Round Pegs and Square Holes: International Law and the Private Sector', in *Regulatory Hybridization in the Transnational Sphere*, ed. P. Jurčys, P. F. Kjaer, and R. Yatsunami (Leiden/Boston: Martinus Nijhoff Publishers, 2013): 29–48 at 45–7.

[49] So far—by Oct. 2014—the UK, the Netherlands, Italy, Denmark, and Spain have launched their national action plans. See: <http://www.ohchr.org/EN/Issues/Business/Pages/NationalActionPlans.aspx>.

[50] A current example can be seen in the directive on disclosure on non-financial and diversity information by certain large companies and groups, adopted on 15 Apr. 2014 by the plenary of the European Parliament.

[51] Jägers in Deva and Bilchitz (2013): 299f.

[52] For further details see also the chapter by Stéphanie Lagoutte in this volume.

instruments within the UNGPs lead in partly different—possibly even conflicting—directions, one important common challenge has ultimately emerged: the need to address non-state actor responsibilities in the arena of international human rights law.[53] Faced with this problem, the UNGPs necessarily enter the dogmatic minefield of the actor/subject debate in general international law. Section 3 will demonstrate that, as with the variety of functional approaches to soft law in the UNGPs, there is no single strategy within the framework for the integration of corporations and other non-state actors in the international human rights arena, but rather a pot-pourri of divergent actions.

3. Consequences of the UNGPs: New Actors and Changing Law-Making Procedures?

If the pragmatic integration of corporations and other stakeholders in the business and human rights nexus into the wider human rights realm is to be fostered via soft law instruments, essential questions must be answered regarding the dogmatic foundations of such an undertaking. A crucial requirement is the clarification of the 'actors' theory of international law and its relation to the fundamental normative question of subjectivity in international law. Initially, it may seem purely academic to impose this discussion in relation to the pragmatic regulative approach of the business and human rights nexus. However, there are good reasons for opening this theoretical Pandora's box: the new soft law developments and their pragmatic broadening of the regulative means touch upon key foundations of international law as a discipline, asking questions such as 'Who is entitled to make law, and who are the legitimate participants in the game?'.[54] Furthermore, this development indicates a critical evaluation of acceptance of the international law system and may be considered a litmus test for the adaptability of new phenomena to the existing international legal system.

In general, the traditional canon of subjects in international law is well known and fairly short: the primary recognized subjects of international law are the states and—to a limited extent—international organizations. Subjectivity overall is thereby defined as the capability of an entity to possess international rights, duties, and the capacity to maintain its rights by bringing international claims. Furthermore, the list of criteria for subjectivity is closely linked to the notion of international legal personality, meaning the inherent capacity to enter into treaties and agreements in the international arena as well as the question of responsibility.[55]

[53] C. M. Bailliet, 'What is to Become of the Human Rights International Order in an Age of Neomedievalism?', in *Non-state Actors, Soft Law and Protective Regimes: From the Margins*, ed. C. M Bailliet (Cambridge: Cambridge University Press, 2014): 95–124 at 120.

[54] A. Bianchi, 'The Fight for Inclusion: Non-state Actors and International Law', in *From Bilateralism to Community Interest: Essays in Honour of Bruno Simma*, ed. Ulrich Fastenrath et al. (Oxford: Oxford University Press, 2011): 39–57 at 40.

[55] See e.g.: J. E. Alvarez, 'Are Corporations "Subjects" of International Law?', *Santa Clara Journal of International Law* vol. 9 (2011): 1–35 at 3; M. Pentikäinen, 'Changing International "Subjectivity"

In the field of international human rights law in particular, this classical notion was fundamentally challenged by the emergence of the individual as an explicit rights holder in international law. Supplemented by the materialization of a limited set of individual obligations in international criminal law, individuals are understood as '"subjects" in some sense', at least 'to the extent that individuals have rights, duties and capacities under international law'.[56] In recent years, the discussion regarding other non-state actors such as corporations or civil society organizations has taken a rather similar direction. The key point from a sociological perspective is the increasingly prominent role adopted by these entities in the process of developing and evolving the international legal system.[57] But one may ask: what does the actor/subject debate have to do with the topic of this volume: the emergence of soft law in general in the human rights field? The issue is an instrumental one: compared to the exclusively state-focused intergovernmental process of drafting 'hard' international law, regulative instruments with soft law content often show a greater ability to translate social realities into normative forms.[58] This is mainly due to the fact that soft law projects profit from the fact that a wider variety of actors participate in the drafting process itself. Coming back to the specific case of the actors/subjects debate, soft law mechanisms have the capacity to translate the factual power of certain actors on the international level into normative terms. Although soft law instruments may only have a relative normative effect,[59] they may provide an opportunity to reduce the dogmatic gap between the normative concept of subjectivity in international law and the reality of international law. This leads us to our next question, namely: how do the UNGPs influence or contribute to this essential and paradigmatic discussion?

Neither the 'Protect, Respect, and Remedy' Framework nor the UNGPs provide an explicit answer to the questions of whether or how non-state-actors could or should be integrated into international law in the specific realm of the business and human rights nexus. The continuous reference to the fact that the UNGPs

and Rights and Obligation under International Law: Status of Corporations', *Utrecht Law Review* vol. 8 (2012): 145–54 at 145; Klabbers in Jurčys et al. (2013): 33; Vincent Chetail, 'The Legal Personality of Multinational Corporations, State Responsibility and Due Diligence: The Way Forward', in *Unité et diversité du droit international—Unity and Diversity of International Law/Écrits en l'honneur du professeur Pierre-Marie Dupuy—Essays in Honour of Professor Pierre-Marie Dupuy*, ed. D. Alland et al. (Leiden/Boston: Martinus Nijhoff Publishers, 2014): 105–30 at 107–10.

[56] K. Parlett, *The Individual in the International Legal System* (Cambridge: Cambridge University Press, 2011): 3 and 359. Regarding the specific role of the individual in International Human Rights Law see also the chapter by Stéphanie Lagoutte in this volume.

[57] From a normative perspective, see e.g.: Chetail in Alland et al. (2014): 110–19 and P. Dumberry, 'L'Entreprise, sujet de droit international? Retour sur la question à la lumière des développements récents du droit international des investissements', *Revue générale de droit international public* vol. 8 (2004): 103–22; from a 'realistic' perspective, J. P. Paust, 'Nonstate Actors Participation in International Law and Pretense of Exclusion', *Virginia Journal of International Law* vol. 51 (2011): 977–1004.

[58] See e.g.: W. Benedek, 'Multi-Stakeholderism in the Development of International Law', in *From Bilateralism to Community Interest: Essays in Honour of Bruno Simma*, ed. U. Fastenrath et al. (Oxford: Oxford University Press, 2011): 201–10 at 210.

[59] D. Shelton, 'Normative Hierarchy in International Law', *AJIL* vol. 100 (2006): 291–323 at 319.

are not to be interpreted as creating new international law obligations creates the impression that the principles have no influence on the actor/subject debate at all. However, a closer look on the concrete second-order effects of the UNGPs calls this general assumption into question. To systematically illustrate the various implications of the UNGPs' soft law norms for the actor/subject discussion, we shall apply the same subdivision according to functional interpretation as in section 2, as different understandings of the soft law function of the UNGPs will lead to different consequences.

3.1 Consequences of the 'hardening' approach

As discussed in section 2, the paramount objective of the hardening approach is the creation of direct international law obligations for corporations regarding their human rights accountability. Such a strategy has various effects on the actor/subject discussion, which can be visualized along the approach's process/consequences line.

Regarding the process, the business and human rights project—as the example of the Ecuador resolution in the HRC clearly shows—evolves entirely in line with the classic notion of the international law system. The HRC decided to establish an open-ended intergovernmental working group to develop a legally binding instrument for transnational corporations and other business enterprises with respect to human rights.[60] Hence, the community of states is the exclusive owner of the process, whereas corporations are subordinated objects of regulation. The endorsed resolution at least provides the option of a degree of secondary stakeholder involvement,[61] but limits its effect to a purely consultative status. Therefore, the top-down process of this approach does not seem to have any effect at all on the evaluation of corporations with regard to the actor/subject question. If anything, one might interpret it as an attempt to strengthen the current system of non-recognition of corporations as subjects of international law.

At present, trying to determine the consequences of such a regulative undertaking is akin to gazing into a crystal ball. Taking the wording of the somewhat rudimentary Ecuador resolution as point of departure, the aim is to 'elaborate an international legally binding instrument to regulate, in international human rights law, the activities of Transnational Corporations and Other Business Enterprises'.[62] Assuming it is actually possible to realize such an instrument in future, this might result in the creation of direct international law obligations for corporations in the international human rights arena. As can be seen from the related discussions on the status of individuals in international law, this could equally be used as an argument in favour of an at least partial or limited subjectivity of corporations in international law. Given the fact that in other fields of international law direct obligations of this

[60] HRC, Elaboration of an International Legally Binding Instrument on Transnational Corporations and Other Business Enterprises with Respect to Human Rights (UN Doc. A/HRC/26/L.22/Rev.1), 24 June 2014, para. 1.

[61] UN Doc. A/HRC/26/L.22/Rev.1, paras 3 and 4.

[62] UN Doc. A/HRC/26/L.22/Rev.1, para. 1.

type already exist for corporations,[63] this new development alone, as a consequence of the UNGPs, is not necessarily a fundamental game-changer in the debate.

3.2 Consequences of the 'governance' approach

Mainly due to their polycentric and multilayered structure, evaluation of the consequences of a governance approach to the UNGPs for the actor/subject discussion is complex, and different aspects must be taken into consideration. In the context of our subject in this chapter, the issue of the role of corporations in the development of new international law norms is of particular interest.

3.2.1 The indirect norm-shaping involvement of corporations and institutionalization of multi-stakeholder dialogues

One of the most frequently given reasons why the 'Protect, Respect, and Remedy' Framework and the UNGPs did not share the fate of their unsuccessful regulative predecessors is the early involvement of corporations and civil society representatives as stakeholders in the drafting process.[64] This multi-stakeholder approach enabled the formal integration of the formerly independent but influential lobbying discourse into the drafting process. To continue using the language of governance, from which this approach is borrowed, the multi-stakeholder approach practised in the drafting process increases the chances of the specific regulations being accepted due to the involvement of different actors as process owners.[65] The emergence of multi-stakeholder dialogues is not a completely new phenomenon in the realm of international law—an early example is the Johannesburg World Summit on Sustainability in 2002—and the incorporation of such forms of participation can mainly be seen in the arena of instruments with soft law content.[66] Yet, in this context the unique aspect of the UNGPs is that the multi-stakeholder approach is not limited to its own drafting process, but at the same time takes root in most of the national and international uptake and concretization processes in the business and human rights nexus. Thus, the UNGPs establish a sectorial procedural benchmark, and due to their element of 'inclusive discourse' are also often glorified as a desirable development towards a democratization of international law. Regarding the actor/subject question, this tendency at least contributes to a formalization and consolidation of the role of corporations in the preparatory stages of new projects for the creation of norms relating to business and human rights.

[63] See e.g.: S. R. Ratner, 'Corporations and Human Rights: A Theory of Legal Responsibility', *The Yale Law Journal* vol. 111 (2001): 443–545 at 475–88.

[64] See e.g.: K. Buhmann, 'The Development of the "UN Framework": A Pragmatic Process towards a Pragmatic Output', in *The UN Guiding Principles on Business and Human Rights: Foundations and Implementation*, ed. R. Mares (Leiden/Boston: Martinus Nijhoff Publishers, 2012): 85–105 at 101–4.

[65] See e.g.: Addo (2014): 145f.

[66] See e.g.: Benedek in Fastenrath et al. (2011): 210.

3.2.2 The direct involvement of corporations in shaping norms and the role of multi-stakeholder initiatives

However, this formalization of the status of the preparatory process represents just one dimension of the changing role of corporations within the international law framework. More important than their involvement in preparing regulative drafts is the establishment of corporations as constituent partners within the direct norm-shaping process itself. This development is linked to the emergence of so-called cross-border multi-stakeholder initiatives in the norm-shaping process. Translated into legal terms, such regulative governance initiatives might best be characterized as public–private partnerships with regulative means. In the area of business and human rights, the actors typically involved in such initiatives are representatives of states, civil society organizations, and corporations. The UNGPs have repeatedly promoted the emergence of such initiatives in the field of business and human rights while at the same time laying claim to a particular role in orchestrating content.[67]

In terms of how the actors/subject question relates to corporations, these initiatives may at first seem of little significance, since they are mainly regarded as operating governance systems beyond the limits of the international law framework.[68] The question is whether this assumption is true for all types of initiatives. Recent research has sought to shed some light on the connections between such initiatives and international law and established the term 'informal international law-making'.[69] From an output-oriented perspective, at least, it seems possible to locate some of these instruments within the realm of international law.[70] The reflexive consequences of these mechanisms on the national and international legal framework are crucial. At the same time, such a categorization has direct consequences on assessment of the actors involved in the norm-shaping process. These consequences will now be illustrated by a brief examination of two cross-border multi-stakeholder initiatives in the business and human rights arena where corporations take a leading role in the norm-shaping process.

3.2.2.1 Practical example I: The Extractive Industries Transparency Initiative (EITI)

According to its own description, the Extractive Industries Transparency Initiative is 'a global coalition of governments, companies and civil society working together to improve openness and accountable management of revenues from natural

[67] Ruggie (2014): 10–12.

[68] J. Pauwelyn, R. Wessel, and J. Wouters, 'An Introduction to Informal International Lawmaking', in *Informal International Law Making*, ed. J. Pauwelyn, R. Wessel, and J. Wouters (Oxford: Oxford University Press, 2012): 1–10 at 1.

[69] J. Pauwelyn, 'Informal International Lawmaking: Framing the Concept and Research Questions', in *Informal International Law Making*, ed. J. Pauwelyn, R. Wessel, and J. Wouters (Oxford: Oxford University Press, 2012): 13–34 at 15–22.

[70] J. Pauwelyn, 'Is it International Law or not, and does it even Matter?', in *Informal International Law Making*, ed. J. Pauwelyn, R. Wessel, and J. Wouters (Oxford: Oxford University Press, 2012): 125–61 at 139–41; similarly G. de Búrca, R. O. Keohane, and C. Sabel, 'Global Experimentalist Governance', *British Journal of Political Science* vol. 44 (2014): 477–86 at 477.

resources'.[71] In short, the basic idea of EITI is to help resource-rich developing countries to avoid the risk of the resource curse and at the same time create a level playing field for any corporations involved.[72] The executive organ of the initiative is the EITI Board, where the implementing states, supporting states, civil society organizations, corporations, and investors are all equally represented. The initiative, launched by the UK government, began with the definition of a set of core 'principles' in 2003 which became 'rules' in 2009. At the EITI Global Conference in Sydney in 2013, the EITI Board adopted the new 'EITI Standard', containing a set of minimal requirements that implementing states must fulfil.[73] Central features are inter alia the creation of an effective oversight mechanism via the establishment of a correlated multi-stakeholder dialogue[74] and clearly defined reporting requirements 'that include full government disclosure of extractive industry revenues, and disclosure of all material payments to government by oil, gas and mining companies'.[75] Furthermore, the reports are subject to an external validation process.[76]

Becoming a member state of the EITI initiative is voluntary, but once a state applies for membership—which requires the head of state or government to issue an unequivocal public statement of its intention to implement the EITI[77]—non-compliance with the EITI Standard and especially with the reporting obligations can lead to suspension or delisting from the initiative.[78] Therefore, from the applying state's perspective the standard, developed exclusively by a multi-stakeholder initiative, works purely on a 'take it or leave it' basis. The procedural parallels with the ratification of an international law treaty or covenant are obvious. Yet, in contrast to classical ratification procedures, no reservations are possible. Currently twenty-nine compliant countries are members of the initiative and seventeen candidate countries are in the process of becoming members.[79]

3.2.2.2 Practical example II: The International Code of Conduct for Private Security Service Providers (ICoC)

A further example, taken from a different field but with similar features in terms of the role of corporations within the international norm-shaping process via multi-stakeholder initiatives, is the International Code of Conduct for Private Security Service Providers (ICoC) established in 2010. The ICoC is a highly illustrative example, since it also demonstrates the partly concurring approaches of governance-driven multi-stakeholder initiatives and state-based legislative procedures in international law. Since the late 1980s the issue of private security provider regulation

[71] Extractive Industries Transparency Initiative, 'What is the EITI?', <http://eiti.org/eiti>.

[72] S. A. Aaronson, 'Limited Partnership: Business, Government, Civil Society, and the Public in the Extractive Industries Transparency Initiative (EITI)', *Public Administration and Development* vol. 31 (2011): 50–63 at 50.

[73] 'The Extractive Industries Transparency Standard', EITI, 11 July 2013, <http://eiti.org/files/English_EITI%20STANDARD_11July_0.pdf>.

[74] EITI (2013), Requirement 1.

[75] EITI (2013), Requirement 4.

[76] EITI (2013), Validation Guide.

[77] EITI (2013), Requirement 1.1.

[78] EITI (2013), Requirement 1.6.

[79] EITI, 'EITI Countries', <http://eiti.org/countries>.

has been discussed extensively within the UN. The establishment in 2005 of the UN Working Group on the Use of Mercenaries as a Means of Violating Human Rights and Impeding the Exercise of the Right of Peoples to Self-Determination was a clear signal of UN regulative ownership, especially regarding the human rights compliance of these corporations. In addition to its monitoring role, the working group's mandate includes a duty 'to elaborate and present concrete proposals on possible complementary and new standards aimed at filling existing gaps, as well as general guidelines or basic principles encouraging the further protection of human rights' as well as 'to seek opinions and contributions from Governments and intergovernmental and non-governmental organizations on questions relating to its mandate'.[80] Surprisingly, corporations are not mentioned as stakeholders of the process at all. To date, the Working Group has not produced any regulative output with regard to its human rights-related task.

The governance-driven approach worked rather differently. The ICoC initiative goes back to a campaign by the Swiss government and the ICRC to clarify the role and obligations of state-related operations by private military and security companies during armed conflict (the so-called Montreux Document)[81] and is strongly influenced by the 'Protect, Respect, and Remedy' Framework discussed in this chapter. Signatory companies commit to the responsible provision of security services so as to support the rule of law, respect the human rights of all persons, and protect the interests of their clients.[82] The central aim of the ICoC is the creation of better governance, compliance, and accountability mechanisms for private security companies. The ICoC was drafted over several rounds of stakeholder workshops involving states, civil society, and business representatives.[83] This approach was also applied to the post-drafting structure of the ICoC Association via the appointment of an equal number of states, civil society, and business representatives to the ICoC Steering Committee and within all working groups.[84] Currently, more than 700 private security companies have signed the IcoC,[85] while the ICoC Association established in 2013 is committed to the creation of an independent governance and oversight mechanism as well as a complementary complaint mechanism.

In contrast to the EITI initiative, the primary addressees of the ICoC are not states but corporations. Nevertheless, the stakeholder-driven code of conduct has

80 E/CN.4/RES/2005/2, para. 12.

81 International Committee of the Red Cross and the Directorate of International Law DIL, 'Montreux Document', <https://www.icrc.org/eng/assets/files/other/icrc_002_0996.pdf>. In Dec. 2014, the participants of the Montreux Document established the so called 'Montreux Document Forum', co-chaired by Switzerland and the ICRC with the aim to 'support national implementation of the Montreux Document and the development of implementation tools, as well as to encourage more states to actively support it. The Forum further aims to strengthen dialogue on lessons-learned, good practices and challenges related to the regulation of PMSCs.' See: <https://www.icrc.org/en/document/private-military-and-security-companies-implementation-montreux-document#.VJRHuUAOBtw>.

82 ICoC, International Code of Conduct for Private Security Service Providers, 9 Nov. 2010, para. 3, <http://icoca.ch/en/the_icoc>.

83 <http://www.icoca.ch/en/history>.

84 ICoC (2010), para. 11.

85 <http://business-humanrights.org/en/intl-code-of-conduct-for-private-security-service-providers-icoc-signatory-companies>.

direct implications for national legislations. A recent example is the Swiss Federal Law on Private Security Services Provided Abroad[86] adopted in 2014: its Article 31 paragraph 1 lit. b makes membership of and compliance with the ICoC a mandatory precondition for private security companies to receive a public contract. This development demonstrates the possible fruitful interrelations between originally governance-driven multi-stakeholder norm-shaping initiatives and their uptake in government driven norm-shaping processes.

The reason for the brief introduction of these two multi-stakeholder initiatives is not to suggest them as paradigms to follow in optimizing the international human rights protection framework. Both initiatives are not without their shortcomings,[87] and it is questionable in general whether this turn to multilayer-governance processes in international human rights law is expedient, particularly in the economic context.[88] Rather, these two examples serve merely to demonstrate how corporations are already strongly involved in the informal international norm-shaping process and that the lines between informal and formal international law-making processes are fluid. This is demonstrated by the reflexive impact of these standards on other 'classic' international and national law domains. Furthermore, both examples clearly show that the involvement of corporations within these initiatives is not limited to the level of preparatory works, but may also cover the standard-setting itself. Returning to the initial question that led us to this short excursion into practice, that is, whether or not the governance dimension of the UNGPs and their uptakes have an influence on the status of corporations within the actor/subject discourse, these fundamental changes in regulative norm-making patterns strongly suggest that a re-evaluation of the theoretical paradigms for the role of corporations in international law is necessary.

4. Conclusion

This short analysis has demonstrated the possibility of varying interpretations of the consequences of the UNGPs on the functional use of soft law instruments within the international human rights framework. In addition to the classical preparatory function of soft law (that is expressed concretely in the expectation to harden the corporate obligation to respect human rights), the UNGPs use and foster soft law instruments to perform a pragmatic shift towards an output-oriented multilayer governance approach. This shift is characterized by institutionalized stakeholder involvement and an openness towards alternative regulative approaches;

[86] Bundesgesetz über die im Ausland erbrachten privaten Sicherheitsdienstleistungen (BPS), Sept. 2013, <http://www.admin.ch/opc/de/federal-gazette/2013/7353.pdf>.

[87] See e.g.: Aaronson (2011): 51; C. Seibert, *Private Military and Security Companies in International Law—A Challenge for Non-binding Norms: The Montreux Document and the International Code of Conduct for Private Security Service Providers* (Cambridge/Antwerp/Portland: Intersentia, 2014): 266.

[88] See e.g.: D. Augenstein, 'The Crisis of International Human Rights Law in the Global Market Economy', *Netherland Yearbook of International Law* vol. 44 (2013): 41–64 at 55–9.

furthermore, it is not limited to the UNGPs, but disseminated across the sector as an underlying benchmark for follow-up projects at the international, regional, and national level.

This pragmatic shift towards new governance approaches challenges the fundamental principles of international law-making. In particular, the active role that corporations play in this regulative process clashes with the dogmatic notion of a limited catalogue of recognized subjects in international law-making processes. One response to this conflict from an international law perspective is simply to ignore it. The inherent risk of this strategy seems to be that the gap between dogmatic and regulative reality in international law would further widen. A more promising response would be to reassess the status of corporations in international law. To a certain extent, the use of soft law by the UNGPs itself offers a possible foundation for reassessment. This is possible not only by fostering the involvement of corporations in the preparation of regulations (participation in multi-stakeholder dialogues), but also by formally granting them an active role in the norm-shaping process (multi-stakeholder initiatives).

13

Soft Law within Participation Rights

Tools in Development

Anette Faye Jacobsen

1. Introduction

Human rights soft law has been expanding immensely over the last decades, not least in the field of development. In this area, many actors have envisaged soft law as a means of clarifying vague hard law, in particular economic, social, and cultural rights. A common strategy has been to expand participation rights, often expressed as a duty for governments to involve or consult with stakeholders in relation to policy or decision-making on water, housing, health, education, and so on.

Participation as a tool for improving economic, social, and cultural rights is one of the cornerstones of the 'Human Rights Based Approach' (HRBA), which has been adopted by all UN agencies, and widely applied among NGOs. HRBA-related soft law has revitalized hopes that human rights in general, and economic, social, and cultural rights in particular, have a pivotal role to play in improving the situation of the world's poor and underprivileged. These increased expectations, however, put treaty bodies and special procedures under pressure to expand and elaborate on hard law instruments via their opinions and recommendations, while at the same time maintaining the credibility of the human rights machinery as a legally based system by ensuring quality and coherence across the different documents that they produce.

The purpose of this chapter is to analyse the development of soft law instruments in the context of the contradictory demands from, on the one hand, development actors outside the human rights community, and on the other hand those evolving from inside the human rights system. The overall question is whether the soft law corpus emanating from the multiple human rights bodies within the UN is in fact providing useful tools for rights holders to claim their rights, or whether these soft law instruments are weakening their claims due to inconsistencies and lack of justification.

The case chosen to illustrate and answer this question relates to soft law contributions, which link participation rights to the implementation of other rights, in particular economic, social, and cultural rights. The chapter will consider whether soft law from the UN human rights machinery, in particular the treaty bodies,[1] has successfully outlined more detailed and improved entitlements to participate in the realization of economic, social, and cultural rights. This enquiry aims to assess treaty body soft law from two potentially contradictory angles: on the one hand, as a tool for monitoring and advocacy by outside stakeholders, including NGOs, activists, and others, and, on the other hand, by testing the sophistication and consistency of this body of law as seen from an international human rights law perspective.

The chapter will address this issue in five sections. Section 2 will outline the wider context, including rationales and concerns, both theoretical and empirical, regarding the expansion of human rights soft law in relation to development. Section 3 will introduce the case study, which is initially examined from a 'vertical' perspective, by comparing different types of soft law developed by one particular treaty body. Section 4 will then supplement this with a 'horizontal' analysis, by comparing soft law *across treaty bodies*. The examples chosen for this purpose will focus on the protection of indigenous peoples' rights through both individual cases and General Comments. A subsection of section 4 will assess the concept of Free, Prior, Informed Consent from the horizontal perspective.

Section 5 will suggest a model, or a taxonomy, to remedy at least partially the confusion and ambiguity arising from the large amount of soft law, by systematizing the terminology for one particular field of rights. Again, the example used is that of participation rights in relation to economic, social, and cultural rights. With a close reading of General Comments from the Committee monitoring the International Covenant of Economic, Social and Cultural Rights (ICESCR), it is possible to determine a detailed and sophisticated terminology in relation to soft law within this particular field.

Finally, section 6 will build on the foregoing theoretical and empirical analyses in order to conclude on the research questions regarding the actual expansion of rights, the receptiveness of the human rights machinery to outside expectations, and the potentially conflicting efforts to secure high-quality soft law sources.

2. The Context: The Expansion of Rights and Conflicting Expectations

For a number of years now the general trend of proliferation of international law has been described and debated among scholars and practitioners.[2] Within

[1] Although a limited selection from the 'soft law market', these are high-status sources. Cf. *International Law and Domestic Legal Systems: Incorporation, Transformation, and Persuasion*, ed. D. Shelton (Oxford: Oxford University Press, 2011): 15.

[2] The proliferation of norms and standards is often discussed together with the issue of 'fragmentation' of international law, see: International Law Commission, 'Fragmentation of International Law: Difficulties Arising from the Diversification and Expansion of International Law' (Report of the Study Group of the International Law Commission) Finalized by Martii Koskenniemi (Doc. A/CN.4/L.682 13 Apr. 2006). See also: S. McInerney-Lankford, 'Regime Interaction and the Fragmentation of International Law', *World Bank Legal Review (Innovation and Empowerment for Development)* vol. 4

international human rights law, this proliferation can be seen through a steady increase in General Comments or Recommendations, views, and observations from treaty bodies. Altogether it has provoked ongoing reform efforts in order to enhance coherence and consistency across the UN monitoring machinery.[3] Simultaneously, new individual communication mechanisms are nonetheless established, as well as the Universal Periodic Review, which produces an astronomical amount of recommendations alongside the many existing recommendations and the newly established Special Procedures.

In addition to this quantitative increase in soft law, a qualitative expansion is also taking place through the dynamic interpretation of existing standards. The practice of the Committee overseeing ICESCR is a good example of this development. During the 1980s the Committee abided by state party consensus, that is, keeping its recommendations in line with at least a majority of states. This interpretative principle transformed in the 1990s into a much broader mode of interpretation.[4] This dynamic trend has continued and has led to more comprehensive and detailed versions of General Comments and Concluding Observations.[5]

Another important trait is the growing involvement of actors other than states in the official human rights machinery. Over the past decades, NGOs and National Human Rights Institutions (NHRIs) have increasingly been invited to participate in the drafting process for new soft law[6] as well as binding standards, most recently the Convention on Rights of Persons with Disabilities (CRPD).[7] Treaty bodies systematically invite NGOs and NHRIs to submit supplementary information as part of the reporting procedures.[8] Hence, the 'interpretive community'[9] for international human rights now includes, on the one hand, civil society actors that are

(2013): 123–60; D. Shelton, 'International law and "Relative Normativity"', in *International Law*, ed. M. D. Evans (Oxford: Oxford University Press, 2010): 141.

[3] Office of the United Nations High Commissioner for Human Rights, *Strengthening the United Nations Human Rights Treaty Body System: A Report by the United Nations High Commissioner for Human Rights*, Navanethem Pillay, 26 June 2012, A/66/860: 25; S. Egan, 'Strengthening the United Nations Human Rights Treaty Body System', *Human Rights Law Review* vol. 13 (2013).

[4] K. G. Young, 'The Minimum Core of Economic and Social Rights: A Concept in Search of Content', *The Yale Journal of International Law* vol. 33 (2008): 150.

[5] B. Saul, D. Kinley, and J. Mowbray, *The International Covenant on Economic, Social and Cultural Rights: Commentary, Cases and Materials* (Oxford: Oxford University Press, 2015): 5.

[6] H. Keller and G. Ulfstein, *UN Human Rights Treaty Bodies: Law and Legitimacy* (Cambridge: Cambridge University Press, 2012): 186–92.

[7] Cf. documents from the Working Group set up by the Ad Hoc Committee mandated by General Assembly Res. 66/168 to work towards a convention, available at <http://www.un.org/esa/socdev/enable/rights/ahcwg.htm>.

[8] All UN treaty bodies have procedures inviting non-governmental organizations and NHRIs to submit supplementary information in relation to the reporting and examination processes of states parties. Cf. e.g. CCPR/C/104/3.

[9] This notion does not imply the parties' shared interest in preserving the overall relationship of the community, as Johnstone has defined it. This cannot be taken for granted when it comes to human rights relationships. I. Johnstone, 'Treaty Interpretation: The Authority of Interpretive Communities', *Michigan Journal of International Law* vol. 12 (1991): 407.

not responsible for implementation of the treaty obligations and, on the other, states members that may be critical to the system.

Simultaneously, other trends pull in the exact opposite direction. Most saliently in the European context, the Brighton Declaration, adopted in 2012 by all member states of the Council of Europe, suggests a series of reforms as a response to what is perceived as failure of the European Court of Human Rights to ensure consistency and high-quality rulings.[10] Some authors have considered this a collective effort by the states parties to regain power taken away from them by a supranational body.[11] Other trends testify more generally to the fragile foundation on which human rights legitimacy is built. For instance, while a steady increase in the number of state ratifications of all UN conventions seems to reflect a greater acceptance of human rights, some have discussed the 'false positive' in terms of states parties that claim to acknowledge human rights but in fact show no commitment to their content.[12]

Despite these challenges and instances of resistance within the human rights system, the growing influence of human rights can be observed almost everywhere in international politics.[13] The development sector is a topical example of this. Major players like the World Bank and the OECD have incorporated human rights in their policy documents.[14] Human rights in the development context are very often linked to the notion, or principle, of participation, which in turn has evolved into a key means of ensuring ownership and sustainability of reforms.[15] At the intersection of human rights and development, participation is a term employed increasingly by activists, professionals, and academics alike.[16] The UN has pushed the 'principle of participation' to the forefront of all its programming

[10] Available at <http://hub.coe.int/20120419-brighton-declaration>. See especially paras 11–12, and 23.

[11] *The European Court of Human Rights between Law and Politics*, ed. J. Christoffersen and M. R. Madsen (Oxford: Oxford University Press, 2013): 238–41.

[12] B. A. Simmons, *Mobilizing for Human Rights: International Law in Domestic Politics* (Cambridge: Cambridge University Press, 2009): 77–80. A similar concept denoting 'tactical confessions' by states is suggested in *The Persistent Power of Human Rights: From Commitment to Compliance*, ed. T. Risse, S. C. Ropp, and K. Sikkink (Cambridge: Cambridge University Press, 2013): 5–16.

[13] E. M. Hafner-Burton and J. Ron, 'Seeing Double: Human Rights Impact through Quantitative and Qualitative Eyes', *World Politics* vol. 61 (Apr. 2009): 360–401. The article is critical of this development, warning that human rights may appear to promise more that can be delivered and may crowd out more appropriate local alternatives, at 392–3.

[14] *World Bank Groups Strategy*. Oct. 2013, para. 9 (p. 6) available at <https://openknowledge.worldbank.org/bitstream/handle/10986/16095/32824_ebook.pdf> (18 Dec. 2014), OECD: 'The Accra Agenda for Action', paras 3 and 13(c), 2008.

[15] See: G. Mansuri and V. Rao, 'Localizing Development: Does Participation Work?' (World Bank Policy Research Report, Washington DC, 2013): 30; OECD: Paris Declaration for Aid Effectiveness and the Accra Agenda for Action (2005/2008): 3.

[16] A. Ling, R. McGee, J. Gaventa, and M. Pantazidou, 'Literature Review on Active Participation and Human Rights Research and Advocacy' (Institute for Development Studies, 2010). Available at <http://www.ids.ac.uk/idspublication/literature-review-on-active-participation-and-human-rights-research-and-advocacy>. P. Gready and W. Vandenhole, *Human Rights and Development in the New Millennium: Towards a Theory of Change* (New York: Routledge, 2014).

activities by proclaiming it as one of the cornerstones of the HRBA.[17] The HRBA has subsequently been adopted as an internal policy or working method among a growing number of human rights and development organizations, including outside the UN.[18]

Human rights professionals and activists in the development contexts have turned to participation rights as a way to create new channels of influence for underprivileged groups, with the aim of enhancing economic, social, and cultural rights. This has brought about a vast number of soft law instruments which aim to define and specify participation rights. Concurrently, academics and activists have growing expectations in terms of the potential of human rights to deliver greater justice.

These trends have imposed a difficult task on the treaty bodies and other UN organs. These bodies must balance aspirations for change and justice that can be achieved through human rights tools with the credibility and consistency expected of a system of public international law.[19] As their interpretation of hard law instruments moves away from a consensus-seeking approach, it increasingly requires other persuasive qualities. Matthias Goldmann suggests seeking reliable concepts of legality as opposed to 'imponderable discourses about legitimacy'.[20] However, the question of human rights legality should not and indeed cannot avoid issues of legitimacy.[21] This does not mean that Goldmann's alternative of 'formalistic arguments' can be set aside as 'legalistic' and exchanged for realistic or even critical power analyses, as David Forsythe comes very close to implying.[22] Rather, as Martti Koskienniemi has suggested, the most fruitful approach features the simultaneous involvement of rigorous formalism and substantive or political openness.[23]

[17] A landmark document for the HRBA policy within the UN is the 'Common Understanding on Human Rights Based Approach to Development Cooperation'. This was issued as the result of a workshop held by the UN administration and its agencies in Stamford, Connecticut, in May 2003, and hence is often referred to as the Stamford Agreement, available at <http://www.undg.org/archive_docs/6959-The_Human_Rights_Based_Approach_to_Development_Cooperation_Towards_a_Common_Understanding_among_UN.pdf>. See <http://hrbaportal.org/>.

[18] At the time of writing (Aug. 2015), documents relating to HRBAs were obtained from the websites of the following organizations; The Global Human Rights Education and Training Centre, Scottish Human Rights Commission, Minority Rights Group International, and ESCRA-Asia.

[19] Similarly, consistency and coherence are high-profile development policy goals in OECD and the EU; S. McInerney-Lankford, 'Regime Interaction and the Fragmentation of International Law', *World Bank Legal Review (Innovation and Empowerment for Development)* vol. 4 (2013): 147–9.

[20] M. Goldmann 'Inside Relative Normativity: From Sources to Standard Instruments for the Exercise of International Public Authority', in *The Exercise of Public Authority by International Institutions*, ed. A. von Bogdandy et al. (Berlin: Springer Verlag, 2010): 665.

[21] The concept of legitimacy in human rights law has prompted a wealth of literature. In the present chapter the meaning is primarily 'output legitimacy', i.e. the degree to which human rights is seen to contribute to fairness, justice etc. See: Keller and Ulfstein (2012): 120 and Ling et al. (2010):141.

[22] D. P. Forsythe and P. David, 'Human Rights Studios: On the Dangers of Legalistic Assumptions', in *Methods of Human Rights Research*, ed. F. Coomans, F. Grünfeld, and M. T. Kamminga (Maastrict: Maastrict Centre for Human Rights/Intersentia, 2009): 59–75.

[23] M. Koskenniemi, *From Apology to Utopia: The Structure of International Legal Argument*, reissue with new Epilogue (Cambridge: Cambridge University Press, 2005): 562–3.

3. Soft Law Delimiting Rights

The Human Rights Committee's (HRC) decisions on individual cases offer detailed considerations on treaty interpretation. In contrast to other soft law documents such as General Comments, the discussions undertaken when examining individual communications are very concrete and specify the contents of a given right as well as delimiting its extent. The sharp and precise wording found in decisions on individual cases cannot be compared to the much vaguer language used by the HRC in its General Comments.

In considering participation rights, we are dealing with Article 25 of the International Covenant on Civil and Political Rights (ICCPR). This article states that citizens have the right and opportunity to 'take part in the conduct of public affairs directly or through freely chosen representatives'. The article is seen as the core *political* participation right relating to the exercise of legislative, executive, and administrative powers. In its General Comment No. 25 (GC 25), the HRC expounded its general interpretation of Article 25.

Article 25 distinguishes between taking part in public affairs 'directly' and 'indirectly'. The two forms are defined in GC 25, so that *indirect* participation refers to citizens' free election of representatives. Several meanings are attributed to *direct* participation: one is the right to run for office and participate directly as an elected representative in political fora; another is casting votes in referendums or popular assemblies where decisions are taken on the spot by a ballot; and a third takes place 'in bodies established to represent citizens in consultation with the government'.[24]

The notion of direct participation has given rise to confusion, as evident in decisions of the HRC. In several instances, it has been claimed that direct participation in public affairs under the meaning of Article 25 entails a right for citizens or groups of citizens to be heard or consulted in decision-making processes. This, however, has been rejected by the HRC. In *Marshall v. Canada*, known as the *Mikmak* case, the Committee explained in categorical terms that:

> It must be beyond dispute that the conduct of public affairs in a democratic State is the task of representatives of the people, elected for that purpose, and public officials appointed in accordance with the law.... Although prior consultations, such as public hearings or consultations with the most interested groups may often be envisaged by law or have evolved as public policy in the conduct of public affairs, article 25(a) of the Covenant cannot be understood as meaning that any directly affected group, large or small, has the unconditional right to choose the modalities of participation in the conduct of public affairs. That, in fact, would be an extrapolation of the right to direct participation by the citizens, far beyond the scope of article 25(a).[25]

[24] ICCPR GC No. 25, para. 6.

[25] Comm. No. 205/1986 *Marshall et al. v. Canada*, para. 5.5. This decision was contested by B. Graefrath in 'Mikmaq-Entscheidung des Menchenrechtsausschusses und deutsche Verfassungsdiskussion', *Neue Justitz* vol. 4 (1992). Graefrath concludes that the HRC's position will exclude all forms of democracy other than a narrow representative model. According to my reading, this is not implied in the decision; rather, the HRC understands the modalities of direct participation

It is remarkable that the HRC in its GC 25 refrained from outlining the limits of the right to direct participation, which it had stated so strongly ten years earlier in the *Mikmak* case. It might be assumed this was because the HRC had softened its position on the question over the years, but a more recent decision shows this not to be the case. In 2005, the HRC rejected an argument that under Article 25(a) a state party must provide an opportunity for interest or activist groups to be included in government decision processes. The Committee explained that the appropriate way to exert influence for such purposes is to participate in public debate, engage in dialogue with political representatives, and organize meetings and similar engagements.[26]

These examples relating to ICCPR Article 25 demonstrate that the soft law instruments of the HRC play different roles. As with other General Comments, GC 25 includes positive and broad language, which rarely excludes any specific understanding of the Covenant wording, even when certain interpretations have previously been ruled out through decisions in specific cases, as we saw with the meaning of 'direct participation'.[27] This format developed for the General Comments conforms well with the external demand for a broader approach to participation, while the more limited and analytical approach in the case decisions has a stronger legal quality—and, consequently, cannot necessarily deliver the results expected from an NGO perspective.

4. Soft Law Expanding Rights

While the HRC has confined an expansive interpretation of the right to direct participation by virtue of Article 25, other avenues have been opened for specific vulnerable groups. The Committee has admitted and decided cases regarding collective rights to participation and consultation by referring to Article 27 of the ICCPR. This provision protects the rights of ethnic, religious, and linguistic minorities to enjoy their own culture, profess and practise their religion, and use their own language.

The article wording expresses only a negative obligation imposed on states, stating that the minorities 'shall not be denied' the said rights. However, in General Comment No. 23 (GC 23) on Article 27 the HRC gave this article an interpretation which goes beyond a mere negative obligation. The HRC underlined that, notwithstanding the negative phrasing of the text, 'positive measures of protection',

to be provided within a constitutional framework. The case is also discussed in light of the right to self-determination in R. Hanski and M. Scheinin, 'Leading Cases of the Human Rights Committee' (Institute for Human Rights, Turko/Åbo, 2003): 402.

[26] Comm. No. 1400/2005 *Beydon et al. v. France*, para. 4.5.

[27] The GC format varies over time, and some GCs refer to previous practice of the HRC. However, it has been particularly difficult to reach a common agreement on whether and how to include case decisions, Keller and Ulfstein (2012): 151–4.

such as legislation, administrative, or judicial initiatives, are required not only in relation to the actions of the state party itself but also the actions of other persons within the state. Furthermore, positive measures are needed to protect the identity of a minority and to adjust any conditions preventing its members from enjoying their rights.[28]

GC 23 also broadened the meaning of 'culture' under Article 27 beyond a narrow everyday understanding. The Committee observed that 'culture manifests itself in many forms, including a particular way of life associated with the use of land resources, especially in the case of indigenous peoples. That right may include such traditional activities as fishing or hunting and the right to live in reserves protected by law.' Hence, the concept of culture also contains key social and economic activities attributed to indigenous peoples and other groups with 'traditional' lifestyles. The HRC further concluded that enjoyment of these rights 'may require' measures to ensure the effective participation of members of minority communities in decisions which affect them.[29]

Even if GC 23 follows the tradition of broad and positive rhetoric, the substance appears moderate in scope. GC 23 was issued only a year after the UN General Assembly had adopted the Declaration on the Rights of Persons Belonging to National or Ethnic, Religious, and Linguistic Minorities. Here minorities' rights include 'the right to participate effectively in decisions on the national and, where appropriate, regional level concerning the minority to which they belong or the regions in which they live, in a manner not incompatible with national legislation'.[30] The Declaration is not reflected in GC 23, as the HRC followed the tradition of using its own wording for statements developed within its own monitoring structures.[31]

The HRC's case law relating to Article 27 has specified certain aspects of minorities' rights to enjoy their own culture, profess and practise their religion, and use their language. At the same time, it has to some extent narrowed the interpretation of this right, compared to the open or vague formulation in the General Comment. In the 1996 case *Länsman v. Finland*, the Committee stated that for economic activities to fall within the ambit of Article 27, they must be '*essential* elements of the culture of an ethnic community'.[32] Consequently, it is not a government obligation to ensure effective participation in every issue of interest to a minority group, but rather in more decisive matters relating to the lifestyle of entire communities. However, impacts on the protected culture should be considered holistically, even when individual activities do not constitute a violation of the rights in Article 27.[33]

[28] CCPR General Comment No. 23 (Doc. CCPR/C/21/Rev.1/Add.5), 1994, ss 6.1– 6.2. This model resembles the tripartite obligations framework that was developed during the 1980s in relation to economic, social, and cultural rights, see: O. De Schutter, *Economic, Social and Cultural Rights as Human Rights* (Cheltenham: Edward Elgar Publishing, 2013): XVII–XVIII.

[29] CCPR General Comment No. 23, s. 7.

[30] Declaration on the Rights of Persons Belonging to National or Ethnic, Religious and Linguistic Minorities. A/Res/47/135, 3 Feb. 1993, Art. 2.3.

[31] Keller and Ulfstein (2012): 156.

[32] HRC Comm. No. 671/1995 *Länsman et al. v. Finland*, para. 10.2 (emphasis added).

[33] HRC Comm. No. 671/1995 *Länsman et al. v. Finland*, para. 10.7.

The quality of the consultation process has also been elaborated on by the HRC. In the *Länsman v. Finland* decision, the Committee found that the participation of the concerned minority group had proved effective because the state party had met with representatives of the group, amended its plans, and balanced the complainants' interests against general economic interests.[34] Other cases from the HRC have emphasized that consultation should include a right to have one's interests considered and adverse impacts minimized before a project is launched.[35]

In a more recent case, *Poma v. Peru*, the Committee took a decisive step as regards the quality of the right to participation. In this case, a government project had diverted water from pasture land with destructive consequences for the local people's llama herding. The HRC found a violation of Article 27. It explained that in relation to development plans, which may lead to a denial of a community's right to enjoy its own culture, there is an obligation for the government to provide an opportunity for effective participation in the decision-making process. This 'requires not mere consultation but the free, prior and informed consent of the members of the community'.[36]

The Committee's use of the phrase 'free, prior and informed consent' (FPIC) is remarkable. The concept is increasingly applied, but at the same time has not been fully defined. The most divisive aspect of this concept is the meaning of 'consent'. The conventional meaning would imply a right to veto a given decision. But is this also the understanding and intention of the treaty body? The Committee explained that if planned measures or projects 'substantially compromise or interfere with the culturally significant economic activities of a minority or indigenous community'[37] they are incompatible with Article 27 unless FPIC of the concerned community is obtained. Unfortunately, the Committee's formulation is not clear in terms of the precise target of the consent.[38] Does consent mean approval of the project plans? Or does it indicate an acceptance of the decision-making process?

The first interpretation might amount to a veto right for the indigenous or minority group (possibly further raising the question of who has the right to define a planned project's degree of impact), while the second would ensure that they be consulted, their opinions taken into consideration, and an assessment made of the project's potential impacts, but would not include the right to reject the results of negotiation. It is most likely the latter interpretation that the HRC had in mind.

[34] HRC Comm. No. 671/1995.

[35] HRC Comm. No. 511/1992 *Länsman v. Finland*, paras 9.6–9.7 and No. 1457/2006 *Poma v. Peru*, para. 7.7.

[36] HRC Comm. No. 1457/2006 *Poma v. Peru*, para. 7.6.

[37] HRC Comm. No. 1457/2006 *Poma v. Peru*, para. 7.6.

[38] In assessing the quality of treaty body soft law I have used the four test criteria offered by John Tobin. These specify that the opinion, comment, or decision must be (1) principled in the sense that it is in line with the general objective of the treaty or the right in question. Furthermore, the interpretation should be (2) clear and practical; (3) coherent in its reasoning and consistent with the international law system, and (4) sensitive to the socio-political context within which it must function in individual states and, more broadly, throughout the international order; J. Tobin, 'Seeking to Persuade: A Constructive Approach to Human Rights Treaty Interpretation', *Harvard Human Rights Journal* vol. 23 (2010): 214–48.

An unconditional right for indigenous communities to veto a development project, even if it substantially interferes with their traditional way of life, would bear a striking resemblance to one of the core traits of the right to self-determination described in Article 1(2) of both Covenants. This politically controversial right has so far not been included in the Committee's complaint competence.[39] As this issue touches on a core aspect of state sovereignty, the right to veto decisions has been rejected widely by states.[40] Nevertheless, FPIC has been advanced strongly through other human rights instruments.

5. The Development of New Rights for Vulnerable Groups

Both in and beyond the UN context,[41] the notion of Free, Prior, Informed Consent has been applied increasingly, primarily in relation to the rights of indigenous peoples and other minority groups with similar 'traditional' lifestyles.[42]

The concept was introduced with slightly different wording by the Committee for the Elimination of Racial Discrimination (CERD) in its General Recommendation on Indigenous People in 1997. It called upon states parties to 'ensure that no decisions relating to their [i.e. indigenous peoples'] rights and interests are taken without their informed consent'.[43] Even though the phrase does not include the words 'free' and 'prior', the recommendation is far-reaching. However, it is worded as a call upon governments and not described as an obligation deduced from the text of the Convention.

A decade later FPIC was adopted as a key concept in the UN Declaration on the Rights of Indigenous Peoples (UNDRIP). One of the most important principles of this declaration is that states shall consult and cooperate in good faith with indigenous peoples' representative institutions at the general policy level in order to obtain their free, prior, and informed consent before adopting and implementing legislative or administrative measures that may affect them.[44] A similar

[39] M. Nowak, *UN Covenant on Civil and Political Rights: CCPR Commentary* (Khel: N. P. Engel, 2005): 26, para. 40 (n. 50).

[40] See: M. Torrance, 'Understanding '"Consent"' in *Free Prior and Informed Consent (FPIC) of Indigenous Peoples: Implications for the IFC Performance Standards and Equator Principles*, available at: <http://lexsustineo.blogspot.dk/2013/02/understanding-consent-in-free-prior-and.html>.

[41] The Inter-American Court of Human Rights has invoked the FPIC and specified the application of the notion of consent in the case of *Saramaka People v. Suriname*, see paras 129–30, 133–4, 28 Nov. 2007, Series C no. 172. The Court's interpretation of the notion of 'consent' is linked to Art. 21 of the Inter-American Convention on the right to property, which is understood to include indigenous and tribal groups' special right to communal property.

[42] Recent major initiatives include the UN Development Group's (UNDG) Guidelines on Indigenous Peoples' Issues, 2009. The Guidelines mention FPIC as a right for indigenous peoples that should be applied in decisions that affect them, p. 10. The UNDG covers UN organizations and other entities active in development programmes. UN REDD Programme (a collaboration between FAO, UNDP, and UNEP on reduction of emissions from deforestation in developing countries), 'Guidelines to Free, Prior and Informed Consent' (Jan. 2013), which are intended as a normative framework for the programme's partner countries.

[43] CERD General Recommendation No. 23 on the Rights of Indigenous Peoples (1997), Art. 4(d).

[44] UNDRIP, Art. 19.

obligation is linked to more concrete projects affecting indigenous peoples' land or other resources.[45]

The UNDRIP requires effective participation and consultation with indigenous groups as a cross-cutting right related to a range of other rights. However, the requirement for FPIC is conveyed via the phrase 'in order to obtain', possibly implying that while the state party may have the intention of obtaining FPIC, it is they who will have the final word.

The Committee of Economic, Social and Cultural Rights (CESCR) has invoked FPIC several times with regards to indigenous peoples in a General Comment to Article 15 of the Covenant (GC 21) on the right to enjoy culture. It is asserted that states should respect FPIC as a general principle in all matters covered by the specific rights of indigenous people. This provision also refers to Article 19 of the UNDRIP and, hence, relates to the more general level of policy.[46] Furthermore, the Committee specifies as a core or minimum obligation that states parties should obtain the free and informed prior consent of indigenous peoples when the preservation of their cultural resources, especially those associated with their way of life and cultural expression, is at risk.[47] Whether this obligation relates to the aforementioned policy level or to the more concrete planning of development projects is unclear. However, the applicability of the obligation in situations when cultural rights are under threat is in line with the HRC's decision in the *Peru v. Poma* case, discussed in section 4.

FPIC also appears in the Concluding Observations (COs) of state party examinations by the HRC, the CESCR, and CERD.[48] The issue discussed again is indigenous peoples' rights, in particular to natural resources. The wording, however, is somewhat inconsistent. The HRC, for instance, sometimes recommends that a state party 'seek' FPIC, and in other situations that it 'secure' or 'guarantee' FPIC.[49]

The CESCR is typically softer spoken on this issue, recommending that state parties 'seek' FPIC. However, this committee also sometimes employs more demanding formulations, for instance that state parties should fulfil 'the obligation to obtain the free, prior and informed consent of those who are affected by the aforementioned economic activities'.[50] Here FPIC is invoked as a binding 'obligation' for decision-making on local activities and is thus not merely a requirement at the more general level of policy, as might be the understanding of the phrase in GC 21. Here, the CESCR builds on Article 32(2) of the UNDRIP and applies a more

[45] UNDRIP, Art. 32 (2).

[46] CESCR General Comment No. 21 (2009), para. 37 and n. 37.

[47] CESCR GC No. 21 (2009), para. 55(e).

[48] All examples of FPIC mentioned in COs are taken from: 'Legal Companion to the UN-REDD Programme: Guidelines on Free, Prior and Informed Consent (FPIC). International Law and Jurisprudence Affirming the Requirement of FPIC' (Jan. 2013): 6–34.

[49] Respectively: Panama, CCPR/C/PAN/CO/3, 17 Apr. 2008, para. 21; Nicaragua, CCPR/C/NIC/CO/3, 12 Dec. 2008, para. 21; Colombia, CCPR/C/COL/CO/6, 4 Aug. 2010, para. 25.

[50] Respectively: Ecuador, E/C.12/ECU/CO/3, 30 Nov. 2012, para. 9 (unofficial translation) and Argentina, E/C.12/ARG/CO/3, 14 Dec. 2011, para. 9.

demanding vocabulary, such as 'obligation', where the UNDRIP requires that states parties consult and cooperate in good faith 'in order to obtain' FPIC.

In contrast to the CESCR and the HRC, the CERD has been more consistent and has recommended that governments 'seek' FPIC with indigenous groups. Now, if one measured the shifting terminology applied in regard to FPIC by the two Covenant committees with the quality criteria set up by John Tobin, the result would not be particularly clear or consistent.[51] The key word 'consent', for example, is often used without an indication of which decisions and at what stages of the decision-making processes the term is applicable.

Based on the treaty bodies' general and country-specific recommendations, it is evident that the notion of FPIC is gaining ground as a new right for certain (indigenous) groups across the UN human rights machinery. This is arguably a clear indication of the monitoring bodies' responsiveness to the heightened demands from active interest groups for human rights to provide safeguards against the increasing pressure on the traditional lifestyles of indigenous peoples.

At the same time, however, the human rights bodies have not succeeded in generating terminological consistency. Both from a vertical perspective, that is, within the soft law corpus prepared by the individual treaty body,[52] and from a horizontal perspective, across treaty-based and other UN bodies, a common terminology has not been applied in soft law recommendations, even where the document type and theme has been the same, for instance across Concluding Observations, and with regard to the application of FPIC.

6. An Example of a Soft Law Taxonomy

As consistency in soft law terminology is not optimal throughout treaty body instruments, this section presents a methodology to assist in a clearer understanding of scope and validity of existing soft law in the field of participation rights. The idea is to establish a hierarchy for the key terms used in a given soft law corpus. Thus, as ensuring the strict consistency of wording even among treaty bodies under the common UN umbrella is difficult, as was demonstrated by the soft law developments of FPIC, it seems more helpful to offer a taxonomy based on uniform soft law sources and within a limited group of rights. This taxonomy will give an example of how, within a given area, a soft law vocabulary may be identified and arranged with the aim of furthering a clear and comprehensive understanding of soft law pertaining to a particular set of rights.

The example below deals with one treaty body only, the CESCR, and concentrates on generating a model for linking participation entitlements to ESC rights based on the GCs, as the most general interpretation tools, from that committee.

[51] Tobin (2010): 214–48.

[52] A similar finding is presented in a study of the HRC soft law production, Keller and Ulfstein (2012): 146.

While such a model cannot claim to be universal or exhaustive, it may be useful to actors in the field of human rights and development.

The Committee monitoring the ICESCR has devoted much effort to strengthening the applicability of the Covenant rights.[53] An important method has been the development of General Comments describing 'obligations and violations', analytically derived from the words of the Covenant. With this discursive shift from individuals' rights to states parties' responsibilities to secure adequate measures, policies, and mechanisms, the Committee endeavoured to recast vague rights as enforceable, adjudicative entitlements.[54]

These interpretative efforts of the CESCR have been discussed and contested.[55] There is no doubt, however, that the rather detailed descriptions of government obligations provided by the Committee in its GCs have offered new tools for civil society groups, NHRIs, and the media to push governments towards implementation through political mobilization. One recurring recommendation of the Committee is to emphasize the responsibility of states parties to secure participation or consultation with stakeholders.

In its first GC on reporting obligations, the CESCR was already suggesting that relevant groups be included more directly in human rights policy-making. It was recommended that states parties 'encourage the involvement of the various economic, social and cultural sectors of society in the formulation, implementation and review of the relevant policies'.[56] Since then, the requirement that governments cooperate with relevant stakeholders has been expanded in a range of ICESCR General Comments, including, in chronological order, GCs on rights to adequate housing, forced evictions, plans of action for primary education, adequate food, health, water, protection of intellectual interests, the right to work, the right to social security, and most recently the right to take part in cultural life.[57]

[53] Saul et al. (2015): 133–73.

[54] See the chapter by Mátyás Bódig in this volume.

[55] See e.g.: Young (2008): 113–75. A critical approach to legal means and remedy as tools to alleviate poverty can be seen in: M. J. Dennis and D. P. Stewart, 'Justiciability of Economic, Social, and Cultural Rights: Should There be an International Complaints Mechanism to Adjudicate the Rights to Food, Water, Housing, and Health?', *American Journal of International Law* vol. 98 (July 2004): 462–515.

[56] CESCR GC No. 1 (1989), para. 5.

[57] CESCR GC No. 4 (1991) on the right to adequate housing, para. 12; GC No. 7 (1997) on the right to adequate housing: forced evictions, Art. 11(1), paras 13, 15; GC No. 11 (1999) on plans of action for primary education, para. 8; GC No. 12 (1999) on the right to adequate food, paras 23 and 29; GC No. 14 (2000) on the right to health, paras 11 and 17; GC No. 15 (2002) on the right to water, paras 16(a), 24, 37(f), and 48; GC No. 17 (2005), on the right of everyone to benefit from the protection of the moral and material interests resulting from any scientific, literary, or artistic production of which he is the author, Art. 15(1) (NB: Here abridged as 'intellectual interests'), paras 32, 34, and 46; GC No. 18 (2005) on the right to work, para. 42; GC No. 19 (2008) on the right to social security, para. 26 (this recommendation differs from the others in that it suggests participation in the *administration* of social security schemes, which is neither policy development nor a decision-making process, as in the other GCs); GC No. 21 (2009) on the right of everyone to take part in cultural life, Art. 15, paras 1(a), 16(c), 29, 33, 36, 37, 55(e).

6.1 The taxonomy's two variables

The CESCR's provisions on participation related to ESC rights show a pattern of interpretation, which distinguishes, identifies, and classifies key notions applied by the treaty body. These notions can be arranged using a taxonomy, or model, featuring two variables:

- The first variable ranks, in hierarchical order, the scope of the obligation put on governments (to secure FPIC, to consult, or to involve).
- The second variable denotes the sphere of influence, either at the more general policy-making level or directly in decision-making processes.

6.1.1 Variable One: type of participation

The left column of Table 13.1 ranks three key notions of participation in relation to ICESCR rights. These have been identified from the CESCR's GCs, and each requires a different amount of effort by the state to meet the requirement. The vaguest words in the Committee's terminology are 'participation'/'involvement'. Hence, they appear in row three of the table's left column. The second row is somewhat more demanding and implies a state party responsibility to secure a dialogue with the target group, and consequently, this group's right to be heard. The strongest participation right, at level one, obliges governments to seek FPIC from a target group.

6.1.2 Variable Two: level of participation

The top row distinguishes two levels of participation, namely the responsibility to invite people/groups to take part in the promotion or protection of a given right at the *policy level*, or to ensure participation at the *decision-making level.*

6.1.2.1 Rights involved

A series of ICESCR rights (right to water, food, etc.) are distributed in relation to the two variables. Thus, one can discover from the table that there is a right to FPIC at policy level as well as at the level of decision-making only in relation to the right to culture (understood as a way of life) and only in relation to indigenous people.

Row one of Table 13.1 indicates that the CESCR follows the general trend of connecting the right to FPIC specifically to the right of indigenous peoples to culture, understood as when 'a way of life' is at stake. The table shows that FPIC also applies to intellectual interests, although again this only concerns 'indigenous authors'.[58] Reserving FPIC for indigenous groups is consistent with the Concluding Observations and the HRC's decisions, described in sections 4 and 5.

[58] GC No. 17 (2005), para. 32. Intellectual interests constitute a special case in many respects. This may explain why this particular field appears so prominently in Table 13.1. It is a property-type right, and as such has a stronger backing in international private as well as public law than most other economic, social, and cultural human rights. Saul et al. (2015): 1225. See also: P. K. Yu, 'Reconceptualizing Intellectual Property Interests in a Human Rights Framework' (Research Paper No. 04-01. Legal Studies Research Paper Series, Michigan State University College of Law, 2007): 1041–9.

Table 13.1 Hierarchy of key terms within participation rights

	Policy Level	Level of Decision-Making
1. FPIC	Right to Culture (= indigenous peoples' way of life)	Right to Intellectual Interests, Culture (= indigenous peoples' way of life)
2. Consultation	Right to Housing	Protection against Eviction; Intellectual Interests
3. Participation/involvement	Right to Plans of Action for Primary Education; Food; Health; Water; Intellectual Interests; Work; Culture	Right to Water; Health; Intellectual Interests; Work

Row two of Table 13.1 shows that 'consultation' is required in relatively few areas.[59] Only the right to housing and protection against forced eviction invoke obligations to consult. The GC on the right to housing asserts that the state party is almost invariably required to adopt a national housing strategy as a means of achieving the full realization of the right to adequate housing and that 'such a strategy should reflect extensive genuine *consultation* with, and *participation* by, all of those affected, including the homeless, the inadequately housed and their representatives'.[60] The Committee has, moreover, issued a GC dealing with forced evictions, in which it prescribes that 'States parties shall ensure, prior to carrying out any evictions, and particularly those involving large groups, that all feasible alternatives are explored in consultation with the affected persons'. Furthermore, the Committee 'considers that the procedural protections which should be applied in relation to forced evictions include: (a) an opportunity for genuine consultation with those affected'.[61] The latter requirement is surprisingly mildly phrased in light of the serious consequences of forced evictions, even if they may in some instances be justified.[62]

At the lowest level of Table 13.1 (row three), the weakest provisions for stakeholder involvement are listed in relation to different rights. The rights to food and water are of greatest interest here because they concern the 'very subsistence of life'.[63] Both rights are derived from Article 11 of the ICESCR (on the right to an adequate standard of living), as is the right to housing, and the Committee has prepared a GC on each of these deduced rights. Similar to the approach suggested for the realization of housing rights, national strategies are suggested in relation to securing the rights to food and water. Regarding the former, the GC states that

[59] One instance has been deemed too narrow to be included in the table at this point: 'consultations should be held with the individuals and communities concerned in order to ensure that the measures to protect cultural diversity are acceptable to them' which appears in GC No. 21 (2009) para. 16(c).

[60] CESCR GC No. 4 (1991) on the right to adequate housing, para. 12 (emphasis added).

[61] CESCR GC No. 7 (1997), paras 13, 15.

[62] CESCR GC No. 7 (1997), para. 11.

[63] Saul et al. (2015): 863.

the 'formulation and implementation of national strategies for the right to food requires full compliance with … people's participation'.[64]

Typical of the more recent GCs, the right to water is described in stronger language and greater detail. The GC on water states that a clear obligation is imposed on states to adopt a national water strategy. It partly reiterates a phrase which also appeared in the GC on food, but adds a new and more demanding specification in relation to decision-making processes:

> The formulation and implementation of national water strategies and plans of action should respect, inter alia, the principles of non-discrimination and people's participation. The right of individuals and groups to participate in decision-making processes that may affect their exercise of the right to water must be an integral part of any policy, programme or strategy concerning water. Individuals and groups should be given full and equal access to information concerning water, water services and the environment, held by public authorities or third parties.[65]

While 'the principle of people's participation' invoked in relation to the national strategies is vague, the obligation to integrate a right to participate in decision-making processes for affected individuals and groups in any policy, programme, or strategy concerning water is considerably stronger. By focusing on the decision-making level, in contrast to the level of policy, and by specifying 'affected' groups and individuals, the GC on the right to water provides a more operational tool for activists than the reference to the broad concept of 'people's participation'. Still, had the GCs on food and water included the same formulation as the GC on housing that all those affected be 'consulted' for the purpose of national strategies, then the approach to the right to participation in relation to Article 11 would have been expanded more consistently.

In other GCs on economic, social, and cultural rights, provisions on participation are established only at policy level, and phrased in vague terms such as for 'people', 'the population', or 'all sections of civil society'.[66] How participation by 'people' or 'the population' (which could include everyone) can be exerted beyond the normal representative channels or via public debate is not evident. Some proactive initiatives on behalf of the government to promote general interest and commitment are, probably, the minimum of what is envisaged. It is therefore more tangible to emphasize the importance of involvement of 'all sections of civil society', even though this phrase too could refer to almost the entire population. However, the term connotes primarily civil society groups, who might find the recommendation useful for their campaigning efforts.

[64] GC No. 12 (1999) on the right to adequate food, para. 23.

[65] GC No. 15 (2002) on the right to water, para. 47. The quotation is from para. 48.

[66] GC No. 12 (1999) on the right to adequate food, para. 23; GC No. 14 (2000) on the right to health, para. 11; GC No. 11 (1999) on plans of action for primary education, para. 8.

6.1.2.2 What the taxonomy tells us about participation rights

The CESCR's interpretation of participation rights in relation to different stakeholder groups thus constitutes a somewhat mixed picture. Clearly, indigenous peoples have gained special status in all matters influencing their culture in decisive ways (i.e. their way of life), and this entitlement includes being consulted and the principle of FPIC, which relates to both the policy and the decision-making level.

The less demanding right to be consulted still entails an obligation for governments to actively consider input from rights holders, but only in relation to housing and eviction. The GC on the right to water comes close to implying a right to be consulted, when it states that a national strategy must allow groups and individuals the right to participate in decision-making processes that may affect their exercise of the right to water. On the other hand, the GC on the right to food contains only a vague reference to 'people's participation' in relation to the national strategy, despite the common origin of these two rights in Article 11 of the ICESCR, with identical recommended measures for implementation. Several other rights are only linked to participation in broad terms, and the scope of stakeholder involvement does not extend further than the aspects of public participation that are already available.

Analysing a specific group of soft law sources, such as the GCs from the CESCR, enables us to generate a detailed and systematic vocabulary in relation to participation and its place among ESC rights. The taxonomy reads that the participation regime is not as consistently and significantly expanded as development NGOs and activists may have expected. However, the pattern and hierarchy of the terminology shows a sophistication of existing soft law which may support and qualify the dialogue between states parties and civil society stakeholders, with the possibility of eventually strengthening participation in development projects and practices.

7. Conclusion

Currently, two opposing demands are imposed on the international human rights machinery: the growing pressure to expand human rights tools for poor and marginalized groups versus a responsibility to sustain the legitimacy of the human rights system through the valid, clear, and consistent interpretation of standards. In the context of such a dilemma, what can be concluded from our examination of the role of soft law?

First of all, this chapter has shown how different types of soft law developed by the UN treaty bodies meet these contrasting demands. The HRC's decisions are cautious and precise in their interpretation of the rights they apply. The General Comments follow a different approach, as they describe the scope of rights in a much broader way. The GCs are generally phrased in a format that meets the demands from NGOs to provide tools for advocacy efforts. These differing soft law approaches bear some risks. One such risk is that of contributing to a superficial understanding of given rights among grassroots activists. The GCs appear to tell only half the story, describing broadly what the maximum realization of rights would look like, while the broader picture, including lawful restrictions and demarcations of the rights, is communicated only in more specialized soft law documents—in particular case decisions, which tend to be buried in databases intended for juridical specialists. In other words, this disparity in soft law interpretations of hard law principles may not contribute to strengthening the many different actors constituting the interpretive community of international human rights, including states parties, NGOs, and others.

An analysis of the application of Free Prior Informed Consent within the UN human rights machinery further demonstrates that FPIC is applied increasingly in treaty body soft law, including a CESCR GC on the right to culture, and in a series of Concluding Observations from the HRC, CESCR, and CERD. Arguably, this reflects the successful advancement of human rights for indigenous peoples expanding throughout the greater human rights community, and thus testifies to the treaty bodies' receptiveness toward current political trends. The types of documents that focus on FPIC include all categories of soft law, that is, case views, GCs, COs, and the Declaration of Indigenous Peoples' Rights. Yet the enhanced attention to protection of indigenous rights in the various categories of treaty body soft law appears uncoordinated and not stringent. This is the case both vertically within the individual organ, as well as horizontally across treaty bodies. FPIC undoubtedly has strong potential to enhance the protection of indigenous peoples' rights, and the DIPR offers a well-considered application of FPIC. In this chapter we recommend that the DIPR should be adhered to by all treaty bodies as a common standard in order to improve clarity and coherence in this field.

This chapter shows that an extended obligation to consult and seek consent of indigenous communities has undoubtedly been imposed on states parties via a process with origins in all categories of soft law across the UN human rights machinery. This development, together with the broad and positive discursive tradition of the more general soft law documents such as GCs, clearly demonstrates the receptiveness of the treaty bodies to demands that human rights be made relevant and useful to grassroots activists and other practitioners. Hence, these developments may be seen as a collective effort by the human rights machinery to ensure that soft law responds to the needs and interests of rights holders and thus sustains the legitimacy of human rights with regard to the outside world.

Finally, a horizontal look at treaty body soft law has enabled us to elaborate a taxonomy of soft law applicable within the field of participation and ESC rights. This provides a clearer overview and deeper understanding of the meaning and scope of state party obligations in this field. It also reveals that there are only a few situations in which state responsibility goes beyond rather vague recommendations for popular involvement.

We may therefore conclude this chapter by stressing the need for a more concerted effort to ensure precise, consistent, and clear soft law terminology within and across treaty body practice. This should be combined with the bold move of incorporating existing limitations of rights, as described in actual treaty body jurisprudence on individual communications, into broader soft law documents such as the GCs. This would ensure a greater clarity of standards in line with what can realistically be expected from international human rights, and simultaneously contribute to the credibility and, thus, the sustainability of the human rights project.

14

The Role of Soft Law in Minority Rights Protection and Diversity Management

Reflections from Practice

Sally Holt, Zdenka Machnyikova, and John Packer

1. Introduction

Minority rights[1] are an important subset of international human rights standards which function to ensure that all human beings, including persons belonging to minorities, are able to enjoy fundamental rights and freedoms on a basis of full and effective equality in law and in fact. Protection and promotion of minority rights serves to redress imbalances arising from the non-dominant position of minorities within states which often leaves them marginalized and disadvantaged in terms of the maintenance and development of their own identities, access to public services and other resources and opportunities, and equal participation in society.

Apart from some key treaty provisions,[2] standards for the protection of minorities include many soft law instruments, including a substantial body of regional commitments adopted by the consensus of participating states of the Organization for Security and Cooperation in Europe (OSCE). In addition, the Council of Europe's Framework Convention for the Protection of National Minorities (FCNM—a 'hard' instrument) has been criticized for the 'soft' nature of its provisions (i.e. their purported vagueness, some of which do not entitle minorities to rights) and for the lack of a supervisory body with significant powers of sanction and remedy.

However, while 'soft law' is generally regarded as inferior to legally binding 'hard law' instruments in its capacity to coerce or sanction states for non-compliance, there is evidence that 'soft' rules can be just as effective in achieving implementation where 'soft' persuasive mechanisms such as dialogue, mediation, and forms of

[1] 'Minority rights' within the context of this chapter mean the rights of national or ethnic, cultural, religious, and linguistic minorities.

[2] Such as within the Convention on the Prevention and Punishment of the Crime of Genocide, the International Convention for the Elimination of All Forms of Racial Discrimination (ICERD), the International Covenant on Civil and Political Rights (ICCPR) (notably Art. 27), and the Convention on the Rights of the Child (notably Art. 30).

effective supervision and assistance are in place. Indeed, lack of 'political will' often translates into non-compliance regardless of the existence of implementation or enforcement mechanisms associated with purportedly 'hard law'.[3] Thus, the actual behaviour of states leads to a focus on the implementation of norms and standards.

This chapter demonstrates that minority rights not only exist in normative terms, but they enjoy an evolving legal character. This is so in terms of the sources of international law expressed in Article 38(1) of the Statute of the International Court of Justice, in subsidiary means of interpretation (with regard to rules), in the evolving standards or as *de lege ferenda*, and in the mechanisms of implementation and their effects. Importantly, this chapter also demonstrates that the interesting and vital aspect of such minority rights is found less in their provenance or source than in their compelling and practical effects which, arguably, is what matters most especially for their intended beneficiaries and for society as a whole.

In this chapter, we argue that while there exists a range of hard and soft law standards on the rights of minorities, the traction—and, thus, significance—of these standards is not determined exclusively or even primarily by their 'hardness' or 'softness'. Indeed, soft law in its capacity to generate detailed rules and more technical standards required for the implementation of treaties may, in the current context of international relations, be better suited than so-called hard law for the *effective* protection of minority rights and complex processes of diversity management. Soft law can provide the necessary flexibility and guidance in the application of relevant standards in different contexts.[4] Voluntary compliance can be effective where viable choices for implementation are made available to responsible authorities and where those authorities genuinely recognize the need for effective frameworks and mechanisms for the peaceful management of diversity and interethnic relations which respect the rights of minorities and majorities alike. Analysis, argument, and suasion through diplomatic, political, and other channels are therefore also required to convince states of this need and support them in negotiating and implementing appropriate arrangements. Arguments of self-interest, notably that respect for minority rights contributes to internal and cross-border security, can hold particular sway in this respect.

In making this argument, we focus on the role of the OSCE High Commissioner on National Minorities (HCNM) as a unique regional mechanism devoted to the prevention of violent conflict at the earliest possible stage through the promotion of international standards of human rights, including minority rights. We demonstrate how the HCNM has encouraged and facilitated states to comply with their international obligations and commitments using a 'quiet diplomatic' facilitative and problem-solving approach which utilizes the full range of available 'hard' and 'soft' norms and standards (including minority rights) to which states have committed. We examine the HCNM's role as a 'normative intermediary' fleshing out the substance of existing norms—regardless of softness or hardness in terms of sources—to facilitate their application in practice. In addition to this 'norm-filling' role, we also examine the HCNM's function as a 'norm-creator' through the

[3] As noted in the Introduction to this volume.

[4] See the Introduction to this volume.

development of soft law that both clarifies and builds on the content of minority rights and other standards (hard and soft) and provides options for effective practice in the form of recommendations and guidelines.[5] We then review the advantages and shortcomings of the HCNM mandate and approach as a whole in supporting states' compliance with their obligations and commitments as we identify enabling and obstructive factors in this regard that might inform the development of mechanisms and processes for conflict prevention through respect for minority rights in other regional or sub-regional contexts.

Lastly, we situate the work of the HCNM in a broader discussion of the substantive nature of diversity management and the relative (dis)advantages of hard and soft law approaches. Focusing as a case study on the 2012 Llubljana Guidelines on Integration of Diverse Societies,[6] we highlight some current issues of contention, including conceptual issues, in the interpretation of existing minority rights and other standards relevant for integration. We also examine whether and to what extent emerging norms from national practice with capacity to restrict rather than protect rights should be reflected in the development of such recommendations and whether and to which extent 'political will' within states should be a factor for consideration. The discussion also provides some insight into the processes whereby HCNM guidelines are debated, elaborated, and agreed.[7] The overall aim of this analysis is not only to highlight the potential of soft law in the realization of minority rights and in building peaceful and cohesive societies, but also to identify relative shortcomings and challenges, as well as areas for potential further development.

2. Background and Framework for the Protection of Minorities

The international protection of minorities dates at least from the 1648 Peace of Westphalia whereby special arrangements were agreed for Catholic, Lutheran, and Calvinist minorities. The contemporary corpus of 'minority rights' is much broader in scope and in detailed content which, importantly, confer *rights* for individuals and groups (as opposed to duties upon states to tolerate some minorities).

Minority rights perhaps more than some other human rights, given their collective nature,[8] lack a clear, agreed definition of the beneficiaries of the rights[9] and

[5] For the set of (so far seven) general recommendations and guidelines elaborated under the auspices of the OSCE HCNM, see: 'Thematic Recommendations and Guidelines', OSCE, <http://www.osce.org/hcnm/66209>.

[6] 'The Ljubljana Guidelines on Integration of Diverse Societies', OSCE, 7 Nov. 2012, <http://www.osce.org/hcnm/96883>.

[7] The authors (under the leadership of John Packer who served as Senior Legal Adviser then the first Director of the Office of the OSCE HCNM from 1995 to 2004) coordinated the process for the initiation and early development of the Guidelines and contributed substantively to their eventual elaboration.

[8] A. Rosas and M. Scheinin, 'Categories and Beneficiaries of Human Rights', in *An Introduction to the International Protection of Human Rights: A Textbook*, ed. R. Hanski and M. Suksi (Åbo: Åbo Akademi): 49–61.

[9] J. Packer, 'Problems in Defining Minorities', in *Minority and Group Rights in the New Millenium*, ed. D. Fottrell and B. Bowring (The Hague: Brill, 1999): 223–73; H. Hannum, 'The Concept and

suffer from a well-known reluctance of states to recognize minority rights for fear that they could threaten the territorial integrity of states. As such, minority rights provide an example of development of an international human rights protection framework that requires enhanced deployment of international cooperation to accomplish the potential of this relatively thin but very important subset. As already noted, the normative framework at the universal level is characterized by a small number of 'hard law' treaty obligations embodied in a few articles of the universal human rights treaties dealing with the protection of the existence of a group, the elimination of discrimination and ensuring equality, and the protection of the cultural, linguistic, and religious distinctiveness of minority groups.[10] At the universal level there are two key instruments that provide specific protection to ethnic, religious, and linguistic minorities, one of them being Article 27 of the International Covenant on Civil and Political Rights (1966) that guarantees the rights to persons belonging to ethnic, religious, and linguistic minorities in community with other members of the group to enjoy their culture, to profess their religion, and to use their language. These rights are essentially guaranteed to an individual, but the article maintains the collective dimension of protection of the identity of a minority group through the collective enjoyment of the minority culture and distinctiveness. The second instrument is a non-treaty-based text: the UN Declaration on the Rights of Persons Belonging to National or Ethnic, Religious, and Linguistic Minorities (the UN Declaration on Minorities), adopted unanimously by the UN General Assembly in 1992. Although the UN Declaration on Minorities (elaborating on Article 27 of the ICCPR, but not necessarily limited to it)[11] offered a more detailed content of the minority protection that states were ready to follow, including the specification of the positive obligation on the part of the state to realize those rights, the provisions remained general, with some important issues concerning minority claims unresolved (such as the right to autonomy). The 1992 Declaration is a reflection of a compromise attempting to strike a balance between the progressive attitude to provide a set of explicit minority rights and the preference of states to define minority rights sufficiently broadly to allow for wide state discretion. These are perhaps the reasons why the UN Declaration has not received wider attention and is much less used and invoked by its beneficiaries than, for instance, the 2007 UN Declaration on the Rights of Indigenous Peoples that provides more detailed guarantees and confirms the right of indigenous peoples to self-determination, recognizing subsistence rights and rights to land, territories, and resources.

A more progressive approach to minority rights has been taken within the regional context of Europe with the adoption of the legally binding Council of

Definition of Minorities', in *Universal Minority Rights: A Commentary on the Jurisprudence of the International Courts and Treaty Bodies*, ed. M. Weller (Oxford: Oxford University Press, 2007): 49–71.

[10] As noted in the Introduction to this volume.

[11] M. Nowak, *U.N. Covenant on Civil and Political Rights, CCPR Commentary* (Kehl: N. P. Engel, 1993): 480–505; A. Eide, 'The Commentary to the UN Declaration on Minorities', E/CN.4/Sub.2/AC.5/2005/2, 4 Apr. 2005.

Europe's Framework Convention for the Protection of National Minorities (1995) inspired by the OSCE political commitments that were formulated in reaction to the rise of nationalism in Europe in the post-Cold War environment. In this regard, it is not without significance to the discussion on the nature of international minority rights norms and standards that the most comprehensive minority rights standard-setting has taken place within the OSCE, an organization that is evidently political in nature and has consistently advanced the idea of its 'commitments' being 'politically [and not legally] binding'.[12] The political process of the OSCE reflects some beneficial attributes when it comes to norm development and respect or conformity ('compliance') thereof. For example, looking more specifically into minority rights standards, the OSCE was able to act quickly, not held back by debates about the legal definition of minorities and without being locked into a long period of treaty negotiation which would miss the political moment of, and opportunity at, the end of the Cold War. Indeed, the then Commission on Security and Cooperation in Europe (CSCE) was able to adopt the 1990 Document of the Copenhagen Meeting of the Conference on the Human Dimension of the CSCE (the Copenhagen Document) in a crucial period—a political opening—when human rights (including minority rights) and democratic governance in Central and Eastern Europe and the former Soviet Union became the major focus of European international relations. The OSCE was able to respond rapidly through a political process of norm-creation and standard-setting resulting in adoption in Copenhagen of a progressive, to-the-point, fairly detailed, and to this day the most comprehensive catalogue of minority rights. The so-called Copenhagen Document was quickly followed by other OSCE documents such as the 1990 Charter of Paris for a New Europe, the 1991 Geneva Report on National Minorities, the 1991 Moscow Document, 1992 Helsinki Document, and eventually the 1994 Budapest Document that formed the basis of the OSCE activities dedicated to protection of national minorities. Together, these instruments—this action—not only rapidly developed the norms and inspired standard-setting in other IGOs (some of it 'hard law') notably at the UN and Council of Europe (CoE), but they contributed to propelling the political change in a virtuous cycle which resulted in constitutional, legal, and institutional reforms in numerous states, conclusion of critical bilateral treaties, and ultimately substantially affected peace, stability, and sustainable development across Europe.

The function of 'soft law' as a precursor to creation of 'hard law' obligations through, for example, a treaty is manifest (as noted above) in how OSCE minority rights standards spurred creation of the FCNM and the European Charter for Regional or Minority Languages.[13] The emergence of the FCNM is directly linked to recognition by states, expressed through their OSCE political undertakings, that

[12] On the nature of the organization see more in: F. Evers, M. Kahl, and W. Zellner, *The Culture of Dialogue: The OSCE Acquis 30 Years after Helsinki* (CORE publication, Centre for OSCE Research Institute for Peace Research and Security Policy at the University of Hamburg, 2005).

[13] On the nature and the character of the Charter, see: D. Ó Riagáin, *European Charter for Regional or Minority Languages: Legal Challenges and Opportunities* (Strasbourg: Council of Europe, 2008): 25–37.

protection of and respect for the rights of persons belonging to national minorities contributes to stability and peace within Europe. Specifically and expressly, the Vienna Summit of Heads of State and Government of the Council of Europe in 1993 decided to transform, to the greatest possible extent, these political commitments of the OSCE into legal obligations. The Preamble and the Explanatory Report to the FCNM directly links its provisions to particular paragraphs of the Copenhagen Document. In this regard the Copenhagen Document is, under international law (i.e. the Vienna Convention on the Law of Treaties, Articles 31 and 32) an authoritative source for interpretation of the FCNM. At the same time, by incorporating the normative content of political commitments adopted within the OSCE, the FCNM strengthens their effective implementation and increases the opportunities for their invocation.

Although both the Copenhagen Document and the Framework Convention provide to date the most progressive normative development, their soft nature has been often pointed out as 'weakness' or deficiency; in the case of the OSCE Documents, their lack of legally binding force, while in the case of the FCNM, the lack of direct applicability of the substantive provisions of the Convention before the state's administrative and judicial authorities and the lack of international judicial control. A large number of the Framework Convention provisions are of a programmatic nature, requiring states to adopt their own domestic policies and legislation to implement the provisions. Some formulations are left (relatively) vague and were drafted as a compromise solution. However, they also aim to encompass the complexity of the differing minority situations, where minorities vary substantially in their minority characteristics, needs, and claims, as well as their settlement, numerical strength, or historic circumstances affecting their position within a state.[14] In addition, fulfilment of minority interests and needs is often viewed as a politically charged and sensitive issue impacting majority–minority relations within a state and requiring dedication of the state's financial and institutional resources (such as delivery of services and education in minority languages).[15] From the positivist point of view, such provisions provide a legal challenge. However, from the perspective of application of minority rights in practice, the programmatic provisions of the FCNM create an opportunity to devise appropriate policies through the political process and enable the diplomatic dialogue of the expert monitoring bodies to consider the fragile balance in majority–minority relations. Perhaps the greatest achievement of these normative developments is that the states are now internationally responsible for proactive realization of minority protection. Reviewing the past twenty-five years of existence and operation of minority rights norms and standards in Europe, the relative (if still far from perfect) success of compliance with the existing norms can be attributed to a number of factors. These include the more detailed elaboration of standards that the soft law norms could

[14] For detailed review of the FCNM's nature, character, and obligations see: *The Rights of Minorities in Europe: A Commentary on the European Framework Convention for the Protection of National Minorities*, ed. M. Weller (Oxford: Oxford University Press, 2005).

[15] See the Explanatory Report to the FCNM, H(1995)010, paras 65–71.

deliver in local contexts, and a process of continuous implementation of the commitments encouraged through political dialogue; the creation of expert dedicated bodies is also key, as will be demonstrated in some detail in the following part, focusing on the case of the OSCE HCNM.[16]

3. The OSCE High Commissioner on National Minorities

Within the OSCE the protection of minorities has been conceived largely as a security issue and the mechanisms that address these commitments are principally security-oriented. The primary recourse is through diplomatic means at interstate or multilateral level. Perhaps the most effective and influential institution within the OSCE context in this regard has been the OSCE HCNM, whose mandate was created in 1992 by OSCE participating states in recognition of the need for an effective mechanism to respond to minority-related tensions following the break-up of the former Yugoslavia and ensuing conflict in the region. As an instrument of conflict prevention, the HCNM addresses minority issues from a security perspective. However, the ill-informed critiques of the 'securitization' of state–minority relations as a risky strategy which can potentially 'problematize' particular communities as a threat to society, prompt or exacerbate vilification, perpetuate negative stereotypes, and lead to restrictive policies do not apply in this case. On the contrary, the HCNM approach whereby (potentially) tense situations involving minorities are addressed using rights-based approaches sits firmly within the 'security-rights nexus' identified by Sasse. The HCNM is essentially a normative actor who aims not only to manage already securitized relations in the short and medium term, but to transform and 'desecuritize' those relationships in the long term.

Accordingly, in this section we examine the HCNM's use of both hard and soft law pertaining to minorities in the execution of his or her conflict prevention mandate, as well as in developing his or her[17] own soft jurisprudence and standards which clarify and build upon the content of minority rights and other standards (both hard and soft) and provide options for effective practice.

3.1 HCNM mandate and approach

The OSCE HCNM is the principal mechanism in the OSCE engaged in the protection and promotion of minority rights. Created as part of the conceptual and operational development of the OSCEs notion of 'comprehensive security' which recognizes the fundamental link between security and, inter alia, respect for

[16] For more on factors affecting compliance with minority norms through the HCNM engagement see: Y. I. Diacofotakis, *Expanding Conceptual Boundaries: The High Commissioner on National Minorities and the Protection of Minority Rights in the OSCE* (Brussels: Bruylant, 2002): 139–42.

[17] Since the present incumbent is a woman we use 'his or her' and 'she or he' when discussing the role, actions, and accumulated experience and practice of the HCNM as an institution. Where the focus is on actions or developments under previous male Commissioners, the masculine is used.

human rights, the HCNM is an 'instrument of conflict prevention at the earliest possible stage'.[18] His or her role is to focus on disputes involving national minorities that have an international character and have the potential to cause interstate tension or to erupt into international armed conflict. The HCNM is above all a political instrument and is not intended to supervise states' compliance with their OSCE commitments or international obligations. The title is significant: as a High Commissioner *on* not *for* national minorities, she or he does not act as an advocate or recourse for individuals belonging to national minorities. The choice to become engaged in a specific situation hinges primarily on the threat posed to international peace and security by the situation in question, not in response to individual or collective complaints or even on the nature or extent of rights violations of minorities per se. In this sense, the HCNM is not a very accessible recourse mechanism since it depends on there being a situation of a certain character which the HCNM in his or her own judgment recognizes and acts upon. Of course, in situations where the rights of minorities are not respected (or this is perceived to be the case) resentments and a sense of historical injustice may be generated and fester, leading to internal tensions. An external dimension is added where the minority has a 'kin-state' poised to protect the interests of 'their' minorities. With this well-established and historically demonstrated understanding, adequate protection of the rights of persons belonging to minorities contributes towards minimizing ethnic tensions that might otherwise threaten to create wider conflict. The HCNM therefore pays careful attention to issues of human rights, especially freedom from discrimination and issues of (in)equality, along with respect for minority rights. As former HCNM Knut Vollebaek observed at a conference to mark the twentieth anniversary of the HCNM, with regard to the HCNM's unique mandate and role:

> Internationally, there are many institutions established to uphold the observance of human rights, but very few have been given the mandate to advise governments on how to achieve the balance between human, including minority, rights and political realities on the ground. With 20 years of efforts in this area to reflect upon, we can say that the HCNM has acted to advance minority rights. However, the key to success has always involved working to strike the right balance between the interests of minorities and majorities in order to minimize inter-ethnic tensions.[19]

3.2 The HCNM's use of norms

Persuading governments to comply with human rights, including minority rights standards, is integral to the process of preventing the escalation of disputes between governments and minorities and between OSCE participating states. The HCNM, in order to analyse the situations in which she or he is engaged, relies on

[18] Conference on Security and Co-operation in Europe, Helsinki Document 1992, 9–10 July 1992, II. CSCE High Commissioner on National Minorities, Mandate, Art. 2.

[19] 'HCNM at 20: The Challenges of Change—Continued', address by Knut Vollebaek, OSCE High Commissioner on National Minorities, to the Conference 'HCNM 20 Years On' held at the European Centre for Minority Issues, Flensburg, 6 July 2012, <www.osce.org/hcnm/92214?download=true>.

international standards to which the state concerned has agreed. In this first regard, the applicable norms provide one important analytical framework within which to assess grievances and scrutinize problems, positions, behaviour, and options. As such, the standards are useful in functioning as a barometer for assessing, inter alia, existing and draft policy, law, and administrative practices impacting on issues and tensions involving minorities in the country or countries concerned. They also provide a framework for dialogue and development of specific recommendations to address the source of tensions, as identified by the HCNM. On the basis of OSCE commitments to uphold *all relevant standards*, she or he may refer to any applicable standard in his or her recommendations regardless of source in order to draw states' attention to their obligations and support his or her arguments. The range of standards at his or her disposal includes OSCE commitments (notably the Copenhagen Document), UN and CoE treaties, bilateral accords, international jurisprudence, as well as domestic legislation and state practice.[20] Reference to existing human rights, including minority rights standards to which the state has voluntarily agreed, also provides the HCNM with a range of possible solutions on the basis of already prescribed norms (sometimes quite specific) and so protects him or her from accusations of arbitrariness or selectiveness. If sometimes general or 'elastic'—a matter to which we will return—the relevant norms and standards are, of course, to be applied by states taking into account the facts (i.e. context) of the particular situation and within a certain margin of appreciation that allows them to devise the specific method of respecting a standard while maintaining its integrity. Within this overall framework, the HCNM has considerable room to work.[21]

As Ratner illustrates, the 'hardness' or 'softness' of a norm or standard has not been the determining factor for the HCNM in deciding which to invoke.[22] In elaborating specific country recommendations and arguing for changes in behaviour, successive High Commissioners have not drawn attention to the source of the norm or standard invoked in support of the argument, but have used all those at their disposal in the most convincing way with a view to impact and effect. They have relied upon the notion of 'international standards' as an umbrella for the accumulated body of law and practice of the OSCE, CoE, and UN regarding minority–majority relations encompassing varying degrees of 'softness' and 'hardness'. The reliance on soft law goes beyond OSCE documents which, as discussed in section 2, are 'soft' in terms of source but possess a significant degree of 'hardness' due to their adoption by all OSCE participating states by consensus at high

[20] J. Packer, 'The OSCE High Commissioner on National Minorities', in *International Human Rights Monitoring Mechanisms: A Textbook on How to Petition and Lobby International Organizations; Essays in Honour of Jakob Th. Möller*, ed. G. Alfredsson (The Hague: Kluwer Law International, 2001): 641–56.

[21] J. Packer, 'Making International Law Matter in Preventing Ethnic Conflict: A Practitioner's Perspective', in 'Colloquy, Minority Disputes in Europe: Toward New Roles for International Law', *Journal of International Law and Politics* vol. 32 (2000): 716–17.

[22] S. R. Ratner, 'Does International Law Matter in Preventing Ethnic Conflict?', in 'Colloquy, Minority Disputes in Europe: Toward New Roles for International Law', *Journal of International Law and Politics* vol. 32 (2000): 591–697.

level as well as the consequences of non-respect or failure to comply. The HCNM has also cited recommendations of the CoE Parliamentary Assembly, for example, as well as thematic recommendations developed by independent experts under his or her auspices, as discussed further in section 4. Such instruments are useful for the specificity of language used and specific behaviour required, not provided by relevant treaties (such as the ICCPR, ICERD, FCNM, etc.) or other instruments.

Where the state is party to a specific convention that directly addresses the issue at hand, this will be referred to and usually forms the basis of the argument, but the HCNM also often makes arguments based on a treaty that the state has not signed or ratified. The HCNM has been strategic in the emphasis placed on different standards even within a particular instrument and on the (legal) argumentation, depending on the international commitments of the state involved and the dynamics of the situation at hand. For example, in engaging with the Latvian government on the use of the Russian language, the HCNM focused on incompatibilities of draft legislation with provisions on freedom of expression and association in the ICCPR and ECHR, although the draft also contravened the rights of minorities to use their own language under Article 27 of the ICCPR. This was a deliberate and pragmatic strategy to achieve a result (respect for the linguistic rights of ethnic Russians in Latvia) in a political climate where many simply refused to accept the Russians' status as a minority based on the size of the population and former status as a (former) occupier. It was not the hardness or softness of the standard, but its character as a universal (rather than minority-specific) provision that was instrumental in this case.

It is notable that the HCNM is not only concerned with adherence to minimum requirements of hard and soft minority rights standards. The High Commissioner's problem-solving approach, which responds to legitimate interests, grievances, and claims articulated by all parties, has often required the HCNM to look for solutions beyond what is provided in the ('hard' and 'soft') minority rights standards to fulfil ideas of good governance within a democratic society and in order to develop tailored solutions that work for all involved. This was the case, for example, with regard to Albanian minority demands for access to higher education in their own language in Macedonia. In this case, the HCNM clarified for both parties—publicly and privately—the content of applicable standards which ensure for minorities the right to establish educational institutions in their own languages, but not to public funding or automatic recognition of diplomas. He also clarified for the government their obligations regarding the recognition of institutions, which cannot be denied solely on the basis of the language used. The clarification provided the framework for discussions between the parties which could then move beyond dispute over applicable rights towards finding a practical solution in line with the standards. Norm clarification and subsequent practical suggestions for a solution—and mobilization of international actors to fund that solution—made possible the move from the abstract to the concrete.[23]

[23] For a full discussion of the HCNM's role as a translator of norms in this case see: Ratner (2000): 625–9.

In this way the HCNM acts as a 'normative intermediary', translating general—and frequently vague and imprecise—standards into specific recommendations for application in specific situations.[24] As the Macedonian example illustrates, in the process of bringing law and policy at national level into conformity with international standards, norms may be invoked, explained, or reinterpreted to render them applicable to the specific circumstances of the case in question and behaviour is modified to fit the norms as a result. This facilitates actual change in real situations, bringing norms and standards to life with tangible meaning for all concerned and, thus, *making them matter*.

3.3 The HCNM as a norm interpreter: 'soft jurisprudence'

In addition to fleshing out the substance of existing norms—regardless of softness or hardness in terms of sources—in some cases, where norms did not yet exist to address certain situations the HCNM has in essence created new ones. This was the case, for example, in the course of engagement with representatives of Ukraine and Crimea, in the absence of any real norms regarding 'autonomy'. The HCNM sought to convince the parties that certain types of relationships between central and regional authorities were generally accepted features of democratic governance to which various instruments referred. In particular, through extensive interpretation and argumentation, the HCNM breathed considerable life into the quite uncertain notion of 'effective participation in public life' expressed in paragraph 34 of the 1990 Copenhagen Document, Article 4 of the 1992 UN Declaration on Minorities, and Article 15 of the FCNM.[25] This and other similar efforts led eventually to a set of ground-breaking generally applicable Recommendations on the subject (i.e. the 1999 Lund Recommendations; see section 5).

The HCNM thus promoted peaceful change not by enforcement or coercion, but by encouraging compliance with norms on their own merit. She or he does this by reminding states of their existing obligations under international (hard and soft) law and providing concrete guidance on options for their implementation in practice, often by creating new understandings and persuading actors to comply with them.

As a former Director of the Office has observed, as a result of careful attention to consistency across varying situations in the invocation of standards and in the often ground-breaking interpretation and application of the standards for conflict prevention the HCNM has become a source of 'soft jurisprudence' drawing upon

[24] Ratner (2000); Packer (2000). In a similar vein, other scholars have since characterized the HCNM as a 'norm entrepreneur'. See e.g.: J. Jackson-Preece, 'The High Commissioner on National Minorities as a Normative Actor', *Journal on Ethnopolitics and Minority Issues in Europe* vol. 12 (2013): 77–82.

[25] Ratner (2000): 644. For a detailed recount of the HCNM's engagement on the topic of autonomy in Ukraine, and specifically the Autonomous Republic of Crimea see: J. Packer, 'Autonomy within the OSCE: The Case of Crimea', in *Autonomy: Applications and Implications*, ed. M. Suksi (The Hague: Kluwer Law International, 1998): 295–316.

international instruments, doctrine, and state practice in the development of his own argumentation to arrive at specific recommendations.[26]

3.4 Reactions to HCNM norm promotion: does the source or status as hard or soft matter?

According to research undertaken by Ratner in the late 1990s, not only does the HCNM use soft law frequently in designing and brokering solutions, but parties also seem to accept these softer authorities as a basis for action. Ratner identifies three main categories of recipient:

1) Those who reject the applicability of international norms to a particular problem on principle regardless of their source and hard/soft status. This may be because they reject the norms per se and/or because they question the legitimacy of the organisations—OSCE, CoE, EU, etc.—who are the source of and enforcers of those norms.
2) Those who accept the importance of international norms but see no reason to differentiate in terms of their hard or soft status. Some may consider major political commitments such as those in OSCE documents to be as significant as, if not more so than, harder legal ones. The willingness of other influential outside actors such as the EU to treat all standards invoked by the HCNM on a par for the purposes of leverage have also helped to erode the distinction between treaties and 'softer' law.
3) Those for whom a distinction between 'soft' and 'hard' remains significant. These include bureaucrats, senior politicians and NGO leaders with exposure to the nature of different legal instruments. Some may simply note that their country's treaty obligations are more significant than politically binding norms embodied e.g. in the Copenhagen Document, with little impact on the reception and implementation of these norms in practice. Others may actively use the legally non-binding nature of a document as a justification for non-compliance with unwelcome recommendations.[27]

Reactions to HCNM norm promotion identified by Ratner thus tend to suggest that the hard or soft status of the norm can be important to—or be invoked by—some actors in terms of acceptance or rejection of norms, but this is by no means a defining factor for 'compliance'. Indeed, the factors that induce compliance with hard legal prescriptions may be identical to those inducing compliance with softer norms.

It is important to note that the political context in which the HCNM now operates is very different from the one Ratner was analysing. States that were newly independent in the 1990s are now more established, have joined—or are on the

[26] Packer (2000): 717.

[27] For a fuller discussion of the significance attributed by respondents to the hardness or softness of a standard and the implications for implementation see: Ratner (2000): 662–5.

way to joining—the 'clubs' such as NATO and the EU that they aspired to in the early days, and consequently have greater confidence and are less receptive to international advice and involvement. As the High Commissioner noted on the occasion of the twentieth anniversary of the HCNM: 'I see more and more frequently how States are erecting hurdles or trying to introduce condition to my engagement.' It is possible that the first and third types of reaction (rejection of norms and the institutions that promote them and/or distinction between types of norms as justification for non-compliance) have increased as the unique openness to international involvement in the 1990s has eroded and resistance to HCNM engagement has grown.

Further updated research into the response of local actors to the norm promotion as an essential part of the HCNMs approach to conflict prevention would not only help to inform a broader picture of the HCNM's relevance and impact. It would also help to clarify the extent to which the soft/hard distinction is genuinely considered relevant and/or is used as an excuse for non-compliance amongst diverse actors. This in turn might help the HCNM in targeted future engagement.

4. The HCNM as Norm Creator: 'Soft Standard-Setting'

4.1 Thematic guidance and recommendations of general application

Successive High Commissioners have also responded to the need for clearer normative guidance in fields where both hard and soft law remain underdeveloped in thematic areas which have recurred in the course of their work as sources of tension within and between states. These include issues of effective participation in public life, education, language use, the media, and policing, among others.[28] The initial three sets of thematic general recommendations were elaborated by international independent experts at the first High Commissioner's request for use by him and his successors in discussions with interlocutors in situations where he/they were involved to provide further support to tailored country-specific recommendations. The thematic recommendations take available international standards—universal and minority-specific and varying degrees of 'hard' and 'soft'—as their point of departure, but offer greater detail where implications and options for implementation are unclear. They also seek to fill the gaps where standards have yet to be explicitly articulated with regard to a particular issue. The approach is similar to that of recommendations made to specific states in that they draw together all available standards pertaining to a particular issue, provide clarification and more detail where necessary, and connect them to options for potential action. However,

[28] For the set of (so far seven) general recommendations and guidelines elaborated under the auspices of the OSCE HCNM see: OSCE HCNM, 'Thematic Recommendations and Guidelines', <http://www.osce.org/hcnm/66209>.

they go beyond the individual country recommendations approach, as they articulate new standards even if expressed as 'Recommendations' or 'Guidelines'. Recommendations are both informed by state practice and serve as an authoritative reference for engagement with specific states. They straddle the line between translation of existing norms and elaboration of new ones. Importantly, states have individually and collectively subsequently endorsed these and so 'hardened' them.

While firmly rooted in international law and international standards, both soft and hard, the HCNM approach appeals to the *self-interest* of states, pointing out that granting minorities equal rights and developing constructive relations between all (majority and minorities) within the state is in the interests of peace and security. Persons who belong to minorities are less likely to pursue policies or survival strategies against the interest of the majority. Kin-states are also less likely to be attracted by irredentist policies if their minorities in other states are treated well. The HCNM has also taken the position that while minorities have rights, they also have duties towards the state. The emphasis is on creating peaceful shared societies in which everyone has responsibilities. This approach is examined in more depth in section 7.

5. Loop Back! How HCNM Soft Jurisprudence and Standards Contribute to Compliance with, or Creation of, Hard Law

5.1 Reference to HCNM recommendations by other IGOs

The thematic recommendations provide a valuable practical tool for the HCNM in his or her own work in discussions with interlocutors to support his or her recommendations. They are also a valuable source for law- and policy-makers. They have been invoked by other IGO monitoring bodies of legally binding treaties pertaining to minorities in their monitoring work or interpretation of states' obligations under such treaty law. The FCNM Advisory Committee of Experts (ACFC) has taken cues from the HCNM's thematic recommendations. In particular, in assessing states' reports on their implementation of the quite general character of Article 15 of the FCNM concerning participation of minorities in public life, the ACFC initially widely used the Lund Recommendations on Effective Participation of National Minorities in Public Life generated by the HCNM in 1999 as a reference. In this respect, Article 15 of the FCNM, as well as other relevant Articles of the Convention underlying minority participation, served as an international law source for elaboration of the Recommendations. Thereupon, the Lund Recommendations were used in the development of the FCNM's own thematic commentary on the public participation of minorities.[29] Such interplay and borrowing became common in

[29] 'ACFC Commentary on the Effective Participation of Persons Belonging to National Minorities in Cultural, Social and Economic Life and in Public Affairs', para. 4 and para. 7.

the early work of the HCNM and the ACFC, and it was followed by others including the European Court of Human Rights.

5.2 Country recommendations

The HCNM's specific country recommendations have also been invoked by other IGOs perhaps most significantly and influentially by the EU. In making accession conditional on compliance with the HCNM's recommendations, the status of those recommendations was elevated so that compliance with the recommendations became a surrogate for compliance with the norms themselves. The HCNM's cooperation with the EU and other international actors is discussed in further detail in the following sections as we consider the factors influencing receptivity to norm promotion among national actors.

5.3 Reference/incorporation into domestic law

The adoption of domestic policy and law and establishment of implementing institutions, in accordance with international standards, is fundamental to the protection and promotion of minority rights. No systematic empirical study of the impact of the HCNM's role as a 'normative intermediary' exists, but the testimonies of relevant officials and case studies are supportive of the argument that soft law used in conjunction with hard law, promoted through processes of political persuasion, has contributed to real changes in behaviours and concrete changes in national law and policy-making as well as institution-building processes.

Frequently, the HCNM has provided states with technical cooperation in drafting domestic legislation concerning protection of persons belonging to national minorities or other relevant laws. The HCNM has played an extensive role in assisting states in their efforts to incorporate minority rights standards, including the legally binding FCNM obligations, in their domestic context and provided them with support and advice in developing their national legal framework for the protection of national minorities, inter alia providing legal advice in drafting the constitutional guarantees and laws on the rights of national minorities across the Balkan region.[30] As noted at the occasion of the Conference enhancing the impact of the FCNM by one of the HCNM advisers: Comparably with judicial bodies or the monitoring mechanisms of the CoE, the HCNM was in a unique position and used his mandate in a complementary way to benefit the implementation of the FCNM. These bodies could not provide such advice and assistance, given that their principal task is reviewing fulfilment of the FCNM undertakings by domestic measures, in particular legal and institutional arrangements.[31] It is notable in this context that drafters

[30] *Quiet Diplomacy in Action: The OSCE High Commissioner on National Minorities*, ed. W. Kemp (The Hague: Kluwer Law International, 2001): 175.

[31] Z. Machnyikova, 'CoE Report on the Use of the Framework Convention for the Protection of National Minorities by the Organization for Security and Co-operation in Europe and the United Nations' (CoE Conference on enhancing the impact of the FCNM, 9–10 Oct. 2008): 6–7.

of the law regulating protection of minorities in the Federal Republic of Yugoslavia included in the initial drafts in their preambles reference to the HCNMs thematic recommendations as 'international obligations'.[32]

While some of the HCNM's interlocutors do (or did) not consider the OSCE particularly prestigious or influential, others have found the link to the OSCE to be critical. More compellingly, states that fail to respect their political commitments may be subject to political sanctions, including exclusion from key decision-making clubs or the benefits of aid and trade. The real effects of these sanctions may be more immediate and significant than the consequences of legal process and sanctions for failure to respect the rights of minorities available under international treaties (e.g. non-respect of Article 27 of the ICCPR). In sum, in the dynamics of international relations the hardness or softness of the standards in terms of sources matters less than the politically or economically costly consequences for non-compliance.[33]

In situations where the carrot and sticks are less compelling, the HCNM must also rely more on governments' self-interest—notably in peacefully solving internal tensions and in being seen to comply with their obligations. Notwithstanding earlier observations about trends away from compliance with the OSCE, the essential point here is that, if (as the HCNM's experience suggests) both 'hard' and 'soft' law largely rely on voluntary compliance which can be achieved through a process of political persuasion then the distinction between 'hard' legal obligations and 'soft' political commitments essentially disappears. Self-interest becomes paramount.[34]

6. The Nature of Diversity Management

As noted in the Introduction to this book, in some cases soft law appears to constitute a primary reference point with no prospect for codification or crystallization into hard law. It also has some advantages in terms of speed and flexibility. Indeed, the subject matter of minority rights is arguably more suited to a soft law approach as contrasted with a more prescriptive hard law one. The open and 'programmatic' wording of minority rights instruments such as the FCNM is often regarded as a disadvantage in that it allows loopholes for states to circumvent their legal obligations. This is undoubtedly the case in some instances both with regard to the scope of application of the instrument (e.g. where states limit enjoyment of minority rights to citizens only) and the failure to implement specific provisions because they are couched in vague terms. However, the 'soft' character (which applies also to

[32] This has transpired in the drafting process of the Law on the Protection of Rights and Freedoms of Minorities of the Federal Republic of Yugoslavia, adopted on 27 Feb. 2002. It is not without a significance regarding the promotion of the soft law standards that just before the drafting process began, the HCNM held a conference on Minority Protection, Integration and Stability in South-Eastern Europe in Bled in Slovenia with the different representatives of the Yugoslav government and minorities discussing extensively the HCNM's thematic recommendations that were translated into the local languages. See: Kemp (2001): 199. This was later deleted, as references to international obligations were not included in the final draft.

[33] Packer (2000): 719.

[34] Packer (2000): 718.

the FCNM even though it is a legally binding treaty) is not necessarily a disadvantage when it comes to conflict prevention through the constructive management of diversity in a normative framework that includes respect for minority rights. As the experience of the HCNM has shown, because soft law instruments at his or her disposal (particularly the FCNM, OSCE commitments notably the Copenhagen Document, and his or her own soft law jurisprudence and standards) do not overly favour standardized and precise formulations they can be flexibly adapted to country-specific circumstances. The diversity of states in terms of size, concentrations, and expressed needs, interests, and claims of its minority populations makes specific prescriptions unsuitable. The Explanatory Report to the FCNM is clear that the decision to include mostly programme-type provisions was based (at least partly) on the fact that minorities' different living conditions demand a more policy-oriented norm setting.[35] The provisions set out objectives which the parties undertake to pursue, but they are granted a 'measure of discretion' in their implementation of those objectives, thus enabling them to take particular circumstances into account.[36] Another advantage of soft over hard law, as identified by Brostig, lies in the ability to address more informal and subtle forms of discrimination in situations permeated by mistrust and the passive acceptance of racist or discriminatory attitudes by politicians and the majority of society. As he observes, hard law instruments appear insufficient on their own to effectively remedy situations where forms of unequal treatment are taking place below the legal threshold.[37]

As also illustrated with regard to the HCNM's recommendations regarding the language(s) used in higher education, the absence of precise norms can also work in favour of minority protection and act as an amplifier. As noted in the Introduction to this book, both states and non-state actors may prefer soft law 'in order to respond more quickly with less paucity and more flexibility'.[38] The potential, however, needs to be actively promoted by monitoring bodies which have responsibility for clarifying unclear norms and preventing the exploitation of legal imprecision.[39] This is essentially what the HCNM does in developing detailed recommendations on state practice within the scope and objective of the relevant instruments. HCNM experience in promoting viable solutions with reference to soft law standards (including those of his or her own creation) illustrates that because soft law provides discretion states actively engage in a norm-creation process themselves.

It should be noted that successful implementation cannot be measured against a desirable 'end state', because contextual conditions will evolve as implementation progresses. This is not to say that progress in norm implementation should not be evaluated, but there is no single moment when a state can be considered to have 'passed the test' with regard to managing tensions in society because this is an ongoing process. The HCNM may decide to scale down engagement or even withdraw,

[35] FCNM Explanatory Report on para. 11.

[36] FCNM Explanatory Report on para. 11.

[37] M. Brostig, 'Implementing Soft Law: The Case of Equality Promotion', *European Yearbook of Minority Issues* vol. 9 (2012): 152.

[38] See the Introduction to this volume.

[39] See the Introduction to this volume.

however, once state practice is sufficiently in line with international standards and the presence of tensions that threaten to escalate into violence has dissipated.

7. Process and Considerations when Developing Innovative 'Soft Law' Standards for Application in Diverse Societies: The Example of the HCNM Guidelines on Integrating Diversity

Recognizing the reality of ethnic, linguistic, and religious diversity within OSCE participating states—which will remain and in many cases increase in the foreseeable future—the HCNM seeks to highlight the positives of such diversity. For this reason, from the beginning the HCNM has encouraged open and peaceful processes of integration which accommodate difference through choice drawing on creative solutions and alternatives which are consistent with human rights standards. This is pursued through specific country engagement and elaboration and application of general recommendation and guidelines as described in sections 3 and 4.

The overall approach adopted and promoted by the HCNM is one of 'integrating diversity'. Broadly speaking this is conceived as a 'two-way process' whereby persons belonging to minorities, acting alone or in community with others, are given adequate opportunity to maintain and develop their distinct identities, while at the same time participating fully in and making a contribution to wider society and respecting the territorial integrity of the state. Integrating diversity goes hand in hand with 'good governance', whereby governing institutions are committed to act in the interests of their whole populations by creating comparable conditions and opportunities for all to pursue their own development and fulfil their own aspirations on an equal basis with others.

In 2009, the then HCNM, Knut Vollebaek, instigated a process to consolidate the HCNM's proven and accepted approach of 'integration with respect for diversity' within one document and across policy areas into a comprehensive whole. The document, as with previous recommendations and guidelines, would be rooted in international soft and hard law and based on real experience and potentially transferable lessons. While thematic recommendations (relating to language, education, and participation in public life, etc.) already existed these would be incorporated and updated in the light of emerging (effective) state practice. New elements (e.g. relating to social and economic participation) would also be introduced. The process eventually led to the elaboration of the 2012 Ljubljana Guidelines on Integration of Diverse Societies.

A review of the process of debating, elaborating, and agreeing the content and text of the Ljubljana Guidelines[40] serves to highlight some current issues of

[40] The authors (under the leadership of John Packer who served as Senior Legal Adviser then Director of the Office of the OSCE HCNM from 1995 to 2004) coordinated the process for the initiation and early development of the Guidelines and contributed substantively to their eventual elaboration.

contention, including conceptual issues, in the interpretation of existing minority rights and other standards relevant for integrating diversity. It also raised some questions concerning the extent to which emerging norms from national practice with the capacity to restrict rather than protect rights should be reflected in the development of such recommendations and whether and to what extent 'political will' within states should be a factor for consideration.

7.1 Consultation process

As with previous thematic recommendations and guidelines, governments were not consulted directly on draft texts—the rationale being that this would raise all kinds of process questions not least in terms of which governments were consulted and whether/how views were incorporated. The HCNM could, however, sound out governments on specific issues. A suggestion to potentially engage with all OSCE participating states by conducting a survey of states' practices with regard to integration in the vein of the *Report on Linguistic Rights* developed as a corollary to the Oslo Recommendations was not taken up.[41] Similarly a suggestion to organize a consultation of mayors to draw on practical experiences at municipal level was not in the end pursued. The HCNM consulted widely with academics, jurists, and think-tanks working on integration issues, addressing some contentious issues in the process. Some of these are highlighted in subsections 7.2 to 7.10.

7.2 Nature and sources

In the course of consultations, some experts suggested that the document 'should not be prescriptive'. It was also suggested that there are few, if any, standards on 'integration' and that prospective guidelines should follow the approach of the HCNM's Recommendations on Policing which draw on practical experience, but make little reference to any standards. However, the 'integration with respect for diversity' approach developed and actively pursued by the Office of the HCNM since its inception is exactly rooted in human (including minority) rights standards as the basis for building peaceful and prosperous societies. To now depart from foundational values of human rights, democratic governance, etc. (which can and should be imposed) would, at best, send mixed messages and, at worst, risk seriously undermining the credibility of previous sets of recommendations and open debate on the normative foundation of HCNM activity and his normative contributions. In fact, as reflected in references in the Structural Principles section of the Ljubljana Guidelines there are a wealth of principles, norms, and concrete standards that support the essential elements of integration integral to the HCNM approach. Consistent with previous recommendations and guidelines, these constitute a mixture of treaty-based and 'softer' standards, including provisions on

[41] A similar survey was undertaken to support the Guidelines on the Use of Minority Languages in the Broadcast Media, see OSCE HCNM website, <http://www.osce.org/hcnm>.

non-discrimination and equality enshrined in UN treaties, as well those pertaining to minority rights as protected by the UN Declaration, FCNM, and other 'softer' instruments.[42] In order to meet the need for more concrete practical suggestions for action, while maintaining the normative value of the document, it was suggested that a commentary elaborating on options for policies and measures to promote integration drawing on the HCNM's practical experience in various concrete situations, could be a useful addition to the Recommendations and Explanatory Note.

7.3 Integration

The term integration is controversial and has many different meanings and connotations (and is equated with assimilation by some). For these reasons it was argued that states may be put off by the title of the Guidelines and/or attribute their own understandings to it. Suggestions for relatively 'neutral' alternatives reflecting the approach and content of the text included 'managing diversity in' or 'consolidation of' multi-ethnic societies—the latter being used in the context of HCNM support for Moldova's development of an 'integration' action plan while avoiding the term integration. Counter-arguments (that eventually won through) were that the HCNM has consistently used the term integration—including in letters of recommendation, speeches, etc.—and continues to do so. To stop now for the purpose of these Guidelines would be inconsistent and possibly also send the wrong signal. It was felt that, so long as the intended meaning and content of the term is clearly set out in the Guidelines (as it is), the HCNM can make a real contribution by taking a controversial and contested term like integration and proposing a principled and practical model which has been shown to work in many contexts where the HCNM has been involved.

7.4 Which minorities?

As with previous HCNM recommendations and guidelines, the Llubjana Guidelines do not specifically limit their application to one group or another. The introduction explains that 'The term "national minority" refers to a wide range of minority groups, including ethnic, religious, linguistic and cultural communities, regardless of whether these groups are recognized by the States where they reside and irrespective of the designation applied to or claimed by them.' With regard to the 'old' versus 'new' minorities debate: from a human rights perspective, the enjoyment of rights does not depend upon 'generations' of migrants and people cannot simply be asked to 'leave their identities at the door' when they enter the jurisdiction of a state. As one expert noted, the needs and interests of minorities and migrants generally overlap and tend to be articulated as similar claims.[43] Furthermore, in many cases in practical terms it does not make sense to differentiate on the basis of

[42] See the Ljubljana Guidelines 7–13 for the full set of references.
[43] Interview with Dr Jennifer Jackson-Preece, London, May 2010.

the individual status (e.g. recent versus third generation immigrant) among those constituting an ethnic minority group when it comes to the realization of rights that benefit the whole community, for example provision of education in a minority language or road signs in the community's language. It was therefore agreed that the substance of any recommendations should be based upon, and respectful of, a normative approach, which de facto makes no distinction between 'old' and 'new' minorities. It was also felt that the Guidelines should include a compilation of practices concerning integration and management of diversity that have proven effective in different contexts. Such an approach would address any attempts by states to contest the relevance of recommendations to their particular situation, including the status of various groups living within their borders. In particular, arguments from states 'West of Vienna' that integration of 'new' immigrant populations presents a different paradigm from that of 'traditional' minorities would be rendered irrelevant.

While experts advised that no explicit reference should be made to particular *categories* of persons ('traditional' minorities, immigrants, non-citizens, etc.) arrangements for integration should nevertheless be considered with respect to their relevance and applicability to the situations of groups who enjoy established and guaranteed minority rights. They should also be examined from the perspective of other groups within the state who are not subject to such special protection. In the latter case, approaches and measures for addressing exclusion based on principles of equality and non-discrimination, inclusion, and the concept of reasonable accommodation, etc. would likely be most relevant and useful. Efforts were made in drafting to reflect an understanding that the specific measures appropriate to different groups will vary according to a host of factors, including group characteristics, migration histories, etc. and that reliable data as well as regular monitoring of outcomes should underpin policies to ensure that they are appropriate and effective.[44] In this regard the soft law nature of the Guidelines provides the necessary flexibility for process-focused development of policies that are adaptable to concrete, local, and often differing situations and thus responsive and effective and consequently acceptable to the state and those affected.

7.5 Rights, responsibilities, and/or duties

It is the role of the state to develop policy, legal, and institutional frameworks within which the legitimate claims of all may be voiced, negotiated, and peacefully resolved. As noted, the HCNM has consistently argued that minorities also have duties as part of a balanced 'two-way' approach which requires everyone to contribute to the building of a peaceful integrated society. The HCNM approach to integration is reflected in the title of the Guidelines which significantly refers to integration *of* societies, which implies that members of all communities should take part in the process of integration, as distinct from the expectation that minorities

[44] See e.g.: Guidelines 15 and 17.

will integrate *into* a majority-dominated society. The emphasis on the responsibilities of all, including minorities, coincides to some extent with the 'rights and responsibility' discourse that has developed in Western European states such as the UK in the last decade. This dictates that minorities not only have rights, but also have a responsibility to play an active role in society and to integrate. This coincidence of terminology is unfortunate in that their approach to integration is often conceived as more of a one-way process (in contrast to the HCNM's) whereby it is only the minorities who are expected to do the integrating.

Politically, the requirement for minorities to contribute to the integration process on an equal basis with others can be regarded as a (probably desirable from a cohesion perspective) part of their 'social contract' with the state. However, HCNM recommendations and guidelines are rooted in international law and under international human rights law individual duties (that pertain to all individuals not just members of minorities) are limited to requirements to respect the rule of law and the rights of others. There is no duty to contribute to integration processes per se. Debate in elaborating the Guidelines centred on whether minorities should be singled out as having a 'responsibility' or (stronger) 'duty' to integrate and on what exactly those responsibilities should entail.

Many experts consulted argued that minorities do not have a duty to integrate per se, but should be encouraged to do so through the creation of genuine opportunities for inclusion and participation. Indeed, persuasive arguments can be made to minorities for why they should make the most of opportunities to participate and contribute (not least that it benefits them). Thus, inclusion and interaction should be encouraged and the benefits of a shared national/community life promoted, but individuals cannot be required to 'opt in'. It was also generally agreed that insofar as any responsibilities are invoked in terms of 'active citizenship' or participation, these should be shared responsibilities and apply across the board and not just to certain (minority) groups. Some also suggested that wider society has a responsibility to make minorities and new migrants feel welcome. HCNM recommendations should therefore acknowledge the need for, and aim to promote, a common sense of belonging and responsibility amongst different communities within a state. Approaches that bring together, and assign responsibilities to, a range of public and private actors (including, e.g., employers and unions in an employment context) were considered to be potentially useful in developing a shared sense of responsibility. The final text reflects this approach of shared responsibility without singling out minorities, but is stronger in its wording ascribing duties (rather than responsibilities) to all members of society. The explanatory text, while reiterating that duties of members of society should be shared by all, asserts that: 'Minorities should participate in all aspects of government in their country of residence and their involvement should not be restricted to areas that specifically concern them.'[45] This goes well beyond what the international standards require and is to a certain extent an inversion of the minority's *right* to public participation into a *duty*. It is true that in

[45] Ljubljana Guidelines: 21.

some states there is a duty to vote that is imposed on all eligible voters, however no particular groups in this regard are singled out in such policies. This debate on rights and duties reflects the challenges of endeavouring to respond to prevalent national or regional discourses regarding 'integration', while staying true to the spirit and letter of relevant international standards. It also demonstrates that the development of soft law does not always follow a steadily more progressive trajectory.

7.6 Is separation inherently bad?

The assumption underlying the discussion on rights, responsibilities, and duties is that separation between communities undermines societal cohesion and that active processes of participation and cross-community engagement are required to strengthen links between different communities. The Llubjana Guidelines take an explicitly non-isolationist approach to minority issues which warns of the risks to society of 'isolation or excessive separation', while acknowledging the need to balance a degree of separation necessary for free expression and development of identity on one hand with the need for cross-community links.[46] There is no space in this model for the peaceful coexistence of separate communities with limited or no contact, but who get along peacefully side by side. This reflects the view expressed in consultations that, while persons belonging to minorities may legitimately choose to opt out of participation in mainstream society, this issue should not be addressed directly in the recommendations.

The approach also reflects a degree of consensus among experts who emphasized the importance of contact between communities and of learning from and about others. The role of educational curricula was emphasized in this respect. At the same time, there was recognition that 'togetherness' cannot be imposed on communities, but can only be encouraged as part of a gradual process determined by what members of different communities are ready for and willing to accept. Challenging fears and negative perceptions of others was identified by some as a key element of this process. It was therefore considered vital that HCNM guidelines challenge entrenched fears and misperceptions about social risks. As a result, specific guidelines support the creation of political and socio-cultural space, including especially intercultural experiences and education, as the route to 'living together' based on actual contacts and knowledge of one another.[47] The HCNM's practical experience of helping the state to manage the challenges of accommodating diversity within one cohesive society in situations where separate parallel structures have developed along ethnic or cultural lines such as Bosnia-Herzegovina is particularly useful in this regard. Again, the approach adopted in the Guidelines, while well balanced

[46] Guideline 7.

[47] See e.g.: the Explanatory Note to Guideline 41, regarding the need to foster 'permanent and ongoing dialogue among and between all minority groups and between minorities and majorities', Ljubljana Guidelines: 50.

and legitimate, can be seen to respond to fears reflected in 'parallel lives' discourses prevalent at the time of drafting (and since).

7.7 Audience

Also connected to questions of rights, duties, and obligations, there was some debate over whether the Guidelines should be addressed not only to governments, but also to minority representatives. It was generally agreed that although the Guidelines should be clear that minorities, like everyone else, have a role in building peaceful integrated societies, they should remain primarily targeted at policy-makers and states' representatives (as are previous sets of recommendations and guidelines). Practical problems in identifying minority representatives as an audience were identified in this connection. However, as the introduction states: 'It is hoped that other actors who contribute in various roles to this process, including civil society and private-sector actors and independent institutions, will also find these Guidelines useful for their work.' The role of different non-governmental actors—and the ways governments might support them—are elaborated in the final text.[48]

7.8 Applicability and utility of the HCNM's conflict prevention approach in contexts across the OSCE?

It was generally agreed among those consulted that there is a genuine link between a lack of integration, societal tensions, and potentially violent intercommunal conflict. It was also acknowledged that integration and conflict are not necessarily strongly linked in all OSCE contexts. Experts agreed, however, that the management of tensions around diversity is an essential challenge for *all* states in their endeavours to build stable and harmonious societies. Although the scope/intensity of tensions and the risk of violent conflict will vary greatly amongst OSCE participating states, this does not invalidate the approach. The aim of the Guidelines is therefore to provide guidance for all states seeking to accommodate diversity and avoid risk of cleavages and tensions developing that can impact on stability and in the worst cases lead to violent conflict.

7.9 Political will

A key consideration in developing the Guidelines was the extent to which sensitivities of participating states and the extent of political will should be influencing factors in deciding on the substantive content. This is critical bearing in mind past experience whereby thematic recommendations developed under HCNM auspices have both drawn on states' practice and become a normative reference for states in terms of what they can and cannot legitimately do under international law.

[48] Recommendations 28 and 29.

Obviously, the HCNM has no interest in incorporating 'bad practice' just because it reflects a trend in states' policies and practices at the time. HCNM staff and experts took varying positions on the extent to which (perceived) existing political will should be taken into account in developing the Guidelines. Some took the line that there would be no point in including provisions which states could be expected to resist (e.g. those relating to restrictions imposed on religious apparel). A variation of this argument is that if states object to one provision it could lead them to question the validity of the document as a whole and ultimately reject the whole thing. The countering view is that provided the provision is rooted in accepted principle and norms and that compliance would probably contribute to social cohesion then it should be included. It was pointed out that the role of the HCNM is not to descend to the lowest common denominator as set by states, but to push the boundaries in terms of what is principled and workable. In addition, as some experts observed, while national public discourses around integration can be negative, states' practice may actually be quite positive in terms of the realization of rights as a tool for integration. The implication for the HCNM is that states will often accept and implement a principled normative approach to integration (as promoted by the HCNM) although this may not always be reflected within the national discourse. In the end, some 'hot' issues for integration such as the ban on wearing of religious symbols in France were not addressed directly in the text. The Explanatory Note to Guideline 41 on Participation in Cultural and Religious Life does refer to 'disproportionate limitations on the public display of cultural or religious symbols and clothing'.[49] However, no guidance is provided as to what kind of actions would be considered disproportionate under international law.

Research into the reactions of states where the HCNM has invoked the Ljubljana Guidelines in situations where she or he is engaged, but also more generally from states, including those 'West of Vienna', would be informative (a) generally in terms of how some of the guidelines considered more sensitive by the drafters have been received, and (b) specifically in terms of whether resistance stems partly from the 'soft' nature of many of the norms relied upon and/or from the soft nature of the instrument itself (i.e. as a set of policy guidelines that can basically be ignored or be rejected as lacking the legitimacy of a consensus-based norm setting).

7.10 The status of the final document as Recommendations or (softer) Guidelines was also discussed at length

The term 'guidelines' was ultimately preferred over 'recommendations' as reflecting a less prescriptive and more practical guidance-oriented approach setting out a range of options. This partly reflects concerns about what states will and will not accept and, thus, the limits of subsequent normative reach and, ultimately, compliance. Indeed, it is vital to avoid overreach which would undermine both the norm and the overall system.

[49] Ljubljana Guidelines: 51.

8. Implications Moving Forward

8.1 Developing new standards

Our analysis in this chapter questions the assumption that hard law instruments are by their nature the most effective for norm implementation. However, this is not to dismiss the potential role and utility of harder forms of law for the protection of minority rights. The continued development of hard law and enforcement mechanisms that are both systematic and less reliant on the mandates, operational techniques, and talents of normative intermediaries such as the HCNM for their effective implementation is therefore to be welcomed in principle. As we saw in section 2 with regard to the development of the soft political OSCE standards (faster, responsive, adaptable, detailed, etc.) versus the legally binding (though essentially 'soft') FCNM, states have to be ready to commit to a Convention. As Brostig notes: 'The advantage of a soft law convention on minority rights is thus the existence of the convention itself.'[50] In our view it is not a propitious time to achieve consensus on the drafting of a universal convention on the rights of minorities. Rather, further development of 'soft' law and the effective implementation of existing norms and standards should remain the focus of efforts to protect and promote minority rights. Progress in this respect would represent a significant step forward.

8.2 Potential transferability of the HCNMs approach?

The current political climate notwithstanding, there might be more chance of success for new standard-setting (hard or soft) at regional level and for establishing mechanisms such as the HCNM in other parts of the world (leaving aside the subject-matter focus on 'minorities', the particular meaning of 'national minorities' in a European context, and variations in normative development between regional systems). While the existence of the institution of the HCNM was the product of a particular European history and set of processes, including importantly regional integration processes, there are certainly universally applicable aspects to the work of the HCNM as a 'normative intermediary', which might well be applied in other contexts at regional or sub-regional level. The HCNM is not entirely unique in the realms of mediation and negotiation in promoting peace and stability with reference to and through the formulation and promotion of norms of behaviour.[51] However contemporary 'peace mediation' has generally been characterized by a preoccupation with 'process' (which is undoubtedly important) focused primarily on 'negotiation' rather than 'compliance' and 'respect' for international standards, including minority rights, with relatively little attention to the substantive points in

[50] Brostig (2012): 152.

[51] S. Touval, 'Does the High Commissioner Mediate?', in 'Colloquy, Minority Disputes in Europe: Toward New Roles for International Law', *Journal of International Law and Politics* vol. 32 (2000): 711.

dispute. The HCNM remains unique in his or her systematic approach towards and reliance upon norms, consistently using a normative framework both for analysis and for solutions to address the substantive issues in dispute. The adoption of some of the defining features and techniques of the HCNM's approach could potentially enhance the work of existing or new mechanisms at regional or sub-regional levels. Interestingly, as the trend towards more and better (i.e. more effective) institutions and actors of 'peace mediation' increases in number and strength, there is an observable focus on 'normative frameworks' (including human rights), their content, and function as well as their wider and consistent use.[52]

9. Conclusion

In this chapter we have sought to illustrate that international law does matter when it comes to preventing ethnic conflict. More to the point in this regard, the protection of minorities and their rights, as well as the effective management of diversity (including respect for human rights), are essential for peace and stability. The system of relevant human rights (especially minority rights) sets some useful parameters for what is both possible and permissible in terms of managing diversity within states and provides important prescriptions and proscriptions for behaviour in terms of policy, law, and practice pertaining to minorities and to interethnic relations both within and amongst states. The HCNM experience suggests that what matters most when using norms to affect change is not the formal characterization of the norm/standards by 'source'—at least not with regard to the particular subject of minorities, their protection and rights, and the peaceful management of diversity. A focus on the HCNM as a 'normative intermediary' reveals a far more complex picture than a simple hard–soft dichotomy allows. Ultimately, what matters most is 'effectiveness' (i.e. impact leading to a change of behaviour). Above all, standards must be sufficiently developed and clear (if also flexible) to be able to offer solutions to real problems. The way those standards are invoked and developed (including 'hardening') is also of fundamental importance for reinforcement and *normalization* of behaviour. In this respect, processes of 'quiet diplomacy' can produce equally (and in some cases more) desirable outcomes in terms of real changes in behaviour than are achieved through coercive mechanisms associated with hard law human rights instruments (e.g. judicial recourses).

To the extent that the HCNM has had a tangible impact as a promoter of international norms, this can be attributed not so much to the nature or status of the norms themselves, but to other factors including the existence of a mechanism dedicated to offering effective solutions to real problems using existing standards, sensitively interpreted and applied through careful recommendations and persistent engagement. Characteristics of the approach—careful substantive work, involving norm clarification and development, and the offer of practical context-specific solutions,

52 See notably the UN Secretary-General's adoption of the system-wide 'Human Rights Up Front'.

modes of engagement (quiet diplomatic, etc.), and mobilizing capacity—have been crucial influencing factors. The HCNM has also contributed to development of a body of norms—both textual/'legislative' standards and jurisprudential—of varying degrees of 'hardness' and 'softness' for addressing minority issues as a source of tensions within the OSCE and by other IGOs including the UN, CoE, and EU. Together, this constitutes a corpus and arguably a system with attributes of legitimacy, foreseeability, reliability, and, indeed, legality which really affect persons, states, and international relations.

Ultimately, the quality of HCNM initiatives and recommendations means they have proven in themselves to be of interest to the parties as useful reference, if not always accepted and implemented solutions to the problems they face. This appears to be a testament to the fundamental universality of the values themselves and to the utility of human rights standards in particular, with varying degrees of hardness and softness, as a means of achieving social justice, peace, and security and ultimately economic and social development.[53] Such a conclusion is important for political scientists, civil servants, diplomats, or those who may be engaged in mediation and negotiation processes who can benefit from a more nuanced understanding of the utility of international standards in reaching principled, just, and sustainable outcomes. The message for international jurists, on the other hand, is that hard legal norms and mechanisms cannot be expected alone to result in such outcomes in real international relations, and so jurists should not preoccupy themselves with the norms per se as much as with the actual effects sought and the way in which this occurs.[54] The example of the OSCE HCNM shows, in respect of minority rights and diversity management, that this is what matters and ultimately gives normative meaning.

[53] Packer (2000): 647. [54] Packer (2000): 724.

Integrated Bibliography

BOOKS

Addo, Michael, *The Legal Nature of International Human Rights*, International Studies in Human Rights, vol. 104 (Leiden/Boston: Martinus Nijhoff Publishers, 2010).

Allen, Stephen, and Alexandra, Xanthaki, *Reflections on the UN Declaration on the Rights of Indigenous Peoples* (Oxford: Hart, 2011).

Anaya, James, *Indigenous Peoples in International Law* (Oxford: Oxford University Press, 2004).

Boyle, Alan, and Chinkin, Christine, *The Making of International Law* (Oxford: Oxford: University Press, 2007).

Christoffersen, Jonas, and Madsen, Mikael Rask (eds), *The European Court of Human Rights between Law and Politics* (Oxford: Oxford University Press, 2013).

d'Aspremont, Jean, *Formalism and the Sources of International Law: A Theory of the Ascertainment of Legal Rules* (Oxford: Oxford University Press, 2011).

Deva, Surya, and Bilchitz, David (eds), *Human Rights Obligations of Business: Beyond the Corporate Responsibility to Respect?* (Cambridge: Cambridge University Press, 2013).

Edwards, Alice, *Violence against Women under International Human Rights Law* (Cambridge: Cambridge University Press, 2013).

Evans, Malcom, and Murray, Rachel (eds), *The African Charter on Human and Peoples' Rights* (Cambridge: Cambridge University Press, 2008).

Fredman, Sandra, *Human Rights Transformed: Positive Rights and Positive Duties* (Oxford: Oxford University Press, 2008).

Gready, Paul, and Vandenhole, Wouter, *Human Rights and Development in the New Millennium: Towards a Theory of Change* (New York: Routledge, 2014).

Hanski, Raija, and Scheinin, Martin, *Leading Cases of the Human Rights Committee* (Turko/Åbo: Institute for Human Rights, 2003).

Kamminga, M. T., and Scheinin, M., *The Impact of Human Rights Law on General International Law* (Oxford: Oxford University Press, 2009).

Keal, Paul, *European Conquest and the Rights of Indigenous Peoples: The Moral Backwardness of International Society* (New York: Cambridge University Press, 2003).

Keller, Helen, and Ulfstein, Geir (eds), *UN Human Rights Treaty Bodies: Law and Legitimacy* (Cambridge: Cambridge University Press, 2012).

Killander, M. (ed.), *International Law and Domestic Litigation in Africa* (Pretoria: Pretoria University Press, 2010).

Morgan, Rhiannon, *Transforming Law and Institution: Indigenous Peoples, the United Nations and Human Rights* (Farnham: Ashgate, 2011).

Murray, Rachel, *The African Commission on Human and Peoples' Rights & International Law* (Oxford: Hart Publishing, 2000).

Murray, Rachel, and Long, Derba, *The Implementation of the Findings of the African Commission on Human and Peoples' Rights* (Cambridge: Cambridge University Press, 2015).

Pulitano, Elvira (ed.), *Indigenous Rights in the Age of the UN Declaration* (Cambridge: Cambridge University Press, 2012).

Radu, Mares (ed.), *The UN Guiding Principles on Business and Human Rights: Foundations and Implementation* (The Hague: Brill, 2012).

Rajagopal, Balakrishnan, *International Law from Below: Development, Social Movements and Third World Resistance* (Cambridge: Cambridge University Press, 2003).

Rehof, Lars Adam, *Guide to the Travaux Préparatoires of the United Nations Convention on the Elimination of All Forms of Discrimination against Women* (Dordrecht/Boston/London: Martinus Nijhoff Publishers, 1993).

Risse, Thomas, Ropp, Stephen C., and Sikkink, Kathryn (eds), *The Persistent Power of Human Rights: From Commitment to Compliance* (Cambridge: Cambridge University Press, 2013).

Russel, Diana, E. H., and Van Den Ven, Nicole, *Crimes against Women: Proceedings of the International Tribunal* (Berkeley: Russel Publications, 1990).

Saul, Ben, Kinley, David, and Mowbray, Jaqueline, *The International Covenant on Economic, Social and Cultural Rights: Commentary, Cases and Materials* (Oxford: Oxford University Press, 2015).

Seibert, Corinna, *Private Military and Security Companies in International Law—A Challenge for Non-binding Norms: The Montreux Document and the International Code of Conduct for Private Security Service Providers* (Cambridge/Antwerp/Portland: Intersentia, 2014).

Sepúlveda, Magdalene, *The Nature of the Obligations under the International Covenant on Economic, Social and Cultural Rights* (Cambridge/Antwerp/Portland: Intersentia, 2003).

Shelton, Dinah (ed.), *Commitment and Compliance: The Role of Non-binding Norms in the International Legal System* (Oxford: Oxford University Press, 2000).

Shelton, Dinah (ed.), *International Law and Domestic Legal Systems: Incorporation, Transformation, and Persuasion* (Oxford: Oxford University Press, 2011).

Shue, Henry, *Basic Rights: Subsistence, Affluence, and U.S. Foreign Policy* (Princeton: Princeton University Press, 1996).

Simmons, Beth A., *Mobilizing for Human Rights: International Law in Domestic Politics* (Cambridge: Cambridge University Press, 2009).

Steiner, Henry J., Alston, Philip, and Goodman, Ryan, *International Human Rights in Context: Law, Politics, Morals* (Oxford: Oxford University Press, 2008).

Thirlway, Hugh, *The Sources of International Law* (Oxford: Oxford University Press, 2014).

Thornberry, Patrick, *Indigenous Peoples and Human Rights* (Manchester: Manchester University Press, 2002).

Viljoen, Frans, *International Human Rights in Africa* (Oxford: Oxford University Press, 2012).

Young, Katherine, *Constituting Economic and Social Rights* (Oxford: Oxford University Press, 2012).

CHAPTERS IN EDITED BOOKS

Alston, Philip, 'The "Not-a-cat" Syndrome: Can the International Human Rights Regime Accommodate Non-state Actors?' In *Non-state Actors and Human Rights*, ed. Philip Alston (Oxford: Oxford University Press, 2005), 3–37.

Bailliet, Cecilia M., 'What is to Become of the Human Rights International Order in an Age of Neo-medievalism?' In *Non-state Actors, Soft Law and Protective Regimes: From the Margins*, ed. Cecilia M. Bailliet (Cambridge: Cambridge University Press, 2014), 95–124.

Bódig, Mátyás, 'Doctrinal Innovation and State Obligations: The Patterns of Doctrinal Development in the Jurisprudence of the UN Committee on Economic, Social and Cultural Rights'. In *Human Rights Protection in Global Politics: Responsibilities of States and Non-state Actors*, ed. David Karp and Kurt Mills (Basingstoke: Palgrave MacMillan, 2015), 49–68.

Boyle, Alan, 'Soft Law in International Law-Making'. In *International Law*, ed. Malcolm D. Evans (Oxford: Oxford University Press, 2010), 122–40.

Buhmann, Karin, 'The Development of the "UN Framework": A Pragmatic Process towards a Pragmatic Output'. In *The UN Guiding Principles on Business and Human Rights: Foundations and Implementation*, ed. Radu Mares (Leiden/Boston: Martinus Nijhoff Publishers, 2012), 85–105.

Chapman, Audrey, 'The Status of Efforts to Monitor Economic, Social, and Cultural Rights'. In *Economic Rights: Conceptual, Measurement, and Policy Issues*, ed. Shareen Hertel and Lanse Minkler (Cambridge: Cambridge University Press, 2007), 143–64.

Chinkin, Christine, 'Normative Development in the International Legal System'. In *Commitment and Compliance: The Role of Non-binding Norms in the International Legal System*, ed. Dinah Shelton (Oxford: Oxford University Press, 2000), 21–42.

Deva, Surya, 'Treating Human Rights Lightly: A Critique of the Consensus Rhetoric and the Language Employed by the Guiding Principles'. In *Human Rights Obligations of Business: Beyond the Corporate Responsibility to Respect?*, ed. Deva Surya and David Bilchitz (Cambridge: Cambridge University Press, 2013), 78–104.

Forsythe, David P., 'Human Rights Studios: On the Dangers of Legalistic Assumptions'. In *Methods of Human Rights Research*, ed. Frons Coomans, Fred Grünfeld, and Menno T. Kamminga (Maastrict: Maastrict Centre for Human Rights/Intersentia, 2009), 59–75.

Goldmann, Matthias, 'Inside Relative Normativity: From Sources to Standard Instruments for the Exercise of International Public Authority'. In *The Exercise of Public Authority by International Institutions*, ed. A. von Bogdanday, A. Wolfrum, J. von Bernstorff, P. Dann, and M. Goldmann (Berlin, Heidelberg: Springer Verlag, 2010), 661–711.

Gómez Isa, Felipe, 'Repairing Historical Injustices: Indigenous Peoples in Post-conflict Scenarios'. In *Rethinking Transitions: Equality and Social Justice in Societies Emerging from Conflict*, ed. Gaby Oré Aguilar and Felipe Gómez Isa (Cambridge/Antwerp: Intersentia, 2011), 265–300.

Hampson, Francoise J., 'The Relationship between International Humanitarian Law and International Human Rights Law'. In *Routledge Handbook of International Human Rights Law*, ed. Scott Sheeran and Sir Nigel Rodley (Oxford: Routledge, 2013), 185–213.

Jutta, Joachim, 'Shaping the Human Rights Agenda: The Case of Violence against Women'. In *Gender Politics in Global Governance*, ed. Mary K. Meyer and Elisabeth Prügl (London: Rowman & Littlefield, 1999), 142–60.

Klabbers, Jan, 'Of Round Pegs and Square Holes: International Law and the Private Sector'. In *Regulatory Hybridization in the Transnational Sphere*, ed. Paulius Jurčys, Poul F. Kjaer, and Ren Yatsunami (Leiden/Boston: Martinus Nijhoff Publishers, 2013), 29–48.

Pauwelyn, Joost, 'Is it International Law or not, and Does it even Matter?' In *Informal International Law Making*, ed. Joost Pauwelyn, Ramses Wessel, and Jan Wouters (Oxford: Oxford University Press, 2012), 125–61.

Shelton, Dinah, 'Law, Non-law and the Problem of "Soft Law"'. In *Commitment and Compliance: The Role of Non-binding Norms in the International System*, ed. Dinah Shelton (Oxford: Oxford University Press, 2003), 1–18.

Steiner, Henry J., 'Individual Claims in a World of Massive Violations: What Role for the Human Rights Committee?' In *The Future of UN Human Rights Treaty Monitoring*, ed. Philip Alston and James Crawford (Cambridge: Cambridge University Press, 2000), 15–53.

Ulfstein, Geir, 'Law-Making by Human Rights Treaty Bodies'. In *International Law-Making: Essays in Honour of Jan Klabbers*, ed. Rain Liivoja and Jarna Petman (London: Routledge, 2014), 249–58.

Vedel Kessing, Peter, 'Security Detention in Peace Operations'. In *Searching for a 'Principle of Humanity' in International Humanitarian Law*, ed. Kjetil Mujesinovic Larsen, Camilla Guldhal Cooper, and Gro Nystuen (Cambridge: Cambridge University Press, 2013), 272–304.

Voyiakis, Emmanuel, 'Voting in the General Assembly as Evidence of Customary International Law?' In *Reflections on the UN Declaration on the Rights of Indigenous Peoples*, ed. Steve Allen and Alexandra Xanthaki (Oxford: Hart, 2010), 209–24.

Zumbansen, Peer, 'Law and Legal Pluralism: Hybridity in Transnational Governance'. In *Regulatory Hybridization in the Transnational Sphere*, ed. Paulius Jurčys, Poul F. Kjaer, and Ren Yatsunami (Leiden/Boston: Martinus Nijhoff Publishers, 2013), 49–70.

JOURNAL ARTICLES

Aaronson, Susan Ariel, and Higham, Ian, '"Re-Righting Business": John Ruggie and the Struggle to Develop International Human Rights Standards for Transnational Firms'. *Human Rights Quarterly* vol. 35 (2013): 333.

Abbott, K. W., and Snidal, D., 'Hard and Soft Law in International Governance'. *International Organization* vol. 54 (2000): 421.

Abresch, William, 'A Human Rights Law of Internal Armed Conflict: The European Court of Human Rights in Chechnya'. *European Journal of International Law* vol. 16 (2005): 741.

Addo, Michael, 'The Reality of the United Nations Guiding Principles on Business and Human Rights'. *Human Rights Law Review* vol. 14 (2014): 133.

Allehone, Abebe, 'The African Union Convention on Internally Displaced Persons: Its Codification Background, Scope, and Enforcement Challenges'. *Refugee Survey Quarterly* vol. 29 (2010): 28.

Augenstein, Daniel, 'The Crisis of International Human Rights Law in the Global Market Economy'. *Netherland Yearbook of International Law* vol. 44 (2013): 41.

Aust, Helmut P., Rodiles, Alejandro, and Staubach, Peter, 'Unity or Uniformity? Domestic Courts and Treaty Interpretation'. *Leiden Journal of International Law* vol. 27 (2014): 75.

Barelli, Mauro, 'The Role of Soft Law in the International Legal System: The Case of the United Nations Declaration on the Rights of Indigenous Peoples'. *International and Comparative Law Quarterly* vol. 58 (2009): 957.

Bellinger III, J., and Padmanabhan, V., 'Detention Operations in Contemporary Conflicts: Four Challenges for the Geneva Conventions and Existing Law'. *American Journal of International Law* vol. 105 (2011): 201.

Bilchitz, David, 'Towards a Reasonable Approach to the Minimum Core: Laying the Foundations for Future Socio-Economic Rights Jurisprudence'. *South African Journal of Human Rights* vol. 19 (2003): 1.

Boyle, Alan F., 'Reflections on the Relationship of Treaties and Soft Law'. *International and Comparative Law Quarterly* vol. 48 (1999): 901.

Bugnion, Francois, 'The Role of the Red Cross in the Development of International Humanitarian Law: The International Committee of the Red Cross and the Development of International Humanitarian Law'. *Chicago Journal of International Law*, summer (2004): 191.

Chinkin, C. M., 'The Challenge of Soft Law: Development and Change in International Law'. *International and Comparative Law Quarterly* vol. 38 (1989): 850.

Davis, Dennis, 'Socio-economic Rights in South Africa: The Record of the Constitutional Court after Ten Years'. *ESR Review* vol. 5 (2004): 3.

de Búrca, Gráinne, Keohane, Robert, and Sabel, Charles, 'Global Experimentalist Governance'. *British Journal of Political Science* vol. 44 (2014): 477.

Dennis, Michael J., and Stewart, David P., 'Justiciability of Economic, Social, and Cultural Rights: Should There be an International Complaints Mechanism to Adjudicate the Rights to Food, Water, Housing, and Health?' *The American Journal of International Law* vol. 98 (2004): 462.

Doswald-Beck, Louise, 'San Remo Manual on International Law Applicable to Armed Conflict at Sea'. *International Review of the Red Cross* vol. 35 (1995): 583.

Ellis, Jaye, 'Shades of Grey: Soft Law and the Validity of Public International Law'. *Leiden Journal of International Law* vol. 25 (2012): 313.

Evatt, Elizabeth, 'Finding a Voice for Women's Rights: The Early Days of CEDAW'. *The Georges Washington International Law Review* vol. 34 (2002–3): 515.

Forsythe, David P., 'The 1974 Diplomatic Conference on Humanitarian Law: Some Observations'. *American Journal of International Law* vol. 69 (Jan. 1975): 77.

Gómez Isa, Felipe, 'Cultural Diversity, Legal Pluralism, and Human Rights from an Indigenous Perspective: The Approach by the Colombian Constitutional Court and the Inter-American Court of Human Rights'. *Human Rights Quarterly* vol. 36 (2014): 722.

Gruchalla-Wesierski, T., 'A Framework for Understanding Soft Law'. *McGill Law Journal* vol. 30 (1984): 37.

Guzman, Andrew T., and Meyer, Timothy L., 'International Soft Law'. *Journal of Legal Analysis* vol. 2 (2010): 171.

Hafner-Burton, Emilie M., and Ron, James, 'Seeing Double: Human Rights Impact through Quantitative and Qualitative Eyes'. *World Politics* vol. 61 (2009): 360.

Harrington, J., 'Special Rapporteurs of the African Commission on Human and Peoples' Rights'. *African Human Rights Law Journal* vol 1. (2001): 247.

Heintze, Hans-Joachim, 'On the Relationship between Human Rights Law Protection and International Humanitarian Law'. *IRRC* vol. 86 (Dec. 2004): 789.

Johnstone, Ian, 'Treaty Interpretation: The Authority of Interpretive Communities'. *Michigan Journal of International Law* vol. 12 (1991): 371.

Kälin, Walter, 'The Guiding Principles on Internal Displacement as International Minimum Standard and Protection Tool'. *Refugee Survey Quarterly* vol. 24 (2005): 27.

Kinley, David, and Chambers, Rachel, 'The UN Human Rights Norms for Corporations: The Private Implications of Public International Law'. *Human Rights Law Review* vol. 6 (2006): 447.

Klabbers, Jan, 'The Undesirability of Soft Law'. *Nordic Journal of International Law* vol. 67 (1998): 381.

Kretzmer, David, 'Targeted Killing of Suspected Terrorists: Extra-Judicial Executions or Legitimate Means of Defence?' *European Journal of International Law* vol. 16 (2005): 171.

Lagoutte, Stéphanie, 'New Challenges Facing States within the Field of Human Rights and Business'. *Nordic Journal of Human Rights* vol. 33 (2015): 158.

Long, Debra, and Murray, Rachel, 'Ten Years of the Robben Island Guidelines and Prevention of Torture in Africa: For What Purpose?' *African Human Rights Law Journal* vol. 12 (2012): 311.

McCall-Smith, Kasey L., 'Reservations and the Determinative Function of the Human Rights Treaty Bodies'. *German Yearbook of International Law* vol. 54 (2011): 521.

McInerney-Lankford, Siobhán, 'Regime Interaction and the Fragmentation of International Law'. *World Bank Legal Review (Innovation and Empowerment for Development)* vol. 4 (2013): 123.

Mechlem, Kerstin, 'Treaty Bodies and the Interpretation of Human Rights'. *Vanderbilt Journal of Transnational Law* vol. 42 (2009): 905.

Nicolaidis, K., and Tong, J. L., 'Diversity or Cacophony? The Continuing Debate of New Sources of International Law'. *Michigan Journal of International Law* vol. 25 (2004): 1349.

Nowak, Manfred, 'The Need for a World Court of Human Rights'. *Human Rights Law Review* vol. 7 (2007): 251.

Orchard, Phil, 'Protection of Internally Displaced Persons: Soft Law as a Norm-Generating Mechanism'. *Review of International Studies* vol. 36 (2010): 281.

Oswald, Bruce, 'Detention of Civilians on Military Operations: Reasons for and Challenges to Developing a Special Law of Detention'. *Melbourne University Law Review* vol. 32 (2008): 534.

Oswald, Bruce, and Winkler, Thomas, 'The Copenhagen Process: Principles and Guidelines on the Handling of Detainees in International Military Operations'. *Nordic Journal of International Law* vol. 83 (2014): 128.

Picciotto, Sol, 'Constitutionalizing Multilevel Governance?' *International Journal of Constitutional Review* vol. 6 (2008): 457.

Randall, Melanie, 'Refugee Law and State Accountability for Violence against Women: A Comparative Analysis of Legal Approaches to Recognizing Asylum Claims Based on Gender Persecution'. *Harvard Women's Law Journal* vol. 25 (2002): 281.

Rodley, Nigel, 'United Nations Human Rights Treaty Bodies and Special Procedures of the Commission on Human Rights: Complementary or Competition?' *Human Rights Quarterly* vol. 25 (2003): 882.

Ruggie, John Gerard, 'Global Governance and "New Governance Theory": Lessons from Business and Human Rights'. *Global Governance* vol. 20 (2014): 5.

Schmitt, Michael, and Watts, Sean, 'The Decline of International Humanitarian Law Opinio Juris and the Law of Cyber Warfare'. *Texas International Law Journal* vol. 50 (2014): 189.

Schrepfer, Nina, 'Addressing Internal Displacement through National Laws and Policies: A Plea for a Promising Means of Protection'. *International Journal of Refugee Law* vol. 24 (2012): 667.

Tobin, John, 'Seeking to Persuade: A Constructive Approach to Human Rights Treaty Interpretation'. *Harvard Human Rights Journal* vol. 23 (2010): 214.

Türkelli, Gamze E., Vandenhole, Wouter, and Vandenbogaerde, Arne, 'NGO Impact on Law-Making: The Case of a Complaints Procedure under the International Covenant on Economic, Social and Cultural Rights and the Convention on the Rights of the Child'. *Journal of Human Rights Practice* vol. 5 (2013): 1.

Viljoen, F., and Louw, L., 'The Status of the Findings of the African Commission'. *Journal of African Law* vol. 48 (2004): 1.

Weil, Prosper, 'Towards Relative Normativity in International Law?' *American Journal of International Law* vol. 77 (1983): 413.

Wettstein, Florian, 'CSR and the Debate on Business and Human Rights: Bridging the Great Divide'. *Business Ethics Quarterly* vol. 22 (2012): 739.

Winkler, Thomas, 'The Copenhagen Process on Detainees: A Necessity'. *Nordic Journal of International Law* vol. 78 (2009): 489.

Wyndham, J., 'A Developing Trend: Laws and Policies on Internal Displacement'. *Human Rights Brief* vol. 14 (2006): 7.

Young, Katharine G., 'The Minimum Core of Economic and Social Rights: A Concept in Search of Content'. *The Yale Journal of International Law* vol. 33 (2008): 113.

OTHER SOURCES

Asplet, Mike, and Bradley, Megan, 'Strengthened Protection for Internally Displaced Persons in Africa: The Kampala Convention Comes into Force'. *American Society of International Law (ASIL) Insights* vol. 16, Issue 36 (2012).

Brookings-Bern Project on Internal Displacement, *Protecting Internally Displaced Persons: A Manual for Law and Policymakers* (Washington, DC: Brookings-Bern Project on Internal Displacement, 2008).

Brookings-LSE Project on Internal Displacement, Internal Displacement Monitoring Centre and Norwegian Refugee Council, *National Instruments on Internal Displacement: A Guide to their Development* (Geneva: IDMC, 2013).

Charters, Claire, and Stavenhagen, Rodolfo (eds), *Making the Declaration Work: The United Nations Declaration on the Rights of Indigenous Peoples* (Copenhagen: IWGIA, 2009).

Cohen, Roberta, *Lessons Learned from the Development of the Guiding Principles on Internal Displacement* (Georgetown University Institute for the Study of International Migration Working Paper, 2013).

General Recommendation 19: Violence against Women, 11th Session, 1992, Contained in Compilation of General Comments and General Recommendations Adopted by Human Rights Treaty Bodies, HRI/GEN/1/Rev.9 (vol. 2), 27 May 2008.

IASC, *IASC Framework on Durable Solutions for Internally Displaced Persons*, Brookings-Bern Project on Internal Displacement (Washington, DC, 2010).

ICRC, *International Humanitarian Law and the Challenges of Contemporary Armed Conflicts 31st International Conference of the Red Cross and Red Crescent* (2011).

ICRC, *International Humanitarian Law and the Challenges of Contemporary Armed Conflicts 32nd International Conference of the Red Cross and Red Crescent* (2015).

Kälin, Walter. *The Guiding Principles on Internal Displacement: Annotations*, 2nd edn, American Society of International Law and Brookings Institution (Washington, DC, 2008).

Levine, S., Bailey, S., and Boyer, B., *Avoiding Reality: Land, Institutions and Humanitarian Action in Post-earthquake Haiti: Humanitarian Policy Group Working Paper* (London: Overseas Development Institute, 2012).

Ling, A., McGee, R., Gaventa, J., and Pantazidou, M., *Literature Review on Active Participation and Human Rights Research and Advocacy* (Institute for Development Studies, 2010).

Mansuri, Ghazala, and Rao, Vijayendra, *Localizing Development: Does Participation Work?* World Bank Policy Research Report (Washington, DC, 2013).

Report of the International Law Commission on its 63rd session, Guide to Practice on Reservations with commentary, UN Doc. A/66/10/Add.1 (2011).

Report of the World Conference of the International Women's Year, Mexico City, 19 June–2 July 1975, E/CONF.66/34.

Report of the World Conference of the United Nations Decade for Women: Equality, Development and Peace, Copenhagen, 14–30 July 1980, A/CONF.94/35.

Sherwood, Angela, Bradley, Megan, Rossi, Lorenza, Gitau, Rosalia, and Mellicker, Bradley, *Supporting Durable Solutions to Urban, Post-disaster Displacement: Challenges and Opportunities in Haiti* (Washington, DC: Brookings/IOM, 2014).

Sudre, Frédéric, *Droit européen et international des droits de l'homme*, Collection Droit Fondamental (11th edn, Paris: PUF, 2002).

UN Human Rights Office of the High Commissioner, *International Legal Protection of Human Rights in Armed Conflict* (New York and Geneva, 2011).

Weiss, E. B., *International Compliance with Nonbinding Accords* (Washington, DC: American Society of International Law, 1997).

Index

The manufacturer's authorised representative in the EU for product safety is Oxford University Press España S.A. of el Parque Empresarial San Fernando de Henares, Avenida de Castilla, 2 – 28830 Madrid (www.oup.es/en or product.safety@oup.com). OUP España S.A. also acts as importer into Spain of products made by the manufacturer.

www.ingramcontent.com/pod-product-compliance
Lightning Source LLC
LaVergne TN
LVHW011911200926
848484LV00002B/590
9780198791409